Private Security and Public Safety

A Community-Based Approach

K.C. Poulin

Critical Intervention Services
President and CEO

Charles P. Nemeth

California University of Pennsylvania
Member Pennsylvania, New York,
and North Carolina Bars

PEARSON

Prentice
Hall

Upper Saddle River, New Jersey 07458

Library of Congress Cataloging-in-Publication Data

Nemeth, Charles P.
  Private security & public safety / Charles Nemeth, K. C. Poulin.—1st ed.
    p. cm.
  Includes bibliographical references.
  ISBN 0–13–112374–2
  1. Community policing—United States.   2. Private security services—United States.   3. Police,
Private—United States. I. Title: Private security and public safety. II. Poulin, K. C. (Karl C.) III. Title.

HV7936.C83N46 2005
363.28′9′0973—dc22

2004007088

Acquisitions Editor: Frank Mortimer, Jr.
Developmental Editor: Korrine Dorsey
Managing Editor: Mary Carnis
Production Liaison: Brian Hyland
Production Editor: Bruce Hobart
Director of Manufacturing and Production:
  Bruce Johnson
Manufacturing Manager: Ilene Sanford

Manufacturing Buyer: Cathleen Petersen
Creative Director: Cheryl Asherman
Senior Design Coordinator: Miguel Ortiz
Cover Design: Carey Davies
Cover Art: Robert Daly, Getty Images/STONE
Composition: Pine Tree Composition
Printing and Binding: Phoenix Book Tech

Pearson Prentice Hall™ is a trademark of Pearson Education, Inc.
Pearson® is a registered trademark of Pearson plc
Prentice Hall® is a registered trademark of Pearson Education, Inc.

Pearson Education LTD.
Pearson Education Australia PTY, Limited
Pearson Education Singapore, Pte. Ltd.
Pearson Education North Asia Ltd.
Pearson Education Canada, Ltd.
Pearson Education de Mexico, S.A. de C.V.
Pearson Education—Japan
Pearson Education Malaysia, Pte. Ltd.
Pearson Education, Upper Saddle River, New Jersey

10   9   8   7   6   5   4   3   2   1
ISBN 0-13-112374-2

Dedication

Charles P. Nemeth

To my oldest daughter Eleanor—musical, voice of an angel, and rooted in the chant of all ages.

To St. Thomas Aquinas

He who does not prevent the theft, whereas he is bound to do so; for instance, persons in authority who are bound to safeguard justice on earth, are bound to restitution, if by their neglect thieves prosper, because their salary is given to them in payment of their preserving justice . . . (Summa Theologica II-II, Question 62, art. 7)

K.C. Poulin

It is not the critic who counts, not the man who points out how the strong man stumbled or where the doer of deeds could have done better. The credit belongs to the man who is actually in the arena; whose face is marred by dust and sweat and blood; who strives valiantly; who errs and comes short again and again; who knows the great enthusiasms, the great devotions, and spends himself in a worthy cause; who at the best, knows in the end the triumph of high achievement; and who, at the worst, if he fails, at least fails while daring greatly, so that his place shall never be with those cold and timid souls who know neither victory nor defeat.

Theodore Roosevelt

Contents

Preface

Few things grow as constantly and predictably as crime in American society. Much to the dismay of a beleaguered culture, the levels of crime and its corresponding rising costs, negatively impact a great number of aspects of daily living. This is a text that suggests a bold and alternative perspective—an increased role for private security in the maintenance of order.

In a general sense the text lays out:

- A thorough and concise review of the security industry from both a philosophical and functional approach, including the contrast between the public and private ideology of public safety.
- Discussion of the trends, the ebb and flow of private law enforcement, with a particular emphasis on the reemergence of the private model in the 21st century.
- Specific suggestions on how the private security industry can intervene and essentially save communities in distress.
- Comprehensive analysis of the role of private sector operatives in community-based integration along with a review of the integration formula and processes only the private sector is capable of.
- Considerable elaboration of the role and function of the Community Protection Officer—that private counterpart to the beat patrol—in the cure of community pathology.
- The specifics of various tactics that security firms can use to win that psychological edge from first contact protocols, shock tactics of various levels of intensity, and other simple steps which announce to the world how crime and criminals have lost their edge in the community.
- A discussion of environmental considerations in the reclamation of crime ridden areas and how private security is better positioned to see the

community in both social and environmental terms and to aggressively alter the landscape to make it less user friendly for the malefactor.

- Suggestions for effective collaboration of public and private entities in the struggle to control crime in a neighborhood setting.

The roots and foundation of private sector justice are fully analyzed in Chapter 1. It makes little sense to advance new theories of policing without a look to how policing in both the private and public sector has unfolded. Indeed our history is too often forgotten in public police circles where the only game in town sometimes excludes the private model. History instructs otherwise with private citizens towing the line in crime and criminality for most measurable time. Clearly the concepts of a posse, a watch and ward, and the idea of feudal protections, rest in the private domain. Even early police fathers arose from the private movement whether Peel, Pinkerton, or Fielding. Hence a strong and vigorous look at the history of private sector justice is worth the investment.

Chapter 2 more specifically reviews the security industry from both a philosophical and functional approach. The trends, the ebb and flow of private law enforcement, are pointed out with particular emphasis on the reemergence of the private model in the 21st century. The concept of privatization is visited keenly. In addition, the chapter lays out the general contributions the industry makes to the law enforcement function and the many tasks it undertakes, from college and university policing to retail and corporate protection. The contrast between the public and private ideology of public safety is also provided.

Chapter 3 debates and critiques the idea of community policing and how public police have bought the approach in efforts to stabilize their relationships with distressed communities. The community policing programs so often witnessed in the public sector are well intentioned attempts to recapture the hearts and minds of those living in crime ridden communities. A major thesis of this chapter is that public police may lack the ideological framework to deliver this form of service and that the private sector counterpart may be better suited to the challenge of restoration in high crime communities. A debate is offered on whether or not community policing practices have failed or succeeded.

Chapter 4 delivers specifics on how the private security industry can intervene and essentially save communities in distress. It is the high crime community so dire in economic, social and other pathological condition where a new approach may be necessary. The public police are rightfully preoccupied with the reactive role of arrest and detention and have scant time to mend the fences in the community setting. Particular suggestions on how to measure the health and condition of a designated community through threat assessment and community profiles are discussed and analyzed. Here again, the private sector appears most capable of effecting change in seemingly unchangeable communities.

Chapter 5 lays out the role of private sector operatives in community based integration and delves comprehensively into the integration formula and processes only the private sector is capable of. The coverage includes a detailed look at the Community-Based Integration Program (CBIP) which allows the private security firm to not only erect a system that repairs, reclaims and restores the community stability but also indicates the types of training and police tactics necessary to effectively win the war on crime in the distressed community. Considerable elaboration of the role and function of the Community Protection Officer—that private counterpart to the beat patrol—in the cure of community pathology is made available.

Chapter 6 outlines the crucial role that communication plays in the delivery of security and public safety services in the community-based law enforcement. Change comes about due to professional tactics assuredly, but even more compellingly, the ability to persuade and change the mindset and outlook of the residents who live in the turmoil of crime. How the private security officers conducts him- or herself, how welcome the officers become in the target community, and how well the private sector justice professionals interact in the marketplace will correlate to the level of success in the community.

Another major contribution of the private security industry will be its ability to alter and metamorphize the landscape in which they carry out their duties. So much of crime and its consequence depend on fear and intimidation. Chapter 7 delineates psychological tactics that take back the streets and restore the appropriate social equilibrium for community tranquility. The unit also specifies various tactics that security firms can use to win that psychological edge from first contact protocols, shock tactics of various levels of intensity, and other simple steps which announce to the world how crime and criminals have lost their edge in the community. Private sector companies are ably placed to change the environment by these psychological tactics.

Environmental considerations in the reclamation of crime ridden areas are the main subject matter of Chapter 8. That a correlation exists between a corrupted environment and the level of criminal activity is now indisputable. Private sector firms and operatives are well placed to deal with community in an environmental sense and to offer recommendations on how the change and modification of the environment will alter the lives of crime. Environmental considerations can be as small as garbage and other eyesores to a lack of lighting and street security and to a host of other issues that announce a collapsing quality of life. Private security is better positioned to see the community in both social and environmental terms and to aggressively alter the landscape to make it less user friendly for the malefactor. Not just imagery and setting but physical security, environmental design and technology in the minimization of crime will be weighed and evaluated.

Chapter 9 ends with the full recognition that the crime problem in the American community can no longer be exclusively dealt with by the public sector. That same recognition leads to an understanding that the private security industry will play a significant role in the elimination and control of crime but probably over the next century will be the most significant player in the delivery of public safety for the American way of life. Simply put, the future belongs to privatization and communities will live or die on the fundamental relationship it builds with its protectors. Given the antagonism so rampant in the public model, the private solution generates resolution by other means and allows the public police system to react while the private model integrates its very essence into the fiber of the American community.

Here is where the future resides: in a system rooted in private prevention and protection. Aligned with the public police model, communities will live or die on the fundamental relationship it builds with its protectors. Given the antagonism so rampant in the public model, the private solution generates resolution by other means and allows the public police system to react while the private model integrates its very essence into the fiber of the American community.

Acknowledgments

This is a project borne out of the passion and professionalism of my co-author, K.C. Poulin. One rarely meets practitioners with as much conviction as he carries, nor will most of us encounter an experienced and seasoned law enforcement specialist who so keenly and emotionally believes in his cause. His ideology of private sector justice and its role in the 21st century is not only appealing but rabidly convincing. He has made me a true believer in his vision of Private Sector Justice. He has convinced me that there is hope and raw ambition in this field and that cynicism and dejection have no place in his horizon. For that alone, I acknowledge this creative and trailblazing individual. Thanks K.C. for the honor of working on this project. For the many practitioners, companies, firms and security operatives, I cannot adequately express my gratitude. While K.C. Poulin and I tackle the problem of private security in America from our unique perspective; the field of private sector justice is filled with able and honorable people who offer up others. Their many contributions allow this text to grow and flourish. My association with Prentice Hall continues to be intellectually rewarding and energizing. Prentice Hall provides a wide array of scholarly materials to the criminal justice community and its willingness to be a flagship in our field can be deduced from the support of this project. To Frank Mortimer, Executive Editor of Criminal Justice and Korrine Dorsey, Editorial Services, I extend my usual heartfelt appreciation for the chance to work with such a great company. To Hope Haywood, long time editorial associate and soon to be a co-author, the plaudits flow forth easily. So much to track and chart, to graph and note, to reference and figure that it leaves me desperate for her type of organizational skill. And as always, she provides with skill and administrative genius.

From the administration of California University of Pennsylvania I experience support and encouragement for these endeavors. President Angelo Armenti continues to inspire faculty to not only be scholars, but leading thinkers in new and emerging fields. He is a true intellectual with an entrepreneurial vision. Just as compellingly supportive has been the university's Provost, Dr. Curt Smith who clearly enjoys his faculty's success in any context chosen. The Provost never envies, never displays jealously, but preferably revels in the achievement of his troops. I rarely meet people who do not fear greatness in others. Curtis Smith always surrounds himself with talented and cutting edge people. For this reason alone he is a fabulous administrator.

Finally, my thanks go to the Dean of Science and Technology, Dr. Len Colelli, who cannot do enough for our operation and the sterling and amazing service of this department's administrator, Laurie Manderino. It is a real joy to be associated with such good people.

To conclude, the family that God's blessings permits continues to prod me into projects in every direction. Large families have many benefits though none is more obvious than the encouragement, love, and affection that come from the enterprise. Without the anchor, the journeys into these intellectual seas would likely never occur. Love to Jean Marie, Ellie, Stephen, John, Joseph, Mary Claire, and Michael Augustine.

In Pittsburgh, across from US Steel,

Charles P. Nemeth JD, Ph.D., LL.M

This book is dedicated to a simple word that some people have never known within themselves during their entire lifetime. A word that symbolizes a concept that many think they understand, but never truly live. A word that has the power to shape peoples lives and, in turn, form their destinies as it has for so many in years gone by. The dedication of this book is to the word *Honor* and what it stands for—a word that has brought a true sense of meaning to the profession of protecting others.

Every good quality in man stems from this one small word. Integrity, respect, truth, strength, and compassion are all embodied in this one principle. It is a word that can teach many of us today, in this blame-free society, to become better individuals and help us become a better people. Today, many people fail to understand that honorable intent alone will create a more lasting impact than any accomplishments that are achieved without it. Creating a family, a business, or a society, without *Honor* shall be, in the end, meaningless. *Honor* is something this country had in abundance at one time, but today can only be sporadically observed.

We also want to dedicate this book to all the frontline security and protection officers who have given their lives in the protection of others. These officers take on assignments that are just as dangerous and, at times, more so than that of their law enforcement counterparts. They patrol apartment communities; protect office buildings, banks, airports, malls, prisons, nuclear facilities, schools, and much more. They do this with little or no recognition and, in some cases, ultimately sacrifice their lives in the protection of others without recognition from the community they serve. Until something drastic occurs, such as the death of an officer, very few in the community realize that the men and women who provide protective services risk their lives for the security of an entire society. These private officers, who are two million strong across the United States, not only outnumber law enforcement, but provide protection that the police cannot. Without their service, law enforcement agencies could never succeed in controlling crime or preventing violence. To quote Christopher A. Hertig, Assistant Professor at York College of Pennsylvania and Director of Accreditation for The International Foundation for Protection Officers, *"The men and women in the private security field are the forgotten soldiers of an invisible empire."* To these officers and their families I can only express my sincerest thanks for your sacrifice.

I would like to first and foremost acknowledge Charles Nemeth and the skill and expertise he has brought to this work. After reading his book called Private Security and the Law, I knew that I wanted to work with this author and was extremely pleased when he accepted the challenge of working on this book. With his guidance and leadership, I believe that we were successful in creating a work that found balance between the world of the practitioner and the academic realm, something extremely hard to accomplish. These two worlds can seem so far apart at times, that it is an amazing achievement to bring them together as a functional and practical work. I take pride and am humbled by being able to call Chuck my friend and colleague.

I also want to thank Michelle Pace, my assistant who worked very hard on transcribing voice notes and organizing thoughts on my thousands of pages of notes.

—*K.C. Poulin*

REVIEWERS

Both authors would like to extend their thanks and appreciation to the following reviewers for their invaluable assistance: Thomas Babcock, California State University—Fullerton, Fullerton, CA; John Eramo, J. Eramo Security Training, Albany, NY; William Parks, University of South Carolina at Spartanburg, Spartanburg, SC; and Patrick Walsh, Loyola University New Orleans, New Orleans, LA.

About the Authors

Charles P. Nemeth, Professor of Professional Studies and Director of Graduate Criminal Justice/Legal Studies for California University of Pennsylvania, has spent the vast majority of his professional life in the study and practice of law and justice. A recognized expert on ethics and the legal system, appellate legal practice and private-sector justice, he also is a prolific writer, having published numerous texts and articles on law and justice throughout his impressive career. His most recent work includes three titles: *Criminal Law* (Prentice Hall, 2003), *Law & Evidence: A Primer for Criminal Justice, Criminology, Law, and Legal Studies* (Prentice Hall, 2001) and *Aquinas in the Courtroom* (Greenwood and Praeger Publishing, 2001). Dr. Nemeth is a recognized scholar in the world of private security. His *Private Security and the Law*, third edition (Butterworth/Elsevier 2005) is regarded as a treatise on the subject. In addition, his *Private Security and Investigative Process* (Butterworth/Elsevier 1999) is deemed required reading for security practitioners.

An educator for more than 30 years, Nemeth's distinctive career in criminal justice is founded on an exemplary education, including a Master of Laws from George Washington University, a Juris Doctor from the University of Baltimore, and a Master of Arts and Ph.D. from Duquesne University. In addition, he was awarded a M.S. from Niagara University and received an undergraduate degree from the University of Delaware. He holds memberships in the New York, North Carolina, and Pennsylvania Bars.

At California University, Dr. Nemeth directs the University's graduate program in Criminal Justice, implemented a new Master's degree in Legal Studies and is developing additional academic programs at CAL-Pittsburgh as Director of Program Development. His previous academic appointments include Niagara University (1977–1980), the University of Baltimore (1980–1981), Glassboro State College (1981–1986), Waynesburg College (1988–1998), and the State University of New York at Brockport (1998–2003).

He is a much sought-after legal consultant for security companies and a recognized scholar on issues involving law and morality.

K.C. Poulin is President and Chief Executive Officer of Critical Intervention Services (CIS) and has over 20 years experience in the fields of law enforcement, security management, and executive protection. Mr. Poulin specializes in the fields of crime in urban communities, critical incident management, terrorism counteraction, juvenile violence and prevention, executive protection, and workplace violence.

He and his team of practitioners developed the premises for this book through the everyday activities and efforts of Critical Intervention Services. The concept called Community and Character Based Protection Initiative (CCBPI) was created by Mr. Poulin and has received worldwide recognition for its effective results in turning around high-crime communities.

Mr. Poulin has received certifications as a Certified Protection Specialist (CPS) through Executive Security International and Certified Protection Officer Instructor (CPOI) through the International Foundation for Protection Officers and is certified in Homeland Security, Level-III by the American Board for Certification in Homeland Security.

Mr. Poulin often testifies as an expert witness in liability cases that require his expertise in terms of inadequate security and premise liability for the limitation of protective operations. He has lectured on a number of occasions to the Florida Chapter of the FBI National Academy Associates and other industry organizations and also serves as a frequent consultant for the news media and has appeared as a subject expert in over 300 television and radio news interviews.

1

History and the Private/Public Distinction

Support your office with spirit, but never use any indecent language or any way insult your prisoner, never strike out but on the utmost necessity.
Henry Fielding, Bow Street Magistrate

It is much better to prevent even one man from being a rogue than apprehending and bringing forty to justice.
Sir John Fielding, Bow Street Magistrate, 1758

Learning Objectives

1. To gain an appreciation for the historical underpinnings that both public and private law enforcement share.
2. To learn about Western tradition in law enforcement and its primary goal of self-help and self-protection.
3. To become familiar with the role of the military in the enforcement of order.
4. To become knowledgeable about early law enforcement efforts, particularly the feudal model of protection, the English and Colonial Watch and Ward, and the commercial protection systems.
5. To study the historical figures that were so instrumental in the development of private and public sector justice, including Sir Robert Peel, John and Henry Fielding, Patrick Colquhoun, Allan Pinkerton, and J. Edgar Hoover.
6. To determine the relationship between public and private models of criminal justice.

7. To discern the interplay between business, commerce, and proprietary interests in the development of law enforcement models.

8. To discover the continuing evolution of private and public justice systems.

9. To question the most appropriate use of the justice model in service to communities.

I. THE SETTING

Few things grow as constantly and predictably as crime in American society. Much to the dismay of a beleaguered culture, the levels of crime and its corresponding rising costs negatively impact a great number of aspects of daily living. The Uniform Crime Report (UCR) summarizes the rates of criminality that impact contemporary culture over the last two years. For the last few years, more than 23,000,000 criminal offenses have officially met the stringent criteria of the FBI's crime report. These figures do not include the unreported or the undetected, nor those cases diverted, alternatively disposed of, or incapable of prosecution; nor do these data signify the watering-down effects of plea bargains. Additionally, the crime figures account only for certain types of criminality that are formally computed in the UCR. Misdemeanors, by way of illustration, fail to find their way into the traditional reporting mechanisms, and a host of criminal offenses have to yet to be cataloged in the arsenal of crime data. Hence, the picture may be different from the numbers manifest. See Figure 1.1.[1]

CRIME INDEX TOTAL

DEFINITION

The Crime Index is composed of selected offenses used to gauge fluctuations in the overall volume and rate of crime reported to law enforcement. The offenses included are the violent crimes of murder and nonnegligent manslaughter, forcible rape, robbery, and aggravated assault, and the property crimes of burglary, larceny-theft, motor vehicle theft, and arson.

Year	*Number of offenses[1]*	*Rate per 100,000 inhabitants[1]*
1999	11,634,378	4,266.5
2000	11,605,751	4,124.0
Percent change	-0.2	-3.3

[1]Does not include arson. See page 61.

FIGURE 1.1   Section II Crime Index Offenses Reported

When violent crimes are assessed, the picture becomes frightening. For over a century, the nation has witnessed an overall escalation in homicidal violence. Although small downward trends have occurred recently, the longitudinal picture paints a negative picture of a culture under siege. See Figure 1.2.[2]

The National Institute of Justice's report *Criminal Justice 2000* appears optimistic about the apprehension of major felons, as recent numbers indicate, but is less optimistic about the rest of the story. As shown by two renowned criminologists in that work, the difficulty with prognostication is obvious:[3]

> Views about future roles of crime in American society are noteworthy for their diversity. One futurologist predicts a society with little crime by the year 2025:
>
>> The most-dreaded types of offenses—crimes such as murder, rape, assault, robbery, burglary, and vehicle theft—will be brought under control in the years ahead by a combination of technology and proactive community policing. Creation of the cashless society, for example, will eliminate most of the rewards for robbers and muggers, while computer-controlled smart houses and cars will thwart burglars and auto thieves. Implanted bodily function monitors and chemical drips (such as "sober-up" drugs and synthesized hormones) will keep most of the sexually and physically violent offenders under control.[4]
>
> By contrast, another futurologist sees a much more crime-ridden society in 2025:
>
>> "fortified, middle-class enclaves in destroyed cities, the latter swarming with drug-crazed, poverty-stricken populations, that finally turn on those who are economically better off"[5]

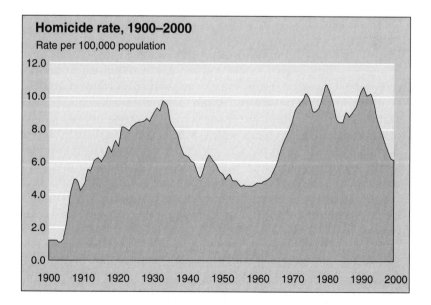

FIGURE 1.2   Homicide Rates

With whom does the responsibility lie to thwart the criminal element? Formal and mechanistic responses to this apparently unceasing plague fall into two major schools of reaction: *public sector law enforcement* and *private sector protective services.*

The subject matter of this inquiry deals with the private security industry and its role in the prevention and elimination of crime. In the latter instance, an industry has emerged that few would have predicted accurately and that is, by every measure, a seemingly unstoppable force. Think tanks, government agencies, and academics all point to a remarkable growth model. The National Institute of Justice's *Private Security: Patterns and Trends,* using statistics from the *Hallcrest Report,*[6] forecasted a continuing upward surge in both personnel and dollar costs through 2012.[7]

Here is where the future resides—in a system rooted in private prevention and protection, aligned with the public police model.[8] In the future, more collaboration will be seen in the crime scene, the terrorist investigation, or the public facility. At present, the list of security functions assumed by the private sector continues its unabated growth. No longer will the public and community merely look only to the FBI, the Department of Alcohol, Tobacco, and Firearms (ATF), or state and local police to carry out myriad tasks.

Today, the public interacts with and depends upon a private sector model whose tentacles reach into every aspect of communal living. The American Society for Industrial Security sees the opportunities present in the field now and in the future, and states that the "demand for heightened security is being increased by theft of information, workplace violence, terrorism and white collar crime. The security industry in the US is a $100 billion a year business and growing. Opportunities exist at all levels with the security industry. All businesses, no matter how small, have security concerns such as fraud, theft computer hacking, economic espionage or workplace violence."[9]

The private security industry possesses an unflappable inertia that will increasingly weave its way into areas of public safety and security. Moreover, public policing and safety entities will welcome the assistance. In housing and apartment complexes, in state and federal installations, at military facilities and correctional locales, at traffic intersections and public transportation settings, in executive protection details and arson/explosives assessments, this is an industry that scoffs at caricatures in the mold of rent-a-cops or retired, unenergetic police officers with donut in hand. Frank MacHovec calls security services police functions that are not performed by police.[10] This is an industry on the cutting edge of technology and operational policy; and it is an industry that public law enforcement now often envies.[11] Less burdened with regulation and free from excessive constitutional oversight, the political interference witnessed in public law enforcement, and driven by efficiencies and corporate creativity, the security industry can only march forward.

In sum, the private security industry provides the bulk of public safety services in America, from public and private facility protection, to public and private housing security: it is an industry with no boundaries. Public responsibility, safety in American communities, crime prevention and deterrence, and asset protection are its hallmark purposes. Private security delivers services in the public realm and generates public trust by delegating the protection of people and property to its skilled personnel. Private security engages citizens even more than its public counterpart, and it has done so without fanfare to match its astonishing rise. David Sklansky's *The Private Police* targets the central implications:

> For most lawyers and scholars, private security is terra incognita—wild, unmapped, and largely unexplored. . . . Increasingly, though, government agencies are hiring private security personnel to guard and patrol government buildings, housing projects, and public parks and facilities, and a small but growing number of local governments have begun to experiment with broader use of private police.[12]

The *Quiet Revolution*[13] of private security could not have greater impacts. More than ever, the enormous public demands piled upon the private security industry call for professional planning and policy making and for a renewed dedication to the advancement of this dynamic industry.

Private security is a steadfast and dependable safeguard in the ongoing war on crime. As distressing as crime rates are, imagine the rates without the participation and integration of the security industry. See Figure 1.3 for some staggering statistics.[14]

Crime fighting and deterrence have come a long way since the days of posses and the "hue and cry." However, for current efforts to be effective, multiple constituencies that include not only crime victims and community groups but also the full range of service providers that are in the security industry must develop a common plan of action. Violent crime rates, the rise of juvenile offenders, increasing levels of incarceration, control of swelling offender populations, to name just a few variables, can no longer be the sole province of traditional public safety. Instead, the community needs multiple approaches to control criminality, and the private security industry plays an essential role here.

Compared with the situation less than a century ago, America now witnesses staggering rates of criminality that public law enforcement can no longer thwart by itself. The National Center for Policy Analysis, a Washington think tank, not only urges the aggressive use of private security but also sees a correlation between lower crime rates and "more individual responsibility and less governmental responsibility."[15]

Throughout America today, security experts, counselors, academics, and law enforcement try to predict and anticipate violence, while simultaneously devising methods of minimizing its impact on the daily life of the public. For public law enforcement personnel, this ambition is simply implausible. They are primarily trained to investigate and enforce, not to prevent crime. The public model now depends on the private sector for some assistance with this distressing state of affairs. The public system has often been accused of the acceptance of the current rates of crime and disorder. Violent crime has become so entrenched in society that the vast majority of the population, in both metropolitan and rural environments, adopts the belief that crime is inevitable and is a permanent element of American society. As if programmed to expect crime to be a way of life, individual citizens reject the actuality of crime control that private security can provide. For too long, the public

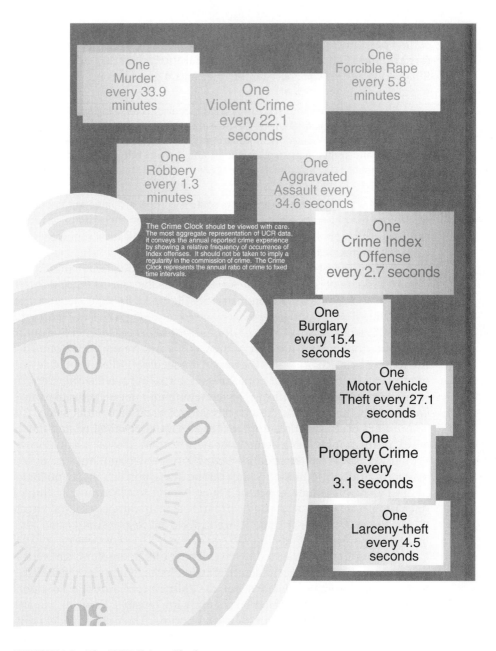

One
Murder
every 33.9
minutes

One
Violent Crime
every 22.1
seconds

One
Forcible Rape
every 5.8
minutes

One
Robbery
every 1.3
minutes

One
Aggravated
Assault every
34.6 seconds

The Crime Clock should be viewed with care.
The most aggregate representation of UCR data,
it conveys the annual reported crime experience
by showing a relative frequency of occurrence of
Index offenses. It should not be taken to imply a
regularity in the commission of crime. The Crime
Clock represents the annual ratio of crime to fixed
time intervals.

One
Crime Index
Offense
every 2.7 seconds

One
Burglary
every 15.4
seconds

One
Motor Vehicle
Theft every 27.1
seconds

One
Property Crime
every
3.1 seconds

One
Larceny-theft
every 4.5
seconds

FIGURE 1.3   The UCR Crime Clock

model, overwhelmed by political and legalistic realities, has set the agenda. Private security delivers a welcome alternative.[16]

Problems with violence and criminality extend far beyond the world of street crime. Escalating rates of violence and inappropriate behavior occur in most customary settings, from workplaces to religious services, from sports and entertainment events to business settings and personal travel. Airlines, for example, report that harassment of flight attendants by passengers has tripled over the last four years.[17] Violence has found its way into everyday life—random spree-shootings, workplace violence, school massacres, and terrorist plots are grim examples of this emerging cultural deconstruction that no public police model will affect alone. Here too lie other types of contributions that the security industry can make.

Predictions of crime problems in the future indicate that such problems will continue, making a central role all the more imperative for the private security industry. See Figure 1.4 for U.S. regional crime data.[18]

All crime rates are expected to rise again. Juvenile rates are most illustrative of this foreboding picture.[19] By the years 2005 through 2007, many experts expect a 20 percent increase in the juvenile correctional population between the ages 14 through 17. By 2010, it is expected that the number of juveniles between the ages of 12 and 19 will reach 35 million. Also, adult incarceration rates will continue to skyrocket, providing a dismal picture of a crime-ridden nation. See Figure 1.5[20] and Figure 1.6.[21] With the current state of affairs and a reliable perception of the future, public police cannot go it alone and will rightfully depend on vibrant and eclectic private security professionals to solve the dilemma.

"Police officers are encountering more children with no hope, no fear, no rules and no life expectancy."[22] In such a stark reality of blank, cold-hearted criminality, the public police system can depend on a professional counterpart that will stand side by side with the police to protect the community. Private security interests stand firm with the same convictions in the battle for community and culture.

Despite the logic of such an alliance, some law enforcement quarters still resist such integration. For some, the clarity of mission and bureaucratic ends precludes the melding of competing entities. In this myopic view, nothing can change—nothing will improve, and the status quo will be maintained. For others, to which this text's project dedicates itself, a dramatic need arises for creative and innovative thinking. The stakes are simply too high to be entrenched by present policing initiatives and methods that are, at least for the most part, largely ineffective. The possible results of collaboration and ingenuity are too compelling to ignore.

What is suggested within the following pages is something radically different from the status quo, since in this analysis, there is conviction about the results of and interplay between a public police system and its private sector counterparts. Here, public police appreciate the wisdom of the private sector model and draw on its strengths and accept its weaknesses. In this case, the private sector compatibly operates in conjunction with public police forces, lending assistance when needed and respecting the boundaries of legal authority. Also, the two worlds merge and blend rather than resist and undermine one another. Private security in

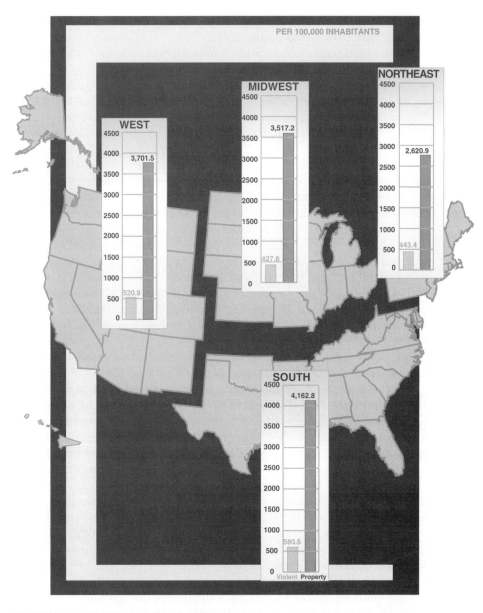

FIGURE 1.4   UCR Regional Crime Data

general seeks not its severance from the public policing model but rather companionship. The two approaches should not be estranged but instead should be integrated. Each should depend on the other and work as team players rather than opponents. Instead of estrangement, there must be a return to the roots of what public safety means. The public model is in its infancy when compared with the private system—but both share a common lineage and genealogy. The stakes are

As of December 31, 2001, there were 2,100,146 United States residents incarcerated in the following facilities:

State and Federal Prisons	1,324,465[1]
Local Jails	631,240
Juvenile Detention Facilities	108,965[2]
U.S. Territorial Prisons	15,852
U.S. Immigration and Naturalization Facilities	8,761
Armed Services (Military) Prisons	2,436
Indian Country Jails	1,912

[1]Excludes inmates in local jails held for federal and state authorities.
[2]As of October 1999.

FIGURE 1.5   Rates of Incarceration

clear in today's society. Novel, innovative approaches to problem solving and effective models for prevention, intervention, and response are mandatory to ensure a better tomorrow.

Public safety needs to be defined in a holistic and multilevel manner, and its operational philosophy and methodology should undergo an extensive reexamination. Only then will the system maximize positive deterrent effects and will preventive measures impact the community and culture.

For example, by properly securing a community, both public and private officers can remove the barrier of fear and, in turn, allow interaction to take place among community members—a fundamental need in the crime prevention effort. The same action also allows businesses to conduct operations free from crime, which directly impacts the costs associated with a business's products or services. As a result, costs to consumers are reduced, and, consequently, a community's standard of living improves. The private sector understands the economic dynamic more

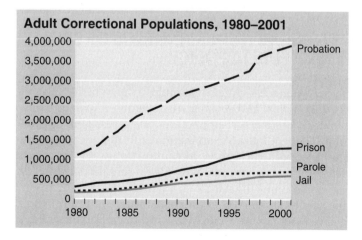

FIGURE 1.6   Level of Prison Population

than does its public counterpart and knows how to upgrade communal quality of life. Private sector operatives work to reclaim the hearts and minds of communities long alienated by a public model that it warily trusts. Security breeds relationships because operations cannot be sustained without satisfied customers. "The security provider's attitude in the relationship should reflect the desire for a long-term partnership with the client."[23]

Private sector police come into the equation with far less baggage and with a willingness to respond rapidly, in contrast to the bureaucratic lethargy that slows down the public response. Here lies the genius of cooperation, the shared and mutually learned experience. Underlying this text's entire approach is the heartfelt belief that private security should be rooted firmly in the American system of law and order, rather than to be treated as an afterthought. This enterprise ennobles both its members and constituents.[24] The private sector allows an entire nation to exist and operate by fulfilling its public responsibility through private means.

Indeed, the private sector philosophy is part and parcel of the American tradition. Self-help, self-reliance, and self-protection represent a way of life in the American experience.[25] Self-help and self-protection signify the essence of a free people who do not await public law enforcement's reaction to crime, but display the moral courage and will to protect its own. The greatness of a nation directly relates to the willingness of its citizenry to stand up and resist the way of life that crime brings. This relationship is true in the nation, the state, the neighborhood, and the business district.[26]

In business and industry, the private security industry shines, since it delivers essential services that the free market depends on. Firms that specialize in protection services can visualize how and why communities live and die, thrive and disintegrate. By providing preventative and protective services to private interests, the private practitioner is ultimately securing the stability of the community. Few would argue that this is not a basic public responsibility.

II. THE HISTORICAL UNDERPINNINGS OF PRIVATE SECURITY AND PUBLIC POLICE

Public safety and its operational philosophy, whether private or public in design, reflect the political and social environment. As with any other type of institution, an evolution occurs. A clear and accurate assessment of private security or public sector justice requires an examination of its historical underpinnings. By assessing societal and political trends, in conjunction with the growth of a formal police model, one gains insight into how the present model emerged. In this case, the examination assumes the nature of a paradigm—its corresponding maintenance or its shift or alteration to other forms. In other words, how did the present system of law enforcement come about? How did the relationship between private security and law enforcement arise? How has it separated? How has it been changed over time? Have there been fundamental changes in the makeup and emphasis of these two entities? An examination of the past is a crucial step in resolving these issues and questions.

Both Thomas S. Kuhn's and Joel Barker's research on the nature of paradigms and paradigm shifts defines a paradigm as a "set of rules and regulations, which does two things. First, some of the rules establish the edges or boundaries of a territory. . . Second, the rest of the rules tell you how to act within those boundaries to achieve some measure of success. . ."[27] The paradigm explains how both private and public law enforcement operate and define their typical and expected norms. Once this is established, Barker indicates that the entrenched paradigm is subject to change when "the rules change fundamentally."[28] Paradigm shifts establish new boundaries; as well as create new problems and new ways of resolution. Law enforcement is not immune to this dynamic and should be aware of these definitions. Barker breaks down the sequence of change into a *Life Span Continuum*, which is composed of three phases, as shown at Figure 1.7.[29]

Phase "A" is the rule clarification phase, in which we begin to figure out what the new rules are. Although problem solving does occur, it is not prevalent. This phase mainly deals with clarifying the foundation of the new paradigm. Phase "B" is the problem-solving phase and begins to gain momentum because the rules begin to be established enough to facilitate better, more effective complex problem-solving. Phase "C" is the toughest problem-solving phase, and as a result, the evolution of the paradigm drastically slows down because of tougher problems, usually

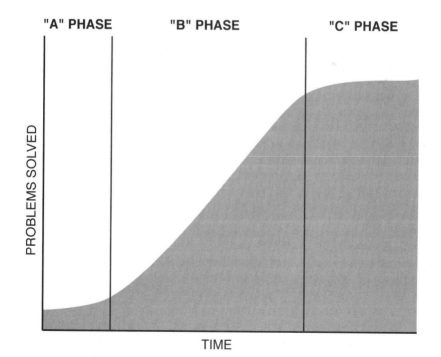

FIGURE 1.7   Evolution of the Law Enforcement Paradigm

reserved for last. As a result of increased difficulty in solving problems in the later phases of the paradigm (in the late "B" phase and early "C" phase), policy makers in any entity shift away from the rules that were developed in phase "A" and expanded during phase "B." This inevitable shift eventually ends the life span of a paradigm and creates an alternative one.

The horizontal line that describes time for completion and the vertical lines that describe the number of problems that have been solved outline the paradigm. As the paradigm evolves and problems are solved, the paradigm line increases in time of existence, and it extends higher and higher after every new accomplishment.

Any understanding of a contemporary paradigm, a way of operating, depends on its historical foundations. Throughout history, our legal predecessors have had to continuously change and adapt methods of government to ensure society's potential for evolution and survival. Laws—aside from moral customs, religious tradition, and ideas of virtue and vice—erect boundaries for acceptable behavior, and they issue corresponding judgments regarding consequences.

The enactment of laws, however well constructed, cannot guarantee the safety of a community. All laws, without the strength and power of enforcement, are really nothing more than admonitions. The paradigm of *law* without enforcement and correctional consequence would remain inadequate. History vividly illustrates this reality. Hence, paradigms shift to other approaches—none more uncommon than the taken-for-granted private security approach. Before Robert Peel first municipal police department in London,[30] the general concept of public safety was undefined. Before the establishment of the first state police departments of Pennsylvania and New York only a few generations ago,[31] what mechanism addressed the enforcement of laws and the apprehension of wrongdoers? The relative modernity of the public policing paradigm should not be assumed.

In fact, what exists today is a far cry from the historical principles of self-help and protection. Instead of an aggressive and a confident public that confronts wrongdoers, our public persona has become rather docile and reactionary. Rather than taking the bull by the horns and ferreting out criminals, our culture waits for professionals to respond. Nothing could be more different from past practice. Thus, the task at hand is the historical understanding of public safety itself. However, it would be impossible to cover all of the field's operational and factual aspects within the confines of this book.

A. The Classical Idea of Public Safety

To say the least, the modern idea of public safety cannot disregard its historical heritage. In most of the Western tradition, *protection, prevention,* and *punishment* were handled by other authorities. For example, the maintenance of law and order in the Greek and Roman empires was primarily the function of the military and its command structure. Order was maintained in those empires not because there was some formal entity but because the power base was rooted in military authority. "Although the word police has a classical origin—the Greek *politeuein* "to act as a citizen of a polis"—the metropolitan police forces we are accustomed to did not exist in the ancient world. A few cities had some form of institutionalized keepers of the peace—"magistrates of the peace"—but municipal police forces are a 19th century phenomenon: the British "bobbies" named for the Prime Minister Robert Peel appear in the 1830s."[32] Protection of both the empire and the emperor was a close police function. The institution of the Praetorian Guard that kept vigil over Caesar could be construed as an early police system.

> [T]his imperial bodyguard was in charge of security of the palace and the imperial family. Splendidly uniformed for special occasions, they often appeared in civilian clothes with weapons hidden . . . Secondly, there were the three urban cohorts of 500 men each. Housed alongside the Praetorians, they apparently acquired daytime police duties and thus kept an eye out for ordinary street crime. Although they could be called out in the event of large-scale violence . . . on the whole they seem to have reacted to rather than sought to prevent crimes. There is no evidence that the cohortes urbanae patrolled on beat, and they were not detectives. Further, they do not seem to have been involved with "high-profile" crimes such as treason and murder.[33]

The Romans were masters at control and order maintenance as a result of wise and efficient use of military units across their wide and sweeping empire. See Figure 1.8.

FIGURE 1.8 Bas Relief of Praetorian Guard

Even the Roman legal and political systems eventually relied on the power foundation of the military. The trial of Jesus Christ represents a curious comparison. Military soldiers carried out the function of arrest, apprehension, and custodial control, as well as the eventual correctional consequence of death. On that day, the justice model knew nothing of correctional guards and police officers, psychologists and court-appointed experts, but instead was driven by the military machine. For hundreds of years, Rome enforced law in this way, as did their Greek counterparts.[34] For the Greeks, the idea of a formal justice system was utterly foreign.

The idea of military control and domination was adopted by the Fascist dictatorships of Hitler's Nazi Germany and Mussolini's Italy during World War II. Both dictators found the public model less effective in their plan for world domination than the military enforcement model. Both dictatorships eventually met their demise because of a complete lack of understanding of a dependable enforcement model. Repression by brutal control never lasts.

B. Feudalism and the Protection of Person and Property

As the Roman Empire disintegrated in the fifth century, the old, dependable military paradigm was shaken to its foundation. Without order and control, chaos emerged in the period called the *Dark Ages.* Order and protection were threatened by nomadic bands of rogues and barbarians, and by territorial fiefdoms and blood feuds. Anguished communities were made captive by hordes of intruders.[35] That period was called dark because the glory of Rome and the protection system that it brought to its citizens lay in ruins. From this period forward, competing lords and land barons controlled the day. Here the concept of feudalism emerges where by the wealthy and powerful landowner gives protection to those who display allegiance and economic cooperation. In this system, small pockets of power develop that are headed by lords and are worked by *serfs,* quasi-slaves in pure service to the landowner. The chief emphasis was on revenge and retribution, with one citizens harming another. In this way, justice was primitive and non-structural. Radcliffe and Corss's analysis of the early English legal system paints an accurate picture:

> An injury done was primarily the affair of the party injured and of his kindred. It was for him and them to avenge the wrong on the wrongdoer and his kin, and to prosecute a "blood feud" against them until the wrong originally done was wiped out by retaliation.[36]

Feuding, blood lust, and tribal rivalries were the order of the day, rather than a professional response from any public safety specialist. In those times, the cultural psyche of neither the commoners nor the elite could envision having *outsiders* addressing disputes. Whereas the elite could depend on loyal servants and bureaucrats, the common people fended for themselves. Self-help and self-protection represented the only way of thinking.[37]

Hence, protection, safety, and security were not assured by any formal policing mechanism or governmental authority, but rather by local landowners and warlords who controlled sectors. The National Center for Policy Analysis addresses the historical resistance to public sector policing in this way:

> Today's heavy reliance on government to control crime is a relatively recent phenomenon. Not too long ago, most protection of life and property in the United States and Europe was personal and private. There were no public prosecutions, and the police were public in name only, deriving most of their income from bounties and shares of revenues from fines.[38]

Although this picture is generalized, it is testimony to how the public police model evident today can claim no heritage from the past.

During the latter Middle Ages, the picture became far more formal. By 1160, the feudal system had evolved significantly enough to require some protection and enforcement structure.[39] Although the historical model of self-help and self-protection remained intact, feudal barons and landowners, along with loyal servants and vassals, required security to hold stable their various holdings. Land, as well as personal property, could continue to accumulate, and the competition for resources made crime a far greater reality in the European countryside. Real property served as the backdrop for the creation of the first structural law enforcement model. Here, land owned by lords and others could be parsed up into various plots or lots known as a *tithing*. Ten tithings were designated a *hundred*, and in these surveyed descriptions emerged the responsibility for safety and security. See Figure 1.9. Each area was responsible for its own protection, and the lord who controlled the land areas pledged safety in return for crops, payment, or other enterprise. "England was inhabited by small groups of Anglo-Saxons who lived in rural communities called tuns . . . Sometime before the year 700, they decided to systematize their methods of fighting by forming a system of local self-government based on groups of ten. Each tun was divided into groups of ten families, called a tithing . . . The tithings were also arranged in tens. Each group of ten tithings (or a hundred families) elected its own chief."[40]

When crimes occurred in the region, the citizens would give out the *hue and cry*, whereby they united to apprehend and prevent the escape of the perpetrator. The entire hue-and-cry system foundationally relies on the self-protection model. The cry is not for the local police to carry out the responsibility but is for the members of the community to band together to root out the perpetrator. As these areas continued to develop, usually into large manors and small villages, the need for a collective response for self-protection grew more urgent. The designation of *constable* emerges in the literature of the times and was primarily descriptive of a designated agent for the manor or small village. The constable assured the integrity of the hue and cry, assessed fines against those not carrying out expected duties, and rooted out those injurious to the land area under his supervision. Although it is more formal, there is little doubt that the system just described is "privatized."[41]

As growth continued, so did the sophistication of the security philosophy. As towns and villages multiplied, the truncated and individualized systems based on feudalism became inadequate. At the center was the King's promise to his subjects that he would institute a *King's Peace* across the land in exchange for fidelity. These

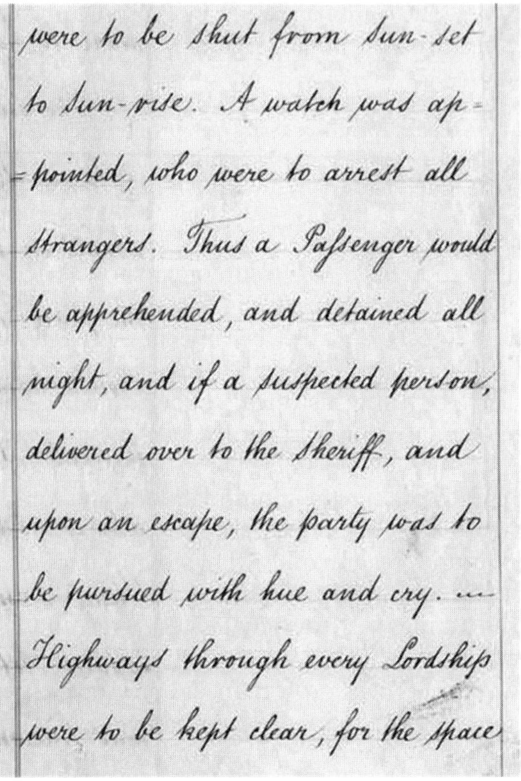
were to be shut from Sun-set
to Sun-rise. A watch was ap-
-pointed, who were to arrest all
Strangers. Thus a Passenger would
be apprehended, and detained all
night, and if a suspected person,
delivered over to the Sheriff, and
upon an escape, the party was to
be pursued with hue and cry. ...
Highways through every Lordship
were to be kept clear, for the space

FIGURE 1.9 Written Description of Safety and Security Procedures in the Later Middle Ages

early English kings created a system of counties, then known as *shires.* A *reeve* oversaw each shire, and constables reported the activities of their tithings to the *shire-reeve.* The term has evolved into the occupational title *sheriff.*[42]

C. The Watch and Ward

During the next developmental phase, in the seventeenth century, especially since urbanization was rapidly occurring, a "watch and ward system" was established. "This consisted of about a thousand watchmen who were paid a shilling or less per night, according to their ward or parish."[43] This system was composed of a justice of the peace, constable, constable's assistants, and night watchmen whose primary function was the care and tending of a designated area of a town or city known as a ward. Even today, political subdivisions are often broken down into the ward structure. See Figure 1.10[44] and Figure 1.11. The watch and ward system also relied on private citizens to scan the horizon for criminal activities and to raise the hue and cry in the event of crime. These practices were systematically integrated into the fabric of English society.

By the seventeenth century, a parish constable and the watch system were London's exclusive way to fight crime. The watch system was essentially voluntary,

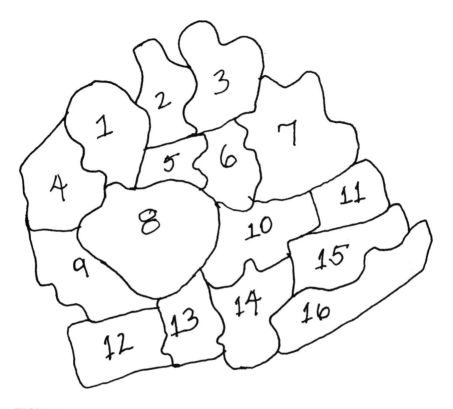

FIGURE 1.10   A Representation of Wards and Subdivisions

and the small pay given for the work required could not overcome the lack of skill and preparation needed for the task.[45] "Little is known about those hired as watchmen. The legislation only stipulated who was *not* to be a watchman: no servants were to be hired as beadles or watchmen."[46] Unfortunately, this group of *crime fighters* were not very effective at apprehending criminals, and the majority of their tour was spent publicly announcing the hours of the night. Unfortunately, the bulk of the watchmen and constables lacked the essential qualities for success.[47] In his book *Hue and Cry,* Patrick Pringle states the following:

> Such is our respect for institutions that when an established system breaks down we are quick to blame people and defend the system; but the lesson of history seems to be that systems must be made for people, because people cannot be made for systems. To be effective, any system—whether political, religious, economic, or judicial—must expect people to be base and selfish and venal.[48]

While there is hyperbole in this perspective, it is undeniable that the London watch and ward was simply incapable of ironing out the escalating difficulties in increasingly urban London. Having constables was a nice idea, but a constable's position was hardly substantial in a professional sense. The constable

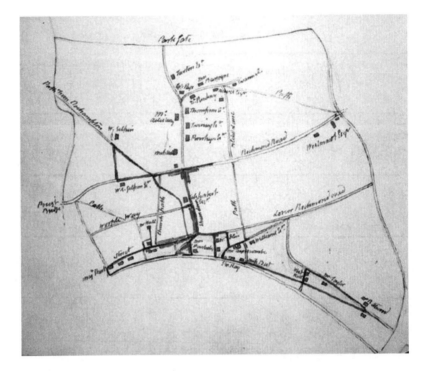

FIGURE 1.11   Wards and Subdivisions Another View

system did not seek full-time careerists but rather part-time participants. See Figure 1.12 for a listing of those serving as constables and "headboroughs" in Rotherhithe for the year 1747.

Over time, professional deputy-constables were implemented as the cities grew and became more intricate and multifaceted. These parish-constables, who were few in number, had very little power to defend against the criminal problems facing their community. All these incremental changes were insufficient to deal with the accelerating problems of crime in the streets of London. Something more than a watch and ward system was crucial to the survival of a way of life.

D. Urbanization and the Changing Security Perspective

Although many regarded eighteenth-century London as one of the greatest cities in the world, its streets manifested a lawlessness and corruption that was rotting its foundation. Watch and ward and the constable models eventually became ineffective, and thus the stage was set for a major paradigm shift in the nature of public safety.[49] But even under the worst conditions, change comes slowly. Londoners, while sophisticated enough to understand the current problem of a corrupted system, lacked the understanding of the type of change that would resolve that problem. In the police paradigm, change into the unknown or previously unseen can

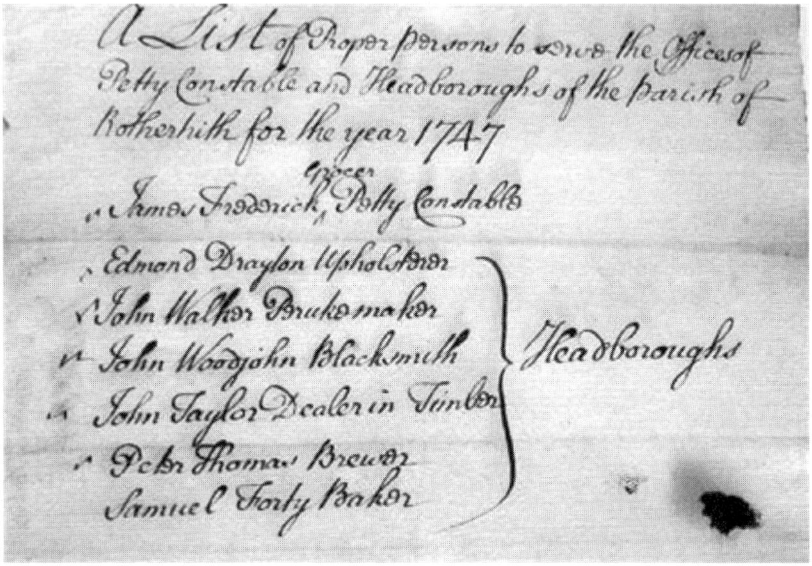
A List of Proper persons to serve the Offices of Petty Constable and Headboroughs of the Parish of Rotherhith for the year 1747

Grocer
James Frederick Petty Constable

Edmond Drayton Upholsterer
John Walker Brickmaker
John Woodjohn Blacksmith
John Taylor Dealer in Timber
Peter Thomas Brewer
Samuel Forty Baker

Headboroughs

FIGURE 1.12 Early Constables

be termed only radical. In addition, a nation-state with little or no exposure to a formalistic, professional, and compensated police model would need powerful convincing. The idea of a compensated police professional was foreign to eighteenth-century citizens. The beliefs in self-help, self-protection, volunteerism in watch and ward, and communal hue and cry were more customary. To engineer an alternative model would require dramatic rethinking. Part of the problem is both cultural and systematic. Londoners were nervous about the establishment of a police force because of potential negative impacts on cherished freedoms. To be free naturally implies resistance to governmental authority. A select committee of the House of Commons, in 1818, reported the general reticence that Londoners had regarding the police force "in a free country":

> [S]uch a system would of necessity be odious and repulsive, and one which no government could be able to carry into execution. In despotic countries it has never yet succeeded to the extent aimed at by those theories, and among a free people the very proposal would be rejected with abhorrence; it would be a plan which would make every servant of every house a spy on the actions of his master, and all classes of society spies on each other.[50]

Even so, change needed to emerge in the English city and countryside. Growth of urban areas, of commercial economies, and of the population was the force that moved the once comfortable paradigm.

1. Thief-Takers. The rise of highway robbery and petty thievery in the English culture could not be effectively addressed by a system of immobile and

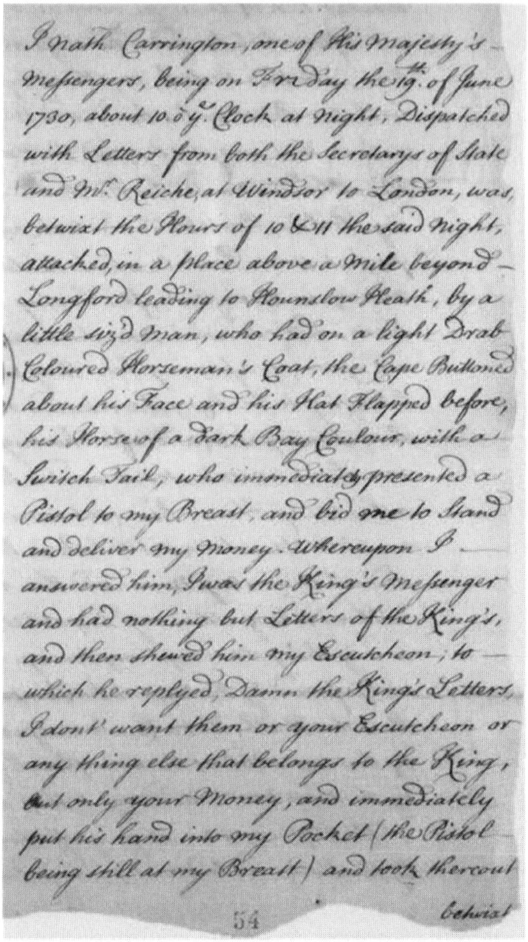
I Nath. Carrington, one of His Majesty's
Messengers, being on Friday the 19th of June
1730, about 10 o'Clock at night, Dispatched
with Letters from both the Secretarys of State
and Mr. Reiche, at Windsor to London, was,
betwixt the Hours of 10 & 11 the said night,
attacked, in a place above a mile beyond
Longford leading to Hounslow Heath, by a
little siz'd man, who had on a light Drab
Coloured Horseman's Coat, the Cape Buttoned
about his Face and his Hat Flapped before,
his Horse of a dark Bay Coulour, with a
Switch Tail, who immediately presented a
Pistol to my Breast, and bid me to Stand
and deliver my Money. Whereupon I
answered him, I was the King's Messenger
and had nothing but Letters of the King's,
and then shewed him my Escutcheon; to
which he replyed, Damn the King's Letters,
I don't want them or your Escutcheon or
any thing else that belongs to the King,
but only your Money, and immediately
put his hand into my Pocket (the Pistol
being still at my Breast) and took thereout
54 betwixt

FIGURE 1.13 Early Crime Report

less than proficient constables. See Figure 1.13, an account by a king's messenger of a highway robbery that occurred in 1730. The watchmen could not keep up with these roving bands of vagabonds. In a blending of an incentive-based model with required immediacy, thief-takers were paid a set amount by the government upon the conviction of a highwayman for his crimes.[51] They were also entitled to the highwayman's property such as his horses, arms, money, and other items, unless those items were proven to have been stolen. The parliamentary rewards given by the government to the thief-takers eventually evolved into a sliding-scale payment system depending on the type of apprehension. See Table 1.1.[52]

Yet despite this innovation, the model of private policing remained essentially intact. Thief-takers were hardly criminal justice professionals or members of the public payroll. Too often these individuals were driven solely by the profit motivation, just as the bounty hunter is, and in some circumstances they made only a minimal effort to catch the true criminals. In fact, many thief-takers worked with

TABLE 1.1 *Parliamentary Awards for Apprehension of Criminals*

Highwayman	£40 possible supplement of up to £20
Burglar/housebreaker	£40
Sheep stealer	£10
Army deserter	£1
Special felon	Up to £100

accomplices who colluded with then, and they also invented various criminal operations for the mere purpose of collecting the stipend. Some thief-takers went as far as planting stolen goods and framing innocent people in order to secure convictions and receive rewards. Many of their prisoners were either framed or seduced into crime by thief-takers, in order for the thief-takers to claim a reward for their services.[53] During the thief-takers' era, bribery was common where the justices, constables, and watchmen were concerned. The ethical standards were at best suspect.

With the systematic flaws in the feudal model that were uncorrected by the watch and ward, the hue and cry, or the competitive thief-taker solution, England was ripe for other avenues in the enforcement of law and protection of persons and property. By the time of the nineteenth-century, London had matured in both a cultural and an economic sense, and it was engaging in a number of public programs that accompany growth and industrialization. Under the existing model, change was a necessity. Public safety simply could not remain in the same inefficient form and ultimately had to shift in order to evolve along with society. In this type of intellectual wellspring, thinkers and innovators like De Veil, Fielding, and Peel began to exert the grade of influence that prompts change in the paradigm.

2. The Bow Street Magistrates.   As England yearned for law enforcement compatible with its cultural ideology and tradition and as it fully accepted the need for alternatives, it was blessed with the person of Thomas De Veil. In 1729, De Veil was appointed to the Commission of the Peace for the County of Middlesex and the city of Westminster. From that day forward, his influence on police and security practice would be so dramatic that it would last a century. Although De Veil is not widely recognized in history, his philosophy clearly set the stage for the eventual institution of Robert Peel's municipal police force in 1829.[54] Even more critically, De Veil used his office as magistrate to perform particular functions that would eventually encompass the ideals of public police officers, detectives, investigators, and private security practitioners everywhere.

The Bow Street Magistrates were just one of several magisterial offices that were sprinkled throughout London. Magistrates, much as they are today, were frontline, street-driven jurists who contended not only with everyday crime but also with trifles between citizens. Magistrate Courts were workhouse courts, of general jurisdictions, and the judges within them had to wear many hats. De Veil, who wore a closetful, set the stage for a professional, public perspective in law enforcement and public safety—a subtle change, yet a far cry from the self-help models that so many had become accustomed to.

As the first Bow Street magistrate, his authority extended to four counties, besides the city of Westminster. De Veil was in fact London's first chief of police, though the title was honorary since no police force had yet to be invented. Instead, he relied on the usual players—the inefficient constables, informers, and thief-takers. De Veil understood and reacted to the concept of crime more than had any of his predecessors, engaging and suppressing criminals and crimes in ways previously not witnessed. He attacked the most powerful gangs, which had previously succeeded in intimidating other magistrates. Also, enforced unpopular and previously disregarded laws, such as the controversial and formerly unenforceable *Gin Act*. Threats and intimidation did not drive him from the bench. Most impressively, De Veil recast and extended the nature of his own position by turning justices and magistrates into activists in the fields of public safety, crime prevention, and crime detection. De Veil used informers, as well his own personal detective capabilities, to collect evidence against the powerful criminal gang leaders of his time. His extraordinary successes came in his aggressive breakup of the London gangs. Within six years of his appointment, he was designated the leading magistrate and was titled a *court justice.*[55]

Aside from having these exceptional qualities, De Veil engaged in novel practices unheard of for his time and shifted the self-help model into a professional template. De Veil was also the first police magistrate in English history to go out of his district to assist in the investigation of a crime. According to Patrick Pringle, De Veil initiated the practice of giving expert detective help to other jurisdictions or authorities in need of professional advice. Before Scotland Yard ever existed, England depended on the Bow Street magistrates. De Veil started the practice of undertaking investigations for private clients and received payments for restoration of a victim's losses, and in turn, set a precedent for the Bow Street Runners. De Veil showed skill in examining persons under suspicion as he developed his detective abilities and utilized them as a magistrate and justice. From every perspective, De Veil opened the door for the public safety field in ways not previously experienced.

3. Protection and Enforcement in the Philosophy of Sirs Henry Fielding and John Fielding. The appointment of Sir Henry Fielding at Bow Street[56] would launch the office magistrate into the forefront of changing London's policing system. Fielding was nominated to the Commission of the Peace for Westminster, and he accepted and assumed the task of creating the first police force of England, although unofficial and very limited in its capabilities. Fielding, who despised corruption, took his role seriously and often displayed a reformist's zeal. Fielding was innovative, because of his lack of experience, and he was comfortable in new settings that his counterparts could not fathom. Not encumbered from the set boundaries of the current paradigm, as were the other practitioners of his day, he was able to look at the crime problem with a fresh perspective. Fielding was able to assess crime from a nonpractitioner's point of view, allowing him to ask profoundly logical questions. His entire vision can be best described as "criminological," with his thrust being a search for root causes in criminality and its interplay with prevention, protection, and enforcement tactics and strategies. Pat Rogers's extraordinary biography of Fielding summarizes this level of inquiry:

> Fielding's general outlook on crime was realistic but also compassionate. He attempts to explore the etiology of deviant behavior, finding the roots of evil in institutions such as gaming-houses. He goes on to illustrate the connection of crime with poverty—a trite message today, perhaps, but one which bore repetition in 1751. He distinguishes between the merely idle and those who are genuinely unable to work through physical or mental incapacity—we should recall that such people were commonly encountered in those days, when hereditary ailments and infant malnutrition produced many crippled bodies and impaired minds. He criticizes the appalling administration of the poor laws.[57]

The times that Henry Fielding lived in were rife with criminal activity. Crime statistics from the eighteenth century manifested a dramatic increase in pickpocketing, street robberies, attacks by highwaymen, gang robbing, defiance of authority, and prison breaks. Fielding's elevation to Bow Street resulted in a new vision regarding how the justice model should deal with enhanced rates of crime.

First and foremost, Fielding believed that his office, as well as Bow Street itself, could play an integral role in the elimination of crime. Instead of solely apprehending, Fielding was in the business of predicting and deterring. Fielding proposed some aggressive shifts in the paradigm common for his time. His approach centered of these issues:

- Active cooperation of the public;
- An institutional police force;
- Crime causation and remediation; and
- Correction of conditions that cause crime.

Eighteenth-century London was a cauldron of problems. "The problems were immense. London was a dirty, ill-lit place which in some quarters became lost in a tangle of impenetrable alleys and festering courts. This made the actual commission of crime easier; and of course it was not an environment conducive to high-minded civil virtue. Poverty, malnutrition, and squalor made life for a high proportion of London residents a short and unpleasant experience."[58]

Fielding developed his new brand of policing by trial and error, developing new concepts at a time when corruption was rampant, when inefficiency was the standard, and when the citizenry was still opposed to public policing. To overcome this resistance, Fielding utilized the media of his day to convince the public that change was good. His office issued what can be best described as "press releases" that announced programs, plans, and recently enacted laws.

As part of the continued effort to educate the public, Henry Fielding funded a small newspaper, the *Covent-Garden Journal*, that included advertisements urging the public to report burglaries and robberies to Bow Street, in an effort to continuously educate the public as to what the criminal justice system was about. Unlike the situation today, when such publications use criminal cases almost solely for entertainment purposes, his publication was specifically designed for the education of the public—and it was very effective. In 1759, his *Covent-Garden Journal* was renamed the *Public Adviser* and shortly thereafter became one of London's leading daily newspapers. Even then, Fielding continued to publish his police notices and information for the public. Fielding's enlistment of public support on the crime issue represented a major alteration in roles. From this day forward, the Bow Street Magistrates' Office entered into a partnership of sorts with the public. See Figure 1.14 for an account of how Fielding spent money trying to catch a highwayman.

Even more significantly, Fielding reconstituted the ragtag constable group into a secret police force. This small, plain-clothed force eventually became known as "Mr. Fielding's people."[59] While not formally designated the "public police," Fielding's organization of the constables, coupled with certain training and preparation, signaled the shift to a public ideology. Fielding trained these men in tactics involving evidence collection, arrest, and safe practices, and he provided professional insight into how to operate clandestinely in criminal circles. These men were still considered thief-takers and private citizens because Fielding lacked the authority to create a police force, even if it constituted only half a dozen men. The existence of Fielding's "secret police" was kept confidential and never revealed until after he died. Fielding's beliefs about crime, punishment, and prevention were much more progressive than De Veil's. Prevention was an effective crime fighter, as this statement indicates:

> Nor, in plain truth, will the utmost severity to offenders be justifiable unless we take every possible method of preventing the offense.[60]

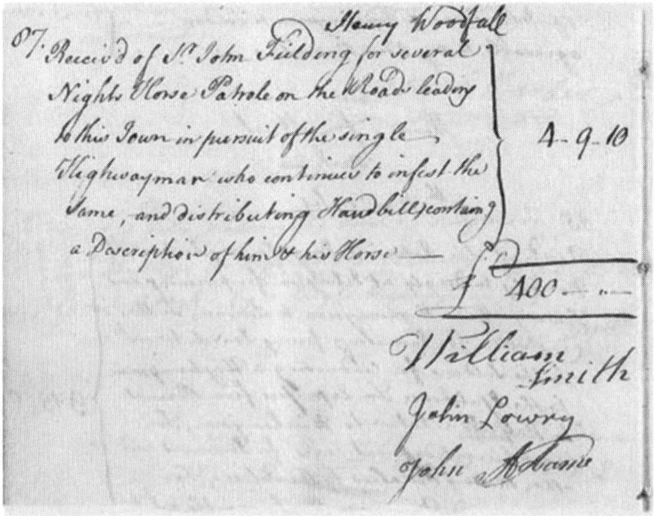
Henry Woodfall
87. Receiv'd of Mr John Fielding for several Nights Horse Patrole on the Road leading to this Town in pursuit of the single Highwayman who continues to infest the same, and distributing Handbills containing a Description of him & his Horse — 4-9-10
£ 4 0 0
William Smith
John Lowry
John Adams

FIGURE 1.14 Notes of Fielding

Within correctional circles, Fielding was equally provocative. Rather than engaging in retribution alone, Fielding suggested a rehabilitative model that would catch the criminal before the act takes place. He was particularly concerned about the excessive use of the death penalty at the time, whereas his colleagues did not give it much thought. If punishment cured crime, Fielding held, why were its rates skyrocketing? His remarks on capital punishment illustrate a behavioral edge that was not part of the current landscape.

> Not only care for public safety, but common humanity, exacts our concern on this occasion; for that many cart-loads of our fellow-creatures are once in six weeks carried to slaughter it is a dreadful consideration; and this is greatly heightened by a reflecting bet with proper care and proper regulations, much the greater part of these wretches might have been made not only happy in themselves but very useful to members of society.[61]

In this sense, Fielding blends the criminological mindset with that of the crime fighter by issuing recommendations on how to deal with the increase in crime; by addressing root causes, such as gambling, poverty, and rampant alcoholism; and by critiquing the inadequacy of criminal procedures available at his time.[62]

Fielding's reputation as a law enforcement thinker continued to grow unabated. In 1753, the Duke of Newcastle requested that Henry Fielding propose a plan that would check the rising tide of murder and robbery in London.[63] It was within the confines of his study that the idea of a true public police system took shape. Fielding laid out the unknown aspects of his Bow Street Runners, the thief-takers and professionalized constables, all of which he argued should be organized into a unified police force, subject to skillful and proper training. Also within the plan were express directions on shift and staffing, resource management, payroll, and qualifications. In place of the old reward and incentive based system, the part-time justice operative, Fielding called for the professionalization of his Bow Street Runners, constables, watchmen, messengers, and informers.[64] Fielding was equally adamant about the allocation of resources to carry out the many tasks of public safety and law enforcement. In other words, government dollars would have to be expended to halt the onslaught of criminality. Unfortunately, Henry Fielding died in 1754 at the age of 47. However, his half-brother John, the "blind beak of Bow Street," took up Henry's cause.[65] In 1754, Sir John Fielding, at the age of 33, took over Bow Street and held that office until 1780.

Although Henry Fielding had outlined the plan and had tinkered with the beginning stages of a public crime control paradigm, it was John Fielding who sought application in the practical realm.[66] Just as had his brother, Sir John believed in the power of the press and the public in the war on crime. He used the *Public Adviser* to print public notices letting citizens of London know that Bow Street's flying squad was able to respond to crimes within a "quarter of an hour's notice." Utilizing the success of Bow Street's more visible and notorious apprehensions, the younger Fielding again placed ads in the *Public Adviser* encouraging the citizenry to contact his Bow Street office with information of any crime. The Runners' reputation evolved toward legendary status.[67]

John Fielding was just as prolific as his brother in using media sources to persuade the public and enlist their support. Publications on robbery prevention, most wanted lists with physical descriptions, and regular press briefings were part and parcel of his office's operation. As had his brother, Fielding investigated the correlation between crime and its causation.[68] He worked diligently to help boys and girls who lived off the street and committed crimes and, in particular, to help girls who frequently turned to prostitution out of necessity. Once Fielding started interviewing the girls, he quickly discovered some of the underlying factors that led to their lifestyle.[69]

John Fielding promoted uniform standards for policing that would eventually transform the Bow Street system into an organized police force. His plan included many creative components including an office for property and money receipt, a treasurer, and a legal advisor to employees. He stated that all fees and fines collected at different offices should be "collected into one fund," which could then be redispersed to pay for expenditures related to the public safety effort. Proposals for stricter licensing of establishments that sold alcohol, stringent controls for pawnbrokers, better street lighting, proper relief of watchmen, and establishment of foot patrols within specific hours were some of his other original recommendations that would surely influence the London police culture.[70]

4. The Public Police Model in Nineteenth-Century England.   Despite all the efforts to deter crime, England increasingly faced staggering rates of criminality. Although the Bow Street system worked hard, it could not realistically be expected to be victorious in the war on crime. Without personnel and resources, and given the complexities of urban and industrialized life, the demands for change continued. Self-help would not work anymore and could not withstand the unceasing number of criminal acts. By the early nineteenth century, England's industrial base had become so sophisticated that cries for the protection of property, goods, and services had become very common. For example, commerce on England's central river, the Thames, had become big business in every sense of the word; however, the infrastructure, which would later assure its safe passage, did not exist at this time. One of law enforcement's most influential predecessors, Patrick Colquhoun (1745–1820), was the man of the hour on the Thames. His treatise *The Commerce and the Police of the River Thames*, which was published in 1800, displays an uncanny understanding of the relationship of commerce and law enforcement.[71] His best-known work on policing is titled *Treatise on the Police of the Metropolis.*

By 1798, the River Thames was considered a center of international trade and one of the world's greatest trading ports. With more than 37,000 employees on the river, many of whom were less than desirable characters, and with millions of dollars of goods and services traversing the waters, a system of policing the river had to be established. Patrick Colquhoun and Captain John Harriet, who were both magistrates, along with the great utilitarian thinker and lawyer Jeremy Bentham, devised a plan to implement policing for the River Thames to be known as the Marine Police Establishment.[72] In 1800, Parliament officially enabled the Marine Police, granting it an initial seven-year charter. At this stage in law enforcement history, the integration of police and government first becomes apparent. The Marine Police dealt with crimes ranging from theft to murder. Eventually, the Marine Police would merge with London's founding police department—the Metropolitan Police.[73] It was operated for thirty years prior to the 1829 *Metropolitan Police Act*, a task assumed by Sir Robert Peel.[74]

Aside from this structural contribution, Colquhoun continued the interest in criminological and behavioral tendencies that had been evident in his precursors by dwelling on social problems and discussing the role of poverty and education in the rates of crime. As part of his prevention efforts, Colquhoun opened kitchens to feed the poor and maintained a fund to help workers retrieve the tools of their trade from pawnbrokers.

5. Sir Robert Peel and the London Metropolitan Police.   Sir Robert Peel, the oldest son of a wealthy cotton manufacturer, was educated at Harrow and Oxford University.[75] See Figure 1.15. A parliamentary seat was acquired for him with his father's money as soon as he became of age in 1809. One year later, he was appointed the undersecretary for war and colonies, and two years later he accepted the position of chief secretary for Ireland. It was during this term that he introduced the Act of Parliament, that would bring about the formation of the Irish Peace Preservation Force.

Peel, widely known as the "Father of Policing," recognized the need for a more effective police force to replace the old watch and ward system as well as the limited capabilities of the Bow Street Runners. He set a standard that allowed the paradigm to continue its evolution in terms of solving problems, refining concepts,

FIGURE 1.15   Sir Robert Peel

and clarifying detailed rules and regulations. Peel believed that by organizing a group of professionally trained full-time police officers, he would be able to reduce the level of crime through proactive prevention techniques instead of relying solely on prevention through punishment. To accomplish this evolutionary process, Peel promulgated new rules for police operations, some of which are included here:

- To prevent crime and disorder.
- To recognize that the power of the police is dependent on public approval and respect.
- To secure the respect of the public means also securing the cooperation of the public.
- To seek and to preserve public favor by constantly demonstrating impartial service to law, without regard to the justice or injustices of individual laws, without regard to wealth or social standing; by exercise of courtesy and friendly good humor; and by offering of individual sacrifice in protecting and preserving life.
- To use physical force only when necessary on any particular occasion for achieving a police objective.
- To recognize always the need for strict adherence to police-executive functions.
- To recognize always that the test of police efficiency is the absence of crime and disorder.[76]

Like his predecessors, Sir Robert Peel passionately believed that it was better to prevent crime from occurring in the first place, than to catch and punish criminals after the commission of an act. In the face of great opposition, Peel ultimately succeeded in getting the necessary laws passed and acquiring the necessary approval to develop London's first real police force on September 29, 1829. See Figure 1.16, which relays some of the public's misgivings regarding a public police force.

Peel's approach was clear and unmistakable when he stated that:

> It should be understood at the outset that the principle objective to be achieved in policing is the prevention of crime. . . .all the other objectives of a police establishment, will thus be better effected by prevention rather than by detection, apprehension and punishment of the offender as he has succeeded in committing the crime.[77]

This prevention mindset was clearly at the forefront of his policing theories. He was determined to establish a professional police force and to ensure that it was an asset to the community. Maintaining the highest standards and implementing effective policies and procedures for his new officers soon followed. From this date forward, England would forego its self-help and protection heritage in favor of the new public bureaucracy, which to this day remains unchallenged. Across the Atlantic, the American experience would blend the Old World in ways unique to its geography, social order, and economic system.

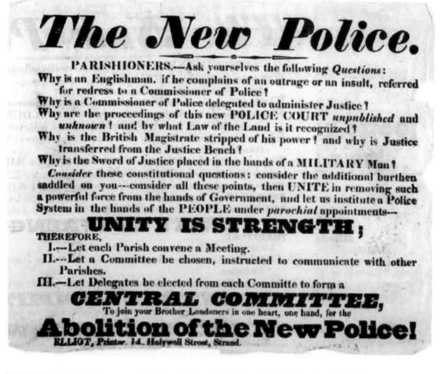

FIGURE 1.16   Propaganda Regarding Abolition of the London Police

III. THE AMERICAN EXPERIMENT WITH POLICING AND PUBLIC SAFETY

While the Peelian dynamic flourished in the English system, the American experience was equally dynamic, but also unpredictable. During the early phase of the colonial period, the thirteen colonies and related territories mimicked the British approach—utilizing self-help and self-reliance as the primary model. The similar use of constables, watch and ward, and part-time citizen hue and cry was evident in the American countryside as well.

The influence of the English culture and tradition in America is quite evident in our legal systems, especially in early colonial law enforcement. Colonial America would incorporate the systems of sheriff, constable, and watch as its earliest forms of law enforcement. However, the concept of a uniform police force was still far in the future. George O'Toole contends in his book, *The Private Sector*, that

> [p]olice, public or private, are not one of America's oldest traditions: the Republic was nearly 70 years old before the first police force was organized, the infant nation had few laws to enforce, and the protection of life and property was largely a do-it-yourself matter in the tiny wilderness communities that made up the frontier.[78]

As in medieval England and Europe, population and geographic factors in colonial America favored a loosely structured communal protection and enforcement system. Generally, the sheriff served in unincorporated areas, and the constables served in towns and villages.

> In Colonial America, the sheriff was charged with the execution of all warranted directed to him, both civil and criminal. He shared with other peace officers special powers of arrest without warrant, but did not serve as an important agent in the detection and prevention of crime.[79]

In 1607, the first constable was appointed in Jamestown, Virginia, becoming the first duly appointed law officer in the New World.[80] As in England, the constable's position was difficult to fill. His duties were many and varied, the pay was minimal, the hours were long, and the prestige associated with the job was low.[81] The constable was, however, the main law enforcement officer for the local American government in the 1800s.[82]

The watch system in America was derived as colonists coming to the New World banded together for mutual safety and business protection.[83] The first night watch was formed in Boston in 1634.[84] Serving as a watchman was the duty of every male citizen over the age of eighteen. The tour of duty usually began at 9:00 or 10:00 P.M. and ended at sunrise.[85] As with constables, finding men of high caliber to serve was difficult. The powers of the night watch were narrower than those of constables; they had no policing power and limited arrest authority.[86]

Primarily, the early colonial need for security did not center on proprietary or commercial interests, but on the fear of fire, vagrants, and Indian attacks. As urban populations grew, the system of sheriffs, constables, and the watch was proving inadequate in meeting protection and enforcement needs. The diversity of the original colonies did not promote any concept of uniform law enforcement practices or a national police. Even with urban congestion and a rising crime rate, little would change in American law enforcement. "Watchmen remained familiar figures and constituted the primary security measures until the establishment of full-time police forces in the mid-1800s."[87]

The seemingly unchanging organization of colonial America's law enforcement was not so much a sign of social stability as it was a wariness of any public or national force that was controlled by a federal government. "The principle of states' rights has a profound and continuing impact upon law enforcement."[88] America, especially right after the Revolutionary War, had been leery of any federal entity that sought to control state and local matters. Law enforcement and security, like other facets of life, were to be controlled by state and local government, which reflected the "states' rights" mentality of the age. Although local and state jurisdictions might have felt politically comfortable with the watch system of security, other factors necessitated a change in American security practices. As it had done in England, the old systems of law enforcement became outdated and inadequate in light of the security problems of the growing nation. "The basic deficiencies of the watch and constable systems rendered them ill-prepared to deal with the unrest that occurred in many American cities during the first half of the nineteenth century."[89] New methods of organizing and defining public and private law enforcement were needed to combat urban problems.

As in England, the American panorama underwent a host of structural changes that surely impacted its vision of law enforcement. Industrialization, urbanization, crime, western expansionism,[90] and population growth were major forces in the development and maturation of the American police model. Although these pressures clearly exerted a mandate for a system of protection, the exact form the system would take was dual in design. Throughout the nineteenth century, law enforcement displayed both private and public qualities, though neither system was entirely up to the task of protecting the citizenry, goods, and services. To be sure, both private security and public law enforcement made contributions, but in a splintered and unplanned way. The theories of self-help and self-protection could go only so far in the world of urbanization and its corresponding maintenance problems. Neither would the public police care for the commercial and proprietary interests of merchants and business people.

The rapid development of the modern police force was in no way the end of private security. On the contrary, private security forces continued to grow, expand, and complement other law enforcement agencies in fighting crime and protecting people and property. Now, two arms of public safety were becoming more closely defined along public-private force lines.

> Thus, by 1830 in England, and within a decade or so thereafter in the United States, the beginnings of a separation of the security function into two spheres of responsibility were taking place. Public police departments, with their sworn duties, were charged with maintaining law and order. The burden of security for private property and personal safety thereon had to be redefined. The world of private security was to be limited.[91]

With public police forces centering their efforts on the enforcing of law and order, private security would expand and grow as guardians of the corporate sector. It became apparent that with the growth of the private business and commercial sector in the United States during the 1800s, the newly created public police agencies were unable or unwilling to provide for their security needs. Public police organizations had little experience or capabilities in handling wide-scale security protection services. With the newly created sworn police serving mainly in metropolitan areas, their jurisdictions were strictly limited to their own territory. Local sheriff and watch were also restricted to local, county, or state lines.[92] Big business and industries found criminal problems surpassing the jurisdictional and functional capabilities of the public police. With interests that often covered vast areas and multiple jurisdictions, businesses and commercial associations began to hire their own protective services.

The transportation industry was instrumental in developing the private security industry. Henry Wells and William G. Fargo had established the American Express Company and Wells Fargo in the 1850s as protective services for commercial shipments both in the East and the Far West. Wells Fargo's security measures included the use of armed guards, ironclad stagecoaches, and an expert investigative service.

The railroad industry also had substantial security needs. As the greatest source of commercial transportation of the nineteenth century, railroads were extremely susceptible to criminal actions. Prior to the Civil War, the railroads contracted with private detective companies, namely the Pinkerton's. After the war, the trend continued and was directed toward developing internal police forces. The railroad police, led by Pinkerton's, became instrumental in pursuing train robbers, watching out for petty theft and embezzlement, and securing the trains from unwanted vagrants.[93] On industrywide problems, the security forces working with different railroad companies often cooperated, increasing the security and efficiency of the industry as a whole. Pinkerton railroad police, with their far-reaching jurisdictions and official powers, would represent the closest thing America had to a national police force. During the latter half of the nineteenth century, "only the railroad police agencies were with full police powers. In many areas, especially the West, the railway police provided the only security services until effective local government units were established."[94]

A. The Influence of Allan Pinkerton

As mentioned before, few players in the history of law enforcement have been as influential as Allan Pinkerton. See Figure 1.17. In 1847, Pinkerton became a policeman and, by 1850, became Chicago's first police detective. Shortly after, he created the Pinkerton National Detective Agency—a private organization that dealt with high-level investigations and protection assignments. Capitalizing on the rapid growth of the country's railroad industry, Pinkerton began to contract his security forces to protect the railroads of the Midwest. The Illinois Central; Michigan Central; Michigan Southern and Northern Indiana; Chicago and Galena Union; Chicago and Rock Island; and Chicago, Burlington, and Quincy Railroads all utilized Pinkerton's protective services.[95] It was through his association with the railroad industry that Pinkerton met George B. McClellan, vice president and chief engineer of the Illinois Central Railroad and later commander in chief of the Union Army during the Civil War. With the outbreak of the Civil War, McClellan would take Pinkerton and his detectives along as the United States's first military intelligence unit.

Pinkerton's early success helped define the role and abilities of the private security industry. For more than fifty years, the "Pinks" were the only officers involved in providing security for interstate activities such as the transcontinental railroads and multilocation industrial concerns.[96] Pinkerton was determined that the public would view his firm as a professional entity, rather than as just a business. James Horan sums up the exemplary construction:

> The Pinkertons fulfilled a need in America at a critical juncture in the nation's history—indeed; their growth was in answer to the strict law of supply and demand. They fulfilled it with fidelity to those who employed them and in accordance with their own moral principles and the ethics of their time. However, in the final analysis the tragic blame for that need must rest upon the shoulders of a society that was,

FIGURE 1.17 Allan Pinkerton

and still is, forced to seek out private police to help it enforce its laws and administer its justice.[97]

Pinkerton authored ethical standards, which his agency operated under, and general principles that are still in existence today. Pinkerton men tracked criminals across the country in an effort to bring them to justice and to terminate their criminal activity; and the Pinkertons were responsible for ending the criminal exploits of many individuals, bandits, and spies. These included men like Billy the Kid, the Reno Brothers, and Jack Canter. Pinkerton's exploits even reached the office of the presidency of Abraham Lincoln.[98]

Allan Pinkerton created the first "secret intelligence service" for the United States government during the Civil War. This secret service was to be utilized to gather intelligence on Confederate activities and to neutralize spying efforts from the South. This new secret organization became very effective in dealing with spies and in gaining information that drastically impacted the war. Pinkerton's adoption of double agents to infiltrate the opposition was another breakthrough. Pinkerton's agency was the only agency, private or public, that compiled and maintained a national system for crime reporting—a seventy-five-year database that the FBI incorporated into a criminal database.[99]

B. Western Expansionism and the Culture of Public Safety

Even though urban and metropolitan police forces continued their growth and even though the interests of commerce and business increasingly demanded the oversight of the private sector, the culture of American law enforcement would be directly impacted by the territorial expansion into the center and Western regions of the nation. Self-help and self-protection remained firmly entrenched in the nineteenth-century West where vigilante groups replaced public figures and where the role of the "posse comitatus," which descended from hue and cry, was readily understood.

Although the labor disputes of the nineteenth century were an important watershed in the development of private security, they certainly did not signal a decline in the use of and demand for private security forces. Pinkerton and other private security forces were attaining a booming business in the as-yet unsettled frontiers of the American West. With Pinkerton controlling the security and investigative services of the railroads, and with Wells Fargo controlling the stages, law enforcement in the towns and territories of the West was largely in the hands of sheriffs or private individuals. The ancient legal tenet of self-help saw its last vestiges of practice in the American West.

As the guilds and businesses had done in a previous age, Western businessmen, traders, bankers, and ranchers banded together for mutual benefit. "Business sponsorship of law enforcement started with the earliest day of the frontier . . . railroads, ranchers, mining concerns, oil field operators . . . all established their own investigating and law enforcement agencies."[100] In some cases, private security was provided by an association of business in the same area of commerce. A system of merchant police was formed in the towns and cities to safeguard mercantile interests. Cattle ranchers in the West joined forces to create associations that frequently employed agents to prevent and investigate cattle rustling.[101] These detectives, although paid by private groups, were often given official state or territorial recognition, and sometimes they were given powers as official public law enforcement officers. Detective forces, each specializing in various forms of business and trade, appeared on the Western scene in increasing numbers. Prassel continues,

> At their worst, such security organizations constituted a combination of the protection racket and violence for hire . . . At its best, a private detective force could provide real services with integrity and discretion.[102]

By contemporary standards, Western justice and law enforcement had less regard for the procedural due process. Vigilantes, who were private individuals with no formal authority and who acted in self-interest or in the interests of a specific group, served as enforcers. The first American vigilantes, the South Carolina Regulators, appeared in 1767, but only really flourished after 1850.[103] Both the Los Angeles and the San Francisco police departments originated as volunteer vigilante forces.[104] "The true vigilante movement was in social conformance with established procedures and patterns of structural leadership."[105] This was not often the case, as abuses of legal power became commonplace. Wyoming had such a distrust of private security forces as to adopt a statute in 1889, which stated the following:

> No armed police, force, or detective agency, or armed body, or unarmed body of men, shall ever be brought into this state, for the suppression of domestic violence, except upon the application of the legislature, or executive, when the legislature cannot be convened.[106]

Other Western states passed similar laws in attempts to curb abuses by private individuals or security forces. For many years, only private security forces served as the quasi–law enforcement agencies in the West. All major transportation systems were protected by security forces in one way or another.

C. The Influence of J. Edgar Hoover

Side by side with the private security industry, the American evolution of public law enforcement grew and flourished. As Allan Pinkerton strove tirelessly to enhance and uplift his colleagues and employees, public police fought similar struggles with incompetence, corruption, and unprofessionalism. Brian Forst's exceptional critique *The Privatization of Policing* zeroes in on the identical dilemmas.

> The police also established reputations for being especially tough on recent immigrants and minorities. Before too long, policing in most large cities became associated with incompetence, corruption, and brutality. Despite receiving salaries about double the level of the average factory worker in 1880, they routinely took payoffs from saloonkeepers, pimps, and gamblers in return for selective non-enforcement, and from peddlers and small businesses—free meals from restaurant owners became the norm in many areas—in exchange for protection. It soon became evident that navy blue uniforms alone did not make for either integrity or effectiveness.[107]

By the turn of the twentieth century, the federal law enforcement system had a firm foundation in the newly established Federal Bureau of Investigation (FBI). Although the Federal Bureau of Investigation was created in 1908 by Attorney General Charles Bonaparte, J. Edgar Hoover may well have had the largest impact on professionalizing American law enforcement. See Figure 1.18. When Hoover was appointed to the Federal Bureau of Investigation, which at the time was called "Bureau of Investigation," there were approximately 650 employees. Hoover immediately terminated agents whom he considered unqualified, and he proceeded to outline a new professional image for the organization, to abolish the seniority rule of promotion, and to introduce standards of universal performance appraisals. He conducted regular inspections of headquarters and field offices. Implementing age limitations and physical requirements, he beefed up educational levels and created a formal training course for new agents. Hoover's sincere concern for professionalism was evident in much of what he wrote:

> The agents of the Bureau of Investigation have been impressed with the fact that the real problem of law enforcement is in trying to obtain the cooperation and sympathy

FIGURE 1.18   J. Edgar Hoover

of the public and that they cannot hope to get such cooperation until they themselves merit the respect of the public.[108]

Hoover, who understood the need for community support, worked feverishly to deliver the message of the FBI to the American people. Skilled in public relations, Hoover would craft an unassailable image of the FBI. This image permeated among all employees at the FBI and fostered professional loyalty that was unrivaled at the time.

Ultimately, Hoover was a tenacious law enforcement professional who believed in professionalism, dedication, and sophistication in the delivery of public safety. He showed foresight in his thinking, agility in maneuvering within the political realm, and ethics that uplifted his cohorts. He believed in law and order, and he treated the subject evenly regardless of the pressures of the time. An example of this belief is the Japanese internment camps, when more than one hundred thousand American Japanese were herded into concentration camps and detained without probable cause during World War II. Hoover described this situation as "a capitulation of public hysteria" and vehemently argued against these unlawful detentions "unless there were sufficient facts upon which to justify the arrests." J. Edgar Hoover, who remained the director of the Federal Bureau of Investigation for forty-eight years, played a central role in the professionalization of the law enforcement community.

IV. THE AMERICAN PARADIGM OF PUBLIC SAFETY: HISTORY AND CHANGE

Change, alteration, adaptation, and evolution all signify the American experience in the world of public safety and law enforcement. Stated succinctly, the American paradigm tends to be a blend of both worlds—fully accepting the necessity of both public police and private security models. It appears that the nation willingly sees the imperative nature of both entities, whether it be the business and commercial services of private security or the felony-based investigative units of the major police departments. But this description of the paradigm is grossly inaccurate, since the crossover between these two dimensions continues to increase day by day. Indeed, justice sector operations are being privatized at rates once deemed unimaginable. Change and integration is the only model left worth pursuing.

Both law enforcement and the private security industry have a moral and legal obligation to open channels of communication and to cooperate professionally. To maintain the current relationship is debilitating to efforts directed at reducing criminality. The continued practice of turf protection, stereotyping, and prejudicial analysis benefits no one. As Kobetz and Cooper relate,

> As soon as the essential unity of a mission is perceived and accepted, the special difficulties of responsibility and approach can be studied in detail. For too long, the other side—our common antisocial enemy—has seen matter in terms of "them versus us." Is it not time that we, the public and the private providers of security, truly end this and in a practical and professional fashion begin to think of "us versus them?"[109]

The call for cooperation and professional interchange is quite substantial. Professional associations and groups such as the American Society for Industrial Security have formulated liaison committees for public and private entities. Additionally, The International Association of Chiefs of Police has emphasized the unique capacities of the security industry, stating that it should be viewed as a complement to public law enforcement.

In short, the law enforcement and public safety paradigm presently in place is an amalgam of sorts, a compression of numerous theories and theorists, in the mold of Hoover and Peel, Pinkerton and Fielding. What presently exists owes its essence to the unraveling of experiment, trial and error, success and failure, and hope and ambition. From this perspective, the times are extraordinarily exciting, especially since the two approaches have never needed each other more than now. Within this dynamic, the paradigm can move and shake as never before. After all, Peel and Pinkerton, De Veil and Colquhoun, were always on the edge rather than the center of change. None of their ambitions ever came to pass in the fullest sense, and partial victories were all that could be mustered. Today, ideas that each of the forerunners individually proposed are now part of the public safety landscape. There is no outright aversion to collective endeavors or to continuing claims to the illegitimacy of public over private sector. Nor is there any argument that states that public law enforcement is capable of assuming the roles and functions of private sector professionals. Neither is there any claim that private sector operatives can perform every public function. For once, there appears a respectful and tolerant view that makes change all the more likely. In this environment, change is natural, and new approaches to public safety can be implemented. It is part of the evolutionary process that enables the evolution of phase "B" to the "C" phase, and ultimately a new paradigm. It helps us to develop and implement new and better ideas as we attempt to deal with future challenges. Ultimately, taking risks, making mistakes, achieving successes, and learning from the instructions of both is what helps define, refine and develop the paradigm of today and tomorrow.[110]

Practitioner Highlight

SekTEK Incorporated

SekTEK provides security and protection for the Goddard Flight Center, National Aeronautics and Space Administration (NASA). This private sector firm is responsible for providing and operating armed uniformed protective personnel directed at the physical protection of this critical NASA facility. Not only are they responsible for providing uniformed security, they also take care of locksmithing, electronic security, classified document control, material destruction, identification services, the analysis of the security for the facility, emergency medical support, as well as a host of other responsibilities.

For the public safety sector, whether private or public, the problems confronted have never been as demanding as those in today's society. Collapse in community and family, unsafe streets and neighborhoods, rampant drugs and sexual violence, dangerous tenements and living quarters seem more common than not. Tragically, the law enforcement sector has even become accustomed to writing off certain community settings as beyond hope. Retreat is shocking enough—to not consider a change in this paradigm is inexcusable. That is the crux of this analysis—to challenge the existing paradigm with change and alteration and to offer hope to communities once thought beyond repair. From this vantage point, the private sector offers an alternative to the existing enforcement model by blending the skills and acumen so apparent in both models and by providing a positive vision for even the most crime-ridden communities. Change in the paradigm of community protection is the solution. Change and innovation should not only be welcomed but also encouraged. The very idea of protecting a "community" rather than forensically and scientifically detecting criminality alone is a shift from the existing paradigm. Public safety, which rests in the twilight of the latter phases of the paradigm, thus is ripe for dramatic change. The new paradigm manifests itself from the mid to the late "B" phase, as problems become harder to solve and new ways must be explored in order to meet those challenges.

In the 1980s, modern policing entered the "C" phase of the paradigm with the advent of community-oriented policing. Change was justified on two fronts. The first is that law enforcement finally realized its inability to successfully combat crime without the support of the citizenry. The second is citizen ownership—a mindset of wanting more involvement and more input in how police operations are conducted within neighborhoods. But the larger question remains, Is the public police system capable of such an undertaking? Can the public police model fully integrate itself into the community setting? Although the argument sounds attractive, have departments substantively proven success in integration? If communities are ever increasingly disconnected from the law enforcement community, if high levels of distrust and animosity exist, and if crime rates and quality-of-life issues cannot be improved, how can public police claim efficacy?[111]

Although the private security industry accomplishes much in a myriad of settings, it is this text's primary thesis that its greatest accomplishments can occur in the community setting. This analysis blends the worlds of private security and protection with public law enforcement, and it offers up a paradigm that rattles common perception about how the public safety and law enforcement communities can impact neighborhood settings. In short, private security is more effective at establishing community-based approaches than is the public police. Private-sector, community-based crime prevention and protection will encompass this new phase in the continuum of change.

V. CONCLUSION

Delivering a general picture of the security industry requires a look back into the heritage and historical underpinnings of this phenomenal industry. Not only does history instruct us regarding where things come from, but also it reminds us of the initial and ultimate purpose of the industry itself—to serve and protect a wide array of interests. Private security is fundamentally rooted in a philosophy of self-help and self-protection, and this self-protection approach is part and parcel of the American experience. Indeed, the concept of a public law enforcement function is clearly a radical departure from our historical foundations. Private sector justice has long been a fixture in the ways of the West. From the idea of royal and military peace-keeping, from the idea of part-time private citizens engaged in the watch and ward, to the idea of commercial hiring of private officers to oversee the safety and sanctity of business and proprietary interest, the public financing of the affairs of law enforcement is a modern phenomena. For nearly 200 years, Graeco-Roman, Western tradition has displayed a preference for the posse comitatus, the hue and cry, the idea of some respectable vigilante reaction to criminality over the publicly funded federal, state, and local police entity. Not until the nineteenth century does any serious effort occur to redirect the plan and purposes of justice operations. Pathfinders in the mold of Sir John and Sir Henry Fielding, Sir Robert Peel, and Patrick Colquhoun blazed the way for a shift of resource to public operations. Comparatively, Allan Pinkerton continued to offer up the alternative to publicly based policing and so intertwined his corporate operations into the fabric of commercial and industrial life, that it is now impossible to deny the importance of the private sector justice. This chapter blends history with the reality of the present, and in many respects the chapter reaffirms the seminal role that private sector justice plays in the maintenance of an equitable and a secure collective.

Notes

1. Federal Bureau of Investigation, *Crime in the United States 2000,* 5 (GPO: Washington, D.C., 2000).
2. U.S. Department of Justice, *Bureau of Justice Statistics Homicide Trends, 1990–1999 Homicide Rate,* at http://www.ojp.usdoj.gov/bjs/glance/hmrt.htm, last visited 10/10/02.
3. Gary LaFree et al., *The Changing Nature of Crime in America,* in Vol. I *Criminal Justice 2000,* 16 (NIJ, 2000). Washington D.C.: National Institute of Justice.
4. G. Stephens, *Crime in Cyberspace* 29 *Futurist* 24, 28 (1995).

5. O. Butler, *Parable of the Sower* 167 (New York: Time Warner, 1993).

6. *The Hallcrest Report,* at pages 236–237, charts employee growth, among a host of other variables.

7. *See* William Cunningham et al., *The Hallcrest Report II—Private Security Trends 1970–2000* (Boston: Butterworth-Heinemann, 1990).

8. The growth, internationally, has been equally dramatic. *See* Jaap De Waard, *The Private Security Industry in International Perspective,* 7 European Journal on Criminal Policy and Research 143, 1999.

9. For more information, *see* American Society for Industrial Security, *Professional Development—What Is Security?* at http://www.asisonline.org/careerwhat.html, last visited 10/10/02.

10. Frank MacHovec, *Security Services, Security Science* 11 (Springfield, MO, Charles C Thomas, 1992).

11. Despite the envy from afar, status perceptions are often vastly different. Deborah Michael's study of security officers shows a negative self-image as "junior partners" when compared with public police officers. Deborah Michael, *The Levels of Orientation Security Officers Have towards a Public Policing Function, Security Journal* 33 (1999).

12. David Sklansky, *The Private Police,* 46 *UCLA Law Review* 1166, 1177 (1999).

13. Sklansky at 1171.

14. FBI, *Crime in the United States 2000* at Figure 2.1.

15. Morgan O. Reynolds, *Review of "To Serve and Protect,"* National Center for Policy Analysis, The Idea House, at http://www.ncpa.org/oped/morgan/mor022100.html, Feb. 21, 2000.

16. Steve Sloan, *Developing a Proactive Approach to Crisis Management: Command Post Exercises and the Crucial Role of the Intelligence Function,* 2 *The Security Journal* 18 (Jan. 1991).

17. So common are these outbursts that one company, Aon Group Aviation, provides insurance policies, underwritten by Lloyd's of London, which specifically cover incidents and injuries arising from "air rage." Just as distressful are "road rage" cases in which acts of violence and insensitivity unravel on roads and highways. These terms imply not only our level of aggression but also the level of violence that filters through common living experiences.

18. FBI, *Crime in the United States* 2000 at Figure 2.4.

19. *See Family First, Kids and Violence—A National Survey and Report* (1991).

20. Bureau of Justice Statistics, *U.S. Prison Population as of Dec. 31, 2001,* at http://www.ojp.usdoj.gov/bjs/pub/press/p01pr.htm, last visited 10/10/02.

21. Bureau of Justice Statistics, *Adult Correctional Populations 1980–2000,* at http://www.ojp.usdoj.gov/bjs/glance/corr2.htm, last visited 10/10/02.

22. John Fireman, International Association of Chiefs of Police.

23. Mark Borchers, *Building Security Relationships, Security Management* (July 1996) at 104.

24. The security industry has shown inconsistent rhetoric in the matter of pay and benefits for its members. Lack of professionalism will never equate with the concept. *See Are Security Officers Dying, Protection News.*

25. Charles P. Nemeth, *Private Security and the Law,* 2nd ed. 1 (1995).

26. Carl F. Horowitz, in his work *An Empowerment Strategy for Eliminating Neighborhood Crime,* highlights the power of the private sector on business and community, and establishes the fundamental reason why the private sector is so vital to the control of crime:

> Local residents, fearing crime, are unwilling to patronize neighborhood businesses during evening hours. Business owners may be willing to bear the risk of

crime in order to attract evening customers, but if residents are too frightened to shop, many of the businesses will not survive. As a result, many inner city residents no longer enjoy the convenience of having neighborhood stores. A lengthy trip thus may be required for groceries, clothing, and other household goods.

27. See Thomas S. Kuhn, *The Structure of Scientific Revolutions* (Univ. of Chicago Press, Chicago, 1970) and Joel A. Barker, *Paradigms: The Business of Discovering the Future* (Harper Business, New York, 1993).
28. *Id.*
29. *Id.*
30. *See* Elaine A. Reynolds, *Before the Bobbies* (Stanford, CA, Stanford Univ. Press 1998); Peter John Stephens, *The Thief-takers* (W. W. Norton, New York 1970.)
31. James Richardson, *The New York Police* 38 (Oxford Univ. Press, New York, 1970); Roger Lane, *Policing the City: Boston: 1822–1885* 7 (Holiday House, New York, 1975); S. Bacon, *The Early Development of American Municipal Police* 44 (1939). On Microform-Penn State Univ. State College, PA.
32. Fred Mench, *Policing Rome: Maintaining Order in Fact and Fiction,* at http://www.stockton.edu/~roman/fiction/eslaw2.htm, last updated 7/25/99.
33. Mench, *Policing Rome.*
34. *See* Plato, *Laws;* and Aristotle, *Nicomachean Ethics.*
35. *See* George Radcliffe and E. L. Corss, *The English Legal System* (Butterworth, Woburn, MA, 1970); Mark Radin, *Handbook of Anglo-American Legal History* (West Publishing, St. Paul, MN 1936); and William Holdsworth, *A History of English Laws,* Oxford Clarendon Press London (1927).
36. Radcliffe and Corss at 6.
37. Frank Prassel, *The Western Peace Officer* 126 (1972).
38. National Center for Policy Analysis, *Using the Private Sector to Deter Crime,* at http://www.public-policy.org/~ncpa/w/w79.html, March 1994.
39. Patrick Pringle, *Hue and Cry* (William Morrow). New York, 1979.
40. National Sheriff's Association, *History* at http://www.sheriffs.org/about/history/middle_ages.htm. (2001).
41. Nemeth at 2.
42. Nemeth at 3.
43. Pringle at 43.
44. For another example, see: Elaine A. Reynolds, *Before the Bobbies,* Map 1.1 (Stanford Univ. Press, 1998).
45. *See* Nemeth at 3.
46. Reynolds at 24.
47. Reynolds at 40–41.
48. *See* Pringle.
49. Pringle describes the situation in eighteenth-century London at pages 29–30 of *Hue and Cry.*
50. Reynolds, *Before the Bobbies* at 107.
51. *See* Pringle at 35.
52. Pringle at 35–36.
53. *See* Pringle at 36.
54. *See* Pringle at 211–213.
55. See a full analysis of the ground-breaking career of De Veil in Pringle's *Hue and Cry* at 69.
56. Pat Rogers, *Henry Fielding* 232–233 (Scribner's). New York, 1979.

57. Rogers at 190.
58. Rogers at 179.
59. Rogers at 180; Pringle at 77.
60. Pringle at 97.
61. Pringle at 96.
62. Rogers at 211.
63. Pringle at 107.
64. Henry Goddard, *Memoirs of a Bow Street Runner* xi (Morrow). New York, 1957.
65. Pringle at 114.
66. Reynolds at 212–216.
67. *See* Thomas Skinner Surr, *Richmond: Scenes in the Life of a Bow Street Runner* vii (Dover Pub., 1976). New York.
68. Pringle at 139.
69. Pringle at 144.
70. Reynolds at 46–50.
71. *See* Patrick Colquhoun *The Commerce and the Police of the River Thames* Montclair, N. J. Patterson Smith 1969 and *Treatise on the Police of the Metropolis.* Montclair, N. J. Patterson Smith 1969.
72. Reynolds at 89–92.
73. Reynolds at 194–195.
74. *See* Reynolds at 211.
75. Reynolds at 211–213.
76. *See* Reynolds.
77. *See* Reynolds.
78. George O'Toole, *The Private Sector* 21 (1975).
79. Lane, *Policing Boston* at 7.
80. Gion. Green, *Introduction to Security* n.13 at 8 (1981). Security World Publishing, Los Angeles.
81. Richardson, *New York Police* at 38.
82. Lane at 9.
83. Charles Hemphill, *Modern Security Methods* 5 (1979). Prentice Hall, Englewood Cliffs.
84. S. Bacon, *The Early Development of American Municipal Police* 44 (1939).
85. Hemphill at 5.
86. Dralla et al., *Who's Watching the Watchmen?* 5 *Golden Gate L.Rev.* 442, 443.
87. *National Advisory Commission on Criminal Justice Standards and Goals Private Security Task Force Report* 30 (1976). Washington, D.C., Gov't Printing Office.
88. Green at 9.
89. Dralla at 443.
90. For a fascinating look at entirely Western law enforcement, *see Lawman* by John Boessenecker (Univ. of Oklahoma Press, Norman, OK, 1998).
91. Milton Lipson, *On Guard* 19 (1975). Quadrangles Books, New York.
92. Lipson at 23.
93. O'Toole at 21–22.
94. Chamberlain at 38.
95. Lipson at 35.
96. Chamberlain at 37.
97. James D. Horan, *The Pinkertons* 516 (Bonanza Books, 1968). New York.
98. During his service to the railroads, Pinkerton became aware of a plot to assassinate the newly elected president, Abraham Lincoln. According to the plot, Lincoln was to be

assassinated prior to his confirmation as the president of the United States. After meeting with President Lincoln, Pinkerton quickly developed a plan to ensure President Lincoln's safety. On the night of February 22, 1861, Timothy Webster, Kate Warne (possibly the first female detective in the United States), and Allan Pinkerton, who were all operatives for the Pinkerton Detection Agency, safely escorted and protected Abraham Lincoln. On March 4, 1861, thanks to Pinkerton's actions, President Lincoln was able to deliver his famous Inaugural speech in front of the Capitol.

99. After many years of service to this country, Allan Pinkerton died on July 1, 1884. His headstone reads as follows:

> In memory of Allan Pinkerton, born in Glasgow, Scotland, August 25, 1819, died in Chicago, Illinois, July 1, 1884, aged 65 years. A friend to honesty and a foe to crime, devoting himself for a generation to the prevention and detection of crime in many countries. He was the founder in America of a noble profession. In the hour of the nation's peril, he conducted Abraham Lincoln safely through the ranks of treason to the scene of his first inauguration as President. He sympathized with, protected, and defended the slaves, and labored earnestly for their freedom. Hating wrong and loving good, he was strong, brave, tender, and true.

100. Frank Prassel, *The Western Peace Officer* 132 (1972). Univ. of Oklahoma Press, Norman, OK.
101. Prassel at 126–149.
102. Prassel at 133.
103. Lawrence Friedman, *The History of American Law* 17 (1979). Simon & Schuster New York.
104. Friedman at 18–19.
105. Prassel at 131.
106. *See* Prassel for an interesting discussion.
107. Brian Forst, & *The Privatization and Civilianization of Policing,* (From Boundary Changes in Criminal Justice Organizations; Criminal Justice 2000 Vol. 2, pp 19–79, 2000 Charles M. Friel, ed.) Washington DC, National Institute of Justice.
108. *See* Forst, *The Privatization and Civilianization of Policing,* (From Boundary Changes in Criminal Justice Organizations; Criminal Justice 2000 Vol. 2, pp 19–79, 2000 Charles M. Friel, ed.) Washington DC, National Institute of Justice.
109. *See The Hallcrest Report* II at 196.
110. *See* David H. Bayley, *Police for the Future.* Oxford University Press, New York, 1994. Even the reprehensible or irresponsible acts of men responsible for public safety should be a learning experience. These actions show us a side of who we are as a society. They show us our shortcomings and alert us to changes needed to better ourselves at what we do. At the time of this writing, a New York police officer by the name of Justin Volpe confessed to sodomizing Abner Louima with a broomstick while Mr. Louima was in his custody. How can a man sworn to protect others commit such an act? Even worse, how can other officers participate in such an act or be witnesses to it, such as in this case, and do nothing to stop it? The lesson we learn here is that societal influences and transgressions create public safety issues that can affect us all—not just the habitual criminal and those who live similar lifestyles. This incident, as well as many others like it, is a clear example of how the extreme behavior seen throughout society has made its way into public safety. This is not at all an isolated case, and it indicates a strong need to reassess the types of attitudes that are infiltrating public safety organizations today.
111. Even in 1933, Dr. J. P. Shalloo's groundbreaking *Private Police* saw the discontent—the inability to see how the public model is incapable of self-sufficiency (at 212).

2

Privatization, the Private Sector, and the Public Safety Paradigm

Law enforcement can ill afford to continue its traditional policy of isolating and even ignoring the activities of private security. Indeed, law enforcement and government officials must be willing to experiment with some nontraditional approaches. . .

Cunningham and Taylor, Hallcrest Report, 1985

Learning Objectives

1. To analyze and assess the impact of privatization in the delivery of justice services.
2. To weigh and discuss the positive and negative consequences of the privatization movement.
3. To zero in on how private sector justice has effectively privatized once-public functions in the justice system.
4. To gain a broad understanding of the security industry.
5. To learn about the diverse occupational functions and roles inherent in the delivery of security services.
6. To become familiar with how public law enforcement increasingly relies on the delivery of its services through the private justice model.

Critical Intervention Services: First Response

It started as a quiet summer evening at an apartment complex in Tampa, Florida. The apartment community housed over two hundred families in the middle of a neighborhood with a consistent crime rate of 300 to 500 percent above normal county statistics. The property was laid out over many acres and had a very large and dense wooded area. Most of the property had very little lighting, and the wooded area was completely dark. In the past, this property had experienced a history of serious felony crime—drive-by shootings, stabbings, open drug dealing, and home invasions. People were terrified to come out at night. They locked their doors and kept their children inside. Criminals loitered in the stairwells, played extremely loud music, dealt drugs on the street corners, and threatened residents with violence. In an effort to combat this problem, the management of the property hired Critical Intervention Services (CIS) to restore safety to the community. Although the CIS team had achieved a great deal of success since its initial deployment, problems still occasionally infiltrated from the surrounding neighborhood, as the security officers assigned to that property were about to discover.

FIGURE 2.1   Security as First Responder

Critical Intervention Services: First Response (cont.)

The two CIS officers assigned to the apartment community arrived for their shift just before dark and began their routine of patrolling the neighborhood and talking to residents. All seemed peaceful on the property. A few hours after sunset, however, a series of chilling screams radiated though the night. The screams continued, echoing throughout the large apartment community. They were clearly the cries of a young girl in a life-threatening situation, fighting for her life. The officers tried to identify the source of the screams, but the echoes around the complex made it extremely difficult to locate the direction that the screams were coming from. The cries for help seemed to come from every corner of the property.

As the screams continued, the officers frantically searched for the victim, while using their radios to call for assistance. They finally turned their focus to the dense wooded area and began an agonizing search. They crisscrossed the woods, listening, calling out to the girl, and using their intuition to guide them. Every scream made them feel increasingly frustrated and helpless as they scanned the dark, dense tree line.

As these officers drew closer to the location of the young girl, they heard the assailant flee through the woods, attempting to reach an adjacent property that was divided by a chain-link fence. One officer gave chase as the other located the victim.

The two officers assigned to patrol duties were both experienced men. One of them was a former Green Beret, and the other had law enforcement experience—they were no strangers to violence. Both officers were well-versed in managing high-stress situations, yet both men found themselves shocked by what they found in that wooded area. On the ground was a twelve-year-old girl who had been raped, stabbed with a knife, and beaten about the head with a large rock. The officers quickly radioed their dispatcher for medical assistance and described their exact location. The communications center then contacted medical emergency services and the sheriff's department. For almost fifteen minutes, these officers administered emergency medical care, keeping the girl alive until rescue units could arrive and take over. In this case, the little girl survived, and the assailant was captured. These officers, with their testimony, helped convict the perpetrator, who received a thirty-year sentence with no possibility of parole.

I. THE SECURITY INDUSTRY: GROWTH AND PRIVATIZATION

On any given day, citizens in this country have a better chance of interacting with security personnel than with public law enforcement officers.[1] As the security industry reached two million strong by 2000, security personnel have become not only primary service providers of prevention and protection but also the "first responders" in many emergency situations. First on location, the security industry continues to be in the forefront of the public safety effort. The "officers" that responded to the little girl in the case scenario above and in countless other events were not police officers or EMTs. Instead, private sector professionals, who risk their lives for the benefit of the public trust, initially responded to the crime scene. Private professionals have historically been a vital part of the public safety system.

Practitioner Highlight

Critical Intervention Services

Since 1998, Critical Intervention Services has provided protective services for the auditors of the Florida Department of Insurance. The auditors are responsible for investigating insurance company fraud, and ultimately, for taking receivership of these firms if criminal activity was detected. CIS has been providing protective services for the facilities and evidence as well.

Public police are neither miracle workers nor magicians. From the sheer load of responsibility to the diminishing resource allocation, public police need and want partners. Economics alone drives this reality. "Public police department budgets nationwide have been growing at about 3 percent a year, but demand for police service is growing much faster. In response, police departments are turning to several alternative service delivery techniques to cut costs and increase service levels."[2] Privatization of once public police functions represents a positive paradigm shift in public safety, since public police have come to depend on the services provided by private sector concerns. Private protection officers have become fully entangled in the daily life of our communities, dealing with violence, crime, crisis, and death, and they are charged with stabilizing situations until public law enforcement arrives. Whereas 2 million private officers labor, only a little over 700,000 don the public uniform. The impact of the private protection officer is far-reaching, and the functions assumed are extraordinarily diverse. Cost efficiency drives the growth model too. Governmental entities soon learn of the extraordinary cost benefits of "outsourcing" services, "funerals, directing traffic, responding to burglar alarms, citing parking violations, prisoner transport, watching over buildings found to be unlocked, dispatching police vehicles and others that do not require sworn officers."[3]

Part of the uniqueness of this shift in services has been its accelerated pace and the way that it seems unquenchable. Professor Debra Livingston's erudite analysis of the private sector summarized this phenomenon.

> By 1990, there were two million private security agents in the United States, as compared to approximately 650,000 public police officers. During the 1990s, the number of private security agents was projected to grow annually at double the rate of the public police. The police, observers noted, have quietly been supplanted in shopping malls, stores, banks, office buildings, apartment houses, single-family residential communities, urban cul-de-sacs, schools and colleges, and factories by private security guards who have become the first line of practical defense against crime in much of modern life.[4]

"Opting out" depicts a system of choice. Public police cannot stop the train.[5] Some see its acceptance as being tied to political ideology. George Rigakos holds that

> In today's neoconservative climate, private prisons, private prisoner transportation, private court security, private forensic accounting, private second-tier policing, and

private security in expansive outdoor residential areas, have all been legitimated, and private policing is no longer just about loss prevention.[6]

Providing security and safety for office buildings, parking lots, seaports, public parks, pipelines, railroads, communities, public housing, even entire neighborhoods, corroborates the substantial inroads of the privatized model. Specialized services in corporate investigations for white-collar fraud cases; executive, dignitary, and celebrity protection; antibomb and explosives tactics and antiterror strategies, further edify the shift. Private companies lead the way in labor dispute security; prisoner transports; protection for nuclear power plants; and privately operated prison systems. Even military organizations, once completely within the public domain, have come to depend on private sector services. The conflict in Iraq illustrates the interplay between military function and private justice. Control and operation of correctional facilities is a staggering private sector story. In less than three decades, the industry has made significant inroads. See Table 2.1.[7]

At a rate of approximately 8 percent a year, the security industry grows and absorbs more public safety duties than ever before.

> Virtually everything that local governments do is being contracted out by some city somewhere, including the provision of fire services, paramedics and ambulance services, road construction and maintenance, water service, parks and recreation services, garbage pickup, tax assessment, court-related services such as "public defenders," police, and jails. State and federal governments also contract for a wide array of services, including prisons and security. Thus, many components of the public sector's criminal justice system are actually being produced by employees of private firms.[8]

Private security, like many of its counterparts in the corporate sector, is amazingly attuned to problem resolution. John Hood's remarkable work *The Heroic Enterprise* pleads the superiority of the private corporation in just about every affair. By *heroic* he means "being courageous and willing to tackle problems head on." Whereas government bureaucrats cringe at the thought of more labor, the private model loves the challenge. Hood remarks as follows:

> My purpose is simply to update and revise this discussion in the context of late twentieth-century American commerce, providing students of corporate social responsibility—in the academy, in the boardroom, in the newsroom, or in the legislative chamber—with specific examples of how businesses can and do serve society through the pursuit of excellence, worker performance, competitiveness, innovation, and profit. Whether business, due to its demonstrable contribution to the common good, can and will be viewed as "heroic" as are other professions or callings is a matter of great importance if free enterprise is to survive and thrive.[9]

In public housing and in agriculture, it is the private system that seems so often to save the day. Hood holds this to be the case in the matter of crime and culture. Hood continues as follows:

> Many businesses, frustrated with the slow response and lack of effectiveness of many urban police departments, have turned to alternative ways of guaranteeing

TABLE 2.1 *Private Prison Vendors Sorted by Number of Inmates*

Company	Number of Facilities	Inmates					
		Maximum Security	Medium Security	Low Security	Minimum Security	None or Other	Total
Corrections Corporation of America	45	1,454 (4%)	21,580 (58%)	2,593 (7%)	10,632 (29%)	985 (3%)	37,244 (100%)
Wackenhut Corrections Corporation	26	1,143 (6%)	8,218 (43%)	2,345 (12%)	7,126 (38%)	169 (1%)	19,001 (100%)
Management & Training Corporation	8	29 (1%)	1,258 (24%)	295 (6%)	3,716 (70%)	0 (0%)	5,298 (100%)
Cornell Corrections, Inc.	4	0 (0%)	629 (18%)	2,282 (65%)	572 (16%)	22 (1%)	3,505 (100%)
Correctional Services Corporation[1]	5	98 (4%)	554 (24%)	157 (7%)	1,536 (65%)	0 (0%)	2,345 (100%)
McLoud Correctional Services, LLC	1	0 (0%)	599 (100%)	0 (0%)	0 (0%)	0 (0%)	599 (100%)
Marantha Production Company, LLC	1	0 (0%)	0 (0%)	256 (50%)	256 (50%)	0 (0%)	512 (100%)
Alternative Programs, Inc.	1	0 (0%)	0 (0%)	175 (50%)	176 (50%)	0 (0%)	351 (100%)
Dominion Management	1	0 (0%)	250 (100%)	0 (0%)	0 (0%)	0 (0%)	250 (100%)
CiviGenics, Inc.	2	48 (58%)	0 (0%)	0 (0%)	0 (0%)	35 (42%)	83 (100%)
Total	94	2,772 (4%)	33,088 (48%)	8,103 (12%)	24,014 (35%)	1,211 (2%)	69,188 (100%)

Note: 1. Correctional Services Corporation operates a facility in addition to the five listed in this table, the Crowley County Correctional Facility. That facility is owned by Dominion Management. Inmates held in the Crowley facility that are under contract with CSC are listed in the inmate totals for CSC. Inmates held at the Crowley facility under contract with Dominion Management are listed in the Dominion Management row of the table.

worker and consumer safety. Indeed, the private security industry has grown dramatically since the mid-1980s. By 1990 . . . private businesses, neighborhoods, and individuals spent $52 billion on private security protection, almost twice the amount collected in taxes for police expenses. These private security personnel are directly accountable for what they do . . . and are responsive to what businesses specifically need. There is evidence to suggest that the boom in private security may well be paying off.[10]

On a grander scale, Hood sees private enterprise as the salvific force in so many lost causes, from urban blight to economic desertion, from failing educational institutions to safe streets. Business is a unique social and legal institution that works with government and charities to achieve the common good.

> The role of business is no less crucial: to find ways to produce the goods and services that individuals want and need at the lowest possible cost in resources and energy output. To expect these institutions to mix and match responsibilities—for businesses to act as standard-setting governments or as environmental charities—is to compromise the unique benefits that each form of social organization can provide.[11]

Entrepreneurship has invaded the delivery of protection services. Market forces are at work in a once untouchable territory. It is "too late to halt the process. Therefore, as an alternative, criminal justice policymakers should seriously consider supporting and even encouraging free and open entrepreneurial discovery, thereby perhaps influencing some of the inevitable developments."[12]

The transference of responsibility from public to private sector is designated "privatization." "Privatization is the trend of making services and functions traditionally performed by public entities, the province of private, for-profit entities, usually companies."[13] The movement toward outsourcing and shared ventures and partnerships is undeniable. Mangan and Shanahan long ago predicted an era of "collaboration and joint ventures between public law enforcement and private security. This is necessitated by the fact that individual and corporate citizens who are policed by public law enforcement are also increasingly becoming the clients of private security."[14]

Wackenhut Services, Inc., for example, has a long record of contracting with local governments to deliver a wide array of protection services. In this private/public partnership, impressive examples of the privatization model appear in every quarter. See Figure 2.2.[15]

Wackenhut delivers the entire police force for the Energy Research and Development Administration's 1,600-square-mile Nevada nuclear test site, and for the Kennedy Space Center in Florida.[16] Florida contracts with Wackenhut for privatized protection at its highway rest stops, and Wackenhut also provides security for courthouses, patrols for the Miami Downtown Development Authority, and guards for the Miami Metro Rail and the Tri-Rail from West Palm Beach to Dade County. The *Hallcrest Report II* charts the emerging transference on a state-by-state basis. See Table 2.2.[17] Thousands of firms offer similar services. See Figure 2.3.[18]

> This public-to-private personnel leasing is the mirror image of the much larger practice of out-contracting, in which government agencies hire private security compa-

The Wackenhut Corporation is a U.S.-based division of Group 4 Falck A/S, the world's second largest provider of Security Services. Group 4 Falch (www.group4falck.com) is based in Copenhagen and has activities in more than 80 countries and is the market leader in over half the countries in which it operates.

Wackenhut is a leading provider of contract services to major corporations, government agencies, and a wide range of industrial and commercial customers. The company's security-related services include uniformed security officers, investigations, background checks, emergency protection, and security audits and assessments. Other services include facility operations and management (O & M), fire suppression and prevention, and airport crash-fire-rescue.

The Company has a nationwide network of customer support centers to insure a uniformity of standards of quality service and professionalism, and close attention to local needs.

The Corporation's training arm, the Wackenhut Training Institute develops and conducts training programs not only for Company personnel, from security officers to managers, but also for outside proprietary security force personnel. It offers college accredited courses, training publications, and programs tailored to the customer.

Wackenhut has over 40,000 employees and its headquarters in Palm Beach Gardens, Florida consists of highly qualified personnel. They are dedicated to providing the organization with a competitive edge—an advantage that enables Wackenhut to realize its vision of being recognized as the premier U.S. provider of contract services to the business, commercial and government markets.

FIGURE 2.2   The Wackenhut Corporation

nies to perform work previously carried out by law enforcement officers. According to one estimate, the fraction of security work contracted out by federal, state, and local governments increased from 27% to 40% between 1987 and 1995. The trend seems likely to continue. Much out-contracted work consists of parking enforcement, traffic direction, and other tasks unlikely to bring the private employees into contact with the criminal justice system.[19]

See Table 2.3.[20]

The cities of Philadelphia and New York, as representative examples, have adopted unique collaborative relationships with private sector police. In Philadelphia, a "security watch" program assists in the Museum and Center City District.[21] "Under the Security Watch Program, security personnel are instructed to report information of a non emergency nature (abandoned vehicles, sanitation violations, etc.) to their agency headquarters."[22] In New York, a central business district plan, known as the "Area Police–Private Security Liaison Program (APPL), was similarly instituted.

> The APPL program encourages personal contact, at each level of the chain of command, between the police and private security. Police commanders and security directors meet monthly on a formal basis, and more frequently on an informal basis, to discuss mutual concerns. In addition, police supervisors and officers interact on a daily basis with security supervisors and guards. By doing this, each gains a better understanding of the others' roles, functions, problems, and goals.[23]

TABLE 2.2 *Sites with Experience in Private Provision of Protective Services*

State	Jurisdiction	Type of Service
Alaska	Anchorage	Parking meter enforcement
		Parking meter collection
		Parking lot security
Arizona	State	Parking lot enforcement
	Flagstaff	School crossing guards
	Maricopa County	Building security
	Phoenix	Crowd control
California	Federal	U.S. Department of Energy facility security
	Hawthorne	Traffic control during peak hours
	Los Angeles	Patrolling streets surrounding private university
		Traffic and security for special events
	Los Angeles County	Building security
		Park security
	Norwalk	Park security
	San Diego	Housing project security
		Park security
	San Francisco	Building security
	Santa Barbara	Airport security
		Prison transport
Colorado	Denver	Building security
	Fort Collins	Building security
Connecticut	Hartford	Sports arena security
Florida	Dade County	Courts, building security
	Fort Lauderdale	Airport, building security
	Pensacola	Airport security
	St. Petersburg	Park security
Hawaii	State	Parking lot enforcement
Idaho	State	Regional medical center security
	Idaho Falls	School crossing guards
Kentucky	Lexington	Housing project security
Massachusetts	Boston	Hospital, courts, library security—city
		Library security—federal
Nevada	Federal	Nuclear test site security
New Jersey	Sport Authority	Sports arena security

(continued)

TABLE 2.2 *Sites with Experience in Private Provision of Protective Services (Cont.)*

State	Jurisdiction	Type of Service
New York	State	Burglar alarm response in state office building
	Buffalo	County security—federal
	New York City	Security compounds for towed cars
		Shelter security
		Human Resources Administration security
		Building security
		Locating cars with outstanding tickets
		Arrests for retail store theft
		Management training: police
		Campus security
Pennsylvania	State	Unemployment Offices security
		Welfare Offices security
	Philadelphia	Parking enforcement
	Pittsburgh	Court security—federal
		Patrolling city park
		High school stadium security
		School crossing guards
		Transfer of prisoners
Texas	Dallas/Fort Worth	Airport security including baggage checking
	Houston	Building security
Utah	State	Building security
		Training for transit police
Washington	Seattle	Building security
	Tacoma	Sports arena security
Washington, D.C.	District of Columbia	Planning and management
		Federal building security

In Toronto, Canada, companies like Intelligarde have became permanent fixtures in the cultural district and have been described as "multi-cliented, multi-tasked, multi-territoried, cooperatively governed police service that closely mirrors the municipal police."[24]

What has caused this shift or at least impetus to do so, toward private-sector operation? It can be argued that privatization is triggered by two major forces: a growing reception, whether actual or perceived, about rising crime rates in America; and the cost-benefit supremacy of private law enforcement versus public operations.[25]

Guardsmark—Our Services
Guardsmark is dedicated to the safety and security of client assets, ensuring that our customers can conduct their business without disruption.
Because business takes place in an increasingly competitive and volatile environment, Guardsmark's expertise extends to numerous areas that are vital to your company's protection:

- **Security services,** including uniformed officers and individualized protection of client assets
- **Investigations,** including undercover agents
- **Consulting,** such as safety and in-depth security program surveys
- **Background screening**
- **Facility design,** including technical and physical security infrastructure
- **Specialized services,** including worldwide executive protection, emergency operations, white-collar crime programs and computer crime programs

FIGURE 2.3   The Guardsmark Company

TABLE 2.3   *Aggregate Demand for Private Contractual Services, 1989–2005 (in millions of dollars)*

A	B	C	D	E	F	G
Business Services						
Revenues (bills $)	249.0	350.0	540.0	760.0	7.0	7.5
% Security	4.70	4.73	4.83	4.84	—	—
Security						
Services Revenues	11708	16550	26100	36750	7.2	7.9
Guard & Investigative	7665	10930	16835	23350	7.4	7.5
Alarm Monitoring	2797	3660	5720	7825	5.5	7.7
Armored Car Transport	695	905	1230	1525	5.4	5.2
Security Consulting	395	620	1050	1550	9.4	9.2
Other Security Services	156	435	1265	2500	22.8	19.5

Source: The Freedonia Group, Cleveland, Ohio, 1995.
Note: e = estimate (projection).
Legend for Chart:
A - Item
B - 1989
C - 1994
D - 2000[e]
E - 2005[e]
F - % Annual Growth: 1989–1994
G - % Annual Growth: 1994–2000

Allied Security—About Allied Security
Some key facts worth noting:

- Allied Security is the largest independent contract security officer company in the United States
- Allied Security is the fourth largest of 13,000 contract security officer companies nationwide
- More than 60 offices serving 2,000 plus accounts in over 250 cities, border to border, coast to coast
- Revenues of nearly $400 million
- More than 16,000 total employees
- More than 100 Fortune 500 companies served
- More than 60 years of industry experience

FIGURE 2.4   The Allied Security Company

The trend toward privatization is indisputable. See Figure 2.4.[26]

In money, resources, and personnel, the statistical picture shows unabated growth in the private sector. Recognition of this shift in role and responsibility impacts policy and budgetary analysis at the state, local, and federal level. However, an honest acceptance of this new reality does not always occur in the public sector. Professional organizations dedicated to the private sector are formidably involved in industry practice. The chief players are the following:

American Society for Industrial Security

International Association of Professional Security Consultants

International Foundation for Protection Officers

National Association of Security Companies (see Figure 2.5)[27]

International Association of Security and Investigative Regulators (formerly NASIR)

NASCO represents private security, the nation's largest protective resource:

- One of the nation's fastest growing industries
- Two and one half times larger than public law enforcement
- Projected employment base of 1.5 million in the Year 2000
- Our purpose is to shape a better future for the million plus who provide private security and the hundreds of millions of Americans they serve by promoting professionalism, safety and education in the industry.

FIGURE 2.5   National Association of Security Companies

These players recognize the reality of privatization more than most. Part of the shift in mentality is coming about simply because the public system has been set up to meet unrealistic, almost absurd expectations. Dollars surely have been invested. See Figure 2.6.[28]

However, dollars alone cannot thwart the contagion for criminality raging through the culture. Public police, who labor under impossible terms and conditions, are expected to be everything from enforcer to social worker, surrogate parent to arresting officer, and child custody referee to commercial protector—to name a few.

Even traditionally protective public law enforcement units, unions, professional associations, and other public police interests can appreciate the emerging picture of radical change. Public police entities increasingly comprehend this dramatic changeover in resource and responsibility. To believe that the police system can significantly affect crime rates and cultural conditions without a complete understanding of the privatization dynamic would now be construed as poor police planning. The benefits of privatization should naturally enlist the public model.

S. Ronald Hauri, a recognized security specialist, sums up the dilemma cogently:

> The days when a law enforcement agency was the be-all and end-all to crime control and prevention within its jurisdictional authority are coming to an end almost everywhere you look. The once clear, well-defined line between public sector law enforcement agencies and private sector security and business has become blurred, and in some areas has all but disappeared.[29]

Private security has shown an uncanny capacity to step in when public police experience difficulty in carrying out its duties. In this sense, change toward its services arises by both opportunity and necessity. Privatization would be here no matter what the story of the public/private relationship. Hill Harper refers to this change continuum on the *Public Police Private Police Change Theory* (PPPP Change

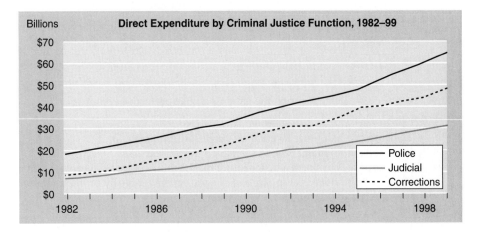

FIGURE 2.6   Rising Criminal Justice Expenditures

Benefits of the Privitazation of Public Safety

Specific advantages presented by the private security alternative to a force of public officers include the following, the first four of which are common to the private sector good and services generally:

1. The buyer of an agency's services can replace the entire agency when it fails to deliver desired levels of service quality.
2. Management can more easily dismiss individual personnel who fail to conform to agency standards.
3. Governmental accounting procedures are biased against efficient resource allocation.
4. Private organizations have strong incentives to respond to specific and diverse user needs, suggestions, and complaints, and they can often do so more quickly, without the requirement that communications wend their way through cumbersome municipal bureaucracies.
5. Private security agencies tend to be more receptive to innovation and risk than do municipal police departments.
6. Private agents have the authority to stop and challenge any person, without probable cause, for trespassing in a designated private area; also, they can make arrests without having to give Miranda warnings to arrestees.
7. Municipal police departments may be able to reduce patrols in areas covered privately, thus freeing up resources for other public needs.
8. The delivery of police services and specific police functions, like the production of other services and goods, is subject to economies of scale—an appropriate size that minimizes costs per unit of service delivered—that private organizations are more likely forces to achieve than are public forces.

Source: Brian Forst and Peter K. Manning, *The Privatization of Policing* 20–21 (Washington D.C. Georgetown Univ. Press, 1999).

Theory): "In the United States, there is a similar pattern. Major private security companies grew in areas where there was concentrated affluence and weak public police."[30] Throughout history, from Western U.S. expansionism to the current crime crisis, the private model steps in. Harper further describes the situation:

> The modern era has seen a proliferation of new companies and new forms of private security, such as varied uses of CCTV, credit cards, and computerized checks on them and other computerized services. There has been a huge increase in proprietary security. Patterns of change arising logically from the differential in organizational structure appear to be supported when examined in this broad historical way.[31]

No longer can politicians and planners look with ignorance on this change in delivery. Public police and the safety of the community need the private sector to survive. Since the eighteenth century, public police have been fully aware of this dependency.[32] Sir Robert Peel, the forefather of the public police model, appreciated the interplay of public and private interests when he remarked, "Police are the public and the public are the police; the police being only members of the public who are paid to give full time attention to duties which are incumbent on every citizen in the interests of community welfare and existence." Peel unknowingly predicted the inevitable merger in public and private services. That vision is as compelling as ever in the contemporary marketplace. Today, private agencies are expected to perform public functions. Specifically, these companies are experts in the fields of information technology breaches, embezzlement, workplace drug abuse, robbery/theft, vandalism, trespassing, breaking/entering, intimidation, threats and assaults, and fraud. Security professionals help clients to address these possible crimes and to develop strategies, and the professionals implement systems and processes to help prevent crimes from occurring.[33]

Practitioners in the private sector find themselves in a special time and at the threshold of opportunity—where only skilled professionals can succeed in the horrid environment that the public safety system labors under. But exactly how privatization should evolve will require much thought and deliberation. What are the targets? What are the roles? How can the public/private collaboration grow and mature? Where are the critical opportunities to impact crime and improve the lot of the community? Herein lies the integral question for an industry experiencing a radical revolution.

II. FUNCTIONS OF THE SECURITY INDUSTRY

The industry weaves its influence at every corner of the American culture. Whether by *individual* delivery, *proprietary* service, or under a *contractual* agreement for services, private security moves at an amazingly fast pace. Contractual services, whereby money is paid for specific services, continue unabated. "The 'private contractual security services' industry encompasses guards, private investigative services, central-station alarm monitoring, armored transport and ATM servicing, security consulting and data security and private correctional facility management services. Niche markets also exist for a wide range of specialized security services, including: bomb sweeps and metal detection; drug testing; pre-employment screening; renting of site secure vaults; radon and hazardous gas testing; and guard dog services."[34] See Figure 2.7.[35] Proprietary services show no hesitation in entering every imaginable market. The proprietary sector offers services directly to the public from property protection to private background checks, from fraud prevention systems to banking security controls. Propriety security reflects the ingenuity and brilliance of its inventors.[36]

Individual services show no signs of stagnation with a surge of private investigators, computer and tech crime specialists, antiterrorism practitioners, and executive protection specialists continuing to emerge. Individual opportunities appear unlimited. Guardsmark, one of the premier private security firms, explains its complex hiring process on the company's website at http://www.guardsmark.com/approach.[37]

Pinkerton's Value Added Services—Risk Management

- Package Control Services
- Classified/Internal Materials Destruction
- Crisis Management
- Hazmat Responder
- Confined Space Rescue
- Clean Room Protocol Officers

Package Control Services
Security officers can receive packages, secure them until the intended recipient arrives to take possession, and take care of internal distribution and delivery of packages. This routine task, though important, can be blended into day-to-day operations at the client site, including coordination with mailroom and shipping departments.

Classified/Internal Materials Destruction
This service includes picking up materials, regulating access, transportation to a destruction site and disposal. All of the chain of accountability paperwork is accordingly completed. Clients are assured that their classified, sensitive or proprietary information is in compliance with internal policies for the protection of intellectual property.

Crisis Management
Crisis management teams can staff emergency operations centers and incident command post vehicles, as well as handle crowd control, incident area perimeter control, and act as external media relations and internal Pinkerton point of contact. Clients benefit from a crisis mitigation team to provide communication, command and control both during a crisis and after the event.

FIGURE 2.7   The Pinkerton Company

The security industry, according to its premier professional association, the ASIS International, breaks down into four major disciplines.

Physical security focuses on the protection of people, property, and facilities through the use of security forces, security systems, and security procedures. Physical security personnel oversee proprietary or contract uniformed security operations; identify security system requirements; assess internal and external threats to assets; and develop policies, plans, procedures, and physical safeguards to counter those threats. Physical security can include the use of barriers, alarms, locks, access control systems, protective lighting, closed circuit televisions, and other state-of-the-art security technology.

Information security involves safeguarding sensitive information. Although information security has traditionally been associated with protection of U.S. government classified information, it can also include privacy data, proprietary information, contractual information, and intellectual property. Information security deals with issues such as who should access the data and how the data are stored, controlled, marked, disseminated, and disposed of.

Personnel security deals with ensuring the integrity and reliability of an organization's workforce. Personnel security encompasses background investigations, drug testing, and other preemployment screening techniques, as well as adjudication of results and granting security clearances and other information access privileges.

Information systems security involves maintaining the confidentiality, reliability, and availability of data created, stored, processed, and/or transmitted via automated information systems. Information systems security personnel develop procedures and safeguards to protect against hackers and other unauthorized efforts to access data, viruses, and a number of other threats to information systems.[38]

Within the major areas, security breaks down into specialties and subfields. Primary designations across the industry are as follows:

- Educational institution security
- Financial services security
- Gaming/Wagering security
- Government industrial security
- Healthcare security
- Information systems security
- Lodging security
- Manufacturing security
- Retail security
- Security sales, equipment, and services
- Transportation security
- Utilities security[39]

Robert Meadows breaks down occupational opportunities of these categories in Figure 2.8.[40]

The security industry breaks down into some major categories of opportunities that shall be covered in the following sections.

A. Unarmed Officers

The classic stereotype of the security industry has long been its caricature of the "guard." While unarmed officers serve as the backbone of this dynamic industry, they are a subset among a series of occupational roles. Officers, according to the United States Bureau of Labor's *Occupational Handbook,* assure diverse functions in the protection end of the business. See Figure 2.9. Qualifications tend to be the least demanding. See Figure 2.10.

Whether in a business or a neighborhood community, private security professionals operate in a patrol capacity. Surveying, detecting, deterring, and integrating patrol, whether by foot, bicycle, or vehicle, opens the door to communal and commercial life. See Figure 2.11 for licensure requirements for a private patrol operator or manager.

Banking and Financial Institutions	Computer Security
General banking institutions	Banks
Bankcard centers	Telephone companies
Savings & loan companies	Insurance companies
Financial centers	Credit card companies
	Crime prevention
Credit Card Security	**Restaurant**
Banks	Large restaurant chains
Retail stores	
Gasoline companies	
Educational Institutions	**Lodging**
Universities	Hotel and motel chains
Junior/Community colleges	
Major school districts	
Fire Resources and Management	**Retail Stores**
Small communities	Department stores
Major firms, aerospace	Grocery stores
	General merchandise stores
Health-Care Institutions	**Transportation and Cargo**
Hospitals	Airlines
Convalescent homes	Trucking firms
Retirement communities	Special couriers
Pharmaceutical firms	Railroads
	Ports/Maritime security
Nuclear Security	**Executive Protection**
Production facilities	VIPs
Power plants	Diplomats
Transportation facilities	Celebrities
Public Utilities	**Community**
Departments of water and power	Apartment complexes
Telephone companies	Afterschool programs
Major power generating facilities	Neighborhood patrols

FIGURE 2.8 Opportunities for Security Services

B. Alarm Companies

Alarm companies sell alarms to protect the consumer's premises; install, service, and monitor alarms; and respond to alarm activations. These companies must be licensed through the appropriate state entity. Retail stores that sell alarm systems only at the store may be exempt. Company operators, managers, and agents must pass criminal history background checks. An alarm company may hire another company to monitor alarms. Assurances must be made, verifying that the company is a licensed monitoring service. Some of the more predominant alarm firms include ADT and Brink's Home Security. See Figures 2.12 and 2.13.

C. Private Investigators

Private investigators may investigate crimes, individuals, the cause of fire, losses, accidents, damage, or injury; search for lost or stolen property; and obtain evidence for use in court. Most investigators primarily investigate civil concerns. In some

Nature of the Work: Security Guards and Gaming Surveillance Officers

Guards, who are also called security officers, patrol and inspect property to protect against fire, theft, vandalism, and illegal activity. These workers protect their employer's investment, enforce laws on the property, and deter criminal activity or other problems. They use radio and telephone communications to call for assistance from an ambulance, wrecker, or the police or fire departments as the situation dictates. Security guards write comprehensive reports outlining their observations and activities during their assigned shift. They may also interview witnesses or victims, prepare case reports, and testify in court.

Although all security guards perform many of the same duties, specific duties vary based on whether the guard works in a "static" security position or on a mobile patrol. Guards assigned to static security positions usually serve the client at one location for a specific length of time. These guards must become closely acquainted with the property and people associated with it, complete all tasks assigned them, and often monitor alarms and closed-circuit TV cameras. In contrast, guards assigned to mobile patrol duty drive or walk from location to location and conduct security checks within an assigned geographical zone. They may detain or arrest criminal violators, answer service calls concerning criminal activity or problems, and issue traffic violation warnings.

Specific job responsibilities also vary with the size, type, and location of the employer. In department stores, guards protect people, records, merchandise, money, and equipment. They often work with undercover store detectives to prevent theft by customers or store employees and help in the apprehension of shoplifting suspects prior to arrival by police. Some shopping centers and theaters have officers mounted on horses or bicycles who patrol their parking lots to deter car theft and robberies. In office buildings, banks, and hospitals, guards maintain order and protect the institutions' property, staff, and customers. At air, sea, and rail terminals and other transportation facilities, guards protect people, freight, property, and equipment. They may screen passengers and visitors for weapons and explosives using metal detectors and high-tech equipment, ensure nothing is stolen while being loaded or unloaded, and watch for fires and criminals.

Guards who work in public buildings such as museums or art galleries protect paintings and exhibits by inspecting people and packages entering and leaving the building. In factories, laboratories, government buildings, data processing centers, and military bases, security officers protect information, products, computer codes, and defense secrets and check the credentials of people and vehicles entering and leaving the premises. Guards working at universities, parks, and sports stadiums perform crowd control, supervise parking and seating, and direct traffic. Security guards stationed at the entrance to bars and places of adult entertainment, such as nightclubs, prevent access by minors, collect cover charges at the door, maintain order among customers, and protect property and patrons.

FIGURE 2.9   Occupational Handbook, 2003–2004

states, they may protect persons and property. Private investigators must be licensed and pass a criminal history background check through the Department of Justice and the FBI.

Comprehensive security firms provide a full range of investigative services, but a significant portion of the investigator force is in the form of sole proprietors.

STATE OF CALIFORNIAó STATE AND CONSUMER SERVICES AGENCY   *GRAY DAVIS, Governor*

BUREAU OF SECURITY AND INVESTIGATIVE SERVICES
P.O. Box 989002
West Sacramento, CA 95798-9002
(916) 322-4000
www.dca.ca.gov/bsis

AUGUST 2002

SECURITY GUARD
(FACT SHEET)

Requirements for Registration

Security guards are employed by licensed private patrol operators to protect persons or property or to prevent theft. To be eligible to apply for a security guard registration, you must meet the following requirements:

- Be 18 or older
- Undergo a criminal history background check through the California Department of Justice (DOJ) and the Federal Bureau of Investigation (FBI); and
- Complete the Power to Arrest training course and pass an examination. This is a three-hour training course covering responsibilities and ethics in citizen arrest, relationship with police, limitations on Power to Arrest, restrictions on searches and seizures, criminal and civil liabilities, terrorism, code of ethics and personal and employer liability. The training and exam may be administered by any private patrol operator or by a certified training facility

Submit your completed Security Guard application, a $40 registration fee and a Security Guard Live Scan form signed by the Live Scan Operator. A $32 DOJ fingerprint processing fee and a $24 FBI fingerprint processing fee must be paid at the Live Scan Site. Send your application package to the Bureau of Security and Investigative Services, P.O. Box 989002, West Sacramento, CA 95798-9002.

OR

Submit your completed Security Guard Application with two fingerprint cards (FD 258) and $96 ($40 registration fee, $32 DOJ fingerprint processing fee and $24 FBI fingerprint processing fee) to the Bureau of Security and Investigative Services, P.O. Box 989002, West Sacramento, CA 95798-9002.

Applications for registration as a security guard are available from private patrol operators or Bureau-certified training facilities.

Once you have submitted your application and the appropriate fees, you may work with a *temporary* registration card as an *unarmed* security guard for 120 days until your registration is issued or denied. *You may **not** work with a temporary registration card if you have been convicted of a crime.*

Firearm Permit:

You may **not** carry a gun on duty without having been issued a firearm permit by the Bureau of Security and Investigative Services. Also, a firearm permit issued by the Department *does not* authorize the carrying of a concealed weapon. You may **not** carry a concealed weapon on duty without a permit issued by local authorities.

FIGURE 2.10   Security Guard Fact Sheet

To apply for a firearm permit, you must:

- Pass a course in the carrying and use of firearms. The 14-hour (8 hours classroom, 6 hours range) training course covers moral and legal aspects, firearms nomenclature, weapon handling and shooting fundamentals, emergency procedures, and range training. The course must be given by a Bureau-certified firearms training instructor at a Bureau-certified training facility. Written and range exams are administered at the end of the course. Costs of training are determined by the training facility. For a list of licensed training schools, call 916-322-4000
- Be a citizen or have permanent legal alien status
- Submit a firearm permit application, pay a $80 application fee, and submit a Security Guard Registration w/Firearm Permit Live Scan form signed by the Live Scan Site Operator. A $28 Firearm Eligibility application, $32 DOJ fingerprint processing fee and $24 FBI fingerprint processing fee *must* be paid at the Live Scan site. Send your application package to the Bureau of Security and Investigative Services, P.O. Box 989002, West Sacramento, CA 95798-9002

<u>***OR***</u>

Submit a firearm permit application, pay a $164 fee ($80 application, $28 firearm eligibility application, $32 DOJ fingerprint processing, and $24 FBI fingerprint processing fees). Send your application package to the Bureau of Security and Investigative Services, P.O. Box 989002, West Sacramento, CA 95798-9002

You may apply for *both* a guard registration and a firearm permit *at the same time* for a total fee of $204.

Note: A firearms qualification card expires two years from the date it was issued. An applicant must requalify four times during the life of the permit: twice during the first year after the date of issuance, and twice during the second year. Requalifications must be at least four months apart.

Tear Gas Permit

The law requires those who wish to carry tear gas on duty to complete two-hour training course approved by the Department of Consumer Affairs. For a list of licensed training schools call 1 (800) 952-5210 or visit the Bureau's license look-up at www.dca.ca.gov/bsis/lookup.htm and search by county.

Baton Permit

To carry a baton on duty, you must be a registered security guard and complete an eight-hour training course from a certified instructor. For a list of licensed training schools, call (800) 952-5210 or visit the Bureau's license look-up located at www.dca.ca.gov/bsis/lookup.htm and search by county. If you have questions about registration as a security guard, call (800) 952-5210. If you have questions about your current guard card, call (916) 322-4000.

FIGURE 2.10   *(Cont.)*

See Figure 2.14. Some organizations and groups dedicated to the advancement of investigative practice in the security industry are the following:

- American Medical Investigator's Association
- Council of International Investigators
- Institute of Professional Investigators
- National Association of Legal Investigators
- National Security Institute (see Figure 2.15)

BUREAU OF SECURITY AND INVESTIGATIVE SERVICES
P.O. Box 989002
West Sacramento, CA 95798-9002
(916) 322-4000
www.dca.ca.gov/bsis

AUGUST 2002

PRIVATE PATROL OPRATOR
(FACT SHEET)

Private Patrol Operator or Qualified Manager

Requirements for Licensure

A private patrol operator operates a business that protects persons or property or prevents theft. In order for a company to seek licensure as a Private Patrol Operator, the Qualified Manager (see below) must have passed the licensing examination. In addition, *each* individual applicant, partner, or corporate officer must meet the following requirements:

- Be 18 or older.
- Undergo a criminal history background check through the California Department of Justice (DOJ) and Federal Bureau of Investigation (FBI); and
- Have committed no offense or violation of the Private Security Services Act that would be grounds for license suspension or revocation

To apply for a company license, submit the $700 company license fee, two recent passport-quality photographs and a Private Patrol Operator Live Scan form signed by the Live Scan Operator. A $32 DOJ fingerprint processing fee and a $24 FBI fingerprint processing fee *must* be paid at the Live Scan site for *each* applicant, partner, and officer. Send your application to the Bureau of Security and Investigative Services, P.O. Box 989002, West Sacramento, CA 95798-9002. (A Qualified Manager who is also an applicant, partner, or officer is not required to send in another set of fingerprints or pay another fingerprint processing fee.)

Insurance

A Private Patrol Operator who employs armed security guards must have $1 million in insurance ó $500,000 for one loss due to bodily injury or death, and $500,000 for one loss due to injury or destruction of property.

Qualified Manager

An individual, partnership, or corporation seeking a license as a Private Patrol Operator must specify in the application the individual who will manage the business on a day-to-day basis.

This individual is called the Qualified Manager. (An owner, partner, or corporate officer may serve as the Qualified Manager, or may hire someone to fill this role.) To be eligible to apply for licensure as a Qualified Manager, you must meet the following requirements:

Be 18 or older.
Undergo a criminal history background check through the DOJ and the FBI.
Have committed no offense or violation of the Private Security Services Act that would be grounds for license suspension or revocation.

FIGURE 2.11

- Have one year of experience (2,000 hours) as a patrolperson, guard, or watchperson, or the equivalent.
- Pass a two-hour multiple-choice examination covering the Private Security Services Act and other rules and regulations, business knowledge, emergency procedures, security functions, and use of deadly weapons. A copy of the Private Security Services Act is available through this link: www.dca.ca.gov/bsis/pssact.htm
- Submit a completed application with two recent passport-quality photographs, a $500 application and examination fee and a Private Patrol Operator Live Scan form signed by the Live Scan Operator. A $32 DOJ fingerprint processing fee and a $24 FBI fingerprint processing fee *must* be paid at the Live Scan site for each applicant, partner, and officer. Send your application to the Bureau of Security and Investigative Services, P.O. Box 989002, West Sacramento, CA 95798-9002.

To request an application for licensure as a Private Patrol Operator or qualified manager, call the Department of Consumer Affairs at (800) 952-5210, or visit our Web site: www.dca.ca.gov/bsis.

FIGURE 2.11   *(Cont.)*

- National Society of Professional Insurance Investigators
- International Association of Arson Investigators (see Figure 2.16)
- National Council of Investigation & Security Services, Inc.
- World Association of Detectives
- National Association of Investigative Specialists
- Global Investigators Network
- Private Eye International

D. Campus Law Enforcement and Educational Institutions

The private sector has a distinguished record of service to colleges and universities. Educational institutions tend to prefer a more humane, professional, and interactive approach than that offered by traditional law enforcement, although a

---

ADT Business Security Solutions

As the nation's premier electronic security provider, ADT can offer your company the comprehensive range of products that will easily meet your growing needs. And because we've been on the forefront of security technology for 125 years, you can count on us to remain there. In fact, as security systems become more and more sophisticated, you can be assured that ADT will continue to offer you unparalleled service and superior integrated security solutions. ADT offers five categories of products to meet your business security needs.

- Intrusion Detection and Control
- Asset Protection
- Access Management
- Video Surveillance
- Fire & Life Safety

Source: ADT Business Security Solutions Webpage at http://www.adt.com/divisions/business/security_solutions/index.cfm.

FIGURE 2.12   The ADT Company

Brinks Home Security—Our History
A Long History of Protection
For over 140 years, Brink's has been a trusted name in the security industry. The same reputation for reliability associated with Brink's famed armored car services is available to help protect your family and home from potential intruders.

Brink's Home Security, Inc. changed the home security industry in 1983 by making high-quality monitored alarm systems affordable to average homeowners.

Brink's Facts:
> In 1859, Brink's began as a delivery company.
> By 1956, Brink's was the world's largest armored car company.
> During its long history, Brink's has been called on to protect some of the world's most valued treasures, including:
> The bat with which Hank Aaron broke Babe Ruth's homerun record.
> The first rock samples brought home from the moon by the astronauts.
> The diamond that Richard Burton gave to Elizabeth Taylor.
> The United States Declaration of Independence.
> The world's largest uncut diamond.

Source: Brink's Home Security, Our History Webpage at http://www.brinkshomesecurity
.com/ab_history.asp.

FIGURE 2.13 The Brinks Company

large number of public and private campuses employ police officers, per legislative acts. Whereas larger state institutions maintain as visible a police presence as the surrounding community, smaller colleges and universities prefer private sector delivery. "Overall, 81% of public campuses had armed officers, compared to 34% of private campuses. Among campuses with 10,000 or more students, 89% of the public campuses had armed officers compared to 59% of the private campuses."[41] See Table 2.4.[42]

Campus security programs are prime illustrations of how public/private cooperation works—and works well. William Best, Director of Campus Safety at Bowling Green State University, and Galen Ash, Director of the Bowling Green Police Department, feel confident that they have mastered the art of interaction. They have listed various essential elements in this recipe for successful cooperation:

1. A mutual assistance agreement
2. Support from the courts
3. Shared training programs
4. Efficient communications (technical)
5. Ongoing administrative working relations
6. Police/Advisory committee participation

Nature of the Work: Private Detectives and Investigators

Private detectives and investigators use many means to determine the facts in a variety of matters. To carry out investigations, they may use various types of surveillance or searches. To verify facts, such as an individual's place of employment or income, they may make phone calls or visit a subject's workplace. In other cases, especially those involving missing persons and background checks, investigators often interview people to gather as much information as possible about an individual. In all cases, private detectives and investigators assist attorneys, businesses, and the public with a variety of legal, financial, and personal problems.

Private detectives and investigators offer many services, including executive, corporate, and celebrity protection; pre-employment verification; and individual background profiles. They also provide assistance in civil liability and personal injury cases, insurance claims and fraud, child custody and protection cases, and premarital screening. Increasingly, they are hired to investigate individuals to prove or disprove infidelity.

Most detectives and investigators are trained to perform physical surveillance, often for long periods, in a car or van. They may observe a site, such as the home of a subject, from an inconspicuous location. The surveillance continues using still and video cameras, binoculars, and a cell phone, until the desired evidence is obtained. They also may perform computer database searches, or work with someone who does. Computers allow detectives and investigators to quickly obtain massive amounts of information on individuals' prior arrests, convictions, and civil legal judgments; telephone numbers; motor vehicle registrations; association and club memberships; and other matters.

The duties of private detectives and investigators depend on the needs of their client. In cases for employers involving workers' fraudulent compensation claims, for example, investigators may carry out long-term covert observation of subjects. If an investigator observes a subject performing an activity that contradicts injuries stated in a workers' compensation claim, the investigator would take video or still photographs to document the activity and report it to the client.

Private detectives and investigators often specialize. Those who focus on intellectual property theft, for example, investigate and document acts of piracy, help clients stop the illegal activity, and provide intelligence for prosecution and civil action. Other investigators specialize in developing financial profiles and asset searches. Their reports reflect information gathered through interviews, investigation and surveillance, and research, including review of public documents.

Legal investigators specialize in cases involving the courts and are normally employed by law firms or lawyers. They frequently assist in preparing criminal defenses, locating witnesses, serving legal documents, interviewing police and prospective witnesses, and gathering and reviewing evidence. Legal investigators also may collect information on the parties to the litigation, take photographs, testify in court, and assemble evidence and reports for trials. Corporate investigators conduct internal and external investigations for corporations other than investigative firms. In internal investigations, they may investigate drug use in the workplace, ensure that expense accounts are not abused, or determine if employees are stealing merchandise or information. External investigations typically prevent criminal schemes originating outside the corporation, such as theft of company assets through fraudulent billing of products by suppliers.

(Continued)

FIGURE 2.14   Occupational Handbook, 2003–2004

Financial investigators may be hired to develop confidential financial profiles of individuals or companies who are prospective parties to large financial transactions. They often are Certified Public Accountants (CPAs) and work closely with investment bankers and accountants. They search for assets in order to recover damages awarded by a court in fraud or theft cases.

Detectives who work for retail stores or hotels are responsible for loss control and asset protection. Store detectives, also known as loss prevention agents, safeguard the assets of retail stores by apprehending anyone attempting to steal merchandise or destroy store property. They prevent theft by shoplifters, vendor representatives, delivery personnel, and even store employees. Store detectives also conduct periodic inspections of stock areas, dressing rooms, and restrooms, and sometimes assist in opening and closing the store. They may prepare loss prevention and security reports for management and testify in court against persons they apprehend. Hotel detectives protect guests of the establishment from theft of their belongings and preserve order in hotel restaurants and bars. They also may keep undesirable individuals, such as known thieves, off the premises.

FIGURE 2.14   *(Cont.)*

   7. Shared crime prevention programs

   8. Cooperative investigations and sharing of information

   9. College educational programs

  10. Informal daily contacts.

Other institutions where cooperative arrangements appear to be bearing fruit are the University of Minnesota (see Figure 2.17) and Purdue University (see Figure 2.18).

The International Association of Campus Law Enforcement Administration (IACLEA) serves as lobby center for private sector justice in educational institutions. For more information on this group, see their website at http://www.iaclea.org.

Primary and secondary schools are part of security's landscape. With school violence rising exponentially,[43] the industry has been called upon to assure safety in the facilities. See Figure 2.19, which highlights the activities of the National Association of School Resource Officers.

National Security Institute—Security Resource Net
The National Security Institute's website is the premier Internet resource for the security professional. The site features industry and product news, computer alerts, travel advisories, a calendar of events, a directory of products and services, and access to an extensive virtual security library.
Source: NSI, Security Resource Net Webpage at http://www.nsi.org/homeframe.html.

FIGURE 2.15   The National Security Institute

International Association of Arson Investigators—I.A.A.I. Membership
What We Have To Offer
I.A.A.I. consists of approximately 9,000 of the best fire investigation professionals in the world, united by a strong commitment to the suppression of the crime of arson. Each member receives a Membership Directory that lists all other Association members. Successful use of this investigative tool just once can justify 10 years of I.A.A.I. dues. We also conduct an Annual Seminar and several regional seminars each year to provide the latest information and technology in the profession to our members.

Our publication, "The Fire and Arson Investigator," contains articles by some of the leading experts in the profession, and is mailed quarterly to each member.

The St. Louis home office is compiling a library of reference materials that members can access. And speaking of access, the home office can now be reached by mail, phone, fax or internet. We also administer the Certified Fire Investigator program in an attempt to ensure a least common denominator body of knowledge in the field of fire investigation.

Lastly it should be noted that I.A.A.I. works in cooperation with other associations and law enforcement agencies to prevent and suppress the crime of arson, including the US Fire Administration, the Federal Emergency Management Agency, The National Fire Academy, the International Association of Fire Chiefs, the Insurance Committee for Arson Control and many others.

Source: I.A.A.I., Membership Webpage at http://www.firearson.com/membership/index.asp.

FIGURE 2.16   The IAAI

TABLE 2.4   *Full-time employees in campus law enforcement agencies serving 4-year colleges and universities with 2,500 or more students, by size of campus enrollment, 1995*

| | | Number of full-time employees | | | | | |
| Campus enrollment | Number of agencies | All employees | | Sworn | | Nonsworn | |
		Total	Median	Total	Median	Total	Median
Total	680	20,067	21	10,651	12	9,416	8
30,000 or more	27	2,525	72	1,258	42	1,267	22
25,000–29,999	30	1,867	52	1,210	35	657	18
20,000–24,999	33	1,663	43	1,092	29	571	17
15,000–19,999	52	2,205	33	1,371	22	834	10
10,000–14,999	108	4,122	30	2,196	18	1,921	10
5,000–9,999	210	4,630	19	2,410	11	2,220	6
2,500–4,999	220	3,060	11	1,114	2	1,946	5

University of Minnesota Police Department—Our Mission
We are a professional police department, dedicated to protecting the people and property of the University of Minnesota community.
Value Statement
We work to provide a safe environment for the students, staff, faculty and visitors to the University of Minnesota. We are committed to fair, professional and equal service for all. We work to maintain a progressive law enforcement organization that embraces the values of the University community.

Source: University of Minnesota Police Department Webpage at http://www1.umn.edu/umpolice/mission.htm.

Figure 2.17 Mission Statement

E. Retail/Industrial

Theft prevention and asset protection has been the staple of the industry since its earliest days.[44] Commercial entities depend on the focused protection system that security provides. See Pinkerton's web page at http://www.pinkertons.com for an overview of the various niches filled by today's private security firms. The future is just as vigorous. Richter Moore predicts property offenses once only dreamt of in science fiction:

> Theft has always been the bane of private security. Loss prevention is a major responsibility of private security today. Its charge is to protect property from theft by outsiders or employees. Theft in the 21st century by criminal organizations will far exceed anything in the 20th century in terms of sophistication and specialization. Piracy at sea, in the air, and at cargo terminals is a major concern of the transportation industry.[45]

In short, the retail and commercial interest remains at the heart of this magnificent enterprise and displays little, if no, signs of change. Private sector justice protects assets in the free enterprise system.

Purdue University Police Department—About the Purdue University Police Department
The Purdue University Police Department supports the University's effort to provide a safe and secure educational environment where diverse social, cultural, and academic values are encouraged to develop and prosper.
    It is our duty and responsibility to professionally provide appropriate police services for all groups and individuals.

Source: Purdue University Police Department Webpage at http://www.adpc.purdue.edu/PhysFac/police/pages/about/ab_mission.htm.

FIGURE 2.18 Mission, Values, and Vision

National Association of School Resource Officers—About Us

With school based policing being the fastest growing area of law enforcement and our membership quickly approaching 10,000 members around the globe, NASRO takes great pride in being the first and most recognized organization for law enforcement officers assigned at our school communities. A wide array of services and programs are available to assist members in developing the most effective program for their community.

NASRO is a member service organization. Students and communities around the globe receive the benefits of NASRO's wide-reaching network of law enforcement members and school administrators all striving to promote a safe and secure learning environment.

The National Association of School Resource Officers was founded with a solid commitment to the youth of the United States. Since 1990, our commitment remains solid to promote the TRIAD concept (Law Enforcement Officer–Teacher–Counselor) of school based law enforcement. Many communities have adopted this philosophy as they blend their SRO program, with the many other community policing programs.

By training law enforcement to educate, counsel and protect our school communities, the men and women of NASRO continue to lead by example and promote a positive image of law enforcement to our Nation's youth. NASRO has made itself available to communities and school districts around the nation in the development of effective school based law enforcement partnerships.

Source: NASRO, *About Us* at http://www.nasro.com/about_nasro.asp.

FIGURE 2.19   NASRO

III. CONCLUSION

This chapter delivers the message of privatization and the undeniability of this movement in the public safety culture. Public police can no longer bear alone the crushing burden of crime in America. Nor can it be expected to work effectively in all settings including the community that demands much from its protectors. Private security consists of creative and inventive energies that simply do not reside in the public framework. The prognosis for the industry can be described only as promising.

Next, the analysis presented a broad overview of the diverse sectors of the private security industry and cataloged the myriad of opportunities in this enterprising field. The reader will surely be impressed with the significant inroads that private sector justice has fashioned in all aspects of communal and commercial life.

Private security is an industry typified by dynamic growth and extraordinary diversity in function and operation. Whether on college or university campus, shopping mall or defense installation, courthouse or nuclear facility, it is now impossible not to come in regular contact with the industry. Coverage here has been to provide a broad overview of the industry, a summary of its functions and duties, and insights into what the future will hold for private sector justice. In more general terms, the chapter's subject matter has extensively dwelled upon the nature and reality of privatization in the delivery of justice functions throughout the American land-scape, from prisons to municipal services, from outsourcing to replacement on once well-entrenched special interests. Private security has now enveloped not only the justice marketplace but also commercial and business interests, neighborhoods, and even governmental services thought at one time to be solely public in design.

Notes

1. For an esoteric look at the distinction between private and public policing, *see* Trevor Jones and Tim Newburn, *Private Security and Public Policing* (London Clarendon Press, 1998).
2. The Reason Foundation, *Cutting Local Government Costs Through Competition and Priva-tization,* Vail Symposium 1997 Briefing Book.
3. Calvert Institute for Policy Research, *Calvert Issue Brief* Vol. 3 (September 1999).
4. Debra Livingston, *Police Discretion and the Quality of Life in Public Places: Courts, Com-munities and the New Policing,* 97 Colum. L. Rev. 551, 569 (1997). "Even more cogent ex-amples can be found in Los Angeles; there, middle-class citizens/consumers have pooled their resources to build private residential enclaves, which are patrolled by armed private security guards. In Canada, closed developments like these have been mainly a regional phenomenon. British Columbia now has many gated communities." George Rigakos, *The New Parapolice* 40 (2002).
5. *See* William Cunningham et al., *The Hallcrest Report II—Private Security Trends 1970–2000* Figure 6.1 (Boston: Butterworth-Heinemann, 1990), for some staggering sta-tistics regarding the growth of the field.
6. George S. Rigakos, The New Parapolice 45 (2002).
7. Federal Bureau of Prisons, *Private Prisons in the United States,* 1999 Table 2 (GPO, 1999).
8. Bruce Benson, *To Serve And Protect* (New York Univ. Press: New York 1998).
9. John M. Hood, *The Heroic Enterprise* xix (The Free Press: New York, 1996).
10. Hood at 84.
11. *Id.* at 197.
12. Bruce Benson, *The Countervailing Trend to FBI Failure: A Return to Privatized Police Ser-vices.* The Independent Institute (May 29, 2001).
13. Charles P. Nemeth, *Private Security and the Investigative Process,* 2nd ed. 3 (Boston, Butterworth-Heinemann, 2000).
14. Terence J. Mangan and Michael G. Shanahan, *Public Law Enforcement Private Security, FBI Law Enforcement Bulletin* at 19 (Jan. 1999).
15. The Wackenhut Corporation, *About Us* at http://www.wackenhut.com/about/index .html, © 1997–2002.
16. Michal Poole, Worker's Participation in Industry 41–42 (London: Boston: Routledge: K. Paul 1978).
17. *Hallcrest Report II* at 275–276.
18. Guardsmark, *Our Services,* at http://www.guardsmark.com/services/services.asp, last visited 10/10/02.
19. David A. Sklansky, *The Private Police,* 46 *UCLA L. Rev.* 1165, 1177 (1999).
20. The Freedonia Group, Cleveland, Ohio 1995.
21. Richard A. Zappile, *Philadelphia Implements Security Watch,* 22 *Police Chief* (Aug. 1991).
22. *Id.*
23. Anthony M. Voelker, *NYPD's APPL Program,* FBI *Law Enforcement Bulletin* 2 (Feb. 1991).

24. Rigakos at 42.
25. Nemeth at 4.
26. Allied Security, *About Allied Security*, at http://www.alliedsecurity.com/pages.html, © 2002.
27. National Association of Security Companies, *Home Page* at http://www.nasco.org/nasco/home.asp, © 2000.
28. BJS, *Direct Expenditure by Criminal Justice Function, 1982–1999* at http://www.ojp.usdoj.gov/bjs/glance/exptyp.htm visited 10/10/02.
29. S. Ronald Hauri, *Public-Private Security Liaison: The Synergy of Cooperation, Crime and Justice International*, (Oct. 1997).
30. Hill Harper, *A Theory of the Relationship Between Private Security and Public Police*, CJ the Americas (Aug.–Sept. 1995) at 15.
31. *Id.*
32. An early commentator, Dr. J. P. Shaloo, remarked that "private police are at the present time practically indispensable," in his 1933 work called *Private Police*.
33. For more information on the many services that these firms offer, see Guardsmark, *Security Issues—Crime*, at http://www.guardsmark.com/issues/issues_sec.asp, last visited 10/10/02.
34. Paul S. Bailin and Stanton G. Cort, *Industry Corner: Private Contractual Security Services: The U.S. Market and Industry*, 31 *Business Economics* (Apr. 1996) at 57.
35. Pinkerton, *Value Added Services, Risk Assessment*, at http://www.pinkertons.com/value/risk.asp © 2002.
36. *See* Pinkerton Security Services USA, at http://www.pinkertons.com/security/together.asp, last visited 10/30/02, for information on the merger of Pinkerton, Securitas, and Burns Security.
37. *See* Guardsmark, *Learning and Development* at http://www.guardsmark.com/approach/approach_sec.asp, last visited 10/10/02.
38. American Society for Industrial Safety, Professional Development-Security Disciplines, at http://www.asisonline.org/careerdisc.html, © ASIS.
39. American Society for Industrial Safety, Professional Development–Security Specialty Areas, at http://www.asisonline.org/careerspecialty.html, © ASIS.
40. Robert Meadows, *Fundamentals of Protection and Safety* 10–11 (Upper Saddle River, NJ, Prentice-Hall, 1995).
41. Brian A. Reaves and Andrew L. Goldberg, *Campus Law Enforcement Agencies, 1995* NCJ 161137 iii (Washington DC, National Institute of Justice, 1996).
42. *Id.*
43. *Kids and Violence—A National Survey and Report* (Family First, Tampa FL, 1991).
44. *Hallcrest Report II at 115.*
45. Richter H. Moore, *Private Security in the Twenty First Century: An Opinion* 18 J. of Sec. *Administration* (1995) at 10.

3

Community and Policing: Public and Private Perspectives

The primary object of an efficient police is the prevention of crime: The next that of detection and punishment of offenders if crime is committed. To these ends all the efforts of police must be directed. The protection of life and property, the preservation of public tranquility, and the absence of crime, will alone prove whether those efforts have been successful and whether the objects for which the police were appointed have been attained.

Sir Richard Mayne, 1829

Learning Objectives

1. To define and critique the idea of community policing.
2. To determine whether public or private police more effectively carry out the community police mandate.
3. To weigh and assess the various community-based approaches in policing.
4. To point the respective strengths and weaknesses in the delivery of community policing by either the public or the private systems.
5. To detail successful examples of community-based policing.
6. To feature cooperative public/private initiatives in the area of community policing.
7. To consider the reallocation of resources from the public to the private police systems for the purposes of community policing.

I. INTRODUCTION

Public safety, whether private or public in design, has certain fundamental purposes. None is more compelling than its relationship with the community. As the policing methodology moves through its various phases of growth and development, central questions are always in need of evaluation. What should the relationship be between the industry and the community? Is the relationship adversarial? Is it reactionary and passive? Is it cooperative? Is it a measurable undertaking—rate of crime and safety being examples? What levels of alienation exist between public safety and the neighborhood? Is there more to the effort than the eradication of crime? Should public law enforcement engage in neighborhood building and social services, or should it be a private endeavor? Can the system befriend the very constituency that it serves? Does the community detach itself from the forces of public safety?

Public safety, in an ideal sense, forever emphasizes the strength of community relationships. But is the talk mere rhetoric? Or underneath the platitudes of community building, are the public police models still primarily engaged in crime detection and deterrence? Assess Table 3.1 for the distinct qualities that traditional and community-based public policing possess.[1] Community protection, in general, emphasizes the development of close relationships with the community.

> Community policing might be expected especially to affect the organizational environment by expanding the range of functions that properly fall within the scope of the police role, and perhaps even by reordering the priorities attached to them. This process might result in greater attention to and recognition of officers' efforts to reduce disorders, solve neighborhood problems, and build rapport with citizens. With these changes, officers might be less likely to adopt a "we versus they" outlook toward citizens and less likely to define their role in narrow terms that emphasize law enforcement. Instead, we might expect that officers will be more likely to internalize a community-policing "philosophy."[2]

Common sense dictates that the elevation of community leads to the reduction of criminality.[3] But exactly how public police perceive the nature and essential qualities of community protection cannot be pinned down. Great variances exist in the command structure. Vogl and Woods's study on the historical departmental definitions is educational because of variety alone.[4] While "partnership" and "problem solving" rank higher, so do other definitions. Definitions are good, but practical implementations are less defined. Helen Greene's study of community policing methods in Virginia relay the inevitable diversity of definitions in novel police concepts.

> The Commonwealth of Virginia has eight cities and four counties serving populations over 100,000. The survey identified nine community-policing programs in these jurisdictions. Seven of the nine were established between 1990 and 1993. The nine programs identified have varying community-policing strategies, features, and activities. Most reported permanent assignment of community-policing officers in neighborhoods, problems solving, and foot patrol. Neighborhood substations were less common. While there were some similarities, there was more variation in

TABLE 3.1 *Traditional versus Community Policing Models*

Question	Traditional Policing (TPM)	Community Policing (CPM)
1. Who are the police?	A *government* agency principally responsible for law enforcement.	*Police are the public,* and the public are the police; police officers are those who are paid to give full-time attention to the duties of every citizen.
2. What is the relationship of the police to other public service departments?	*Priorities often conflict.*	The police are *one department among many responsible* for improving the quality of life.
3. What is the role of the police?	Focusing on *solving crimes.*	A broader *problem-solving* approach.
4. How is police efficiency measured?	By detection and *arrest rates.*	By the *absence of crime and disorder.*
5. What are the highest priorities?	*Crimes* that are high value (e.g., bank robberies) and those involving violence.	Whatever *problems* disturb the community most.
6. What specifically do police deal with?	*Incidents.*	Citizens' *problems* and concerns.
7. What determines the effectiveness of police?	*Response* times.	*Public cooperation.*
8. What view do police take of service calls?	Deal with them only if there is no *real police work* to do.	Vital function and great *opportunity.*
9. What is police professionalism?	Swift/effective response to *serious crime.*	Keeping close to the *community.*
10. What kind of intelligence is most important?	*Crime intelligence* (study of particular crimes or series of activities crimes).	*Criminal intelligence* (information about individuals and groups).
11. What is the essential nature of police accountability?	*Highly centralized,* governed by rules, regulations, and policy directives; accountable to the *law.*	Emphasis on *local accountability* to community needs.
12. What is the role of headquarters?	To provide the necessary *rules and policy directives.*	To preach *organizational values.*
13. What is the role of the press liaison department?	To *keep the "heat" off* operational officers so they can get on with the job.	To *coordinate* an essential channel of communication with the community.
14. How do the police regard prosecutions?	An as *important goal.* .	As *one tool* among many.

operational strategies, features and activities. This supports two commonly-held beliefs: (1) programs are tailored to meet local needs, and (2) the community policing
banner is often used inappropriately.[5]

Community deterioration is accompanied by the panoply of social ills and
criminal effects so evident in a host of communities across the nation. Drugs, prostitution, dilapidated housing and living centers, gang warfare, skyrocketing rates
of all felony categories—these all paint a miserable picture of death and decay.
Community life can be a fragile enterprise, and the public police system is only too
aware how crucial its operational integration is in thwarting this continued decline.

The nature of crime has also changed. Crime is more violent and indiscrimi-
nate. Everyone seems vulnerable, and fear of crime is a constant in many urban
communities. Little about the current state of affairs differs over the last forty years.
Since the riotous 1960s, communities have dealt with fear, crime, and social decline
never before dreamed possible. The decline in community quality appears in every
facet of daily life. Stan Stojkovic, John Klofas, and David Kalinich summarize the
occupational impotence and professional frustration that seem part and parcel
within the culture:

> Despite the fact that for the past 50 years the police have been promoting themselves
> as crime fighters, devoting enormous resources to the effort, taking credit for drops
> in the crime rate and criticism for rises in it, the best evidence to date is that no mat-
> ter what they do they can make only marginal differences in it. The reason is that all
> of the major factors influencing how much crime there is or not are factors over
> which police have no control whatsoever. Police can do nothing about the age, sex,
> racial, or ethnic distribution of the population. They cannot control economic condi-
> tions; poverty, inequality; occupational opportunity; moral, religious, family, or sec-
> ular education; or dramatic social, cultural, or political change. These are the "big
> ticket" items in determining the amount and distribution of crime. Compared to
> them what police do or do not do matters very little.[6]

Public police systems struggle with such complexity and yearn in good faith
for solutions. The status quo does not work as capably as the systems wants, but
these agencies have been down the path of "fad"—whether they are new programs
or technological improvisations. Change has visited these entities in a host of other
circumstances. Change, which in general is happily received, is unnatural to the
bureaucratic model. The police bureaucratic model, which emphasizes "the values
of neutrality, conformity, impersonality, and crime control,"[7] can no longer accomplish its primary aim of community involvement. Something different envelops
the horizon.

II. THE PROMISE OF COMMUNITY-BASED POLICING

One of the most-often-touted solutions to crime is "community policing." It is the
contemporary rage of police planners, bureaucrats, and academics. The allocation
and reallocation of police officer positions to community policing has been remarkable by any measure. See Figure 3.1.[8]

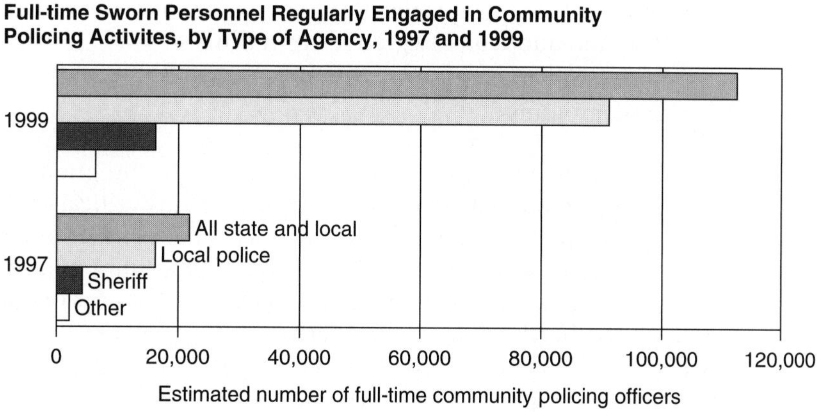

**Full-time Sworn Personnel Regularly Engaged in Community
Policing Activites, by Type of Agency, 1997 and 1999**

FIGURE 3.1 Low Enforcement in the Community

Long advocated as a panacea of community ills, community policing promises far more than is capable of delivery. Trojanowicz and Bucqueroux describe the principle of community policing as "both a philosophy and an organizational strategy that allows the police and community residents to work closely together in new ways to solve the problems of crime, fear of crime, physical and social disorder, and neighborhood conditions."[9] Framed in the belief that people in the community should have input into the police process, in exchange for their participation and support, community-policing attempts to make community members stakeholders in the crime effort. Additionally, community problems can be resolved only when people and institutions are free to explore creative approaches in neighborhood crime. Simply put, the community and law enforcement cooperate with "corporate management, employees, tenants, visitors" and benefit "from the team and systems approach to security management."[10] Trojanowicz and Bucqueroux delineate further components of the concept known as "community policing":

- Community policing is team-driven rather than singularly controlled.
- Community policing produces a new breed of officer—the CPO (Community Police Officer).
- Community police officers are the liaisons with police agencies and community neighborhoods.
- Community and police contract to fight crime and deliver services.
- Police and community alter type and timing of traditional police services.
- Police deliver a broader spectrum of services to the community.
- Police target focused groups prone to victimization: elderly, juveniles, and the infirm.
- Police favor human interaction and interpersonal relationships over technology.

- Police employ all resources of government and community to solve problems and adopt an integrative approach.
- Community policing provides decentralized, personalized police service to the community.[11]

Others challenge the naïveté of thinking that this programmatic change cures ills of the proportion that are witnessed today. "Many critical analysts believe that the community policing model mystifies or covers up police use of coercive force, which they regard as the essence of policing. Community policing seems to be 'a romantic delusion, not for the world we have lost, but for one we never had. It harks back to a harmonious idyll, where the police were everyone's friend. It was thus never, and it is unlikely that it ever will be.[12, 13']"

Community policing is by no means an earth-shattering proposition, since "policing" on any level should revolve around the community. Police work better when working from within a community rather than as an occupying force or as outsiders. Community policing and problem oriented policing require helping the citizenry or the community solve problems that may or may not be related to traditional police services. To accomplish this goal, the police agency would need to secure commitments from other supporting community entities and organizations, such as family services, sanitation, neighborhood planning and zoning, code enforcement, welfare and housing, child and youth services, and other human service offices. In doing so, law enforcement coordinates and brokers the community and its supportive organizations with the overall crime picture. Officers cannot be reactive, but should be proactive. "Officers get out in the neighborhoods and solve problems, without waiting for directions from headquarters."[14] In other words, crime is perceived holistically—not merely as criminological phenomena, but a social, cultural, and economic issue to be reckoned with. The Bureau of Justice Statistics charts the typical constituencies consulted. See Figure 3.2.[15]

As a result, law enforcement would no longer be the exclusive agency that deals with the elimination and eradication of crime, and traditional policing would be reengineered for this multidimensional approach rather than crime fighting alone. In this sense, community policing solves wider problems in conjunction with the narrower ones known as criminal acts. Arguably, the current police model in place in most American jurisdictions sees community less broadly and concentrates the bulk of its energies on crime resolution. Police, for the most part, are inadequately trained in matters of community. From another perspective, proponents for the model believe that the camps—of public police and the community—are fusible, capable of being enjoined. Idyllically, the advocates think that these factions can be brought together. Consider these suggestions for making this outcome happen:

- Hold regular local meetings with police to raise concerns and to talk about what to do to make things better.
- Set up a community police academy or other training to learn more about the police's job. "Ride along" programs with police on patrol help teach people about this.

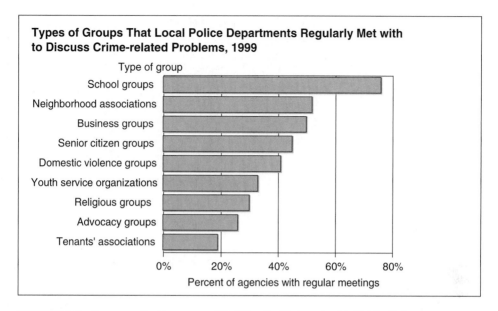

Types of Groups That Local Police Departments Regularly Met with to Discuss Crime-related Problems, 1999

FIGURE 3.2   Community Groups and Entities that Interact with Public Safety

- Work together on projects like community gardens, after-school programs, and block parties. Work with the media to create guidelines on how to cover stories fairly for both citizens and police.
- Have officers work in one neighborhood for a long time. Have more foot or bicycle patrols. Give officers enough time on calls to get to know the people they serve.
- Make a strong commitment to community-oriented policing. Everyone in the police department should be involved, not just a few units or officers.[16]

Needless to say, the policy initiatives sound sensible, but are they plausible?

Community policing has its primary support from those who believe that its method solves problems. Various factors, which most police departments will not take credit for, have resulted in a decrease in the current crime rate. See Figure 3.3.

Hence, community policing is often identified as "problem oriented policing" for which the police are responsible for finding and implementing solutions within the community. On the surface, a problem-oriented approach does sound logical and even foolproof. Are the major players in policing convinced of its utility and soundness? Even a "consortium" of organizations have banded together to promote these practices. "The Consortium is in partnership with the International Association of Chief's of Police (IACP), the National Sheriff's Association (NSA), the National Organization of Black Law Enforcement Executives (NOBLE), the Police Executives Research Forum (PERF) and the Police Foundation."[17]

However, when one evaluates the dynamics involved in the community-oriented approach, the problem-solving aspects on a larger scale, the implementation is easier said than done.

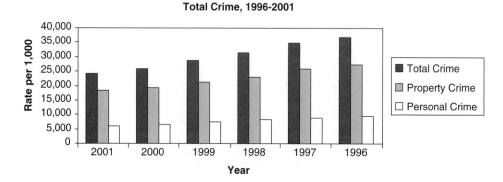

FIGURE 3.3   Crime Rates and Types: Short-term

III. COMMUNITY-BASED POLICING AND THE CULTURE OF PUBLIC LAW ENFORCEMENT

Community-oriented policing requires a major transformation, away from the re-actionary model, under which public police departments have trained and oper-ated for generations. Community policing, to be effective, needs a reorientation of sorts, generally foreign to the American police model, and a "significant departure from the way American police departments have operated throughout the better part of the twentieth century."[18] Debra Livingston's esoteric assessment of the new policing sums up the issue:

> The theories of community and problem-oriented policing are based upon a funda-mental reassessment of the purposes, strategies, and bases of legitimacy of modern policing. To understand these theoretical developments thus requires a somewhat extended discussion of both the historical emergence of the community policing phenomenon and the ideas contained within community and problem-oriented policing.[19]

Change of this magnitude does not occur instantaneously, since community policing is a philosophy that substantially broadens the role of police in our soci-ety. Statisticians Matthew Hickman and Brian Reaves of the Bureau of Justice Sta-tistics recognize the drastic reorientation in traditional police thinking. "The community policing approach to law enforcement seeks to address the causes of crime and reduce the fear of crime and social disorder through problem-solving strategies and police-community partnerships. A fundamental shift from traditional reactive policing, community policing strives to prevent crime before it occurs."[20]

"Community policing is people-based as opposed to being bureaucratic or militaristic. It is about improving citizens' quality of life. . . . Although law en-forcement is important, it is recognized that it is only one part of the overall re-sponsibility of the police."[21] Hence, the traditional law enforcement approach rests uncomfortably in the community policing philosophy. Historically, law enforcement was primarily driven by its natural mandate to enforce laws and ensure domestic tranquillity. Abandoning this long-held view causes a professional nervousness that the mission and purpose of public law enforcement would be undermined, that control would be relinquished to those set on social and cultural destruction, and that the change in role and purpose would drastically alter the legal system.[22] There has been substantial reexamination about the role and function of policing. To be candid, some policing entities have resisted the community policing ideal—not out of malevolence but occupation unease. This type of role reorientation takes time.

Yet the push for these new responsibilities for police officers is evident throughout the philosophies behind community policing.[23] Many practitioners have jumped on the bandwagon of community policing without having supportive data as to whether or not community policing actually works. Jerome Skolnick and David Bayley in their book *The New Blue Line*, for example, identify the components of community policing that make it the "wave of the future" as the following:

1. police-community reciprocity;
2. a real decentralization of command;
3. reorientation of patrol; and
4. civilization.[24]

As a result, in an effort to increase good community relations and enhance "police-community reciprocity" and meet the challenges of "decentralization of command," many public practitioners are implementing techniques such as substations or storefront stations. Levels of resistance vary but are institutionally obvious in most quarters. Traditional procedures die hard, problem-solving methods are still under development, and no one knows for sure how successful the approach will be. As a result, no police agency has adopted the approach fully or consistently. Though success stories abound on the news and in academic quarters, for some sectors of public law enforcement, the community-based approach has historically been embraced.[25] In fact, many proponents of the practice view community integration as almost a sentimental journey to the past way of doing things. Beat cops, permanent duty precincts, less technology, and lots of interaction are measures of "days gone by," and departments need only to resurrect them. Proactive was the norm—reactive a sign of unpreparedness. Chief Michael J. Heidingsfield of Scottsdale, Arizona, thinks that the clamor and fuss over community policing belies common sense:

> So where [is] the Chief's definition of community-based policing after all of this? Here goes: It is a philosophy shared by police officers who appreciate that they alone cannot insure the safety of a community and must turn to the wisdom, resources and support of the citizenry as a partner in that effort. Community-based policing is an attitude that each officer brings to work every day in which there is a willingness to look beyond the situation at hand for all possible solutions and to treat each and every human being as we would wish to be treated.[26]

Problem-oriented policing is a realistic response to the limitations of traditional, incident-driven policing.

A. Public Police Professionalism and the Resistance to Community Policing

Since the civil rights revolution of the 1960s, when unrest and urban tumult became the focal point for a once very stodgy police system, the public police philosophy has trended to "professionalism." Professionalism was urged in all police quarters, from education to forensic science, from technology to police planning and management.[27] The "professional model" was a confident mix of science and self-assurance whereby police actually felt, and many still do, that crime resolution was within their grasp and that given enough resources and professional preparation, there would be no problem that could not be remedied. Police, like so many other professions, came to believe in a sort of professional invincibility that could tackle the troubling issues with learnedness and preparation and could affix an intelligent prescription to any negative dilemma. The "professional" police mentality relied on forensic and engineering technology, electronics and computers, chemistry and psychology, profilers and behavioral specialists. For each offense, there emerged an arsenal of responses that would not only identify the criminal agent but also predict patterns of criminality and offer up a therapeutic regimen that cured the offender. Police, as well as correctional specialists, judges, and caseworkers, all seemed to believe in a professional approach incapable of failure.

By stark contrast, community policing holds otherwise, and it poses alternatively a humbler, more realistic vision of what the policing profession can and cannot accomplish. In some ways, the two schools of thought directly contradict one another. At its foundation, the professional policing model emphasizes the enforcement of laws while maintaining a neutral posture with the citizenry it serves. Predominantly still the case—the twentieth century witnessed the evolution of a public police model that detached itself from the very constituency it served, standing aloof of the fray of criminals and victims and hoping somehow to resolve crimes through professional acumen. In addition to lessening political influence, efforts to enhance the effectiveness of police services and reduce corruption were the impetus behind professional policing.

The inconsistencies and differing viewpoints are evident in other ways. Professional policing insists that its officers maintain a healthy distance from the community, and by doing so, that they enforce criminal law in a fair and impartial manner. Lack of personal involvement proves the integrity of the police process, whereas a lack of intimacy in the community policing design would intimate the very opposite perspective. The Chicago Alternative Policing Strategy, a recent and very frequently studied community-based initiative, starkly contrasts the historical design. Officer training, among other things, includes a three-day skills training curriculum.[28]

Next, today's professional policing system, in order to be effective, adopts rapid, professional, incident management. Officers are expected to handle service calls expeditiously, while simultaneously patrolling designated areas.[29] The concern lies first and foremost with the incident, and secondly with the players in the community experiencing the crime activity. The professional would not care for issues of root cause or deterrent solution. In short, police officers react—"You call and we will respond." To aid in this process, practitioners have implemented large, complex computerized systems in order to maintain track of their vehicles and to facilitate dispatching officers to the community in need. This model of policing effectively fills the requirements set forth by society: to provide protection and immediate response to life-threatening situations. Within this model, police find themselves restricted in many areas of prevention, especially the development of meaningful relationships with community members. The "professional police" model cannot afford such sideshows and distractions, since its penultimate purposes are the enforcement of criminal law and "fighting crime." Citizens report crime, and police react. The task of preventing crime as a primary focus is simply impossible to accomplish when one looks at the "professional incident management" services that communities depend on—the ones that police must provide—because no other entity can. As a result, there was a clear need to establish a well-trained professional system to accomplish the crime-fighting task. In *The Privatization of Policing*, Brian Forst highlights the contradiction of purpose:

> The notion that police were the experts contributed to police arrogance and a sense among the police that members of the community were inferior. Effective use of technology and emphasis on efficiency need not interfere with a healthy relationship between the police and the public, but the leaders of the professional era managed to replace a friendly service attitude with a cool, detached one and thus to severely damage that relationship. Police in many jurisdictions further alienated the public by spending less and less time on the street. . . . The reform era of policing was largely a response to public disgust with rampant police corruption. The community-policing era emerged, as central elements of "police professionalism" revealed themselves to be not only ineffective but also often counterproductive, stimulants of frustration and anger in minority communities. August Vollmer and Orlando Wilson's concepts of professionalism in policing surely were not designated to promote arrogance, insensitivity, and brutality, yet professionalism nonetheless became a cloak within which those evils came to masquerade. Proponents of community policing would certainly do well to ensure that their good intentions are not similarly corrupted.[30]

Nor can the public police system be all things to all people. Police are not superhuman, and they certainly are not as multi-occupational as desired. Chief of Police Mike Shanahan truly discerns the difficulties:

> There are those that romanticize the value of the beat cop from days gone by and the importance the figure played in community life half a century ago. Today's modern counterpart, however, has a vastly expanded agenda and weakened social support institutions upon which to draw. Currently, officers face enormous challenges in coping with out-of-control social programs.[31]

B. The Efficacy of Professional Public Policing

So desperate are some politicians and policy makers, criminologists and think-tank advocates over the ravages of crime in America that the endless call for community police designs seems to disregard the measure of its impact. For many, the model has been less than effective, and in some cases, an abject failure. The statistics show that however "professional" the system becomes, the criminals appear a step ahead in every direction. Unfortunately, history shows that the traditional policing, nor even the contemporary novelties "can cope effectively with serious crime. Admittedly, the rates of serious crime in recent years have continued to decline, but these may have as much to do with the maturing of the baby boomers out of their most crime-prone years and the unprecedented strength of the sustained economic boom, as well as the contribution the police have made in quadrupling the number of people behind bars in recent years. The fact remains that this society continues to suffer rates of serious crime that would be considered intolerable in other industrialized Western nations. This reality has sparked and continues to fuel a radical reassessment concerning whether police departments might find better ways to approach the challenge posed by crime."[32] Even with the plague of recidivists and habitual offenders, categories of criminal perpetrators readily discernable to the police system, police are still impotent in thwarting their felonious activity. Despite incarceration, a new crop of repeat offenders and other malcontents simply take their place. The influence and impact of juvenile crime continues its meteoric rise, and the professional police force seems incapable of halting this march either. Prison incarceration rates rise without interruption. In sum, more than 6 million people are subject to some type of court imposed-behavior control because of criminal activity. David Anderson, Associate Professor of Economics at Centre College in Danville, Kentucky, illustrates the staggering rates of criminality in the culture:

> This study estimates the total annual cost of criminal behavior in the United States. While past research has typically focused on particular costs, regions, or crime categories, this general study estimates all of the direct and indirect costs of every type of crime for the entire nation. In addition to aggregating expenses commonly associated with unlawful activity, it considers ancillary costs that have not yet been included into an overall formula for the cost of crime. Beyond the expenses of the legal system, victim losses, and crime-prevention agencies, the burden of crime includes the opportunity costs of victims', criminals', and prisoners' time, the fear of being victimized, and the cost of private deterrence. More accurate information on the repercussions of crime could guide our legal, political, and cultural stance toward crime and allow informed prioritization of programs that curtail criminal activity. The net annual burden of crime is found to exceed $1 trillion.[33]

Any reasoned view of efficacy in policy making pines for better figures or for better evaluation methods. Hence, despite the extraordinary investment of time, resources, and personnel—a quid pro quo under the professional policing investment—the results are yet at the level that policing can be happy about. Some in deterrence-mode police management appear undaunted as they clamor for more of the "past." Indeed, "most police managers have developed an amazing tolerance for ineffectiveness because they concentrate so much on efficiency. . . . Fixation on efficiency leads inexorably to obsolescence because people become rooted in convention . . ."[34] George Kelling and Catherine Coles conclude that the professional policing model has not been very successful at fighting crime because the philosophy "does not recognize the links between disorder, fear, serious crime, and urban decay. And, the criminal justice system model has also failed because it ignores the role of citizens in crime prevention."[35] Although the picture may not be this bleak, the crime data, at least in longitudinal terms, are not a pretty picture. Wherever improvements can be implemented, the public police should welcome them.

Oddly enough, much of current inefficiency in the contemporary police model, including evaluation methods, directly correlates to a lack of understanding of role and function. If numbers do not lie, then police need to look honestly at the picture. Police need to discern both strengths and limitations and to adopt strategies that feasibly can impact the flood of crime in communities. This goal cannot be achieved while standing fast to propositions that do not deliver positive and measurable results of crime rate decline.[36] Successful traits of any community-based public safety organization are depicted in Figure 3.4.

The pattern of fund and fail will no longer fly at the governmental level. Accountability is on the rise. James Brooke summarizes the dilemma in this way:

> The inevitable result of these programs will be an increase in the costs associated with law enforcement services. This is so because the police are taking on a broader mission by attempting to deal with the root "causes" of crime. Clearly, this enchanced mission requires significant time and service commitments. Given budgetary constraints, how long can the government afford widespread implementation of "community policing"? The next logical question is, if the police do not provide these services, who will? The answer in large part is private security.[37]

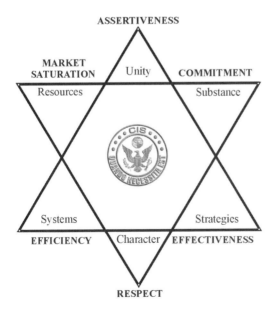

FIGURE 3.4 The Community-Based Policing Philosophy of Critical Intervention Services

Funding and the Private Sector Solution

Much of the inefficiency in the public model is directly related to its reliance on public funds to carry out its mandate. Public outcry over the dramatic rise in publicly funded everything is now commonly heard. The growth of taxpayer-supported governmental activities shows no signs of abating. Law enforcement is no different from other government operations. Private sector justice delivers its product in a completely different way.

First, it is market driven. To succeed in the private marketplace, the proponent must demonstrate that not only the product or service is worthwhile but also that its usage makes good economic sense. Private sector companies expend extraordinary energies convincing a wide array of constituencies of its value. It has to do so, since in order to survive the marketplace, it must be successful in how it operates and in what it delivers. Hence, the private sector is by nature entrepreneurial, and its philosophical perspective is vastly different from that of public sector counterparts.

Second, the companies and service providers of private security can operate only if the revenue necessary for its plan and purpose is generated. This goal requires that the company and its agents "contract" proprietarily with interested parties—both private and public entities, in the delivery of its services. Thus, private sector justice is primarily a contractual design, offering up services for compensation and intent on maintaining the balance sheet. Most security firms execute contracts such as is evident in Figure 3.5.

Security companies must track expenses with unusual vigilance in order to achieve the bottom line and also must track activities to be certain that staff and resources are used intelligently and efficiently. Private sector justice always worries about the bottom line. See examples of time and expense forms in Figures 3.6 and 3.7.

Third, private sector justice increasingly relies on public assessments and even tax receipts in the delivery of its services. When transportation facilities hire companies by contract or agent, these public entities divert public funds to pay for privately delivered services. Other examples of the public transfusion into the private marketplace are the following:

Courts	Housing and parking authorities
Private prisons	Transportation of prisoners
Traffic enforcement	Traffic enforcement
Collection of judgments	

This list continually grows. Even business communities and commercial districts exact fees to deliver services that the public sector cannot provide alone. New York City's alliance, by way of example, charges a set sum per square foot of office space for its alliance services, which include traffic, security, and other community maintenance needs. See Figure 3.8. This money is collected by the city and redistributed to the business improvement district for their utilization. The New York Alliance, with this type of resource, can deploy 65 officers for this area, covering 24-hour-a-day security using officers on foot, bicycles, and electric scooters. In New York alone, there appear to be over 30 such districts implemented across the city; many of them with security departments. Hundreds of cities and municipalities across the nation are comfortable with the transfer of publicly collected funds to the private sector.

In short, the private sector draws its economic power from many quarters, and its future appears bright because there is a corresponding accountability.

SERVICE AGREEMENT

1. Parties: Critical Intervention Services, Inc. a Florida Corporation, located at 1261 South Missouri Avenue, Clearwater, 33756 ("CIS"), and _____ ("Client"), having a principle place of business at _____ hereby enter into this Agreement on the date last set forth below.
2. Location of Services: CIS will provide services at the physical location _____ ("Property").
3. Duration of Agreement
   A. _____ to _____
   B. This agreement shall automatically renew for successive periods equal to that set forth above.
4. Charges for Services:
   A. Client agrees to pay CIS the following rate for services rendered (only checked lines apply):
      ____ $____ per officer hour worked
      ____ $____ per day that services are provided
      ____ $____ per day per radio transceiver for radio communication services
      ____ $____ Other:
   B. Client agrees to pay CIS one and one half (1 1/2) times the hourly rate for all hours worked on the following holidays: New Years Day, Memorial Day, Easter, 4th of July, Labor Day, Thanksgiving and Christmas Day.
   C. It is agreed that if the Federal Government raises the minimum wage, Social Security, or Medicare, or institutes other new programs which increase the cost of labor, or if Workman's Compensation or liability insurance rates or premiums increase, the rate per this Agreement shall be raised a like amount.
   D. CIS will be paid $.00 per hour for all the time expended in connection with preparing for or attending a deposition, hearing, or trial in any criminal or civil case in any way connected with the Property or any alleged criminal or tortuous acts which occurred wholly or partially thereon.
   E. CIS has the right to double the officers assigned to the Property on July 4th and on December 31st should CIS determine in its sole discretion that same is necessary to carryout its duties on the Property or to protect its officers and Client will pay for same. Nothing herein shall obligate CIS to deploy additional officers on those dates.
5. Billing and payment procedures:
   A. Client and CIS agree to the following (only checked line apply):
      ____ Client agrees to pay CIS a refundable deposit of $_____ which will be refunded upon the Client's full performance of this Agreement.
      ____CIS will bill the client on a weekly/seven (7) day billing cycle.
   B. All invoices are due when rendered. If any bill is not paid within 15 days after the invoice date, CIS will terminate this Agreement on the 16th day, according to Paragraph 10C.
   C. All balances over 30 days old will be subject to a service charge of 1.5% per month applied to the over-due balance.
   D. Client will pay CIS for all its collection costs, including but not limited to, reasonable attorney's fees incurred in pre-litigation, litigation, appellate and bankruptcy related work and all court costs and litigation related expenses, expended in an effort to protect or enforce CIS' rights under this Agreement.
   E. Client will pay a $50.00 service charge for checks returned due to insufficient funds.
   F. The parties agree that upon each renewal period as set forth in Paragraph 3B, above, all applicable charges shall increase by five percent (5%).
6. Statement of Services:
   The purpose of the service CIS is providing to the Client is to assist the Client in protecting the Client's physical property only, through crime prevention techniques. The primary technique employed will be the deterrent effect of having a uniformed CIS employee at the Property during the agreed-upon hours which employee may but is not obligated to intervene to prevent a crime against the Property. CIS is not being hired to protect residents, patrons, employees, invitees, guests, vendors, or other persons on the Property or the personal property of such persons. Client understands and agrees that should CIS determine that another CIS client has a security emergency, which requires the immediate dispatch of additional CIS officers, CIS may temporarily remove the officer assigned to Client's property to assist with the emergency without being required to send a replacement or back-up officer to the property. Client acknowledges that even if this Agreement calls for unarmed security services, a CIS employee who happens to be armed may enter the Property as needed to assist, supervise, or relieve a CIS officer on the Property.
   If a CIS employee observes a crime in progress or a suspicious individual on or near the Property, it will be at the employee's discretion to decide whether to intervene to prevent the crime, to call the police, to take other action, or to take no action at all. Client acknowledges that CIS is under no obligation to intervene to prevent or stop a crime or to recover any tangible personal property. The Client will instruct their employees to

FIGURE 3.5 Security Contract for Services

immediately call the "911" emergency number in the event of an emergency or if they have any concerns for their persona safety, safety of their customers/residents, or protection of the Property.

Client agrees that CIS will not be responsible for and Client hereby waives, releases, and discharges CIS from all liability to the Client for any and all loss and damage including personal injury damages, property damages, and all other damages including punitive damages, whether caused by the negligence of CIS or otherwise, unless such loss or damage is directly caused by the grossly negligent act of a CIS employee. Client also acknowledges that this Agreement does not create an independent obligation on the part of CIS to any person not a party to this Agreement.

CIS, in its sole discretion, may deem it appropriate to instruct its personnel to engage in what may be deemed "non-traditional security measures". These include but are not limited to attendance at neighborhood watch or community association meetings, activities designed to increase rapport with members of the community (such as playing basketball with the neighborhood children). The Client agrees to pay for these non-traditional security measures in accordance herewith.

Not withstanding the above, CIS may choose, at its sole discretion, to provide, at no expense to the Client, a community resource officer to meet with people in the neighborhood.

Client understands that CIS is highly proactive with the community and at times throughout the year CIS will sponsor community outreach programs. Client agrees to pay up to $25.00 per year to help offset the costs incurred by purchasing materials for the community such as coloring books, stickers, and the Careport identification system, just to name a few. At no time will the yearly fee be used to pay for personnel, CIS will provide personnel at no cost.

7. Licensing and Insurance: CIS shall be properly licensed by the Florida Secretary of State and shall carry the required liability insurance coverage mandated by the State of Florida. Client may request to be placed as additional insured on CIS' policy at a cost of $250.00 per year.

8. Method of Operation: CIS will provide services to the Client as are consistent with the Agreement, and in its discretion and experience, necessary and appropriate to providing patrol services at the Property. CIS is not required to make any arrests or to recover any tangible property. CIS does not guarantee against personal injury or property damage.

9. Exclusive Services: So that CIS may effectively provide the required security services, Client agrees that no other security/protection firm or person will be used unless provided by CIS.

10. Cancellation and Suspension:
   A. Termination: The Client may cancel this Agreement at any time with documented, due cause by mailing a 30 day written notice via certified mail to CIS' offices.
   B. CIS may cancel this Agreement at any time and for any reason by giving 24 hour written or fax notice to be sent to the designated client representative.
   C. CIS may suspend its provision of security services hereunder during any period of time when the Client is in default of its payment obligations hereunder by giving the Client 24 hours written or telephone notice. During any period of suspension, Client shall pay CIS the liquidated damages as set forth in Paragraph 11 below.

11. Liquidated Damages: If the Client breaches its obligations hereunder by refusing to permit CIS to provide the services agreed to hereunder or if CIS invokes its right under Paragraph 10C, above, to suspend its performance under this Agreement due to Client's failure to pay CIS for services rendered, CIS shall be entitled to recover from Client liquidated damages to be calculated as follows: (1) the charges incurred by Client form the beginning of the Agreement through the date services are suspended will be, (2) divided by the number of days between the beginning and suspension date of the Agreement, (3) which result will be multiplied by the number of days remaining under the terms of the Agreement, (4) which sum will be multiplied by forty percent (40%) to arrive at the liquidated damages amount. Client agrees that this liquidated damages provision is necessary as the damages to CIS in the event of Client's breach are not readily ascertainable. Client agrees that this provision is reasonable, not a penalty, and that Client substantially limits its financial liability hereunder in the event of default by virtue of CIS being limited to the recovery of damages as calculated above. Client acknowledges that CIS has substantial sales, marketing, recruitment, education, training, supervision, and other costs which it incurs before and at the beginning of this Agreement and that this provision is designed to reimburse CIS for those costs and its lost profits. The payment due under this paragraph is in addition to and not in place of Client's payment for services already rendered.

12. Hiring by Client of CIS Personnel: Client agrees that it will not hire as an employee, independent contractor, consultant, or otherwise, whether directly or indirectly, any person who is employed by CIS or who had been employed by CIS within six (6) months of the date of hire. If the Client does so, the Client will be responsible for paying two thousand five hundred dollars ($2,550.00) to compensate CIS for employee recruitment and development costs.

FIGURE 3.5   *(Cont.)*

13. Agent of Client: Client appoints CIS and its agents and employees involved in rendering services under this Agreement as the agents of Client for the purpose of:
    A. Issuing trespass warnings about, swearing out complaints regarding, or otherwise handling violations;
    B. Performing other protection functions in order to carry out the purpose of this Agreement;
    C. Executing and delivering cease and desist notices to residents committing violations, pursuant to Florida Statute 83.56.
14. Indemnification: Client agrees to defend, hold harmless, and indemnify CIS against loss, including attorneys fees and litigation costs, from any and all claims or actions, including claims for contribution, brought by any person or entity, in any way arising out of or relating to the injury or death of any person, or, to damage to any personal or real property, which occurred partially or wholly on the Property, or, to persons on, visiting, or living on the Property, and which injury or damage was the proximate result of an unauthorized, illegal, or criminal act of a person not employed by CIS.
15. Rules of Construction:
    A. This Agreement shall be construed according to the laws of the State of Florida.
    B. If any part of this Agreement is found to be illegal or unenforceable, both parties agree that the remaining terms of this Agreement will remain in full force and effect and, that all terms of this Agreement shall be construed, where possible, to provide full enforcement of the Agreement.
    C. The rule of construction that ambiguities will be resolved against the drafting party shall not apply in the interpretation of this Agreement.
16. Successor and Assigns: This Agreement shall be binding on the heirs, executors, administrators, legal representatives, successors, and assigns of the respective parties.
17. Entire Agreement and Amendment: This Agreement represents the entire Agreement between the parties and all other agreements, whether oral or otherwise, are merged into this Agreement. This Agreement may be amended by the mutual agreement of the contracting parties in writing to be attached to and incorporated into this Agreement.
18. Consent to Jurisdiction and Venue: Client consents to personal jurisdiction and venue, for any action brought by CIS arising out of a breach or threatened breach of this Agreement, in the United State District Court for the Middle District of Florida, Tampa Division, or in the Circuit Court in and for Pinellas County Florida, Clearwater Division. Client agrees that any action arising under this Agreement or out of the relationship established by the Agreement shall be brought only and exclusively in the two referenced courts.
19. Waiver of Jury Trial: Client agrees that any controversy which may arise under this Agreement or out of the relationship established by the Agreement would involve complicated and difficult factual and legal issues and that, therefore, and action brought by either party, alone or in combination with others, against CIS, whether arising out of this Agreement or otherwise, shall be determined by a Judge sitting without a jury.

DATE: _____ By:_____

Its:_____

DATE: _____ Client Representative:_____

FIGURE 3.5 *(Cont.)*

David H. Bayley's critique of the contemporary police mindset cogently lays out the argument of some:

> The police do not prevent crime. This is one of the best-kept secrets of modern life. Experts know it, the police know it, but the public does not know it. Yet the police pretend that they are society's best offense against crime and continually argue that if they are given more resources, especially personnel, they will be able to protect communities against crime. This is a myth.[38]

For Bayley and many other commentators, there is a dearth of hard and conclusive evidence that correlates and connects the investment of officers, time, resources, and public expenditures and crime rates. No matter what the fad or trend,

ABC Protective Services 123 Security Street Anytown, US 00000 (000) 000-0000				*Weekly Time Sheet*			
Employee Name		Social Security No.		From (Date)		To (Date)	
Date	Client Code	Location	Office	Travel	Surveillance	Contact	Total Hours
			Totals				
Employee Signature:						Date:	
Supervisor Signature:						Date:	

FIGURE 3.6   Security Firm Time Sheets

the police policy will have marginal impact on the relative rates of crime in the community. While this position may be extreme and somewhat pessimistic, data on crime rates and victimization do not logically refute this position. It even appears that some departments implement community-based policing strictly in order to receive grant money or to comply with demands from local politicians. Utilizing all the "buzz words," these policy makers lack any dedicated effort directed at the effective implementation of community-based policing and problem solving. As Brian Forst states, "Many, perhaps most, police departments have embraced the form and rhetoric of community policing and largely ignored its substance."[39]

If with all the system's inventiveness, numbers remain consistently high, what can the public police really do in the community? As long ago as the early 1970s, the Police Foundation's comprehensive study, *The 1974 Kansas City Preventive Patrol Experiment*, foretold what now appears consistently true—that the public police initiative seems incapable of any significant success in the community that it serves.[40]

Granting some level of inefficiency, it would be unfair to label the effort futile. On any given day, public police with courage and zeal have certainly reaped positive benefits for communities with its efforts in the areas of drugs and guns, by way of example. Patrolling city streets with uniformed officers in marked patrol cars may or may not equate to crime prevention. However, this same patrol will deter and apprehend offenders and will prevent other activities from taking place.

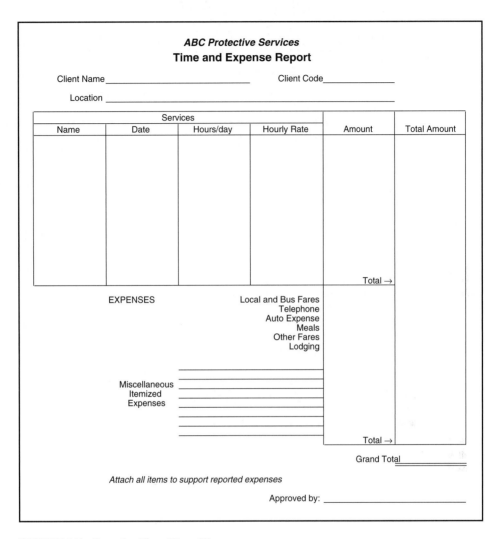

FIGURE 3.7   Security Firm: Time/Expense

Although the police may not be the best protection from crime or the best prevention of crime, the police system is the most effective offense against it. The ridiculous expectations thrust upon the police model—expecting not only social services and social engineering from a law enforcement tenacity but also solutions to circumstances and conditions over which it has absolutely no control, exacerbates the problem. In many circumstances, the sobering truth is that these issues need solutions that are well beyond the capabilities of police officers. The growing gap between rich and poor, the homeless, the blight of the inner city, racism and racial

The Downtown Alliance's Public Safety force work hard to ensure a safe and comfortable Downtown neighborhood for all. We do this through a variety of community programs aimed at increasing the sense of security in Lower Manhattan.

The Ambassador Program
The Downtown Alliance's Ambassador Program is a face-to-face way by which we can gather information and address problems faced by merchants in our district. Our public safety supervisors personally visit every street-level retail business on their beat in order to find out who the owner is and what number to call in case of an emergency. These supervisors also leave a calling card, inviting business owners to contact us with problems of any size.

Safe Corridor to the Subway
The Downtown Alliance's public safety department operates a "Safe Corridor to the Subway" program that offers extra protection for homeward-bound commuters, especially those returning to their Downtown residences late at night. From evening rush hour through 9 pm, our public safety officers are stationed on the streets near key subway entrances and nearby residential buildings in the Financial District. Our aim is to create a safer atmosphere for returning Downtown residents as well as for workers and visitors heading home for the night. The Downtown Alliance Website, Public Safety at http://www.downtownny.com/neighborhood_public.asp.

FIGURE 3.8   The Downtown Alliance—Downtown New York–Neighborhood Services

tensions, teen violence, teen pregnancy, substance abuse, lack of community ownership and involvement by its members, as well as a host of others difficulties, are beyond the purview of the police system. Police can and do make remarkable differences in the lives of people contacted every day. To imply that no matter what is done is only marginal is harsh and inaccurate, because it is the police who are contacted when violations occur or emergencies are unfolding. Emergency 911 calls are routed to police officers, not social workers. Furthermore, it could be argued that the enforcement of many of our laws equates to active prevention of victimization. In other words, the enforcement model generates immediate and ongoing benefits for the whole community. For example, driving under the influence arrests may prevent serious injury, as does the intervention of police in an abusive spouse case. Each police interaction prompts rippling effects throughout the community and in this way positively impacts the life of the community. But the reactive nature of the public police model will never be able to truly immerse itself into the community. Inevitably, public police will, knowingly or not, remain above the fray, outside the arena, and less integrated than another community design—that delivered by the private security industry.

In the final analysis, only those who are the community can effectively protect the community, and only those whose occupational perspective is not inexorably bound up in a professional image of resource and technology, of criminal apprehension and criminal investigation. To the police in the community it calls for something radically different. See Figure 3.9.

C. The Incompatibility of Public Police and Community-Based Policing Initiatives

As frustrating as it may be, the public police model may fundamentally and inherently be inconsistent with the ideals of community policing. Even the most standard policing techniques interfere with the theoretical view of community policing. For example, utilizing vehicles, instead of face-to-face patrols diminishes the citizens' ability to naturally communicate and interact with officers patrolling their neighborhood. Community police officers "must be freed from the isolation of the patrol car and the demands of the police radio, so that they can maintain daily, direct, fact-to-face contact with the people they serve in a clearly defined beat area."[41] Police training, criminal investigations, communications systems, and personnel deployment are also all geared for providing reactive services to the community rather than the integrative dynamics of the community-based model.

Many aspects of traditional police operations undermine human interaction—vehicle preference to foot patrol, from tinted patrol car windows to even uniforms

FIGURE 3.9   Preventative Interaction: Community Toy Drive

An Example of Incompatibility

Failing to recognize the ineffectiveness of current community policing efforts often creates a false sense of security, rendering the community vulnerable to tragedy. For example, in the early 1990s, the city of St. Petersburg, Florida, implemented a number of new community policing initiatives aimed at improving relations with the community. Their community policing program and new economic development programs for the inner city were lauded as a model of success by cities all over the country. All proceeded well until October 1996, when a riot erupted after a police officer used deadly force to stop a vehicle about to run him over. Until that time, everyone in the local government believed that the community policing effort had secured the complete support of the citizenry and had eliminated the need for concerns such as riot control training and contingency planning.

Then, on November 13, 1996, the officer in question was cleared of all charges by a Pinellas County Grand Jury. The community, divided in its members' beliefs over the incident, once again plunged into darkness. Looting, arson, and random gunfire punctuated the community's frustration as tensions once more erupted into a night of rioting. The community-policing program, despite its noble efforts, had failed.

and equipment that give the appearance of an outsider instead of a community member. How can a department expect officers to implement true community policing when policy creates barriers?

The public policing culture—the aura of occupational policing itself—may at times, be antagonistic to any change in the operational model. Command, line, and staff personnel change with more reticence than other occupations. Much of this mentality is further fostered by the "thin blue line," "the brother and sisterhood," which generally resist change or challenge. Put another way, protectionism and even suspicion are natural and, in many cases, justified. Police are wary of academic theoreticians, legal activists and community groups, liberal judges and lawyers forever proposing new and grand plans that have turned out to be ineffectual and even preposterous. People, including police, do not want to be interfered with on the job. New duties, questionable assignments, and other experiments are typcial in the lives of police officers. Policing is what they are after, and community policing seems to undermine the occupation. In a recent study of line officers, "ninety-eight percent of officers agreed that assisting citizens is as important as enforcing the law, but 88 percent also said that enforcing the law is an officer's most important responsibility. Almost all officers agreed that citizen input about neighborhood problems is important, but 25 percent said they have reason to distrust most citizens."[42]

Further complicating the issue, the police union may have objections to the types of programs or approaches being implemented or to the way that officers are deployed, and therefore the union may create more roadblocks and justification for the attitudes of the rank and file. In his work *Police for the Future*, David H. Bayley expands upon this situation:

Police departments have to struggle to enlist the full and enthusiastic cooperation of their own members in community policing programs. Community policing goes against the grain of police organizations. Departments are also often preoccupied with other matters and do not believe they can devote the resources that might make community police programs succeed.[43]

Time is required in community policing—the type of time for human interaction. Stephen Mastrofski understands the time demands of community policing better than most:

> One theme of community policing is encouraging officers to spend more time with the people who are invested, or could be persuaded to become more heavily invested, in "community" and to work with police. These people are frequently identified as residents, businesspeople, members of neighborhood organizations, and others invested in the areas, such as those who work in schools and belong to churches and other collectivities. A central element of this community building, problem-solving process is tending to fears and anxieties about crime and disorder. Making people feel safe has become as important as making them safe; invariably this entails being visible, responsive, and physically present.[44]

Politicians who have the power to influence practitioners and to acquire funding for crime prevention efforts are promoting community policing as an effective tool in solving the crime issue. Even in the face of hard data, many politicians choose to defend their positions of support of these programs. A good example of a community-oriented policing program that does not seem to have been as effective as some politicians and practitioners wished is the federally funded Community Oriented Policing Services (COPS) program.

Clearly this program has been the center of controversy since the government's own watchdog, the General Accounting Office (GAO), disputed the infusion of 60,000 new officers. In an audit of selected agencies, it found that nearly four of every five police agencies (78 percent) that received grants to reassign officers from desk jobs to street patrol "either could not demonstrate they re-deployed officers or could not demonstrate that they had a system in place to track the re-deployment of officers into community policing."[45] COPS's primary aim was community-based, yet most studies of the program find the usual government shifting of resources for other purposes. Add to this state of affairs the instability of politicians, and another reason why public police cannot deliver community-policing services emerges.[46]

Research conducted by the Heritage Foundation's Center for Data Analysis concludes that COPS, as well as a predecessor program that also funded community policing, added, at most, only some 40,000 full-time officers to the nation's police ranks during 1993 through 1998. A release made by the foundation claims that given the rapid growth in police hiring that began prior to 1993, the true number of police hires attributable to COPS may be considerably lower.[47]

Realistically, even if the street-level officer were brought into the community-policing fold, attempts would have to be made to establish the proper frame of mind for dealing with the community. Reeducation of role and function is no minor undertaking. William Oliver further relays the definitional confusions about what "community policing" means.

> What is the future of this new paradigm in the academic world? Is it important? Is it a fad? How can one convince a fellow educator that the topic of community-oriented policing is needed and desired as an academic course rather than a single chapter in a mainstream policing textbook? People often ask how community-oriented policing is different from police-community relations.[48]

Oliver recommends that street officers be exposed to the following:

Community-oriented policing;

Problem-oriented policing;

Crime prevention;

Strategic-oriented policing;

Neighborhood-oriented policing;

Concepts and philosophy of policing;

Pedagogical and practical applications;

Changing role of police;

The community, the police chief, and midlevel management;

Organizational structure; and

Management and leadership styles.[49]

These officers have already been habituated in another direction—high-risk patrolling, vehicle pursuits, swat team actions, warrant executions, life and death situations—and are now expected to adopt the warmer, more social interactive style of community policing. Those who are highly trained and specialized in emergency response and crisis management cannot switch gears without a philosophical switch in direction.[50]

For the public police officer, the occupational lifestyle can be challenging. Naturally hardened over time by high-stress situations, one of the often-seen remedies is disassociation, alienation, and a growing and unstoppable cynicism, as well as the adoption of an attitude of "us versus them." Eventually, the "blue line" becomes its own wall that blocks out the public and community at large.[51] Interaction is limited to fellow law enforcement people who give comfort unreservedly. In some agencies, police commanders attempting to implement community policing have had to develop policies that force their officers to have face-to-face contact with citizens in a positive and proactive context. Unfortunately, these types of policies cannot be force-fed but instead call for significant training and education. Community policing embraces the formation of relationships with its citizenry. Its goal is to protect the vulnerable and to enhance the lives of the community members through providing crime prevention and protection services, in addition to responding to other calls and emergencies. Is it plausible to expect public police officers to assume these tasks? Can officers switch like chameleons and shift personalities to fit the regimen? From swat team to special victims unit; from drug task force to organized crime team; from enforcer and apprehender to counselor, caretaker, community guardian, and friend—is this a request that can be honored? Of course, these adaptations can occur, but institutional accommodations will need to be made. Directives alone will not suffice.

Practitioner Highlight

Dyncorp

Dyncorp functions as a staffing resource for government-sponsored international police programs in locations such as East Timor, Kosovo, and Iraq. The company also has a security services division that provides security deployments throughout these countries in crisis, in addition to protecting U.S. government facilities.

Dyncorp was also responsible for the protection of facilities within Kuwait and in Afghanistan after the military interventions occurred. They are currently responsible for the security of the physical palace in Kabul, Afghanistan, as well as for the dignitaries and staff within it.

Community policing tends to get law enforcement, from executives to line officers, advocating practices not usually heard of. For example, many chief executives of police departments talk about and even have gone as far as advocating the need to operate their agencies more like a corporation—one that is consumer friendly and results oriented. Service to community members as any other constituency is urged as the improved approach. Given the nature of public police and the bureaucratic structure of departments, as well as the subject matter of usual business, is this plan possible? A corporation's mode can hardly be established when carrying out government functions, though intentions are surely grounded in good faith. The public police system cannot equate its operational essence with that of the profit-driven corporation. Regimentation, structure, rules, and procedures, instead of creative thinking and problem solving, is more likely the public police ethos. Whereas corporations are competition driven in budgeting, marketing, and strategic development, public police are functionally minded. Police departments are not in competition with others in their industry and primarily are attuned to their public safety mission. Here again, public safety depends upon a full-scale and heartfelt reconsideration of its role and function.

Bruce L. Benson, in his book *To Serve and Protect*, recognizes with insight this critical distinction:

> Police chiefs do not have to see that their departments make profits in order to survive, and they do not generally have to compete with other producers for the atten-

Police Substations

Getting in touch with the community to some community police advocates calls for altered geographic placement. In Rochester, New York, for example, "Net Stations" were disbursed out of the centralized district into neighborhood programs. The program has met with intense debate.

In Florida, Hillsborough County, the police substation program produced less than impressive results. One particular substation, a very small, single-story building located within a high-crime area in the east side of Hillsborough County, Florida, seemed to provide little deterrence to the open drug dealing conducted across the street (a two-lane road) in nearby parking lots. In fact, there was so much activity that the small apartment community across the street needed armed security officers to patrol the area all night to ensure that dealers did not operate in that community. The murder of Elizabeth Swanson, aged 38, who was beaten to death inside her Palms Cleaners and Laundromat at 401 45th Avenue, South, in Coquina Key Plaza in St. Petersburg, Florida, near the substation, further amplifies the difficulties. This violent crime, in which the victim was severely beaten about the head, occurred in a strip mall in broad daylight, five doors down from a police substation. The incident occurred between 2 P.M. and 4 P.M. on a weekday. The Community Resource Center (police substation), which was open at the time of the incident, is located only 66 feet from the dry cleaners.

tion of consumers (they may have to compete for their appointment, of course, but their organization has a virtual monopoly over production of the service within its jurisdiction).[52]

To successfully operate like a corporation, police agency operations would have to undergo a draconian reformulation. Budget dollars would be tied to productivity and effectiveness, promotion and staffing would be as apolitical as possible, and the utilization of civilians in key positions would be commonplace, especially in managerial and financial areas. Personnel deployment and shift decisions would also be altered. Instead of commanding, the upper echelon police leaders would manage first and would order second. Public police officers earn respect through service, not cost efficiencies. The subculture of policing would be turned on its head—as it needs to be if community policing will ever function.

Corporations are proactive, whereas police departments are naturally reactive toward crisis, crime, and emergency. The security giant Pinkerton-Burns rests its operational philosophy on this set of "core values," some of which public law enforcement may find foreign:

- Satisfy client needs;
- Empower and respect our people;
- Embrace high ethical standards;
- Work as a team; and
- Reward innovation and constant improvement.[53]

In these values resides a vastly different mentality from that of most police departments.

A major shift in policy making and planning would be mandatory. From training to education, from police academy requirements to promotion and job reviews, the culture of public police would have to shift dramatically. Public police are incapable of this level of transformation. Private sector organizations, already rooted in the nonbureaucratic ideal, have a better chance of rising to the community policing challenge than do their public counterpart.[54] Bickering about turf and jurisdictional lines would have to cease in the public model before any inroads into community policing could occur. In Florida, for example, multiple small police departments operate independently from each other, alongside a County Sheriff's Office.[55] Operating in this fragmented manner fosters miscommunications, raises costs, and heightens political tensions. Public policing will never be capable of eliminating all these dilemmas. Corporations merge, consolidate, and reorganize for maximum effectiveness and in turn reduce costs or utilize excess revenues for the betterment of their service. Public law enforcement never willingly downsizes or streamlines its operational mandate. None of this tendency is surprising to Bruce Benson, who fully appreciates the entrepreneurial nature of the private protection industry:

> This should come as no surprise, since private entrepreneurs—unlike public bureaucrats—are under constant competitive pressure to discover new ways to improve their products and services, including discovering new ways to improve community cooperation. Clearly, private entrepreneurs and the public they work with deserve much of the credit for falling crime rates.[56]

The level of commitment to the complex tasks of community policing are lofty, yet attainable goals, but getting to these ends will not be easy. Stretched beyond their limits already, public police agencies have little room to experiment or think outside the box. Community policing mandates a novel flexibility. Departments have to adjust an entire operational plan to approach citizenry within each neighborhood, interact, and enlist support and encourage involvement in crime reduction efforts. These steps are not afterthoughts but are crucial programmatic requirements in community policing. Face-to-face daily interaction, with specific training directed to those ends, is not optional but is essential to success.

For a substantive relationship to exist between the community and the police, the majority of interaction between the two must revolve around natural, nonconfrontational encounters, which are usually not associated with enforcement and crime issues. The environment needs to be one of trust and respect, of neighbor-to-neighbor, and one in which sufficient noncriminal interaction occurs to allow this relationship to flourish. Public police must dedicate themselves to much more than the crime demands of the communities served. Community policing might have a tendency to become window dressing in the eyes of command officers operating under a reactionary mentality. Community policing wants guardians, not enforcers.

In high-crime environments and minority neighborhoods where many people do not trust the police, and in business districts that fret over the customer base, positive interaction between a citizen and its protector is becoming a thing of the past. Foot patrols give community members a sense of security, as well as allowing them to develop a relationship with the officer and the agency represented, enables the development of mutual trust, and builds a foundation of respect and cooperation. Neighborhoods besieged by poverty and crime pine for police interaction beyond the investigation and arrest mode. Community policing depends on the trust relationship. Raids, sweeps, and other highly visible tactical actions add to the paranoia that undermines the trust. Carl F. Horowitz stresses the importance of the relationship between police programs in low-income neighborhoods and imparts that "a police anti-crime program in low-income neighborhoods requires maximum fact-to-face communication with resident leaders."[57] This is a tall order.[58]

Add to these requirements public policing's obsessive concern about incident management systems, collation and collection of data, and political influences, and public policing's efforts toward community policing are further distracted. Instead of flexibility, the modern public police system ties itself to programs and crime reports, which essentially guide its rudder. Foot patrols are replaced with directed and targeted deployments. Constituency building is not on the list of priorities for the typical police department. "The demise of foot patrols and beat integrity in favor of directed patrol over large geographic area prevented officers from becoming knowledgeable about specific problems and individual people on their beats."[59]

For a few police officers, the characteristics of community policing are beneath the training and sophistication of the position; community-driven activities are for underlings, they believe. Benson, a professor at Florida State University, addresses this point:

> Unfortunately, public police in major cities are well aware that community policing requires them to act like security guards . . . they tend to be insulted by the idea that they should do so.[60]

In the final analysis, such resistance is the greatest of ironies, since it is bona fide and aggressive community policing that will thwart criminal activity more effectively than most other police strategies. Adoption of its modus operandi will actually achieve the noble ambitions of the public police model—to serve, to protect, to arrest and apprehend, and to assure safe communities, whereas current police tactics will not. The means is right under the noses of a system that has difficulty embracing the ideals of community policing wholeheartedly, because of the reactionary nature of the policing system.

IV. THE COMPATIBILITY OF THE PRIVATE SECTOR IN COMMUNITY PROTECTION: THE NEW PARADIGM

As the community policing definition and purpose has been formulated, its constituency targeted, and its many influences discussed, from the political footballing to the unionist's objection, from the entrenched police structure to the psychology of officer resistance, our conclusion is single-minded—that the private sector coupled with public entities represents the best approach in community protection and crime prevention. Public police cannot carry out this mandate alone. Some would argue that the venture is a plan destined to fail. Yates, Pillai, and Humburg describe the public officer excursion into the world of public policing as one of "frustration" and "strain" and "conflict."[61] In their comprehensive survey of English and U.S. officers in two jurisdictions, their findings are indicative of stress. Two significant findings include officer levels of *frustration and strain*[62] and levels of *commitment.*[63] Although not universally binding, the results illuminate the dilemma.[64]

As already observed, the need for change is more than commonplace. Moreover, the essence of change in the community-policing paradigm must be radical and dramatic. That the police system as presently understood is solely or exclusively capable of carrying out the community-policing directive is not debatable. What is imperative is "a significant departure from the way American police departments have operated throughout the better part of the twentieth century."[65] That departure would be the transference or sharing of community policing functions to private sector operatives. Such transference would not only be sensible and compatible with the philosophy but also complimentary to it. Public police must forego any provincial or proprietary turf and must appreciate not only the wisdom of the delegation but the efficiency that it will bring to the system at large. Private sector companies can effectively and comprehensively deliver the ambitious agenda of community-oriented services, whereas public police can reorient their plan of attack to the nexus of the public approach—crime.

Presently, public police often tangentially or reluctantly deal with the community policing mandate. Turning over the responsibility to the brothers and sisters of the private sector will relieve them of this burden and free up precious time, energy, and resources. In addition, high-crime areas, the most frequently neglected clientele in the pressed public police model, will experience positive interaction and the type of care that all citizens are entitled to. See Figure 3.10.

The strategy of fighting crime by utilizing public law enforcement can include a problem-solving approach, but never will problem solving be at the forefront of service delivery as long as contemporary policing systems are required to perform from a reactive infrastructure. Furthermore, law enforcement is by far the leading component charged with the control of crime, and as long as this remains the case, crime will never be effectively controlled. David H. Bayley, author of *Police for the Future*, properly concludes,

> In modern democratic societies the police bear the primary responsibility for ensuring public safety because law enforcement is viewed as the primary solution to crime. For several reasons this total reliance on law enforcement is unwise and should not be allowed to continue.[66]

A public safety effort must be composed of law enforcement balanced with prevention. Prevention is the centerpiece of the community-oriented model. Increasingly, police practitioners realize that police organizations are incapable of this level of service. With this understanding, the seminal question becomes, which

FIGURE 3.10   Community Integration by Preventative Interaction

entity is better suited to engage in community problem solving and crime prevention? After consideration of the relative merits, strengths, and weaknesses of the two cultures, it appears that the private sector is better suited to these purposes, because in the private security industry, entrepreneurial spirit runs free, the corporate model dominates unabated, accountability rules over personnel and unions, and success motivates. All of these factors assure success.

In addition to these considerations, private security practitioners are neither saddle-bound nor laden with the bevy of responsibilities that would distract from the mission. Public policing must serve more masters than the private sector could ever envision. Neither does the private sector come to the table with excessive baggage, whereby ill will blinds sensibilities and agendas seem perpetually part of the landscape. This is a new creature in a new world, unshackled from the usual constitutional claims,[67] civilian review boards, and activist groups looking to carve out examples in the public sector. This finding does not suggest public policing's inherent inadequacy in carrying out the plan, but the fact remains that to require this of public entities is to further burden an already overburdened environment. The private sector offers a remedy that benefits the public safety system as a whole. The story of exactly how that program plays out comprises the pages that follow. It is a story that is mostly yet to be told, and indeed, the propositions here are new to the ear. Fundamentally, logic cannot avoid the inevitability of this choice; and if this choice is adopted, the implications for the criminal justice system and society in general are staggering. The conceptual framework is in a gestational period, but its viability is assured. The proposition could be argued to be at the "C" phase of the proposed paradigm, but it may be more appropriately described as a new vision altogether. Change is inevitable, but exactly who or what will assume the burden is this text's question. For some, change will not take place in police organizations. Jahong Zhao comments as follows:

> It took approximately 50 years of change before the bureaucratic model crystallized in the 1950's. During this transition, a considerable number of boundary-spanning units appeared and were later institutionalized into American law enforcement practices and police agency structure. The same phenomenon may be occurring again as police organizations try to be more responsive to their external environments. It may take another 30 years for the COP (community oriented policing) model to be finalized with respect to organizational domain, technical core and task environment . . . American policing is likely engaged in a long process of evolution rather than a fast-moving revolution. Although many scholars of policing might say that the direction of change is favorable, it appears to be more creeping incrementalism than decisive advancement.[68]

To find solutions that allow practitioners to maximize public safety and meet the new paradigm shift, we are being forced to abandon traditional methods and find new, innovative approaches; this need is what has mandated a shift to community crime prevention and problem solving. It will be exciting no matter how you look at it.

V. CONCLUSION

Any true understanding of the private/public systems of justice requires heavy comparative analysis. What makes these two systems tick? What are the ends and aims of these two approaches? Are they compatible, complementary, or antagonistic? When applied to community settings, the differences can be quite striking. Laying out the nature of community policing is another end of the chapter, and exactly how the public and private police square with the definition is a regular consideration. For some, there can be only frustration in the eventual molding of community with public police. For others, there appears to be a fundamental incompatibility between the public, professionalized policing and the skills and tactics so essential to success in the community. Whereas the public model tends to gravitate toward the enforcement and deterrence model, coupled with a strong apprehension philosophy, the private sector seems more dedicated to the theories of community integration. In the private sector, a stronger realization exists that success in the community depends on conquering the hearts and minds of its members. This chapter attempts to lay out the implications of these fundamental differences in tactical strategy and ideological designs.

For community policing, the implications are quite serious. While the public model puts its eggs in this basket, a debate rages as to whether or not the fit is possible. While new programs and initiatives crop up everywhere and funding sources are endlessly directed to new and avant-garde community strategies, one can only wonder whether public law enforcement is capable of this sort of delivery. Private security is posited as the more apt player in the world of community integration, since its operational foundation is more accustomed to service and measures of efficacy. The public police are simply overwhelmed with a myriad of activities to be as effective in community-based policing as the private sector is. This chapter lays out all the competing visions so relevant to success in the community.

Notes

1. M. Sparrow, *Implementing Community Policing, Perspectives on Policing,* 8–9 (1988), cited in Robert Trojanowicz et al., *Community Policing: A Contemporary Perspective,* 2nd ed., 23 (Anderson, 1998).
2. Eugene A. Paoline, III, et al., *Police Culture, Individualism, and Community Policing: Evidence From Two Police Departments,* 17 Just. Q., 575, 581–582 (Sept. 2000).
3. The document "A Strategic Plan for Reinventing the Chicago Police Department" describes many of the reasons why the police are reaching out and attempting to develop community support. It states the following:

   > Changing demographics, a shifting economic base, deteriorating schools, the breakdown of families, chronic drug and alcohol abuse, racial tensions—all contribute to a spiraling crime rate and a growing sense of fear and disorder in many neighborhoods. These changes in society and an increasingly diverse and demanding public placed new demands on the police at a time when their traditional workload was already expanding because of illegal drugs, street gangs, and the presence of increasingly powerful firearms.

4. Joanne Ziembo-Vogl and Devere Woods, Jr., *Defining Community Policing: Practice versus Paradigm,* 19 *Police Studies,* 33, 39 at Table 1 (1996).
5. Helen Taylor Greene, *Community-Oriented Policing in Virginia,* 19 *Police Studies,* 17, 28 (1996).
6. Stan Stojkovic, John Klofas, and David Kalinich, *The Administration and Management of Criminal Justice Organizations: A Book of Readings,* 3rd ed. 29 (Long Grove, IL, Waveland Press, 1999).
7. Jihong Zhao, *Why Police Organizations Change: A Study of Community-Oriented Policing* 6 (Washington, D.C., Police Executive Research Forum, 1996).
8. Matthew J. Hickman and Brian A. Reaves, *Community Policing in Local Police Departments, 1997 and 1999,* BJS Special Report, NCJ 184794, at 1 (Feb. 2001).
9. *See* Robert Trojanowicz et al., *Community Policing: A Contemporary Perspective,* 2nd ed., 23 (Anderson, Cincinnati, 1998).
10. Thomas F. Raymond, *A Case Study in Affordable Security,* 54 *Journal of Property Management* 58, 59 (May–June 1989).
11. *See* Trojanowicz et al. at 23.
12. P. Waddington, *Community Policing: A Skeptical Appraisal,* 84–96, in P. Norton, ed., *Law and Order and British Politics* (1984).
13. Thomas Feltes, *New Philosophies in Policing,* 17 *Police Studies* 29, 35 (1994).
14. Edward C. Byrne, *Back on the Street, Law and Order* 43, 45 (May 1997).

15. Hickman and Reaves, Figure 4 at 7.
16. Study Circles Resource Center, *Protecting Communities Serving the Public* 13 (Pomfret, CT, 2000).
17. John Hoffmann, *Community Policing Consortium, Law and Order* 126 (May 1997).
18. Trojanowicz et al. at 135.
19. Debra Livingston, *Police Discretion and the Quality of Life in Public Places: Courts, Communities, and the New Policing,* 97 *Columbia Law Review* 551, 564, (April 1997).
20. Hickman and Reaves.
21. Trojanowicz et al. at 23.
22. The Vera Institute study on community-based policing programs, for example, reveals that these programs have not been extremely effective in large cities and concludes that there is a wide gap between promises made and the reality of neighborhood conditions.
23. The lobby or political groups dedicated to the concept multiply. Some examples are National Center for Community Policing, National Center for Neighborhood Enterprise, National Crime Prevention Council, National Latino Peace Officers Association, Neighborhoods USA, National Organization of Black Law Enforcement Executives, and the Officer Next Door Program.
24. Jerome Skolnick and David Bayley, *The New Blue Line: Police Innovation in Six American Cities* (New York, Free Press, 1998).
25. For examples, *see* Judith E. Sulik, *Police Excellence in Bridgeport, CT, Law & Order* 114 (Oct. 1997) and Alan S. Elias, *Pro-Active Approach Successful, Law & Order* 111 (Oct. 1997).
26. Michael J. Heidingsfield, *Community Policing: A Chief's Definition, Law & Order* 196 (Oct. 1997).
27. Brian Forst and Peter K. Manning, *The Privatization of Policing* 7 (Washington, D.C., Georgetown Univ. Press, 1999). *See* Stan Stojkovic, John Klofas, and David Kalinich, *The Administration and Management of Criminal Justice Organizations: A Book of Readings,* 3rd ed. 29 (Long Grove, IL, Waveland Press, 1999).
28. *See* Gail Dantzker et al., *Preparing Police Officers for Community Policing: An Evaluation of Training for Chicago's Alternative Policing Strategy,* 18 *Police Studies* 45, 56–57 (1995).
29. *See* P. J. Ortmeier, *Public Safety and Security Administration* at page 61 (Butterworth, 1999).
30. Forst and Manning at 12.
31. Michael G. Shanahan, *Surviving the Policing Paradigm Shift,* 1 *Beretta USA Leadership Bulletin,* at 3 (April 1995).
32. Trojanowicz et al. at 23.
33. David Anderson, *The Aggregate Burden of Crime:* (January 1999) at http://www.ssm.com/abstract_147911.
34. Chris Braiden in *Police Management: Perspectives and Issues* 95 (Larry T. Hoover, ed., Police Executive Research Forum, 1992).
35. George L. Kelling and Catherine M. Coles, *Fixing Broken Windows* (New York, Simon & Schuster, 1996).
36. David L. Carter keenly observes: "Even the aspects that are being implemented do not seem to have the intended effect on crime or on improving basic community relations. The relationship between the police and community in America has been like a flesh wound that would not completely respond to treatment. As we apply salves to the wound and treat it carefully, it begins to heal. Then, without warning, we turn our head and re-injure the wound, once again looking for medications and "wonder treatments"

that will cure the injury with finality [Carter]" Police Management: Issues and Perspectives by Police Executive Research Forum, Washington, D.C. (1992) (Hoover, 61).

37. James Brooke, *Police/Security Partnerships: Privatization Models That Impact Crime,* CJ The Americas Online 1/28/97.

38. David H. Bayley, *Police for the Future* 3 (New York, Oxford Univ. Press, 1994).

39. Forst and Manning at page 14.

40. In an effort to measure the impact on crime, the Kansas City experiments required redeploying police units. For the purpose of this experiment, the city was divided into 15 sections where police officers patrolled the areas using one of three separate methods involving levels of patrol. Some sections were overrun with patrol cars that were highly visible at all times. Other sections received less than normal patrol, and others remained unchanged. The results illustrated that there is very little, if any, difference in the crime rate whether a neighborhood is flooded with patrol cars, the amount of patrol stays the same, or whether it is decreased.

41. Trojanowicz et al. at 23.

42. Roger B. Parks et al., *How Officers Spend Their Time with the Community,* 16 *Justice Quarterly* 483 (Sept. 1999).

43. Bayley at 118.

44. Parks et al. at 483.

45. (Bruce Cameron COPS: A Political Football Law Order Oct. 2000)

46. In an article by Bruce Cameron called "COPS: A Political Football," published in the *Law & Order* magazine, (Oct. 2000) Cameron quotes Senator Joseph Biden with such a position. Senator Biden wrote: "I could not disagree stronger with your editorial . . . Contrary to your assertions, the COPS program has delivered on its goal of 100,000 new police officers under-budget and ahead of schedule. In fact, to date, police departments in large cities and small towns nationwide have received funding to hire more than 100,000 new officers—with more than 60,000 on the streets already." "According to COPS office officials, the office's first systematic attempt to estimate the progress toward the goal of 100,000 new community policing officers on the street was a telephone survey of grantees done between September and December 1996. COPS office staff contacted 8,360 grantees to inquire about their progress in hiring officers and getting them on the street. According to a COPS office official, a follow-up survey, which estimated 30,155 law enforcement officer positions to be on the street, was done between late March and June 1997. The official said that this survey was contracted out because the earlier in-house survey had been extremely time-consuming. The official said that as of May 1997, the office was in the process of selecting a contractor to do three additional surveys during fiscal year 1998." Community Policing: Observations on the COPS Program Midway Through Program Implementation. (GAO/T-GGD-00-33, Oct. 28, 1999).

47. (Bruce Cameron COPS: A Political Football, Law Order Oct. 2000)

48. Willard M. Oliver, *Moving beyond "Police-community Relations" and "The Police and "Society": Community-oriented Policing as an Academic Course,* 9 *Journal of Criminal Justice Education,* 303 (Fall 1998).

49. Oliver at 310.

50. Parks, Mastrofski, Dejong, and Gray have shown that community policing specialists spend less time interacting with the community than do generalist patrol officers. See Roger B. Parks et al. at 16.

51. Trojanowicz et al. at 23.

52. Bruce L. Benson, *To Serve And Protect* New York Univ. Press, New York, 1998.

53. Pinkerton Service Corporation, Core Values, at http://www.pinkertons.com/ company/info/company_profile.asp visited 9/4/2002.

54. Private security can be said to labor under wholly different perceptions. For an interesting examination, *see* Anthony Micucci, *A Typology of Private Policing Operational Styles*, 26 *Journal of Crime and Justice* 41 (Jan./Feb. 1998).

55. St. John's County Sheriff's Office, *Bridging the Gap Between Law Enforcement and Private Security Agencies*, 1998 St. Augustine, Fl.

56. Bruce L. Benson, *Growing Private Security Investments Help Crime Rates Tumble, The Detroit News* editorials and opinions online edition, 12/16/99.

57. Carl F. Horowitz, *An Empowerment Strategy for Eliminating Neighborhood Crime, Backgrounder Number* 814, The Heritage Foundation, at http://www.heritage.org/library/categories/crimelaw/bg814.html, 3/25/91.

58. Kelling and Coles further corroborate how public police are pulling out, when staying visible is what is mandatory for community policing. *See* George L. Kelling and Catherine M. Coles, *Fixing Broken Windows* (Simon & Schuster, New York 1996).

59. City of Chicago Strategic Plan Working Group, Together We Can: *A Strategic Plan for Reinventing the Chicago Police Departments* City of Chicago, IL, Oct. 1993.

60. Benson, *To Serve and Protect* at 335.

61. Donald L. Yates et al., *Frustration, Strain and Commitment to Community Policing: A Comparative Analysis of American and English Police Officers*, 19 *Police Studies* 1 (1996).

62. Yates et al. at 8.

63. Yates et al. at 9.

64. Wesley Skogan in his book *Disorder and Decline* gives us an accurate picture of the cause and effect associated with today's policing system and the reason why it is extremely difficult to implement the community approach designed by the academic body: "One consequence of these changes in the organization and mission of big-city police was a dwindling interest in disorder. Other problems always seemed more pressing. This was in part because the way they are now organized and managed means the police are most 'effective' (as they measure it) at responding to complaints about major crimes. As the volume of those complaints skyrocketed in the 1960s and mid-1970s, the commitment to respond to every emergency call as quickly as possible absorbed most of the police resources. In effect, not the top brass, but thousands of individual citizens dialing '911,' set the day-to-day agenda for many police agencies. Departments had to meet these growing demands in the face of shrinking resources, for by the beginning of the 1980s many big-city departments were smaller than they were a decade earlier. With efficiency in mind, police managers adopted call-prioritizing schemes, which guaranteed a rapid response to 'man with a gun,' 'burglary in progress,' and other emergencies, but put most complaints concerning disorder at the bottom of the stack. Many stoutly resisted providing services which were not 'productive'—which did not give them wide-area coverage and speed their response time, or did not generate arrests. One early victim of productivity was foot patrol." At 88.

65. Trojanowicz et al. at 135.

66. Bayley.

67. One of the often-seen criticisms of the private sector justice is its irrelevancy to constitutional oversight. See Lynn M. Gagel, *Stealthy Encroachments upon the Fourth Amendment: Constitutional Constraints and Their Applicability to the Long Arm of Ohio's Private Security Forces*, 63 *U. Cin. L. Rev.* 1807 (Sum. 1995).

68. Zhao at 81.

4

Private Sector Community Profile and Threat Assessment

There is no "quick fix" for many of the forms of disorder that plague city neighborhoods. Solutions need to be carefully matched to the specific problems facing individual communities, and in many cases it will take a combination of approaches to make a significant difference in the lives of area residents.

Wesley G. Skogan, Author of Disorder and Decline at 186.

Learning Objectives

1. To become familiar with the various methods to assess community composition and state.
2. To appreciate the role that private security plays in developing an accurate profile of the target community.
3. To learn how to construct a general Community Profile.
4. To see how policy making depends upon an accurate and full understanding of the community to be served.
5. To become capable of identifying specific community threats.
6. To catalog and type community threats.
7. To develop proactive strategies in the elimination of a community's more typical threats.
8. To author policy that prevents and deters the growth and escalation of community threats.
9. To author and compose a Community Profile and a Threat Assessment.
10. To see how private sector justice plays a critical role in the analysis and interpretation of community data and characteristics.

I. GENERAL PERCEPTIONS OF COMMUNITY LIFE

Any sensible plan of community-based protection depends on a substantive understanding of community composition and makeup. To integrate, to imbue, and to become part of the community calls for full assimilation into the life of the community. Practitioners must acquire a clear picture of the setting. Both profile and assessment open the door to prevention, prediction, and deterrence.

Most would agree that the concept of community in a generalized sense has undergone dramatic change in the last hundred years. The pressures, stresses, and negative evolution appear everywhere. Security specialists cannot avoid the broad sociological implications. In fact, these professionals must master the comprehensive view of what community trends are. Any preordained conceptions of community have long been undermined by the radical revolution of the last three decades. Instead of a collective mindset, a view of common over individual goods, the general approach has been one of individualism and self-interest. The picture is not pretty: "Communities characterized by (a) anonymity and sparse acquaintanceship networks among residents, (b) unsupervised teenage peer groups and attenuated control of public space, and (c) a weak organizational base and low social participation in local activities face an increased risk of crime and violence."[1]

To control a community requires a look at the collective fabric. What may become apparent is the loosening of the threads that once bound communities together. The security industry perceives the dynamics and tensions of collective and individual interests in each and every assignment given. Community protection will not be effective without recognition that individuals think themselves above the common purpose.

Drugs, liberalized views on the nature of authority, and the outright rejection and defiance of authority have become more commonplace. Barriers and behaviors were undermined, and new thresholds for moral tolerance were accepted as what society is today. The hippie movement, the Students for a Democratic Society, the Weather Underground Organization, the Black Panthers, the abortion movement, the Watergate scandal, Vietnam, sexual revolution, political distrust and revolution, contempt for authority, and the loss of religious fervor are just a few of the extraordinary changes that the culture has absorbed. Values and ethical boundaries have become relative, and fixed moral answers are hard to come by. Means justify the end that is sought, and the idea of "me" overtook the concept of the whole. The parts were all that mattered, rather than the sum of the whole. In short, community disintegrated or evolved into other, less defensible formats. The self-centered, self-absorbed citizen replaces the person of sacrifice.

The panoply of social ills and cultural shifts infects the community in direct and subtle ways. Obsession with leisure over work (or vice versa), inordinate desire for physical over intellectual pleasures, rates of illegitimacy and divorce, promiscuity and unchaste existences, rates of prostitution and drug and alcohol dependency—these are other unfortunate signs of the shift in community life. Civics is replaced with fun and self-interest. Bizarre clothing, self-mutilation, binge drinking, and other forms of substance abuse tell a miserable tale of uncontrollable mores.

Media, from television to movies, music, and theater no longer uplift and educate but instead prefer shock and titillation. If it sells, produce it. Shock television, rampant and blatant sexuality, and entertainment devoid of all artistic, scientific, and educational value are now normative. The community is flooded with artistic distress.[2] Television statistics in Table 4.1[3] are illustrative of the problems.

Violence is a staple for all media, and the young are specifically targeted for offensive and unceasingly violent portrayals. Even the traditional news shows dwell on violent or scurrilous stories over factual journalism. Rates of juvenile crime are now at epidemic proportions. Aside from a general upward trend, the bulk of criminal conduct is now committed by those below the age of 20. See Table 4.2.[4]

The longitudinal picture is just as disturbing. Evaluate the levels of arrests during the period 1970 through 1997 in Figure 4.1.[5]

Communities are in distress. Brian Forst's *The Privatization of Policing* lucidly remarks as follows:

> I see the decline of basic human virtues related no less to other factors: the growth of freedom and leisure without enlightenment, the absence of major societal crisis such as war to bind people, cynicism bred by media obsessed with the imperfections of well-known people and institutions and often conspicuously uninterested in their contributions, the glorification of self-indulgent behaviors, and the atomization of family and community bonds.[6]

In communities riddled with sociopaths, indifference, and violence, the task of private sector operatives will not be easy.[7] These settings present special challenges not witnessed a generation ago. See Figure 4.2.[8]

Desensitized and cold-blooded, an ever increasing number of community members do not abide by historical controls.[9] The private sector professionals must be prepared to root out the worse for the benefit of the better. Gangs of juveniles now prey on the innocent. Some commit unthinkable abuses towards people, animals, and objects without any sense of guilt, shame, or remorse. When confronted or caught in the act, they provide absurd defenses and generally blame others.

TABLE 4.1 *Violent Acts, 6 A.M. to midnight, April 2, 1992, on Major Networks*

Act	Number of Scenes	Percentage of Total
Serious assaults (without guns)	389	20
Gunplay	362	18
Isolated punches	273	14
Pushing, dragging	272	14
Menacing threat with a weapon	226	11
Slaps	128	6
Deliberate destruction of property	95	5
Simple assault	73	4
All other types of violence	28	1

TABLE 4.2 *Victimization Rates for Persons Age 12 and Over, by Type of Crime and Age of Victims*

Type of crime	Rate per 1,000 persons in each age group							
	12–15	16–19	20–24	25–34	35–49	50–64	65 and over
All personal crimes	**110.7**	**110.3**	**79.8**	**56.1**	**35.6**	**15.6**	**6.9**
Crimes of violence	107.0	107.7	78.8	54.8	33.8	14.0	5.9
Completed violence	32.4	37.0	22.3	15.7	9.3	2.4	1.6
Attempted/threatened violence	74.5	70.6	56.5	39.1	24.4	11.6	4.3
Rape/Sexual assault	2.2	5.7	3.0	2.0	1.4	0.1[*]	0.0[*]
Rape/Attempted rape	1.3[*]	4.6	1.8	1.5	0.9	0.0[*]	0.0[*]
Rape	1.1[*]	3.3	0.7[*]	0.7	0.5	0.0[*]	0.0[*]
Attempted rape[1]	0.2[*]	1.3[*]	1.1[*]	0.8	0.3[*]	0.0[*]	0.0[*]
Sexual assault[2]	0.9[*]	1.1[*]	1.2[*]	0.5[*]	0.5	0.1[*]	0.0[*]
Robbery	9.5	9.0	10.8	6.9	4.7	1.8	1.3
Completed/property taken	5.8	4.7	7.1	4.9	3.2	1.1	0.8
With injury	1.1[*]	1.7	2.1	1.2	1.1	0.4[*]	0.1[*]
Without injury	4.7	3.0	5.0	3.8	2.0	0.7	0.7[*]

(continued)

113

TABLE 4.2 *Victimization Rates for Persons Age 12 and Over, by Type of Crime and Age of Victims*

Type of crime	Rate per 1,000 persons in each age group						
	12–15	16–19	20–24	25–34	35–49	50–64	65 and over
Attempted to take property	3.6	4.3	3.7	1.9	1.5	0.7	0.5*
With injury	1.1*	1.1*	0.9*	0.5*	0.4	0.1*	0.0*
Without injury	2.6	3.2	2.8	1.5	1.1	0.6*	0.5*
Assault	95.2	93.0	65.0	45.9	27.7	12.1	4.6
Aggravated	15.4	24.4	15.2	11.6	6.8	2.6	1.3
With injury	4.4	8.5	3.3	3.0	2.0	0.1*	0.2*
Threatened with weapon	11.0	15.9	11.9	8.5	4.8	2.5	1.0
Simple	79.9	68.6	49.8	34.4	20.9	9.5	3.3
With minor injury	20.4	19.4	10.3	6.6	3.2	1.1	0.6*
Without injury	59.5	49.2	39.5	27.8	17.7	8.4	2.8
Purse snatching/Pocket picking	3.8	2.7	1.1*	1.2	1.8	1.6	1.0
Population in each age group	15,575,940	14,539,170	17,813,630	41,138,060	60,635,010	34,451,280	31,556,350

Note: Detail may not add to total shown because of rounding.
*Estimate is based on about 10 or fewer sample cases.
[1]Includes verbal threats of rape.
[2]Includes threats.

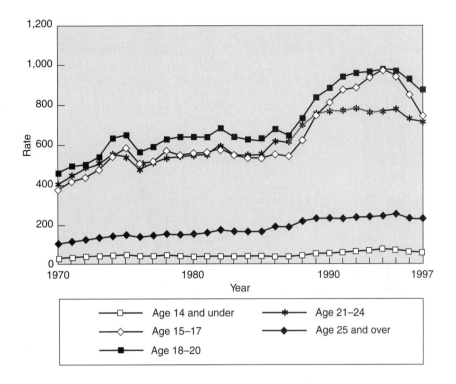

Note: The Violent Crime Index includes the offenses of murder and nonnegligent manslaughter, forcible rape, robbery, and aggravated assault.

Source: U.S. Department of Justice, Bureau of Justice Statistics. 1999. Arrests by age group, number, and rates for total offenses, Index offenses, violent offenses, and property offenses, 1970–97. Spreadsheet. *Crime and justice electronic data abstracts.* Retrieved 3 January 2000 from the World Wide Web: http://www.ojp.usdoj.gov/bjs/dtdata.htm.

FIGURE 4.1   Exhibit 2. Arrest Rates for Violent Index Offenses per 100,000 Population, by Age Group, 1970–1997

These same individuals engage in staggering rates of violence and care little about the consequences. The descendants and offspring of the current crop of delinquents may become even more threatening in the years to come.[10] Many in the community sorely lack the emotional and spiritual socialization that leads to productive lives. These deficits lead to erosion of empathy—the sense that others and their problems matter.

To gain a broad overview of the community state of health, consult the template in Table 4.3. Here the profiler reviews geography, people, crime, health data, housing, economic conditions, and lifestyles, rates of poverty, and corresponding services. See also Table 4.4, which pinpoints existing levels of collective cooperation and lays out opportunities for collaboration.

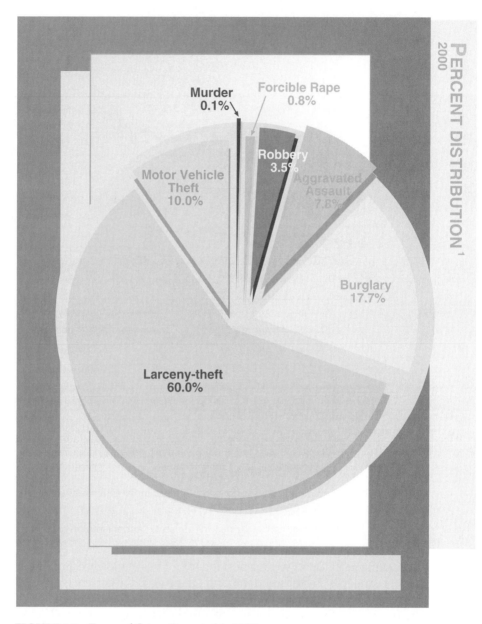

FIGURE 4.2   Types of Crime Reported in UCR

TABLE 4.3 *Indicators to Be Discussed with Different Agencies*

Theme	Indicators at Community Level
Maps	• Neighborhood • Health authorities • Urban/Rural • County
People	• Population numbers by age group and gender • Projected future population trends by age group • Population density maps (persons per hectare) • Components of population change • Change in populations • Household types/family information • Ethnic breakdown of the population
Crime	• Number of reported crimes by significant breakdown of crime • Total reported crime per 1,000 population • Reported crime per 1,000 population by significant breakdown of crime • Age profiles of offenders and of victims (violent crime and burglary of dwellings) • Cost of crime for burglary of dwellings (value stolen) and criminal damage (value damaged) *Map.* Location of police stations
Health	• Leading cause of death • Standardized mortality ratios (SMRs) for top ten causes of death • Premature deaths (Years of life lost) • Limiting long-term illness, health problem, or disability • Hospital admissions (registered population) • Information on unhealthy lifestyle factors (smoking, alcohol consumption, obesity levels, physical inactivity, cholesterol levels) *Map.* Location of health facilities and organizations
Housing	• Average house price • Number of housing units by house type • Number of HUD/affordable housing units by house type • Number of unfit dwellings • Number of housing units without central heating • Estimated need for housing by group • Number of homeless seeking advice/assistance with finding accommodation

(continued)

TABLE 4.3   *Indicators to Be Discussed with Different Agencies (Cont.)*

Theme	Indicators at Community Level
Local economy	• Employment trends (full- and part-time jobs) • Employment trends by sector • Growth in economically active population • Unemployment, monthly totals and rates • Number of businesses by number of employees • Average weekly earnings
Poverty	• Percentage of population on public assistance • Number of households on public assistance • Percentage of children living in households on public assistance • Number of pensioners receiving Social Security benefits
Social services	• Percentage of population in receipt of disability *Map.* District offices and facilities
Service capacity	• Web links to home pages of agencies
Community capacity (including multiagency partnerships and voluntary services)	• Strategies, plans, partnerships, contact persons • Web links to voluntary and community organizations • Community organizations • Information services for children
Education and lifelong learning	• Class sizes • Unauthorized school absence (primary and secondary) • Examination results • Percentage of workforce trained • Pupil forecasts • Provision of nursery and preschool places *Maps.* Location of education facilities including libraries
Community safety	• Road accidents • Fatalities
Lifestyles/Surveys	• Community appraisals
Environment	• Water quality • Pollution incidents
Leisure	• Web links to district pages

TABLE 4.4 *Partnership and Collaborative Opportunities*

Area of Work	Yes/No	Contact Details
Community strategy		
Local economy		
Children's services		
Social care, housing, and health		
Social inclusion strategy		
Lifelong learning		
Community safety strategy		
Environment		
Travel and transport		
Performance plan		
Joint asset management		

A. Community Structure: Organized/Disorganized Environments

Perceptions about a community can be further broken down into the state and health of its underlying structure. In other words, communities can be measured by their respective levels of organization and/or disorganization. Communities that are well-organized tend to have fewer problems than those operating in chaos and disorder. Disorganized communities yearn for the type of order that builds individuals and institutions that shape a neighborhood. Disorganized environments lack structure in schools, recreation, commerce and economic growth, and family and general safety. Private security specialists, who can discern the factors that lead to disorganization, can utilize ingenuity to change the environment.

Disorganization is represented by a community in disarray, whose members care little for the quality of life experienced. Criminals attack disorganized environments as if on a feeding frenzy, since they know only too well that misdeeds will likely go unreported, if not undetected. In fact, "crime-prone people are attracted to the neighborhood, while law-abiding people get out if they can. This pattern results in high crime rates that tend to persist even when there are complete turnovers in the people who live there."[11] This disorganized impression is detrimental to the community, since it paints a picture of hopelessness and simultaneously invites further victimization. Wesley Skogan's *Disorder and Decline* highlights this distressing reality:

> Three aspects stand out in the process of community change. First, disorder undermines the mechanisms by which communities exercise control over local affairs. It fosters social withdrawal, inhibits cooperation between neighbors, and discourages people from making efforts to protect themselves and their community. Second, disorder sparks concern about neighborhood safety, and perhaps even causes crime

itself. This further undermines community morale, and can give the area a bad reputation elsewhere in the city. Third, disorder undermines the stability of the housing market. Disorder undercuts residential satisfaction, leads people to fear for the safety of their children, and encourages area residents to move away. Fewer people will want to move into the area; the stigmatizing effect of disorder discourages outside investors, and makes it more difficult for local businesses to attract customers from outside. All of this erodes the value of real estate in disorderly communities, contributing to the further deterioration and abandonment of residential and commercial buildings.[12]

Security professionals must identify the signs of a disorganized community. Without this understanding, the tactics and strategies of community-based protection cannot be properly constructed, because the combination of disorder and disorganization fosters "suspicion and distrust, undermine[s] popular faith and commitment to the area, and discourage[s] public and collective activities. Disorder may also undermine individual morale and the perceived efficacy of taking any positive action."[13]

In disorganized environments, the best-planned tactics will not work unless they are created in light of the community dynamic. Practitioners must address the core factors that lead to this disintegration and must erect mechanisms that undermine the disorganization and create an organized environment. If an apartment complex, for example, allows open drinking, loud music, hanging out in the parking lot, or open drug dealing, the location is disorganized under any reasonable definition. Felons sense this delicate state and seize the opportunities. Citizens know this to be the case and forlornly lose faith in a system that allows the disorganization to exist. Apathy sets in, and the disorganization becomes even more entrenched. Not all agree that disorder triggers crime and have questioned the "broken windows" theory of crime causation. Instead, the functionality of community is the measure—its "collective efficacy."[14] Robert J. Sampson and Stephen W. Raudenbush have argued from a different angle than disorder theorists are used to, claiming that "the implication is that disorder and crime have similar roots: The forces that generate disorder also generate crime. It is the structural characteristics of neighborhoods, as well as neighborhood cohesion and informal social control— not levels of disorder—that most affect crime. Where collective efficacy was strong, rates of violence were low regardless of socio-demographic composition and observed disorder."[15] In the meantime, as this criminological novelty plays out, it is a fair assumption that disorder promotes the climate of crime more than the organized, structural setting.

Crimes are committed freely and without much concern for active citizen reporting. Good citizens eventually give up. The cycle of despondency furthers the disintegration and the disorganization. Good residents eventually relocate, leaving less reputable parties to fill the vacuum. The cycle of flight and repopulation precipitates the decline in organization. Here is where the practitioner attacks the problem. Undercut the negative force, and a positive force will replace it. Eliminate fear in the community, and the citizens will stand fast.[16] Create a plan of organization, and the elements that prey on a disorganized community will flee.

Practitioner Highlight

Wackenhut Corporation

The Wackenhut Corporation provides high-end public safety specialties. The United States State Department has contracted with Wackenhut Corporation to provide specialized antiterrorism assistance in terms of training resources to over 19,000 law enforcement personnel from 104 countries around the world. The Anti-Terrorism Assistance Program, which has been implemented since 1983, trains countries in learning how to protect their national borders as well as protecting vital installations within their country. The program assists in training how to respond and resolve terrorist incidents and to conduct and manage postterrorism investigations.

A community unwilling to tackle the hotbed problems that give impetus to criminality is a community destined for permanent disorganization. But a community willing to target the malefactors has within its power the essence of change, organization, and growth.[17] When the negative elements of a community are eliminated, the felony cycle begins to break down. Vehicle theft and vandalism rates drop, property values rise, and citizens again claim the turf as their own, business investment surges thereby creating jobs.

The task is stopping "the "spiral of decay" by cleaning up trash, graffiti, and so on; increasing the social relationships between adults and teenagers through organized youth activities; reducing residential mobility by enabling residents to buy their homes or take over management of their apartments; scattering public housing in a broad range of neighborhoods rather than concentrating it in poor neighborhoods; maintaining and increasing urban services, such as police, fire, and public health services, especially those aimed at reducing child abuse and teen pregnancy; and generally increasing community power by promoting community organizations."[18]

In short, community is nothing more or less than a reflection of its activities and members. Eliminate the negative aspects of the community, address the problems, and disorganization will melt into the horizon. Yet the issue is organization in a moral, legal, spatial, and communal sense.[19] Organization requires orderly thinking and prioritization; otherwise, energy and resource will be dissipated. Order and organization will reign supreme.

B. The High-Crime Community: Challenges and Opportunity for Change

Although community can be broadly defined, the unique demands evident in the high-crime areas of this remarkable country present extraordinary challenges and opportunities for change by public safety practitioners. High-crime areas need the security industry as do no other sector of America. The data for urban environments are indisputable. See Figure 4.3, which charts urban/suburban comparisons, as well as rates of racial victimization.[20]

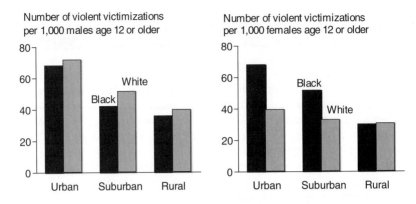

FIGURE 4.3   Rates of Violent Victimization, by Sex, Race, and Locality of Residence

The security industry can advocate an approach that goes far beyond mere maintenance but that is a sure path to cultural benefit. Today, high-crime communities labor under a mighty load where terror, hopelessness, and apathy are combated with Band-Aids and political sloganeering. Community members fight for survival while policy makers debate legislative designs and new fads. High-crime areas do not have the luxury of experiment and political posturing. Levels of victimization attest to the ineffectiveness of the public remedy. Violent crime rates are charted from 1960 to the present at Figure 4.4.[21] Although some recent improvement can be seen from these data, the historical picture speaks for itself.

In high-crime environments, community members live and work in isolation, and they have an outcast mentality that further generates a declining neighborhood identity. "Poverty, family disruption, and high residential mobility are community characteristics that result in anonymity, the lack of social relationships among neighborhood residents, and low participation in community organizations and in local activities."[22] With the residents being seen as outcasts in communities

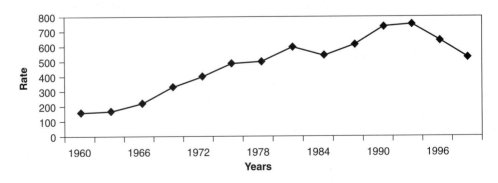

FIGURE 4.4   Crime Rate, 1960–1999

unworthy of investment, the role and purpose of public law enforcement does little than order maintenance or reaction to crimes. This approach will not elevate the high-crime community but will simply assure its demise. Businesses retreat and refuse to invest, residents must venture beyond their own physical space for necessities, schools deteriorate, and the inevitable cycle of negativity is fostered. Any sense of community is lost in the misery of decline and corruption. Lost additionally is that sense of activism, involvement, and personal integration in the communal life. Putnam articulately produced evidence of this withdrawal from civic involvement as follows:

> This dismaying trend began to accelerate after 1985: in the ten short years between 1985 and 1994, active involvement in community organization in this country fell by 45 percent. By this measure, at least, nearly half of America's civil infrastructure was obliterated in barely a decade.[23]

See Table 4.5.[24]

The same downward trend exists in other forms of participation from churches and various clubs, to civic engagements of any sort. Although it is a national problem, it is exacerbated in the high-crime major metropolitan areas. See Figure 4.5 for a comparison of households experiencing crime in rural, suburban, and urban areas.[25]

Transportation is limited, business development is unlikely, and growth in any quarter is a pipe dream. Even the most elementary practices, from ordering pizza to finding pay phones, signify the contrast between the cultures of high-crime and secure neighborhoods. Check cashing is frowned upon, store clerks work behind Plexiglas and steel bars, ATM machines are unavailable, medical facilities are rare, and most of the elementary facets of life taken for granted in safer neighborhoods are looked upon as luxuries in high-crime sectors. These apparent "little things" amount to an undeniably bleaker picture. High-crime areas lack neighborhood convenience stores, gas stations, and other mercantile establishments. Tradespeople sometimes balk at visiting these areas.

In a way, these indirect forms of victimization are harder to differentiate and understand than the more blatant variety. The effect of victimization is far-reaching in high-crime communities because without a stable, communal foundation, freedom and any sense of participatory democracy remain impossible. The poor have far less freedom to engage in life-achieving endeavors because their main focus is survival, both from an economic and a personal perspective. From children playing in environments polluted with needles, broken bottles, gang members, drug dealers, and an assortment of other types of criminals and hazards, to abandoned infrastructure and crack houses, high-crime communities represent the worst form of human distress. Putnam clearly summarizes the effect of a less cohesive society, one that is bound to lead to chaos. He states the following:

> When people lack connections to others, they are unable to test the veracity of their own views, whether in the give-and-take of casual conversation or in more formal

TABLE 4.5 *Percentage of U.S. Adults reporting community participation, by selected characteristics, 1996*

Characteristic	Number (thousands)	Type of Community Participation							
		Member of an Organization		Attended Religious Services once a Month More		Did Ongoing Community Service		Participated in All Three Types[1]	
		Percent	s.e.	Percent	s.e.	Percent	s.e.	Percent	s.e.
Total	188,233	59	1.3	50	1.3	39	1.2	25	1.0
Age									
18–24	21,345	46	4.7	38	4.1	30	4.6	13	3.0
25–39	64,157	52	1.9	42	2.0	41	2.3	22	1.9
40–54	50,442	62	2.2	52	2.8	42	2.6	28	2.4
55–69	31,396	66	2.6	61	2.8	38	2.7	30	2.7
70 and older	20,893	72	3.8	64	3.5	33	3.4	28	3.3
Sex									
Female	98,437	59	1.8	55	1.6	42	1.7	28	1.4
Male	89,795	58	1.9	45	1.9	35	1.9	21	1.5
Race/ethnicity									
White, non-Hispanic	143,297	60	1.5	48	1.5	39	1.5	24	1.3
Other race/ethnicity	44,936	55	2.1	57	2.3	39	2.2	26	2.0
Highest level of education									
Less than high school	23,823	45	4.4	50	3.8	19	2.7	13	2.6
High school diploma/equivalent or vocational education	73,185	49	1.8	49	2.4	33	2.0	21	1.8
Some college	47,621	62	2.8	49	2.7	44	2.9	28	2.5
Bachelor's degree or higher	43,604	78	1.8	53	2.4	52	2.5	34	2.3

(continued)

TABLE 4.5 *Percentage of U.S. Adults reporting community participation, by selected characteristics, 1996 (Cont.)*

Characteristic	Number (thousands)	Type of Community Participation									
		Member of an Organization		Attended religious Services once a Month More		Did Ongoing Community Service		Participated in All Three Types[1]	
		Percent	s.e.	Percent	s.e.	Percent	s.e.	Percent	s.e.
Household income									
$15,000 or less	38,583	47	2.9	51	3.3	29	2.7	17	2.1
$15,001–30,000	47,833	53	2.9	51	2.8	36	2.5	25	2.1
$30,001–50,000	49,502	60	2.3	47	2.4	39	2.1	24	1.9
$50,001 or more	52,315	71	2.0	51	2.2	48	2.5	31	2.1
Parent with child age 18 or younger in household[2]									
Yes	71,646	57	1.9	50	2.1	48	2.3	27	1.8
No	116,587	60	1.7	50	1.6	33	1.7	23	1.3

[1] Member of an organization and attended religious services once a month or more and did ongoing community service.
[2] This question was asked of all respondents whose households contained members age 18 or younger and who were at least 12 years older than those children. "Parent" includes stepparent or guardian.

Note: s.e. is standard error. Numbers may not add to totals because of rounding.

Source: U.S. Department of Education, National Center for Education Statistics, National Household Education Survey, 1996, Adult Civic Involvement component.

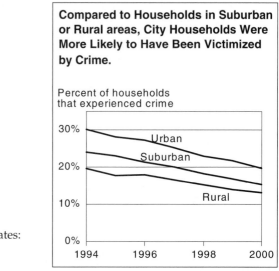

FIGURE 4.5 Crime Rates: Urban/Suburban Comparison

deliberation. Without such an opportunity, people are more likely to be swayed by their worst impulses.[26]

Within these cauldrons of human frustration, the criminal often rules the roost. The security industry and its experienced practitioners are positioned to assist its public counterpart in effecting its general aims. For example, "a federal investigation and trial have produced evidence of the Gangster Disciples (gang members) control over inner-city life. Seven Gangster Disciples leaders were convicted in federal court for running a multimillion-dollar drug conspiracy. The convictons included charges that they used narcotics proceeds to fund 21st Century VOTE, which finances candidates, allies, and voter-registration drives."[27]

In high-crime communities, the tone can be described only as "survival of the fittest." As a result, individuals, who compose the essence of what community means, withdraw and alienate, isolate and aggressively react to the normal channels of public law enforcement.

Public police are intensely consumed in the deterrence facets indigenous to high-crime communities, as is only natural. If anything has to give, it would be the integrative aspects of their jobs. Public police protect from occupational obligation alone, not from the self-interest of a vested community member.[28] With so much distraction from crime rates to social problems, community members perceive a neglect and a disregard for community tranquility. In retaliation, high-crime community members sometimes exhibit less than cooperative attitudes, toward, and a general mistrust of, the law enforcement effort. Eventually the relationship sours and produces little positive benefit to community order. Carter labels the chaos as a "flesh wound"[29] that will be difficult, but not impossible, to heal.

Victimization, Victimizers, and Community Control: The Gangster Disciples

In an article called "A Community Turns to Its Tormentors" (vol. 88, 3/28/96 at 1) in the *Christian Science Monitor,* Ann Scott Tyson relays concrete examples of gang victimization phenomenon. She explains that against a backdrop of vacant lots and boarded-up storefronts, poverty, and joblessness, many residents accept the gang's drug business and fleeting protection much as they do the metal gratings on their windows. Since public police tactics have failed, in some neighborhoods people ironically turn to the criminals, the very victimizers, for help. Mrs. Washington, one of the residents who were interviewed, phoned 21st Century Voices of Total Empowerment (VOTE), a gang-run political group, to get protection from shootouts occurring around her home. Soon, streetwise envoys from Chicago's biggest gang, the Gangster Disciples (GD), showed up at her door. Within days, she says, the gunfire virtually stopped. "They came—nobody else," recalls Washington, who still cooperates with the gang members.

Many other South Side residents of Chicago, like Mrs. Washington, have turned to the GDs when police protection fails. When Rev. T. L. Barrett complained about someone's attacking his home with bricks, gang leaders responded. Within two hours they had two young men kneeling before Barrett, apologizing for the vandalism. Gang leaders placed the youths on guard duty outside his home, Mr. Barrett said. Former South Side NAACP director Sidney Finley used to pay a visit to the local gang leader whenever his hubcaps were stolen. "Within an hour" the caps would be back, "either the exact same ones or new ones," recalls Mr. Sessoms.

Tyson goes on to explain that from housing projects to schools and churches, the 30,000 strong Gangster Disciples has used its muscle, money, and manpower to impose a brute order on neighborhoods. It has infiltrated police and security forces, monitored school hallways, mobilized protesters, and registered voters. In this case, the GD, without doubt, controls neighborhood life, victimization, and even the dispensation of justice.

It is ironic that in this age of international terrorism and domestic threat our agencies of government seem incapable of recognizing the crumbling neighborhoods in close proximity. High-crime communities represent a more formidable threat to national security than does any foreign entity, because the ravages of community instability, so intensely rooted in the high-crime community, cannot bear positive social fruit. Urban decay, poverty, victimization, crime waves, decrepit housing, and educational entities blight the horizon in high-crime communities. By now, the public model should have mastered the community problems and be better able to predict outcomes. See Table 4.6 for statistics regarding the degree of fear suffered by residents from twelve major cities in the United States.[30] Communities can attack the historical troublemakers and anticipate future patterns of crime.

Philadelphia's Badlands Revival

On the morning of June 15, 1998, with sirens blaring, police cruisers, garbage trucks, tow trucks, and various other law enforcement vehicles rolled into Philadelphia's Badlands with a mission—to clean up and revitalize the neighborhood. Called Operation Sunrise, a collaboration of more than a dozen city, state, and federal agencies, the effort was an attempt to restore to its former state the area in North Philadelphia called the Badlands. Since the 1970s, the area, which once housed hard-working blue-collar families, has gone through a slow decaying process to become an economically depressed area inhabited by drug dealers, criminals, and low-income families.

Within three weeks of the initial effort, a noticeable improvement was seen by the residents. Bernadette Sterling, a resident for 25 years, stated that "it's 75 percent better than it was less than a month ago" (Andrea Fine, "Philadelphia Launches Dragnet to Rid the 'Badlands' of Drugs," *Christian Science Monitor,* 1998). The jobs of area community and church leaders were made much easier and safer because of the effort of law enforcement agencies. Rev. Luis Centeno, a former youth gang member and the recipient of The Robert Wood Johnson Foundation Community Health Leadership Program award in 2001, has preached in the area for 25 years. "Mr. Centeno is not preaching to the converted, but to the unknowns here in the 'badlands' of North Philadelphia: to the curious adults who watch from the sidewalk; to the teens who pause briefly on their bicycles and ride on; to those eight drug dealers gazing with solemn intensity from across the street" (David O'Reilly, *Philadelphia Inquirer,* 6/21/01). The Rev. Centeno's mission is not to convert the neighborhood, he states to the crowd: "We didn't come here to take your money or get you to join our church . . . We just want you to know we're here for you" (David O'Reilly, *Philadelphia Inquirer,* 6/21/01).

Working with private protection professionals, communities not only can predict but also can strengthen a way of life.

Contemporary police methodology, which includes the utilization of coercive power, struggles with the humanity of the place where it labors. Instead of being vested in the community, in many neighborhoods the public police are inaccurately perceived as oppressors and antagonists. When communities and neighborhoods routinely witness enforcement actions such as raids, the use of police tactical units, racial profiling, unwarranted individual searches, and other confrontational activities, then distance and alienation set in. This is not to say that public police pursue these methods without restriction or never use better alternate approaches. Dedicated public officers risk life and limb daily in the pursuit of order maintenance. Motivation is not the issue, but the means and the methods are. Public police, when compared with their private sector counterpart, operate under a very different stream of demands and occupational roles. As was noted in Chapter 3 on community policing, the need to be both the public officer and the community member is in some ways incompatible. No public officer is capable of fixing

TABLE 4.6   *Residents in 12 Cities, by Degree of Fear of Crime in Their City, 1998*

| | | Percent of residents age 16 or older | | | | | |
| | | Fearful | | | Not Fearful | | |
	Estimated Number of Residents	Total	Very Fearful	Somewhat Fearful	Total	Not very Fearful	Not at All Fearful
Total	12,440,671	71%	18%	53%	29%	21%	8%
Chicago	1,970,708	74	20	54	27	19	8
Kansas City	337,094	73	17	56	27	22	6
Knoxville	121,960	62	12	51	38	28	9
Los Angeles	2,737,851	80	24	56	20	14	7
Madison	151,352	36	2	34	64	51	13
New York	5,142,188	68	17	51	32	22	10
San Diego	894,738	58	9	49	42	35	8
Savannah	96,190	73	18	55	27	19	8
Spokane	141,827	62	10	52	38	30	8
Springfield	104,175	77	23	53	23	16	7
Tucson	352,353	70	15	56	30	23	7
Washington, DC	390,235	74	21	53	26	18	8

Note: Don't know responses and refusals to answer are excluded from analysis. Detail may not add to total because of rounding.
Question: "How fearful are you about crime in your city? Are you very fearful, somewhat fearful, not very fearful, or not at all fearful?"

the calamities so obvious in troubled neighborhoods. However, the private security industry offers a community-based model that works—even in the worst neighborhoods and under the most precarious conditions. The argument here is not about less enforcement but about a balanced implementation of prevention efforts that resolve community problems.

Public police also operate under heavy scrutiny. Every mistake is magnified by media frenzy, and the actions of a few taint the whole. Undeniably, abuses of power, use of excessive force, and unfortunate beatings cast a long shadow over the public police. With scandals and sensationalized cases, public police operate under a microscope. The prevalent and unfortunate belief that the police in high-crime communities systematically engage in illegal searches, racial imprisonment, torture, invasion of privacy, and a host of other violations of individual rights persists. Whether in agreement or not, the high-crime community will alter its makeup only with another approach—the chief thesis of this text, the private sector's involvement with public safety.

The Effects of Police Brutality on the Image of the Private Practitioner

Adding to the perception of oppressive behavior on the part of the police is the often one-sided media coverage of police officers engaging in behaviors that violate a person and the person's rights. Abuses of power, uses of excessive force, beating, and even torturous actions all have a definite and long-lasting impact on how these communities view police. Incidents such as a New York police officer's sodomizing a man in his custody with a broomstick while other officers looked on, and the Los Angeles police gang unit's executing an unarmed suspect, planting evidence, and selling confiscated narcotics, reinforce the notion that the police are oppressive and brutal.

In the end, it becomes a prevalent belief that police everywhere are engaging in illegal searches, racial imprisonment, torture, invasion of privacy, and a host of other violations of individual rights, when in reality it is only a very small minority who commit these crimes. As a result, many people don't trust or even hate the police and the government that the officers represent. In response, many people don't cooperate with the police, and they even aid and harbor criminals. They see the police as the real oppressors, rather than the criminals.

Because of this view, private security specialists must take extra care when establishing a relationship with the community. Although they are not police officers, the community's view of authority in general may transfer to the private security specialists. Establishing trust will take time and effort on the part of the security operative to demonstrate that the officer is there to protect the citizens from the criminal element in their community.

Security practitioners can effectively establish trust and respect in the public safety effort, as the public sector has done. Trust solidifies when communities see positive results. Public justice must honestly accept its own inability to be the exclusive change agent in distressed high-crime communities. A fundamental shift in resources, strategy, and policy is mandatory. For nearly five decades, the public sector has struggled, but has fallen short of its lofty goals. Given the demands, how could it be otherwise? Communities remain riddled with the same dilemmas— poverty, criminal victimization, drug and alcohol addiction, violence, illiteracy, unemployment and underemployment. The human and social decay is indisputable.

II. THE COMMUNITY PROFILE

Implementing community-based protection is much like the way a physician treats a patient. Prior to administering any treatment or prescribing any medication, the physician must evaluate the extent of the illness. The doctor's assistant checks the vital signs and obtains a description of the problem. Blood and tissue samples are collected for lab testing; MRIs and CAT scans are conducted. This process—diagnosis—is the first step in determining a program of medical treatment. It is illogical for anyone to attempt to create change or establish control within an environment without actually taking the time to evaluate and understand what makes that environment the way it is. Public safety professionals cannot continue to establish techniques or programs unilaterally. The medicine varies depending on the illness.[31] "Whether neighborhoods become high-crime areas seems to be mediated by what happens with the people in the community. In some communities with sparse friendship networks, unsupervised teenage peer groups, and low levels of organized participation, high crime rates develop."[32]

Prior to the design of any community-based approach, the practitioners need to conduct a Community Profile. The format of the profile can be broken down in various ways. A sample template is provided at Figure 4.6. Profiles should be au-

Forward	• Purpose of profile
	• Relevance to community development
	• Status
	• Development—needs to be worked with locally and improvements identified for the future. Should lead to local commentary on key issues and identification of key priorities for action, with targets wherever possible. Key indicators should be identified for future tracking.
	• Establish "editorial board" to oversee developments and modifications.
Structure	The profile will comprise:
Introduction	• Maps of the area involved
	• Basic information re: demography, inward and outward migration
	• Key towns and population centers surrounding the area
Themes	• Prosperity
	o Economic conditions
	o Poverty
	• Social services and health care
	• Children's services
	• Education, lifelong learning, culture, and leisure
	• Community safety (inc. crime)
	• Environment
	• Housing
	• Access and transport
	• Community development
	• External funding
	• Crime rates
	• Drug and alcohol usage/abuse rates

FIGURE 4.6 Community Profile Template

thored under widely democratic circumstances. The assessor should not be averse to soliciting a wide array of opinion. Potential sources for participation are laid out in Figure 4.7. The collection process should adhere to specific guidelines, since the level of participation can easily bog down the process. Employ the Project Meeting Template in Table 4.7. The analysis process begins with a thorough survey of social, economic, and environmental factors woven though the entrusted area. The profile will encompass a number of issues that are not specifically criminal in nature but that depict the climate for criminal activity. It is imperative to remember that the community under scrutiny may be as small as a housing complex or a city block and that the atmosphere of the community can change from street corner to street corner.

Hence, the view is cultural, political, and economic in scope. The profile gauges the lifeblood of the community in question. In particular, how criminal

☐	Youth clubs, scouts	☐	Funding agencies	☐	Religious groups
☐	Archaeological groups	☐	Health workers	☐	Residents
☐	Archaeologists	☐	Homeless people		groups/associations
☐	Architects	☐	Industrialists	☐	Rural community
☐	Builders	☐	Journalists		councils
☐	Businesses	☐	Land managers	☐	Schools
☐	Chambers of Commerce	☐	Landowners	☐	Senior citizens
☐	Charities	☐	Landscape architects	☐	Shopkeepers
☐	Children	☐	Lawyers	☐	Sports groups
☐	Churches	☐	Local authorities	☐	Town managers
☐	Civic groups	☐	Local history groups	☐	Statutory agencies
☐	Colleges	☐	Media groups and	☐	Street cleaners
☐	Community associations		organizations	☐	Student groups
☐	Community-based organizations	☐	Migrants	☐	Surveyors
☐	Community leaders	☐	Minority groups	☐	Teachers
☐	Environmental groups	☐	Planners	☐	Tenant groups/
☐	Companies	☐	Museums		associations
☐	Conservation groups	☐	Nongovernmental	☐	Wildlife groups
☐	Engineers		organizations	☐	Utility providers
☐	Craftspeople	☐	Parent-teacher	☐	Urban designers
☐	Designers		organizations	☐	Universities
☐	Developers	☐	Public works	☐	Transport companies
☐	Disability groups		departments	☐	Young people
☐	Ecologists	☐	Photographers	☐	Postal workers
☐	Economists	☐	Property owners	☐	Police
☐	Financial Institutions	☐	Professional groups	☐	Ethnic groups
☐	Publications	☐	Farmers		

FIGURE 4.7   Community Profile Participants List

TABLE 4.7 *Project Meeting Template*

Meeting	Event	Topics	Attended	Process Decisions
	Meeting	District profiles identified as a project		
1	Project meeting	Discuss project format for profile. Indicators: population (people profile)		
	Training	Project management training (2 days)		
2	Project meeting	Agree process and monthly meetings. Indicators: Population and maps (refer to GIS project)		
	Milestone	Send project remittance		
3	Project meeting	Accept project remittance Indicators: Crime, health, people, poverty		
	Milestone	Final project remittance submitted		
4	Project meeting	Presentation of data on the web. Indicators: Crime, housing, local economy		
	Meeting	Progress report		
5	Project meeting	Indicators: crime, housing, health		
6	Project meeting	Indicators: Social services		
	Project review			
7	Project meeting	Discuss launch of site. Indicators: Social services, community capacity, health		
	Milestone			
8	Site review	Discuss feedback. Indicators: Social services, education, community capacity		
	Project meeting			
9	Project meeting	Review indicators and work still to be done.		
	Project review			
	Progress report	Progress report		
	Transition point			
10	Project meeting	Discuss community planning process Questions: Key themes of community plans? Responsibility for compiling community planning profiles? Indicators: community capacit		
	Milestone			

activity manifests itself will vary according to a host of demographic issues: age of population, race and ethnicity, political corruption, reputation of police in sector, attitudes of business and commercial residents, economic opportunity and job rates, and perception of nonresidents about the state of the community. More specifically, the profile paints a picture of what the quality and composition of life is like in the most general terms. See the *Community Profile and Threat Assessment* at Appendix A for an example.

Combined with an assessment of the physical environment, a reliable picture begins to emerge. Community profiles can be characterized in many ways—from ordered to disordered, from violent to peaceful. The target is not the stable community but the one beleaguered by the ravages of social decomposition. Communities in decline are composed as Skogan describes here:

> Two general classes of disorder: social and physical. Social disorder is a matter of behavior: you can see it happen (public drinking, or prostitution), experience it (catcalling or sexual harassment), or notice direct evidence of it (graffiti, or vandalism). Physical disorder involves visual signs of negligence and unchecked decay: abandoned or ill-kept buildings, broken streetlights, trash-filled lots, and alleys strewn with garbage and alive with rats.[33]

Crime, in the final analysis, can only germinate in rotted soil and will die in resistant strains. The Profile delineates the factors that generate the fertile environment for crime to grow in. High rates of resident turnover, a preponderance of burglar bars on windows, abandoned vehicles, graffiti, consumption of alcohol and drunkenness, open prostitution, and gang activity all portray an environment descending downward while the criminal agents move to a supreme position in the rabble. The profile identifies other variables that speak loudly of the potential for criminal activity. Practitioners should constantly survey residential and commercial areas for the items shown in Figure 4.8. Public safety initiatives should integrate the survey into operational policy. See Figure 4.9.

☐ Loitering	☐ Vagrant activity
☐ Open alcohol	☐ Uncollected garbage
☐ Loud music	☐ Unprofessional security
☐ Poor lighting	☐ No access control
☐ Open drug activity	☐ Poor landscaping
☐ Building decay	☐ Social disorder
☐ Vandalism	☐ Poor police relations
☐ Graffiti	☐ No community interaction

FIGURE 4.8   Variables of disintegration

A diverse list of variables will eventually create a reliable community profile. Not only will the physical condition of community mold perceptions, so will the styles of interaction and street activity typically witnessed. The National Institute of Justice's Strategic Approaches to Community Safety Initiative (SACSI), in Table 4.8, covers all the bases.[34] A few of the more salient indicators are reviewed in the following sections.

- Restricted -	Critical Intervention Services	- Restricted-
Title: Patrols		**Uniformed Division Order Series:** 430.00
Intent: To establish guidelines for patrol duties and personnel.		
Effective Date: January 12, 1997		**Page:** 2 and 3

Responsibilities of Patrol

1. **Suspect Vehicles:**

   A. Record information on vehicles in area.
   B. Record descriptions of suspicious vehicles and all occupants for possible later identification.
   C. Observe, record, and report any suspicious vehicles loading furniture, equipment, boxes, or merchandise.
   D. Record and report vehicles obviously being operated by an alcohol or drug impaired individual.
   E. Record and report any vehicle being used for any criminal purpose.

2. **Survey Residential and Business areas for:**

   A. Signs of breaking and entering.
   B. Vandalism.
   C. Prowling and loitering.
   D. Thefts.
   E. Criminal activity.
   F. If any of the above situations should develop, DCO/Ops must be contacted to request police assistance.
   G. Records must be kept of the time, date, exact location (address, business name, etc.), events, and descriptions of suspects and/or vehicles. DCO/Ops must at all times be kept informed about the events, location, and officer well being during these occurrences.
   H. Upon arrival of the police, the CIS officer must relay all available information and should <u>not</u> assist unless requested to do so. The police officer(s) must be allowed to perform their duties. However, officers should stand by to provide assistance, should the situation arise.
   I. Information police officers need most:
       1. What, when, and where the incident occurred.
       2. Has anyone been hurt?
       3. License plate numbers
       4. Vehicle descriptions
       5. Direction of travel
       6. Description of suspects
       7. Are there any weapons/firearms involved?

Communications

1. Transmissions should be held to a minimum, consistent with the need.
2. Transmissions should be brief, clear, and concise.
3. Common codes, such as Ten-Codes or Communication Signals, should be used.
4. Officers should check their radio operation with DCO or OPS when beginning their patrol, and at regular intervals thereafter.
5. A back-up channel should be selected should the primary operational channel become congested with traffic.
6. Any transmissions of profanity, music, or advertising are prohibited by FCC.

FIGURE 4.9   Patrol Policy

Use of K-9 on Patrol: Vehicle and Foot	Uniformed Division Order #430.002

Purpose: Officers who are trained to use K-9 on sites will use them for the following purposes:

1. Community & Character Based Protection Initiative
2. Public Relations
3. Officer Safety

Defense: A K-9 will be used in the following situations as a defensive tool:

1. In defense of another person who is in danger of bodily harm, or worse, from an assailant.
2. In defense of another officer or oneself when there is a threat of bodily harm, or worse, from an assailant.
3. If the K-9 is attacked.

Use of force involving K-9: In situations where a K-9 has injured someone, the following procedures will be strictly adhered to:

1. Medical assistance will be called immediately for immediate response.
2. The supervisor on duty will be notified of the incident.
3. K-9-1 (Director of K-9 Division) will be notified of the incident.
4. In serious incidents, the CIS Internal Affairs officer shall be notified immediately.
5. The CIS Incident Report and Use of Force forms shall be completed.

K-9 Log: All K-9 officers shall immediately start a personal log incorporating the following:

1. Shifts worked, to include:
   a. Date
   b. Hours worked
   c. Any unusual occurrences
2. All training days, to include:
   a. Date
   b. Hours worked
   c. Type of Training

Foot Patrol of Residential Property	Uniformed Division Order #430.003

Patrols shall be performed to include all common areas, i.e. grounds, laundry rooms, swimming pools, recreation/club house, vacant units, and other areas that the owner/manager might direct officers to patrol. This pertains to all foot patrols and vehicle patrols when authorized. These patrols are for the client's physical property and not for the residents' security or their personal property.

Occupied units will not be entered unless:

1. An emergency situation exists that requires the officer to enter to preserve or protect life;
2. The owner/manager requests the officer's presence; or
3. The officer is requested to enter by law enforcement, EMT, fire rescue, or other emergency service.

Foot Patrol of Retail Areas	Uniformed Division Order #430.004

CIS policy on foot patrol of retail areas is based upon a 90/10 rule, i.e., the officer(s) will spend 90 percent of their patrol time in the common areas, such as outside sidewalks, indoor and outdoor parking lots, and roof tops (where needed). This is to deter damage to the physical property. No set patterns shall be established: the patrol routes will be random, using double-back and crisscross patterns. The other 10 percent of the officer's time shall be spent briefly checking on the tenant(s) and doing random walk-throughs. Officers will not stay in stores for an extended amount of time unless requested to do so by the client and/or supervisor, or if it is warranted by circumstances. A high profile/high visibility approach is to be maintained at all times.

FIGURE 4.9   *(Cont.)*

TABLE 4.8 *Sample Master Data List*

Feature	Object	Attributes
Abandoned/boarded-up houses	Point	Type, date, address/location
ABC permit holders	Point	Name, type, owner, address/location, violations
Accidents	Point	Accident number, contributing cause, fatality, time, date, address/location
Adult establishments	Point	Owner, name of business, type of license, address/location
Arrestees	Point	Name, charge, date, address, work address
Arrests	Point	ID, name, charge, date, time, location, crime type, MO, victim age, race, gender, type(s) of drugs, address of arrestee
Assessment neighborhood	Polygon	ID
ATF database		Serial number, crime linked to
Calls for service	Point	ID, address/location, type, date/time, contact, status
Car dealerships	Point	Name, makes sold, average # of vehicles, address/location
Child fatalities	Point	Age, date/time, cause, address/location, child's address
Churches	Point	Name, denomination, address, phone #, programs
Community map	Point	Name, address, program name, program description, geographic area
Community Watch area boundaries	Polygon	Name, contact name, contact address, contact phone number, police liaison
Community Watch meetings	Point	Group name, address of meeting, date/time, usual attendance, notes
Convenience stores	Point	Owner, name of business, address/location, type of license, hours of operation
Counties	Polygon	Name, ID, state
County neighborhoods	Polygon	ID, name
Crime incidents	Point	Incident number, crime type, MO, time, date, address/location, status, suspect, victim
Crime victims	Point	Incident number, age of victim, suspect name, suspect description, victim home address
Day care	Point	Name, enrollment, address/location
Demographic characteristics	Polygon	Population, age distribution, race distribution, Hispanic origin, income distribution, education attainment, poverty status, polygon ID (block, block group, tract, etc.)
FDZs	Polygon	ID
First line directory	Point	Name, address, program name, program description
First-time mothers	Point	Address, birth date
Foster/adoptive parents	Point	Name, address, telephone number, type, age of child, sex of child, name of child, age of parent(s)
Gang territories	Polygon	Gang name

A. State of Public Police/Community Relations

How the public police interact with the community tells much about the current health of the neighborhood. A community festering in antagonism and distrust will usually be one in some sort of upheaval. Are the police proactive in their approach to the community? What is the state of planning and institutional interaction between police and community? Can police identify problem areas and regions in the area of responsibility? Are police willing to intervene, or have they adopted a hopeless approach to problems in the community? What is the quality of police-citizen interaction, of police with community leaders, and of overall openness of the department? Do police exhibit professionalism? Do they converse with the citizenry, or do they intentionally avoid contact? Do police use the car as a shield or barrier? Are police willing to work closely with children, or do they respond as a matter of nuisance? If the results portray an embedded alienation, the profile will be troubled.

B. Level of Juvenile Delinquency and Gang Activity

Juvenile activity should be analyzed to determine the number of gangs and their members, social and economic status, and attitudes toward the justice system. Age is a significant factor, since preteens tend to be more malleable than the stubborn teenager whose opinion is already shaped. Children and youth at the poverty level present special and clearly tougher challenges than those with sufficient resources.[35] Thus, the profile should separate youth according to income levels. If possible, the profile should include demographic data on what the composition of the family is, what the divorce rates are, and whether or not the juvenile has a two- or single-parent influence. Finally, do sufficient social institutions exist that would allow networking with the young? Regarding church groups, Scouts, athletics, and social clubs, are the youth of region able to forge a social existence? High levels of juvenile crime foretell an area in substantial distress. The U.S. Surgeon General has repeatedly worried that a nation's health is measured by the state and condition of its young. Criminal statistics are not pretty. See Figure 4.10.[36] In the absence of ordinary social structures, have gangs emerged? Is the gang motivated by pleasure, money, criminal enterprise, or defiant behavior? Is the gang cross-cultural or singularly exclusive? What is the level of loyalty among its members—will they fight for one another, are they willing to die or kill for each other?

The profile must account for the gang mentality in the community, since the gangs' lifeblood often replaces the ordinary community infrastructure. High gang rates are indicia of a troubled community.[37] See Figure 4.11 for various gang identifiers.

C. Business Climate and Economic Conditions

The community profile examines the economic vitality of a community.[38] What level of business and corporate activity exists? What are the prospects for jobs? What corporations have expressed a willingness to relocate out of the region? How many

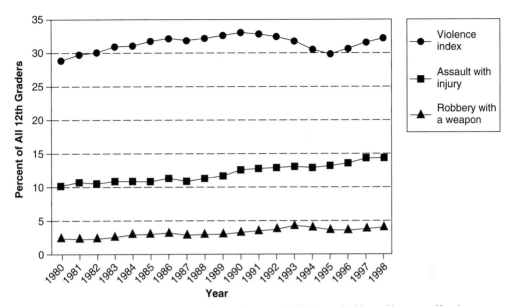

Sources: Rates for violence index: Johnston, 2000; rates for assault with injury and robbery with weapon: Maguire and Pastore, 1999.

Entries above are 3-year running averages of the prevalence of each of the specified acts. The violence index is defined as the percent committing any of the specified following five acts, with no missing data allowed: hit an instructor or supervisor; gotten into serious fight in school or at work; taken part in a fight where a group of your friends were against another group; hurt somebody badly enough to need bandages or a doctor (assault with injury); used a knife or gun or some other thing (like a club) to get something from a person (robbery with a weapon), 95% confidence intervals for the violence index are all less than ±2.5% for assault, less than a ±2%; for robbery less than ±1.1%.

FIGURE 4.10   Levels of Criminality of 12th Graders

businesses have relocated to the region? What is the tax base? How many major corporations and businesses are negotiating for tax amnesty, breaks, and other special treatment to remain in the community? In the place of mainline business growth, have other forms of business development taken root? Businesses that cash checks, rent furniture, make loans, sell liquor, and pawn things seem on the rise, whereas traditional business growth decays. What are the business-owner perceptions of the community? How does management feel about the current environment? What does management and business ownership think of the current state of affairs? The profiler should not hesitate to contact business owners to conduct face-to-face interviews. Business leads the way—in either decline or resurrection.

   During this interview, the profiler should question whether the business needs intervention of any sort to address criminal conduct. How can the security firm aid the business? What steps would management like the firm to take? Be open to all suggestions. If business and management have become indifferent and lethargic about the problems, the profile will note the lack of real optimism for community change. This lack of cohesion and support will surely affect subsequent community-based efforts.

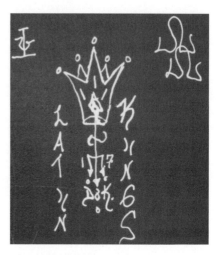

FIGURE 4.11   Gang Insignia
Markings

D. Private Security Professional Perceptions

The last component of the community profile measures the attitudes of security personnel already in place. The profile will evaluate the private security perspective and will contrast the results with public police. This form of examination delivers cross-professional insights and seeks to identify uniform reactions about the state of the community. The attitudinal survey has educational qualities, too—instructing the new firm about mistakes, miscues, and bad policy making.

The profile results will evaluate and advise security firms on the contemporary setting, the strengths and weaknesses of the community, and the issues of most pressing concern. If the existing security service has been effective, transference of power and authority will be an easier step. However, if the security experience has been ineffective, indifferent, and intolerant of criminal activity or marked by mistreatment of the community, then the profile will stress avoidance of identical pitfalls and problems. Once an accurate assessment of the security posture has been conducted, the security firm is ready to target, in a more particularized way, threats that impact the community. At the end of the profile process, an evaluation should be conducted. See Figure 4.12.

III. THREAT ASSESSMENT

The identification of potential and actual criminal activities is called a threat assessment. The threat assessment precedes any deployment of manpower, determination of specific protective strategies, and authorship of security measures. A threat assessment attempts to answer the "what," "when," "how," and "where" of criminal activity. "The threat assessment process involves identifying, assessing, and managing individuals who might pose a risk of violence to an identified or identifiable target."[39] See Figure 4.13.

Name: Organization (if any):
Address: Position (if any):
Title of Activity: Date/s of Activity:
Nature of Activity: Date of evaluation:

1. What is your role in the activity?
2. How did you become involved?
3. What do you think are/were the aims?
4. What do you think motivated people and organizations to get involved?
5. What effect, if any, has your personal contribution made?
6. What effect has the activity had on the physical environment?
7. What effect has the activity had on the local economy?
8. What effect has the activity had on local organizations?
9. What effect has the activity had on individuals?
10. Was the activity worthwhile? Why, or why not?
11. What improvements would you make if the activity was being done again?
12. What would be your advice to others organizing a similar activity?
13. What additional information sources would be helpful?
14. Any other comments?

Thank you for your time during the project and for answering this survey!
Please return this form to:

FIGURE 4.12   Evaluation Form: Community Profile

Once the broad picture has been determined from the community profile, the analysis turns to criminological questions. Exactly what drives the criminal element in this community? The assessment raises these fundamental issues:

- Who engages in a criminal lifestyle?
- How are criminal designs carried out?
- Where do criminals reside?
- When will the criminals act?
- What conduct can the community expect from the criminal?

In threat analysis, the world and the community are viewed through the eyes of the enemy. The evaluation assesses the weaknesses and vulnerabilities of the target environment, identifies the root causes that nurture negative elements, and searches for the common denominators that bind environment to the threat. Finding out where the community's criminals operate is a good starting point. Threat assessment analysis will be effective if the practitioner adheres to fundamental principles. They are as follows:

- Targeted violence is the end result of an understandable, and oftentimes discernible, process of thinking and behavior.

1. Contact Information
2. Property Description
   2.1 Layout and Construction
   2.2 Resident Population
   2.3 Surrounding Environment
3. Criminal Activity
   3.1 General
   3.2 Violent Offenses
   3.3 Nonviolent Offenses
   3.4 Rules Violations
   3.5 Gang Presence and Activity
   3.6 High-Activity Areas
   3.7 Surrounding Environment

4. Community Attitudes and Integration
   4.1 Crime Perceptions
   4.2 Community Unity and Trust
   4.3 Community Care and the Environment
   4.4 Perceptions About Law Enforcement
       and Property Management
   4.5 Resident Interviews

5. Physical Site Survey
   Daytime Survey
      5.1 Grounds and Outdoor Community Areas
      5.2 Apartment Buildings
      5.3 Pools and Clubhouses
      5.4 Parking Lots
      5.5 Surrounding Neighborhood
   Nighttime Survey
      5.6 Lighting
      5.7 After-Hours Activity
6. Policies and Management Practices
   6.1 Applicant Screening
   6.2 Community Orientation
   6.3 Resident Problem Resolution and
       Eviction
   6.4 Trespassing and Outsider Interdiction
7. Local Resources

FIGURE 4.13   Environmental Threat Assessment and Residential Property
Security Survey Outline

- Targeted violence stems from an interaction among the person, the situation, the setting, and the target.
- An investigative, skeptical, inquisitive mindset is critical to successful threat assessment.
- Effective threat assessment is based on facts, rather than on characteristics or "traits".
- An "integrated systems approach" should guide threat assessment investigations.
- The central question of a threat assessment is whether an individual poses a threat, not whether the individual made a threat.[40]

Threats will vary in intensity. The U.S. Department of Justice categorizes three levels of threat.

Low level: A threat that has been evaluated as low level poses little threat to public safety and in most cases would not necessitate law enforcement investigation for a possible criminal offense. (However, law enforcement agencies may be asked for information in connection with a threat of any level.)

Medium level: When a threat is rated as medium level, the response should in most cases include contacting law enforcement agencies, as well as other sources, to obtain additional information (and possibly reclassify the threat into the high or low category).

High level: Almost always, if a threat is evaluated as high level, immediately inform the appropriate law enforcement agency. A response plan, which should have been designed ahead of time and rehearsed by both private security professionals and law enforcement personnel, should be implemented, and law enforcement should be informed and involved in whatever subsequent actions are taken in response to the threat.[41]

Case by case, the assessor must systematically weigh circumstances and conditions that qualify the threat. Some predictable method is mandated. "A standardized approach will help security firms construct a database, with information on the types and frequency of threats, which may help evaluate the effectiveness of policies. Consistency in threat response can deter future threats if criminals perceive that any threat will be reported, investigated, and dealt with firmly."[42]

Concentration should then turn to the more immediate problems stemming from quality of life issues and from the "who," "what," "when," and "where" of criminal activity. The real insight is the actual evaluation of ongoing and current problems, situations, and criminal activity. The evaluation of these elements will deliver reliable insight into the causal factors that promote the felonious lifestyle. When conducting a threat assessment in an effort to get answers to the issues just discussed, the practitioner will have to conduct physical inspections of the intervention areas. By surveying the environment, practitioners are able to locate drug paraphernalia such as empty plastic bags, broken glass pipes, and syringes. Organized gang activity can be gleaned from graffiti on buildings and sidewalks, much of which forms the basis for communication between rivals and internal members. Abandoned homes and crack houses filled with vagrants, drug dealers, or gang bangers edify the threat problem and zero in on the suspected criminal players.

Practitioners need to work cooperatively with police agencies by reviewing data, crime reports, and police activity logs. Using historical data to spot trends and crime patterns can reap solid results. Alleged victimless crimes, such as prostitution and vagrancy, should not be discounted in the threat assessment. If anything, the emphasis on these types of offenses should be heightened. Although the past is not always predictive, it is always educational. Interpreters of data must keep in mind their inherent reliability, particularly in high-crime neighborhoods where only a small percentage of crimes committed are actually reported by citizens to the police. The threat assessment team can also review "security threats to facilities, materials, and activities. The team also conducts liaison activities with the community, law enforcement, and other Federal agencies in support of its threat."[43]

Additionally, the types of crimes reported are somewhat disproportionate to the actual rate and incidence of criminal conduct. Naturally, the most commonly reported crimes are those that directly affect the residents themselves (robbery, battery, sexual assault, etc.). Many crimes that "indirectly" affect residents are rarely reported, despite their impact on the overall status of the community. Citizens in high-crime areas, for example, rarely report drug dealing and prostitution, although they may be notorious in the area. The same is true for crimes that do not result in physical harm or loss of property, such as a gang member's threatening a resident with a gun (aggravated assault). Fear of reprisal often overtakes the urge to report. Although assessors should evaluate crime statistics over long periods of time, gaining a snapshot of police and criminal activity, the statistics should not be relied upon as an accurate picture of the level of victimization occurring in the community.

During the same physical inspection, the practitioner should interact with residents, seeking feedback and input. Find out about the quality of life and the associated threats by those who reside in the neighborhood. The skills and training necessary for threat assessment are varied and demanding. The assessor needs the following:

- A questioning, analytical, and skeptical mind-set;
- An ability to relate well to members of the community, colleagues, and other professionals;
- Familiarity with childhood and adolescent growth and development, the school environment, the need for safe schools, and the community;
- A reputation within the community for fairness and trustworthiness;
- Training in the collection and evaluation of information from multiple sources;
- Discretion, as well as an appreciation for the importance of keeping information confidential and of the possible harm that may result in the inappropriate release of information; and
- Cognizance of the difference between harming and helping in an intervention.[44]

Residents who live in the "combat zone" may have reliable intelligence on criminal activity, so that professionals, both public and private, should seek out the information wisely to build trust in the sources. Threat assessment requires observation, surveillance, and intelligence gathering over extended periods to confirm information received. Threat assessment examines "traditional crime data, including calls for service and alcohol and drug-related arrests. The evaluation will also measure outcomes important to the practice of community policing, such as changes in citizen participation in reporting crime, the level and extent of problem-solving collaboration between police and community members, and citizen satisfaction with police services."[45]

The Association of Threat Assessment Professionals sets standards for these practices. See their webpage at http://www.atap.cc/aboutatap.htm.[46]

A. Preincident Indicators: A Tool for Threat Assessment

Threat assessments must be conducted on a regular basis to keep up with environmental changes. Threats should be somewhat predictive—that is, the protection specialist becomes adroit in identifying the signals of trouble to come. Factors worth continual evaluation are labeled *preincident indicators.* The indicators fall into two main classifications: *trend* and *individual* indicators. *Trend* indicators target particular social, economic, and cultural factors such as the following:

- Crime incidence rates
- Results of juvenile surveys
- Types of crime
- Levels of gang activity[47]
- Levels of poverty
- Rates of drug activity

Much in the same manner as the state and federal Uniform Crime Reports, the assessment looks at these variables for policy making purposes and for justification in the implementation of community tactics.[48]

The second type of indicator is *individual.* These indicators focus on individuals with known propensities for criminal conduct, whether by drugs or domestic violence, weaponry or school violence. Individuals are matched to potential situations and circumstances in the target community where these behaviors can occur. The data reveal that a specific individual or situation is developing a potential for victimization.

Juvenile indicators are instructive. Being young can be tumultuous under ordinary circumstances, but extreme conducts are signs of a personality out of kilter. Troubled youth usually possess a few of the traits and characteristics shown in Box 4.4. Employ Figure 4.14 as an investigative tool to focus on troubled youths.[49]

Recent school violence incidents illustrate the utility of pre-incidence indicators. In many instances, the perpetrator foretold intent to commit criminal acts. Letters, notes, and e-mails to innocent and conspiratorial parties announce intentions. These same individuals may have substantial criminal or juvenile histories that make recidivism a sure bet. Weapons, previous altercations, threats, and sociopathic behavior can be targeted in individual cases.

Workplace security specialists must be on the lookout for preindication signs. Larry Moore's *Preventing Homicide and Acts of Violence in the Workplace* highlights three phases that trace the evolution of violent behavior.

Juvenile Behavior Indicators

Moody/withdrawn	Exceedingly reclusive
Secretive	Destructive/antisocial behavior
Rude/obnoxious	Resistance to discipline
Argumentative	Resentful of authority
Spiteful toward parents/siblings	Extended periods of depression or anger
Self-conscious/self-critical	Sexual promiscuity
Sensitive to criticism	Nightmares
Short outbursts of anger	Repeated runaway attempts
Restless/bored	Frequent accidents/illnesses
Acts tough	Drug use
Testing limits/"No Fear"	Self-mutilation
Problematic teen behavior	Dramatic change in appearance
Difficulty concentrating	Indulging in satanic rituals and experimentation
Forgetfulness	Truancy/failing grades

Trigger Phase . . . can be triggered by other people, events, situations . . . Responses may be as unique as the individuals themselves; however, in many instances, triggers can be identified and managed.

Escalation Phase . . . first clear warning sign . . . is a noticeable change in behavior . . . triggers begin to accumulate . . . Recognizing this stage facilitates . . . an appropriate response.

Crisis Phase . . . The individual has lost the ability to cope. The key is to keep the agitated person talking . . . Law enforcement research shows that an armed person seldom pulls the trigger while talking . . .[50]

Once individual indicators are identified, the practitioner has the ability to develop a rapid response to the potential situation and effectively intervene prior to acts of violence. Hindsight, unfortunately, is always more intelligent than the assessment of what could happen. Human beings cannot always be predictive.

In order to be able to develop a clear picture using multiple preincident indicators, an effective communication network must be established between many entities (parents, teachers, other students, as examples). A proactive effort must be implemented to encourage communication between parents, students, school staff, and community leaders. Unfortunately, the larger the school or community, the harder this analysis becomes. The United States Department of Education offers up what it terms "attack-related behaviors" to ferret out dangerous individuals roaming the schools. Violence is predictive if the student exhibits the following:

The Steele Foundation—Behavioral Sciences—Workplace Strategy

Threat of Workplace Violence . . . What Are Your Options?

An employee is terminated for insubordination. The supervisor of the former employee receives threats, as does your corporate office. Police take a report of the threats and advise you to call should anything happen. What are the appropriate steps to take to protect your employees and mitigate liability? What resources are available to your company?

This is an event that many companies are facing more frequently; however, the resources to proactively counter such risks have been limited. The response to a workplace crisis has traditionally been an increase in visible security that is sometimes accompanied by the counseling services of the organization's employee assistance program. How long should the increased security remain? When is the threat really over? The Workplace Violence Intervention Group program provides immediate resources necessary to make informed and proactive decisions.

Threat of Workplace Violence . . . An Active Approach With Depth

The Steele Foundation has developed a program that assists businesses during workplace crises. The Steele Foundation's Workplace Strategy Group (WST) offers an immediate response to a developing crisis or violent incident in the workplace. The team is comprised of professionals who possess key academic and practical experience in addressing deviant workplace incidents, aberrant behavior, and employee misconduct.

Source: The Steele Foundation, Behavioral Sciences, Workplace Strategy at http://www.steelefoundation.com/services/behavsciences/workstrat.php.

- Ideas or plans about injuring himself/herself or attaching a school or persons at school;
- Communications or writings that suggest that the student has an unusual or a worrisome interest in school attacks;
- Comments that express or imply that the student is considering mounting an attack at school;
- Recent weapon-seeking behavior, especially if weapon-seeking is linked to ideas about attack or expressions about interest in attack;
- Communications or writings suggesting that the student condones or is considering violence to redress a grievance or solve a problem; and
- Rehearsals of attacks or ambushes.[51]

What private security offers is a more aggressive approach to pre-incident prevention than can possibly be exhibited by its colleagues in the public sector.

The Individual Indicators in the Case of Kipland Kinkel

Kipland Kinkel was arrested the day prior to his planned school-shooting spree. The arrest and apprehension took place while he attempted to purchase a stolen weapon. His school history alone delivered a bevy of "individual" indicators. In a literature class at Thurston High School, Kinkel routinely stood in front of his classmates and read intimate portions of his diary that included plans to "kill everybody." Dozens of classmates said that they had noticed Kinkel's strange behavior for about two years. On January 4, 1997, police charged him with throwing rocks at cars from an overpass. On his Internet profile, Kinkel described his hobbies as "Role-playing games, heavy metal music, violent cartoons/TV, sugared cereal, throwing rocks at cars and EC Comics." Under occupation designation, he listed this: "Student, surfing the Web for info on how to build bombs." According to other students, he also delivered an organized and authoritative talk on how to make bombs. It was illustrated with a detailed picture of an explosive charge connected to a clock. A student had even heard him say that he would bring a gun to school to kill a few people and save a bullet for himself. Ironically, his fellow students had voted him "Most likely to start World War III."

Security officers are not besieged and overwhelmed with every imaginable demand that public officers now experience. Security officers, looking to the principles of efficiency and economy, and driven by the underlying quest for success in the marketplace, can focus on these trends a little more. Security officers are the pivot points for information and the interpretation of information in communal settings.

By knowing the collective, that body of individuals that comprise the common social order, the security officer dwells on individual conduct in both a positive

Columbine and the Discovery of Threat

In the case of the Columbine shooting in Colorado, the School Resource deputy assigned to that school had received a number of pre-incident indicators that (if handled differently) could have been a history-changing action. The *Rocky Mountain News* in Denver reported that Neil Gardner, the Deputy Sheriff stationed at Columbine, received a report in March 1998 that the subjects Harris and Klebold were detonating pipe bombs and talked of committing mass murder. The Brown family had filed a report with the Sheriff's Office on March 18, 1998, that included printouts of Harris's Internet threats that he was ready to kill. One quote from that printout stated, "God, I can't wait until I can kill you people." Another quote stated, "I'll just go to some downtown area in some big [expletive] city and blow up and shoot everything I can."

Identifying Information:
Name:
Description:
Date of birth:
Social Security No.:

Background Information:
Residence:
Home situation:
Academic performance:
Social network:
History of relationships/conflicts:
History of harassment:
History of violence:
Attitude toward violence:
Criminal behavior:
Mental health status:

Substance abuse history:
Access to/use of weapons:
Known grievances/grudges:

Lifestyle Information:
Stability of home situation:
Relationships/support network:
Losses of "status":
Current grievances/grudges:
Perceptions of unfair treatment:
Coping/stress difficulties:
"Downward" progression of social, academic,
   behavior, psychological, aspects:
Suicidal thoughts, hopelessness, despair:
Pending crisis:
Change in circumstances:

FIGURE 4.14 Youth Assessment Form

and a negative way. Foretelling violent situations, zeroing in on troubled settings where violence reoccurs, and realizing that reaction will be too late and that intervention in advance is the better response, security officers can often tackle threats before their germination.

These practitioners must be aware of all constituencies in the community, the stable and dependable, as well as the "outsiders," the "loners," and the "misfits." By getting to know people with issues and problems and by being able to assess the potential for violent behavior, practitioners can gauge these preincidence indicators. Being familiar with common motives for adult and juvenile violence, the officer can predict when events may occur. There is nothing all that magical about this skill. Those entrusted with community protection should be mindful of these pre-incident indicators.

- Gang conflicts, both within gangs and between rival gangs;
- Neighborhood and ethnic conflicts, often over "turf";
- Contributing feuds between individuals over perceived insults or disrespect;
- Disputes over girlfriends or boyfriends;
- Acquisitive violence, such as extortion or robbery;
- Preemptive or strategic violence, that is, "I'm going to get him before he gets me";
- Dating violence; and
- Ritualized violence, for example, gang initiations.

V. CONCLUSION

Success in the eradication of crime and the assurance of peace in the neighborhood cannot occur without some serious analysis; otherwise, the public safety effort is no more than hit and miss. Planned and rational in design, the community profile and the threat assessment seek to paint a picture of what the community is composed of—both good and bad. The analysis should be as broad as possible, and as narrow as necessary, and should encompass as many players as feasible. In community profiles, the practitioners work to accurately characterize the community by not only its membership but also the recurring types of problems that the community is confronted with. By cataloguing trouble spots and zeroing in on target locations, the community plan can focus on where it needs to act and react first. The profile also identifies leaders and cooperative groups that will assist the community integration officers in carrying out specific tasks. Working with teachers, for example, can focus on pre-incident indicators, and potential problems can be thwarted. Community members who have the desire and the means to develop a safe community can figuratively brand troublemakers and criminal recidivists. In the workplace and schools, the same dynamics apply. Studies and investigations reveal, for example, that in most incidents of workplace violence, many employees knew or suspected that violent acts and actors were possible, given the history of the employee.[52] Predictability can be based on statements and behavior that could only signify trouble in the future. An assessment that formalizes the general suspicions can literally mean the difference between a successful proactive prevention effort and a potential or an actual catastrophe. Specific suggestions in the compilation of threat assessment documents, which guide the community officers in plan and strategy, are also provided. Special emphasis on targeting troublemakers and environmental settings where crime can flourish is provided. Extensive consideration of a generous list of pre-incident indicators has been developed and offered. Formats for threat assessment are laid out for the reader.

Notes

1. Robert D. Putnam, Bowling Alone: *The Collapse and Revival of American Community* 307–308 (New York Simon & Schuster, 2000).
2. Shock generated television programs like *Worlds Most Shocking Moments Caught on Tape,* and this obvious new generation of "shock comics" have all emerged to satisfy society's need for stimuli. MTV's Tom Green show shocks our kids by showing real scenes of obscenity. Episodes include Tom Green eating worms, appearing to be sexually assaulting a dead moose on the side of the road, and suggestively sucking the milk from a cow's udders as though he is committing a sexual act of oral copulation.
3. Center for Media and Public Affairs, cited in Harry Waters, "Networks under the Gun," *Newsweek,* July 12, 1993.
4. Bureau of Justice Statistics, *Criminal Victimization in the US, 1995,* table 3, at 10 (U.S. DOJ, 1995).

5. Harris et al., *A Century of Juvenile Justice in The Nature of Crime Continuity and Change* at Exhibit 2, 387.

6. Brian Forst and Peter K. Manning, *The Privatization of Policing* (Washington, D.C. Georgetown Univ. Press, 1999).

7. *See* Joel Blau, *The Visible Poor,* (New York Oxford, 1992).

8. *Federal Bureau of Investigation' Uniform Crime Report, 2000,* Figure 2.3.

9. *See* Gregory Gibson, *Goneboy, A Walkabout* (New York Kodansha, 1999)

10. James Q. Wilson's *Thinking about Crime* delivers a provocative look into a failed justice vision. "If it is hard by plan to make the good better, it may be impossible to make the bad tolerable so long as one seeks to influence attitudes and values directly. If a child is delinquent because his family made him so or his friends encourage him to be so, it is hard to conceive what society might do about his attitudes. One can imagine families being changed through the expert intervention of skilled and patient counselors. But no one knows how a government might restore affection, stability, and fair discipline to large numbers of families lacking these characteristics; still less can one imagine how a family once restored could affect a child who has passed the formative years and has developed an aversion to one or both of his parents." 45–46.

11. George B. Vold et al., *Theoretical Criminology,* 5th ed. 129. Oxford Univ. Press, New York, 1992

12. Wesley Skogan, *Disorder and Decline* 65. Univ. of California Press Berkely, CA 1992

13. Skogan at 72.

14. Collective efficacy is "defined as cohesion among neighborhood residents combined with shared expectation for informal social control of public space, is proposed as a major social process inhibiting both crime and disorder. Disorder was measured by direct observation rather than through the subjective perceptions of neighborhood residents. The informal social control mechanism of collective efficacy (and the broken windows thesis as well) focuses on what is visible in public places." Julie E. Samuels, *Disorder in Urban Neighborhoods—Does It Lead to Crime? NIJ Research in Brief,* NCJ 186049 1 (U.S. DOJ, 2001).

15. Samuels, H. *See also* Robert H. Langworthy, ed., *Measuring What Matters: Proceedings from the Police Research Institute Meetings,* Research Report—NCJ 170610 (USDOJ, NIJ & Office of Community Oriented Policing Services, July 1999); and George L. Kelling, *"Broken windows" and Police Discretion,* Research Report—NCJ 178259 (USDOJ, NIJ, Oct. 1999).

16. As far back as 1967, we can clearly see that the fear of crime is strongly related to the presence of disorderly conditions within communities (as elaborated in the President's Commission on Law Enforcement and Crime).

17. Forst and Manning conclude that community members are the ultimate designers of the environment and that private sector specialists should "encourage citizens to protect themselves in crime prevention and to provide information . . . to facilitate the solving of crimes." at 39.

18. Vold et al., at 133–134.

19. Paul M. Whisenand, *Crime Prevention* 290 (Boston Holbrook Press, 1977).

20. Bureau of Justice Statistics Figure 16, at 56.

21. Bureau of Justice Statistics, *Violent Crime Rate for the Years 1960 to 1999 from State Level Crime Trends database* at http://149.101.22.40/dataonline/search/crime/state/runcrimetrendsinonevar.cfm., 9/2/02.

22. Vold et al., at 129–130.
23. Putnam at 60.
24. U.S. Department of Education, National Center for Education Statistics, *National Household Education Survey*, 1996, *Adult Civic Involvement Component. See also* Putnam, Figure 10 at 60.
25. Patsy A. Klaus, *Crime and the Nation's Households*, 2000 NCJ 194107 (Bureau of Justice Statistics, September 2002). *See also* Putnam, Figure 50 at 206.
26. Putnam, at 288–289.
27. Ann Scott (Tyson A Community Turns to its Tormentors, Christian Science Monitor 3/28/96 1996).
28. For a thorough analysis of failed police practices, *see* George Kelling and Catherine Coles, *Fixing Broken Windows* (Simon and Schuster, New York 1996)
29. David L. Carter, *Community Alliance in Police Management: Perspectives & Issues,* in Police Management: Issues and Perspectives Larry T. Hoover, ed. (Police Executive Research Forum, 1992)
30. Steven K. Smith et.al, *Criminal Victimization and Perceptions of Community Safety in 12 Cities*, 1998 NCJ 173940 (Bureau of Justice Statistics, May 1999).
31. Forst and Manning suggest viewing the public served as customer rather than servant and that policing must become more "service oriented and attentive to customer demands and needs, and eventually to precipitate customer-based modes of evaluation of products and services." at 85.
32. Michael Rutter et al., *Antisocial Behavior by Young People* 229 (Cambridge Univ. Press, Cambridge England 1998).
33. Skogan at 4.
34. National Institute of Justice, *Strategic Approaches to Community Safety Initiative, Appendix D: Sample Master Data List* at http://www.ojp.usdoj.gov/nij/sacsi/sacsi_12.html, 9/3/02.
35. The stark world of juvenile crime and desperation receives increasing attention from policy makers forlorn about changing adult criminality. *See* Philip W. Harris, Wayne N. Welsh & Frank Butler, A Century of Juvenile Justice, in Vol. 1 The Nature of Crime: Continuity and Change-Criminal Justice 2000 U.S. Dept. of Justice Washington, D.C.; July 2000. Alex Kotlowitz, *There Are No Children Here* (New York Anchor Books, 1992); and David Blankenhorn, *Fatherless America* (New York, Harper, 1995).
36. Rates for violence index, Johnson 2000 and rates for assault with injury and robbery with weapon Maguire and Pastore 1999, at http://www.surgeongeneral.gov/library/youthviolence/images/fig28.gif.
37. See Florida Department of Corrections, *Gang and Security Threat Group Awareness* at http://www.dc.state.fl.us/pub/gangs/sets.html. "The department has identified for delinquency prevention and early intervention program development, four components that impact a child's healthy development both in the family and in the community. Research indicates that staying in school, keeping busy, living violence-free and getting a job are areas which, if effectively, addressed at the prevention and early intervention level, will reduce the rate of delinquency." Florida Department of Juvenile Justice, Preventing Delinquency: A Path to the Future 4 (1997).
38. *See also* W. Michael Cox and Richard Arm, *Myths of Rich and Poor* (New York, Basic Books, 1999).
39. Threat Assessment in Schools: A Guide to Managing Threatening Situations, and to Creating Safe School Climates, U.S. Secret Service, U.S. Dept. of Education Washington, D.C. May 2002 at 29–30.

40. Ibid.
41. National Center for the Analysis of Violent Crime: Critical Response Group, *The School Shooter: A Threat Assessment Perspective* 27 (U.D. DOJ).
42. National Center for the Analysis of Violent Crime at 25.
43. Nuclear Regulatory Commission, *Threat Assessment* at http://www.nrc.gov/what-we-do/safeguards/threat.html, 8/29/02.
44. Threat Assessment in Schools: A Guide to Managing Threatening Situations and to Creating Safe School Climates at 38. U.S. Secret Services & U.S. Dept. of Education Washington, D.C. May, 2002
45. Stacy E. Curtis and Meg Townsend, *What Works: A Change of Focus*, (Washington DC U.S. Dept of Justice, 1999). at 2.
46. Association of Threat Assessment Professionals Website, *Welcome to ATAP*, at http://atap.cc/aboutatap.htm, 8/29/02.
47. *See* Jackie Ripley, *Deputy Points to Signs a Gang Is Trying to Take Root, St. Petersburg Times*, April 5, 2002.
48. The Florida Department of Education, for example, produced a study of youth violence in Florida public schools for the years 1996 through 1997. The statewide study revealed that there were 227,872 reported incidents of violence for a total student population of 551,456. This would be a very good example of a trend indicator. This type of indicator allows the practitioner to foresee the strong influential trends that are in place. If we continue with the Florida example, the practitioner would then assess whether the trends apply to the specific community that he or she is responsible to protect. In this case we will use Hillsborough County. By using the same survey, we find that Hillsborough has the third highest rate of school violence in the state. By looking at the statistics, we can clearly see that the county averages are very similar to the overall state figures. Out of 33,763 students, Hillsborough had 13,694 reported violent crimes in its public schools. By observing this trend indicator, it would be clear to any practitioner that the school violence issue is very applicable to the Hillsborough school environments. In turn, the practitioner can identify the need for prevention planning and can adjust the desired techniques to eliminate or minimize the potential for violence and crisis. It also enables the development of tailored contingency planning in the event of an occurrence of violence on a large scale. Florida Department of Juvenile Justice.
49. Threat Assessment in Schools: A Guide to Managing Threatening Situations and to Creating Safe School Environments 49–50. U.S. Secret Service and U.S. Dept. of Education, Washington, D.C. May 2002.
50. Threat Assessment in Schools: A Guide to Managing Threatening Situations and to Creating Safe School Environments at 50. U.S. Secret Service and U.S. Dept. of Education, Washington, D.C., May 2002.
51. *See* David L. Berger, *Industrial Security* 2nd ed. 255 (Woburn, MA Butterworth-Heinemann, 1999).
52. Larry R. Morre, *Preventing Homicide and Acts of Violence in the Workplace* 42 *Professional Safety* (July 97). *See Dealing with Dangerous Employees, Security Management* (Sept. 1993) 82; *Homicide in US Workplaces: A Growing Trend, Police Chief Magazine* (1993) 70; and, *Violence in the Workplace: A Cry for Help, Occupational Hazards* (Oct. 1993) 31. *See also* George E. Hargrave, *Risk Assessment of Workplace Violence: Ethical and Procedural Issues in Evaluating Employees* (Journal of Threat Assessment Vol. 1 pp. 1–20 2001); Vivian B. Lord, *The Implementation of Workplace Violence Policy in State Government* Violence and Victims, Vol. 16 pp 185–202 (2001); Duncan Chappell and Vittorio DiMartino, *Violence*

at Work, 2nd ed. (Geneva: International Labour Organization 2000); Asa Corinne Peek, Carol W. Runyan and Craig Zwerling, *The role of Surveillance and Evaluation Research in the Reduction of Violence against Workers* (Am. Journal of Preventative Medicine Vol. 20, pp 141–148 2001); and Michael D. Kelleher, *New Arenas for Violence: Homicide in the American Workplace* (Westport, CT: Praeger Press 1996).

5

Private Sector Officers in the Community: Community-Based Integration Tactics

Learning Objectives: _____

1. To learn about CBIP, Community Based Integration Programs, and its various tactics of implementation.
2. To discuss the various strategies for integration in the community and to weigh and assess the efficacy of the tactics chosen.
3. To differentiate integration from other common police practices—such as observation and surveillance, arrest and apprehension—and to distinguish integration from the idea of occupation.
4. To review the most productive methods of training for community integration and evaluate curricular designs for the CPO—the Community Protection Officer.
5. To discern which type of character and professional proficiencies are most compatible with CBIP.
6. To compare and contrast the public police model for integration with that offered by private sector specialists.
7. To find that private security and its operational plan is more compatible with community integration than its public counterpart.
8. To learn about specific operational methods in deterring, detecting, and defusing of troublesome community situations.

I. INTRODUCTION

Given the natural frustrations of the public model in the comprehensive delivery of community services, the proposal offered touts the suitability and compatibility of private sector community-based public safety. The security industry has a unique

155

opportunity to complement and effectuate the policy making of law enforcement within designated communities. At its disposal are the manpower and resources needed to establish a philosophy of community that the public police model can only dream of. Community-based services for the private sector apply to residential and neighborhood environments, rather than the investigation of crimes and apprehension of criminal offenders that public police are directed toward. Private sector services could not be better attuned to the communal role. Whether at offices, schools, community parks, or housing complexes, private police can and will gratefully incorporate the community-based approach. Additionally, private officers author an agenda that is based on community integration. Wherever assigned, the security firm enables both its corporate design and corresponding economic viability with the communities served. The private model cannot disregard the needs of client and community, and it cannot take lightly the demands of clientele, since its funding sources depend upon customer satisfaction. The future of the enterprise depends on community tranquillity although the same cannot be said of its public counterpart. Healthy and happy communities lead to success in the private security industry, whereas the opposite will not bode well for either the firm or the constituency it serves. Here lies the advantage of the private sector in the community debate. To survive, private sector operations must please the customers and succeed in the community. Although the public model is obviously supported by the public largesse, the honest reality is that funding sources from this coffer are less likely to evaporate. Funding comfort does impact the performance philosophy.

America's most successful corporations have long appreciated the interplay between community integration and the generation of profits. Companies that prey on local resources, with little regard for the residents, are passing ships in the life of the community. Corporations that engage in outreach regarding matters of day care, gym facilities, car-pooling programs, or free counseling services for the families and employees foster an environment of loyalty and contentment. Other business entities, such as General Electric Corporation,[1] pledge volunteer hours to help in community programs. Art, cultural institutions, parks and recreation sponsorship, social services, and crisis intervention are just a few other examples of how the private sector integrates its essence into the life of the community. The security industry has an identical capacity for "outreach," which in turn increases its own effectiveness in crime prevention and community order. Anthony Miciccu refers to this mindset as one of stakeholder—something the industry must do to succeed. Aside from crime fighting, security must "compromise this position and had to begin promoting a style of security that focused more on service provision than on crime fighting. This compromise position was explained largely by the fact that these officers, unlike either the crime fighters or the guards, were formally held accountable for security policy both by their administrative superiors and by influential client groups within the institutional environment. These stakeholders wished to see in place a model of security that was cost effective, service oriented, and integrated with the institution's central mission."[2] As the private security industry anchors itself as the primary provider for community protection, it will need a solid and defensible plan of action. Outreach without method is rarely effective. The plan for community integration by and through the private security industry follows.

II. COMMUNITY-BASED INTEGRATION PROGRAMS (CBIP)

Community-based integration programs (CBIP), or *comprehensive communities programs (CCP)*, operate on two fundamental assumptions. First, support must emanate from the citizenry and community served. Alienation or distance between the community and its protectors undermine the very idea of community-based programs. Second, the private sector protection agency must be fully integrated into the life of the community it serves—not just as employees who visit during normal working hours, nor as an occupying force or as crowd controllers. With community integration, the program must live within and become part of the very community that the protection officers serve. In place of communal distrust and alienation, a cooperative and welcoming atmosphere and a collective spirit of cooperation and dependency take over. In the absence of these two variables, the impact of community-based programs will be negligible.

Without an intense and intimate relationship between the private sector force and the community served, problems and conflicts will stubbornly remain a part of the communal fabric. Practitioners must understand this tendency and acknowledge the underlying relationship that exists between them and the community. Once private officers are assigned to patrol a given area, it becomes their own community where brothers, sisters, parents, and friends live and work. This relationship is vitally important to facilitate information gathering, build public support, assist in restoring the community's self-esteem, and create a reassuring sense of security.

In today's world of modern protective services, the private security industry can and must integrate these principles in each area of responsibility. Community-based integration programs must be implemented consistently for all types of protective assignments—whether protecting a television station, a retail store, residential area, or a nuclear plant. Integration calls for an intimate and a heartfelt investment on the part of the proponent. Integration weaves itself into the lifeblood of a community, without reservation or contempt and with good faith.

The idea of private protection officers as a catalyst to community integration is rather new; however, the industry is slowly recognizing the need for this innovative model. Seasoned companies, such as Critical Intervention Services, walk point on this innovative model. See Figure 5.1.

The tactics for effective integration share these essential qualities:

- Bring together people most affected by crime problems.
- Give each stakeholder a meaningful role in solving problems.
- Apply a deliberate planning and implementation process.[3]

FIGURE 5.1   CPO Community Interaction

A. *Integration versus Observation*

To fully integrate into community life requires more than criminal apprehension and enforcement functions performed by public justice agencies. The private sector can fill this gap using the basic tactics of observation, integration, prevention, deterrence, and reporting. From a twofold format, preventative and proactive, private sector specialists weave into a community. Preventative interaction involves communication, trust building, commitment and caring for community members. Proactive intervention involves many techniques that revolve around officers creating interference, interdiction, harassment, and enforcement. Hence, a major philosophical distinction emerges from the outset of this discussion. The use of observation and reporting of criminal activity alone fails to catch the essence of a community-based integration program. Integration, prevention, and deterrence methods, which also are central, insist on a heavier investment of time. Resource and program integration recognizes that crime can be conquered only from a web of varying angles and that using only enforcement and reporting will not find favor with the community. Interaction with the community is key.

   Enforcement alone will gain even less, especially in high-risk communities, since the central mission of law enforcement inhibits the types of interaction that will foster and assure community tranquillity. In rare cases, the public system sometimes avoids interaction, preferring to stay detached. Private security firms should not resist the fullness of integration because it is crucial to successful community building, but these firms are always mindful of liability issues. A bona fide community-based integration program cannot tremble over a potential lawsuit, and in fact, could argue that a lack of intervention may spawn even greater liabilities. CBIP encourages officers to interact. Control of an environment and maintenance of community trust come only from close interaction.

The esteemed thinker Amitai Etzioni insists in a "reinvention" of American society, a return toward the components that envelop the life of a community—put another way, a return to "communitarianism":

> There are ways to enhance public safety, the most elementary requirement of community life, and rebuild the Communitarian nexus without relying on specific institutions, such as local schools or the police. People can work directly with one another. Crime watches, in which people undertake to watch out for one another's safety and property, and citizen patrols, in which people volunteer to patrol their neighborhood, if properly carried out, are activities that contribute to a community need and build community bonds among the participants.[4]

Community integration implies an affirmative intervention—not crossing one's fingers hoping that nothing happens, or reacting only when something does happen. Community intervention pushes the security player into the proactive mode. To edify, youth crime is a given problem. In community integration, officers anticipate and intervene, and they attempt to prevent the incident from ever being considered. See Table 5.1 for examples of how youth violence can be tackled, according to the Surgeon General.[5] In reality, many of these practices have proven effective, even though rated ineffective by the Surgeon General. Examples include boot camps, behavioral modification programs, individual counseling, and redi-

Practitioner Highlight

Security at Toyota Manufacturing of Indiana

There are three divisions within the Security Department at TMMI: Central Dispatch, Security, and the Emergency Response Team. These divisions are responsible for securing and responding to incidents on a 2-mile by 1-mile piece of property that houses two plants, a day-care center, and a staging yard. There are about 4,000 employees who produce about 800 vehicles a day. Central Dispatch is the backbone of the everyday operations of the security department. The Central Security Officer not only monitors various cameras and access panels but also operates an in-house phone system, dispatches officers, and monitors the radio system.

The second division is the Security Division. This division is responsible for all the perimeter security and access to the plant. This requirement is accomplished by seven or eight fixed posts, including vehicle and pedestrian gates.

The final division is the Emergency Response Team (ERT). The ERT patrols both the perimeter and internal roadways and the interior of the plant. The team members respond to all medical and fire calls, hazardous materials incidents, and security-related emergencies. They are equipped with patrol vehicles, modified E-Z-GO emergency carts, three fire trucks; one *pumper*, one *rescue*, and one *brush truck*.

TABLE 5.1   *Rating Intervention Strategies*

Effective Strategies	Ineffective Strategies
Primary Prevention: Universal	**Primary Prevention: Universal**
Skills training	Peer counseling, peer mediation, peer leaders
Behavior monitoring and reinforcement	Nonpromotion to succeeding grades
Behavioral techniques for classroom management	
Building school capacity	
Continuous progress programs	
Cooperative learning	
Positive youth development programs	
Secondary Prevention: Selected	**Secondary Prevention: Selected**
Parent training	Gun buyback programs
Home visitation	Firearm training
Compensatory education	Mandatory gun ownership
Moral reasoning	Redirecting youth behavior
Social problem solving	Shifting peer group norms
Thinking skills	
Tertiary Prevention: Indicated	**Tertiary Prevention: Indicated**
Social perspective taking, role taking	Boot camps
Multimodal interventions	Residential programs
Behavioral interventions	Milieu treatment
Skills trainings	Behavioral token programs
Marital and family therapy by clinical staff	Waivers to adult court
Wraparound services	Social casework
	Individual counseling

recting behavior. The individual and the agencies involved must be thoroughly evaluated when appropriate tactics are being considered.

CBIP in general actively looks for opportunities to interact with the community. Various limitations to this general philosophical approach are bound to undermine any positive results. Any hope of effective integration will mandate a transformation in how police services are delivered. These critical goals are the following:

- Suppress violence and restore the sense of community well-being that is needed to recapture the security of neighborhoods.
- Focus on the problems and concerns of communities and their neighborhoods by initiating comprehensive planning and improving government-community relationships.

- Develop a comprehensive, multiagency strategy within each community to identify the causes of violence and to control and prevent violent and drug-related crime.
- Use community policing and other efforts to encourage citizens to take an active role in problem solving.
- Coordinate and concentrate existing federal, state, local, and private agency resources in the program communities to maximize their impact on crime reduction.[6]

B. Personnel and the CBIP

Given the unique nature of this strategy, the quality of personnel for the tasks associated with integration must be elevated, and required traits must be reassessed. With these needs in mind, officers must be carefully screened and selected during the hiring process. Rather than attempting to change the current mindset of reactive personalities, discerning compatible professionals from the outset is crucial to eventual success. At the hiring level, candidates need to be selected according to personality testing, psychological testing, interview scores, experience, and training. In all aspects of the hiring process, attention should be given to the officer's ability to adopt the philosophical approach of the CBIP. Community officers must have many talents that are not necessarily witnessed in their public colleagues. Instead of a street fighter, a "people specialist" is required. The community officer must be open to the following:

- New job description
- New patrol duties
- Fixed or permanent duties
- Visibility
- Media interaction
- Community partnerships
- Problem identification and solving
- Acting as a referral source[7]

The level of sophistication and interactive, verbal communication and personal skills must be high for the community specialist. In general, as Dr. Shalloo notes in *Private Police,* too much care cannot be exercised in determining the qualifications of an applicant and the way that those qualifications are prioritized. He states that the most important trait in an applicant is *character;* the second is *moral courage;* the third is *judgment,* and finally the fourth is *education.*[8]

As in all occupations dealing with the public, CBIP targets candidates who possess strong written and oral communication and negotiation skills. Community officers by necessity must be master communicators. As such, the CBIP does not insist on undergraduate preparation in the field of criminal justice or legal studies but is just as enthralled with those who are well prepared in the liberal arts, from

Critical Intervention Services and CBIP

In 1993, a pilot program aimed at developing "community based integration programs" was created by Critical Intervention Services (CIS) to address what it saw as a community in crisis. When the program was initially developed, it was strictly focused on apartment communities but was later expanded into neighborhoods and business operations. Today, these concepts are being successfully adapted to a range of commercial and residential environments with quantifiable results.

Originally, CIS was retained by the management of an apartment community that had been completely overwhelmed by high levels of criminal activity. Unable to control the property with regular law enforcement involvement, property management brought in CIS officers to start patrolling the grounds. CIS's assignment was to regain control of the property in crisis; the question was how to do it effectively. Initially, five officers were given the task of identifying the criminal elements and removing them by any legal means necessary. But officers quickly realized that more effective approaches would have to be used in order to ensure the success of the assignment. CIS practitioners realized that in such high-crime areas, better concepts had to be outlined and specific tactics developed to meet the needs of the environment, or they would meet the same failures of past security firms and the local police department. There is no question that CIS and its success today started with what was, essentially, an unproven experimental process. Through trial and error, CIS learned that ingenuity (a major component to the art of this profession)

FIGURE 5.2   Team of Security Professionals Dedicated to Better Communities

Critical Intervention Services and CBIP (cont.)

could solve many of the problems it faced. Shifting its mindset away from traditional security thinking and rewriting the book on protective services for high-risk communities, CIS invented the community-based integration program (CBIP).

CIS officers developed a concept of community-based "protection," in contrast to policing. Although policing sometimes implies prevention responsibilities, the main focus of the CIS program was proactive prevention and protection. Although there were numerous tactics involved, primary attention centered on attacking the quality-of-life factors that created the image of an unorganized property. CIS approached the high-crime environment with one simple premise: *The true cornerstone to solving the dilemma of criminal actions in a community is controlling the elements that lead the criminals to believe that they can perpetrate their crime without fear of apprehension.* Simply said, the disorganized environment contributes to victimization, and victimization interferes with establishing community fiber and ultimately the investment of social capital.

The CIS prototype emphasizes that this premise must be at the foundation of any proactive public safety effort, and this perspective exists at every level of the program developed by CIS. Additionally, CIS's concepts, policies, and procedures are derived from the following three fundamental beliefs that serve as the foundation for corporate operations.

1. All people have a right to safety from criminal activity regardless of their status or income. Crime should not be expected and accepted as part of a community's daily life.
2. Children within a given residential environment, conventional or subsidized, have a need for positive influences and role models in their environment. This is absolutely necessary if practitioners are going to stop the cycle of crime that continues in many communities, from generation to generation.
3. The community must be encouraged to interact and communicate with each other, with community leaders, and with public safety officials. This is essential to unify the community into a force that can resist and oust the criminal element.

With these fundamental beliefs, CIS created the foundation under which its Uniform Services Division operates today. This foundation was established to create a direct path to positively impact on the living conditions of the residents within a targeted area. . Upon their initial deployment, the CIS officers experienced an almost complete lack of interaction with the community because the community had withdrawn from interaction with public safety officials.

CIS officers felt firsthand the lack of connection between the community members themselves and with the "police" who were there to protect them. In high-crime environments, the lawful citizenry lock themselves up not only against crime but also against their own police. If CIS practitioners were to be successful, they would have to devise specific tactics to get attention and support from the residents. Only after gaining the residents' attention would communication and involvement become possible. During this process, many tactics and techniques were developed to meet this goal.

The initial focus for CIS was to create an environment that enabled trust and, subsequently, the participation of the community. The first step to accomplish this was to ensure that visible criminal activity was subdued. Only the absence of crime could allow

Critical Intervention Services and CBIP (cont.)

interaction to begin. While the criminal activity was being eliminated, CIS focused on tactics directed at destabilizing the criminal element enough to create a vacuum caused by the absence of criminal activity. Removing the visible criminal behavior simply allowed community members to stop being intimidated by the criminal. As a result, residents participated fully in the life of the community without having to fear retaliation from the criminal element. Once this approach was developed, the actual concepts were refined and then interwoven into training, interaction, communication protocols, and all aspects of the agency's operations.

FIGURE 5.3   Community Integration Activities—Preventative Integration

English to history, from philosophy to science. Interaction, interpersonal relations, problem solving, and dispute resolution are required attributes for the CBIP officer. In general, officers need to possess certain attributes and skills that make the philosophy of CBIP credible. H. John Bernardin's article regarding security officer profiles (SOP) sets the minimum standards in Figure 5.4.

C. Training for Community Integration

Historically, police academy training spent less time on community integration strategies in favor of other traditional police strategies. Although there is a move afoot to place greater emphasis on the former, community-based policing generally

CIS Character Statement

The first item a potential private protection officer sees upon applying for a position is CIS' Character Statement, shown . . . [in Figure 5.4]. This statement, written by officers and supervisors, is an explanation to new officers about what is expected from them by their fellow employees.

Critical Intervention Services, (CIS) is an elite forerunner in the security industry. This is signified by a history of success hallmarked by individual integrity and organizational pursuit of excellence. Our mission statement is:

"The staff of Critical Intervention Services is dedicated to providing each client with the finest quality of protective services available."

"Our commitment and dedication to professional, ethical and protocol conscious service is our trademark."

"Preserving, projecting and protecting our clients' image and interest is our business."

To fulfill the mission statement and maintain our success, CIS is looking for employees who have the ability to achieve, the responsibility to proceed and the leadership to influence others. Our approach to meeting our clients' needs is known as Community and Character Based Protection Initiative (CCBPI). Character is the single most important trait in a CIS employee. Character includes integrity, honesty and loyalty, which are the trademarks of our agency. At the very foundation of our success is the honorable conduct of all who represent us.

If you meet our standards of character and excellence and wish to become part of our team of professionals, your potential to succeed will be limited only by your self-determination. We expect commitment to excellence from you and, in return, you will receive unwavering support from us.

plays second fiddle to the complexities of criminal investigation, apprehension, high-speed driving tactics, and the like. Trojanawicz and company label the move toward community policing as nothing short of a "radical departure."[9] Public police organizations prioritize according to the urgency of the task. Rapists, robbers, and murderers generate a reactive quality that will always shy away from innovation and novelty. Such resistance cannot be read as antagonism and skepticism but is more likely the product of necessity and immediate pressing concerns. Public police adopt new tactics and strategies slowly and deliberately, since it is laden with a multiplicity of tasks. Community-based policing is a serious business that requires serious dedication. Public police appear inclined to advancement in the techniques of community integration, but accomplishing this goal will take time.

Community-based public safety efforts call for intense and dedicated training that cannot possibly be delivered in customary police circles. Subject matter for training must be reality based and must endlessly stress human interaction and people skills. Examples of the type of training skills that benefit the community integration philosophy are the following:

Summary of Abilities and Other Characteristics

- Willingness to work rotating shift or overtime, any day of the week including holidays;
- Reading comprehension ability at the 12th grade level;
- Investigative interests: inquisitive; curious; interested in learning how things work;
- Willing to dig for information to solve a problem;
- Normal peripheral visual field (150–180);
- Visual acuity: ability to distinguish small details from a complex background; ability to read indicator numbers from a normal viewing distance;
- Depth perception;
- Auditory acuity: ability to hear changes in pitch or loudness of equipment noises; ability to distinguish spoken language from a noisy background;
- Ability to respond appropriately under stress;
- Emotional stability/low neuroticism;
- Analytical ability: ability to reason, problem solving; detect trends, plan action in a logical, orderly manner;
- Ability to retain and recall information;
- Attention to detail: ability to perceive and interpret small details;
- Conscientiousness in checking and caring for equipment;
- Ability to communicate oral information clearly and accurately in English;
- Ability/willingness to follow set routines/procedures;
- Ability to work closely with other people;
- Ability to remain vigilant and efficient over long, uneventful shift periods;
- Ability to react quickly in dangerous situations;
- Ability to size up situations and take action;
- Ability to control one's temper/low aggressiveness;
- Ability to remain alert despite a boring task;
- Ability to adjust to unusual work schedules;
- Ability to remain calm in difficult situations;
- Ability to stay alert for possible unlawful activities;
- Ability to follow directions carefully.

The above items were judged by over 65% of the supervisory respondents to be necessary to perform one or more of the essential functions of the job at a minimally acceptable level.

FIGURE 5.4   Character and Qualifications for Community Protection Officers

- Character building
- First contact protocols
- Community-based protection initiative
- Deescalation techniques
- Individual communication skills
- Phased or gradual community bonding
- Trespass warning effectiveness
- Juvenile interaction

- Law enforcement relations
- Criminal interaction/intimidation techniques
- Chemical munitions certification
- Impact weapon certification
- Defensive tactics
- Handcuffing
- Weapon retention
- Edged weapon defense
- Advanced officer survival
- Advanced firearms courses
- Other courses as specific needs are identified

Subsequent to classroom instruction, community-based security officers need to be regularly tested in the field to ensure that the requisite levels of interactive people skills have been achieved. Some people suggest the implementation of a field training officer program in which prospective officers are tested in actual situations. When combined with training in human relations and traditional police practice, the certification/licensure ensures that the officer understands the legal and statutory responsibilities in the role assumed. No community-based officer should lack regulatory certifications or licensures. Beyond these basic requirements, community-based officers should receive regular sessions of in-house corporate training that continually emphasizes the integration approach and the importance of effective communication with the residents served. Continuing education or other available training that complements the basic preparations is an added plus. Specialized training in investigative and intelligence activities is also a helpful addition for the community protection officer.

Undergraduate courses in criminal justice, with a heavy emphasis on human relations skills and professional conduct, would also be a welcome addition. Nalla, Christian, Morash, and Schram's comprehensive study of undergraduate curriculum in security studies illustrates a general security firm awareness of this need. Aside from the traditionally expected topics, the practitioners call for, by importance, the following:

- Public speaking presentation skills
- Public relations skills
- Effective writing skills
- Knowledge of group dynamics
- Competency in preparing computer graphics
- Ability to type or use a word processor[10]

The findings are instructive, since a draconian shift occurs on many fronts. Reactive policing methodology needs to be replaced with human relations—that "art" of interchange and interaction—because the primary focus is not apprehension, but prevention. More than forensic science is called for, since the analysis suggests "a dramatic shift in the views of respondents from certain industry groups that traditionally were perceived as following military/law enforcement police models. Such a finding indicates their recognition that security professionals must understand management skills to compete successfully in today's market."[11]

The urgency of education in the lives of community officers is derived from the demanding functions they must perform. Bertus Ferreira wisely sums up the need for such education:

> Examples of this include: studying psychology to better understand the human mind and interpersonal relationships; learning another language to better communicate with more members of a community; studying law and court cases to understand when to arrest somebody or search and seize property; and studying arts, humanities and social and natural sciences to better understand the world we live in and how we relate to others in our world environment.[12]

Educating the officer on standard operating procedures (SOPs)—as well as liability issues regarding the agency, the community, and the clients—is another valuable training excursion. Other training that supports community integration could include gangs, gang symbols and language, race relations, poverty and other community stresses, drugs and the law, and tactics for economic empowerment.

On a more practical front, the community officer needs preparation in fundamental policing skills. Additionally, officers who carry secondary weapons, such as OC spray (pepper spray) or expandable batons, are required to complete the necessary certifications. Weapons certification and technological training in detection equipment are also mandatory for the community-based officers if used in the field. CBIP officers are first and foremost human relations specialists, but they cannot forego the specific policing skills necessary for survival in the rigorous environments that are assigned.

D. Fundamental Skills in the Community Protection Officer

The guiding principles that community protection officers must always abide by are fourfold: Deter, Detect, Defuse, and Defend must be the operational cornerstone of any public safety strategy. These guiding principles will bring a reduction in criminal activity and will increase citizens' quality of life. Agencies should develop training curriculums and should indoctrinate protection officers as to the importance

---

The Philosophy of the Community Protection Officer

1. Deter crime.
2. Detect issues.
3. Defuse problems.
4. Defend the community.

of these principles, especially when they are deployed in high-crime environments. This method should be utilized as the standard approach for handling all non-life-threatening situations. The method progresses systematically from proactive contact to resolution and utilizes enforcement only as a last resort. Being on the offensive in community operations manifests the will to succeed and the necessity of strong convictions when neighborhoods are at stake.

1. Detering Crime.   Deterring crime is part and parcel of the community integration package, though the emphasis here is on the latter three criteria of officer conduct. Undeniably, any law enforcement philosophy stresses the deterrence end of its business, but what private sector justice so amply realizes more than its public counterpart is that deterrence depends on other forces at work in the community. For example, the public model holds that stiff punishments "deter," and although this assuredly may be so in individual cases, the community integration plan must create communal conditions and an infrastructure that naturally deters criminality. Within this framework, the deterrence model works effectively, for a community protection plan depends on the spirited cooperation of its members. Security officers dedicated to community integration tackle the problems step-by-step when deterrence fails. See Figure 5.5. Deter includes officers checking buildings to ensure security. It involves insuring that lighting is adequate. It also requires the officer to survey fencing, report any breaches or disrepair and note overgrown landscape. It means that officers must stop unrecognized individuals and identify and escort them to a secure area.

2. Detecting Issues.   Whether the issues are general (relating to community life and characteristics, such as red light districts, poor street lighting, lack of sidewalks, etc.) or individualized issues that contribute to the larger picture (such

---

All CIS officers assigned to STOP (see p. 182) operations are thoroughly trained in the three "D's":

1. **Detect**
In the CCBPI Methodology, accurate identification of the community's unique problems and quality of life issues is essential. STOP officers give tremendous attention to problem definition to ensure that the CCBPI plan is complete.

2. **Defuse**
Once problems are identified, STOP officers focus on proactively defusing and intercepting problem situations. In addition to conflict de-escalation, this principle also includes controlling environmental factors that contribute to crime and community disorganization.

3. **Defend**
When de-escalation has been ineffective, decisive action must be taken to prevent victimization of the community. Defense may include law enforcement, trespass warnings, and other forms of direct action to force criminals to abandon their activities.

FIGURE 5.5   The Three "D's" of STOP Operations.

as drug activity, prostitution, domestic disputes, and others), each must be accurately identified and understood in order to be resolved. Before any protection agency can achieve success in a community, officers must be able to define and understand the problematic issues of that community. Identifying issues of concern is imperative if officers are to effectively tailor their approach to solving not only high-crime issues but also community instability and deterioration. Although arrests solve a host of community problems that contribute to a disorganized environment, arrests alone are not always the answer. Public police have long recognized the crucial role that "discretion" and "diversion" plays in effective policing. However, the demand for lower crime statistics tends to thwart officer discretion. Solid community policing requires case-by-case intervention. In fact, relying on arrests as a solution may contribute to the further decline of individual members, which in turn leads to an overall community decline. At times keeping the target out of the police action and out of the justice system contributes to the common good.

The ability to identify issues can arise only from officer integration with the community. Through this process, protection officers become part of the community that they protect and begin to experience for themselves the common dilemmas of the target area. The only true way that this process can be done is by assigning dedicated protection officers to foot/bike patrols (depending on area size). These officers should be assigned exclusively to community interaction and be free from responding to emergency calls that current law enforcement typically must respond to. Community building takes time and dedication. By freeing officers from most emergency call response, officers are able to establish relationships with the citizenry and truly become familiar with the issues that the community is experiencing.

Therefore, every aspect of the officers' professional existence must be focused on ensuring that community members know who they are and what their purpose is. One example of how officers can achieve this is by implementing a proactive "move-in" policy, whereby community protection officers are responsible for greeting and welcoming new residents as they move into a community. This tactic indicates a sincere willingness to work with the community and lays out professional and personal expectations of the officers and residents.

Another emphasis must relate to the young community members. Children know and see more of the world around them than adults do when it comes to juvenile activities and crimes. They are often exposed to information that many practitioners are unaware of. The reasons for this tendency are simple. Children are rarely perceived as a threat to criminals operating around them, and as a result, children are often privy to information that officers could never get on their own. Another reason is that children have an immense network of contacts within the juvenile arena. This network includes not only the neighborhood but also their school and other kids whom they know from social clubs and outings. Needless to say, tapping into those networks is vital to officers who intend to implement prevention activities. The interplay of officers and the young plays a critical role in the elements that negatively influence a child's development. Sitting around and talking with kids, throwing ball, or just spending time with them regularly has a long-term impact that can literally change a child's future and drastically affect crime trends in a given area. As these children grow up, they become well-known to officers and open to interacting with them. Here is where real fiber between the community and the "police" can truly become interwoven in a positive manner and can have a long-term impact in police/community relations.

The quality of life issues identified during the detect responsibilities should be documented and combined with uniform crime reports (UCRs) to improve the assessment and causation factors within a given area. Although there is no question that tracking index crimes is an important function of law enforcement, it could be argued that more benefit for the private practitioner would come out of conducting neighborhood surveys and assessments directed at identifying the social and physical disorders that the community is exhibiting. This function could be conducted by protection officers in coordination with the crime specialists of the local law enforcement agency. The findings should be shared with the law enforcement agencies of the area in order to assist them in obtaining a clearer picture of the community. These indicators would give law enforcement and protection personnel better focus at directing resources.

3. Defusing Issues. Once officers have identified the community issues, they can then begin to implement techniques and tactics tailored to defuse identified problems. To defuse is to prevent crime and problems from occurring in the community setting. Defusing tactics usually involve the intervention or interception of criminal activity before it reaches full force. Hence, prostitution is unlikely to occur on street blocks that residents picket and challenge. Drugs are less likely to be dealt when officers are walking the premises and video cameras track dealers and customers alike. Reactive organizations in the traditional police mold operate after the fact and have no serious impact on community alteration. The problem disappears for the moment only to reappear soon after. Defusing tactics work at eliminating the problem altogether.

Defusing the issues requires management and analysis of those factors that contribute to crime. Whether the situation takes ten minutes or ten days to resolve, when the possibility of de-escalation and resolution exists, officers must follow that path. This undertaking is what they have been chartered to do.[13] Part of being able to defuse issues requires officers to utilize skills in de-escalating confrontations. In many cases, officers can observe threats evolving if they pay attention to warning signs. By observing and recognizing threat cues, the officer will be able to shift, refocus, or terminate an escalating threat by using de-escalation skills.

4. Defending the Community. Defending the community against victimization requires concrete action when defusion has failed. Obviously, law enforcement officers can conduct arrests in an effort to prevent community victimization, such as when a crime of battery is committed or when drug sales are perpetrated in the open. Working with law enforcement to conduct those actions should be part of the defend approach.

Practitioner Tip

Security firms control troublesome situations in both direct and very subtle ways. For example, how an officer acts or portrays his or her position will sometimes enhance or diminish problems. To de-escalate, the officer must understand not only the science of control but also the art of prevention of a problem. Both verbal and body language send clear messages.

Officers must utilize the art of de-escalation, and they must understand that de-escalation also involves controlling body language. Regardless of what is said verbally, body language or actions will speak just as loud as the officer's words. For example, many officers have a habit of keeping their thumbs dug into the front of their gun belt when talking to people or having their hands on hips while rocking back and forth; not only is such a posture interpreted as threatening to an individual and is not tactically sound in terms of safety, but it also sends a message of arrogance and supremacy to the observing community. Another nonverbal escalation technique includes invading personal space, which is also very unsafe to the officer and is a sign of extreme rudeness to outside observers.

Communicating, in an effort to de-escalate, is not about just body language. What an officer actually says is also very important in the de-escalation process, yet officers are usually given very little training in verbal communication skills. What is important is not only what is said but also how it is said, and the latter is where most officers fail to verbally communicate with the community. Officers must use clear and simple language, and they must not try to communicate above the comprehension level of the people they are dealing with. They should not use professional-related jargon such as 10-codes or advising the subject that he or she is in violation of such and such a state statute. That is not the manner in which people talk to each other. The use of jargon when talking to the general public is often interpreted as the officer's being condescending. This interpretation in itself can escalate the situation. Officers should always talk with respect to another person, regardless of who that person is,—even if the subject is being placed into custody. Although this is simple advice, carrying it out is not seen very much in policing.

- Trespass warnings
- Eviction warning notices
- Monitoring a known criminal
- Interaction with neighborhood sources
- Overseeing troubled youth
- Interacting with civic organizations, local churches, and community leaders
- Boycotting of certain types of businesses that allow criminal activity
- Organizing community activities
- Crime prevention programs
- Creating social functions and activities that help unify the community

FIGURE 5.6   Defend Strategies for the CPO

In addition, utilize nonreactionary techniques that have a more long-term in effect. These include, but are not limited to, those shown in Figure 5.6. The defend component can also utilize techniques such as interacting and working with civic organizations, local churches, and community leaders to help either solve the problems or, more specifically, apply pressure to do the same. The boycotting of certain types of businesses that allow criminal activity would be an example.

Organizing community activities aimed at crime prevention or increasing community awareness should also be part of the defuse strategy. The proactive arsenal available to agencies is limited only to the resources and imagination of the individual officers and the program developers. The focus for those practitioners should be to keep from establishing neighborhood crime watch programs that are structured and "official."

Furthermore, it is almost impossible to establish crime watch programs in communities where the residents don't trust the police. Rather, practitioners should focus on creating social functions and activities that help unify the community, particularly in high-crime or high-turnover areas (such as apartment communities). Implementing a "canned" crime prevention program will usually fail at the outset. Practitioners must focus on the fiber of the community prior to attempting any organized crime prevention efforts. One cannot exist without the other.

Use of civil courts for eviction and abatement purposes has been a remarkably adept tactic at rooting out drug dealers and other undesirables. "In fact, it might be one of the most effective strategies that police or citizens can use to combat neighborhood drug problems. This tool applies nuisance abatement ordinances to close down or confiscate properties that are sites for drug sales."[14] In abatement, property owners are ordered to press corrective actions for nuisance activities—in the same way an owner might be told to rid property of health hazards. In eviction, landlords are affirmatively requested to not renew leases or to exercise some eviction right in the existing contract. The purpose is "displacement" of the offender and rehabilitation of the environment.[15]

By applying the Deter, Detect, Defuse, and Defend approach and by focusing on the disorder of the environment, officers, in the long run, will be able to reduce the turnover of or the exodus of good residents from the area. As a result, officers will increase community interaction and foster trust. CPOs must be constantly evaluated for the necessary attributes for success in community integration. From appearance to patrol, officers should be scrutinized. See Figure 5.7 for a sample evaluation sheet.

III. A SYSTEM'S APPROACH TO COMMUNITY INTEGRATION

Understanding the officer's role and function in community integration is fundamental to any future success in a plan of action. Once achieved, the approach must be systematic. Etzioni entreats the diverse facets of community life to join in the effort:

	Instructed	MS	FS	NA
Name: Date:				
Call Sign: Purpose:				
Evaluator:				
1. Appearance:				
a. Uniform Standards	___	___	___	___
b. Personal Appearance	___	___	___	___
2. Attitude:				
a. Toward the Security Profession	___	___	___	___
b. Toward CIS	___	___	___	___
c. Toward Accepting Feedback	___	___	___	___
i. From Supervisors	___	___	___	___
ii. From Peers	___	___	___	___
iii. From Citizens/Residents	___	___	___	___
iv. From Law Enforcement	___	___	___	___
d. Job Attendance	___	___	___	___
e. Self Initiated Activity				
3. Job Knowledge Skills:				
a. CIS Policies	___	___	___	___
i. Chain of Command	___	___	___	___
ii. General Orders	___	___	___	___
iii. SOPs	___	___	___	___
iv. Bulletins/Pass Ons	___	___	___	___
b. Patrol Requirements/Geographics	___	___	___	___
c. Communications	___	___	___	___
i. Radio Codes/Signals	___	___	___	___
ii. 10 Series	___	___	___	___
iii. Radio Ids/Unit Ids	___	___	___	___
d. Documentation	___	___	___	___
i. Form Recognition	___	___	___	___
ii. Form Application	___	___	___	___
iii. Form Distribution	___	___	___	___
iv. Form Composition/Accuracy	___	___	___	___
e. Equipment Maintenance/Use	___	___	___	___
i. Firearm/Ammo	___	___	___	___
ii. Speed Loaders	___	___	___	___
iii. OC	___	___	___	___
iv. Baton	___	___	___	___
v. Handcuffs	___	___	___	___
vi. Web Gear	___	___	___	___
vii. Ancillary	___	___	___	___

FIGURE 5.7 Officer Evaluation Report (OER)

4. Performance Skills:	Instructed	MS	FS	NA
a. Patrol Functions	___	___	___	___
i. W/Assigned Vehicle	___	___	___	___
ii. Foot Patrol	___	___	___	___
iii. Detect Suspicious Activity	___	___	___	___
iv. Interaction w/Others	___	___	___	___
(1) Residents	___	___	___	___
(2) Citizens	___	___	___	___
(3) Peers	___	___	___	___
(4) Supervisors	___	___	___	___
(5) Law Enforcement	___	___	___	___
v. Assist Other Agencies	___	___	___	___
vi. Conduct Personnel Stops	___	___	___	___
(1) CCBPI/Public Service	___	___	___	___
(2) Trespass/Warning	___	___	___	___
(3) Other	___	___	___	___
vii. Traffic Control	___	___	___	___
(1) Mobile	___	___	___	___
(2) Parking	___	___	___	___
viii. Exhibit Officer Safety	___	___	___	___
(1) W/Assigned Vehicle	___	___	___	___
(2) Foot Patrol	___	___	___	___
(3) Conduct "Safe" Interview	___	___	___	___
(4) Weapon/Firearm Safety/Retention	___	___	___	___
(5) Building/Residence Searches, Clearance	___	___	___	___
ix. Recognize and Utilize Use of Force Continuum	___	___	___	___
x. Information Awareness	___	___	___	___
b. Documentation Functions	___	___	___	___
i. Collect, Secure, Process Evidence and Information	___	___	___	___
ii. Maintain Field Notes	___	___	___	___
iii. Maintain Personal Record File	___	___	___	___
iv. Maintain Vehicle Log	___	___	___	___
v. Prepares Reports, etc.	___	___	___	___
vi. Records Attendance Record, Training Data Pass Ons, etc.	___	___	___	___
vii. Maintains FS Statute References	___	___	___	___

MS—Meets Standards   **FS—Fails Standards**   **NA—Not Appraised**

Evaluator:

Officer:

Supervisor:

FIGURE 5.7 *(Cont.)*

OFFICER EVALUATION REPORT
CONTINUATION SHEET

EVALUATOR COMMENTS:

Reference:

OFFICER COMMENTS:

Reference:

FIGURE 5.7   *(Cont.)*

The level of crime is deeply affected by the total community fabric. It is not enough for families to be strong, or schools to be fine educational institutions, and so on. To minimize the crime, all of these elements must reinforce one another. Thus, in those parts of the country (and the world) where families are strong, schools teach moral values, communities are well intact, and values command respect. In Utah, for instance, crime is much lower than in places where these factors are absent. The national violent crime rate in 1990 was 730 per 100,000; in Utah it was 284. In the first part of this book we saw what works in situations such as Utah is that families, schools, and communities—all the factors that go into making the moral infrastructure—come together to support moral conduct. In effect, they work not merely or even mainly to fight crime, but to sustain civility and values in general. Prevention of crime is a bonus of a moral and civil society.[16]

Effective and successful community integration follows progressive steps until the community controls its own destiny and roots out the malefactors. While differences in tactics are permissible, certain elements should always be present in the integration strategy:

Strategic planning. Ongoing planning by all key stakeholders is essential for any progress in developing this public safety strategy.

Management and operations. An individual or a team coordinator must be given authority to oversee this multifaceted strategy throughout its development.

Evaluation. A sound public safety strategy must include an evaluation component to help determine whether goals are being met and whether to improve or modify the strategy if needed.

Sustainment. The strategy must be viewed as a long-term effort, requiring ongoing commitment and support from stakeholders.[17]

Community integration programs initially determine how the environment is impacted by street-level felony crimes and the corresponding rates of victimization. The process has both global and particular qualities. Effective community tactics can start block by block, facility by facility, complex by complex, and eventually move toward a grander geography. Whenever and wherever the criminal and his or her cohorts feel comfortable, change is essential. It is the environment that must be changed.

Without alteration of the corrupted environment, no amount of community policing will matter. The environment represents the underlying problem. In bad environments, the criminal runs free, because he or she not only believes in his or her ability to perpetrate crime, but also more boldly believes the impossibility of his or her apprehension and prosecution. See Figure 5.8.[18]

Community integration programs zero in on and change environments by removing negative quality-of-life characteristics and nuisance problems. Dirty and dilapidated grounds, roving juveniles, abandoned cars, loud music, prostitution, and open alcohol and drug consumption—all lead the criminal subconsciously to believe in his or her own invincibility. Trojanowicz and his colleagues categorize the types of disorder that community programs must overcome in Figure 5.9.[19]

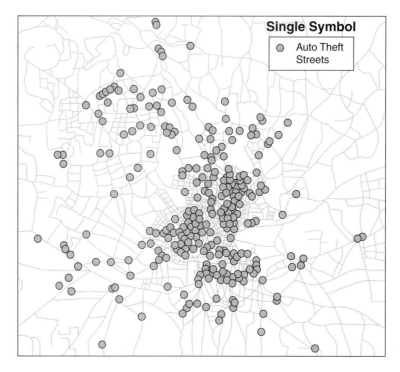

FIGURE 5.8   Auto Theft Incident Rates by Street on Block

These environments can be described only as troubled and disorganized. A viable community-based program hopes to alter the environment and reputation of a community and to uplift the quality and character of life for average residents. CBIP transforms the area into a neat, tight, organized, and controlled environment with many positive influences—an environment where criminals no longer rule the roost, children play, and residents interact without fear of reprisal. Change in the envi-

---

Problems to Overcome
Street prostitution and related robberies.
Thefts from autos in parking lots.
A high rate of burglaries in run-down apartment buildings.
Abandoned cars on public housing property.
Repeat calls over a period of years regarding drugs and violence.
Absentee owners who allow illegal activities to take place in their businesses.
Poor outdoor lighting at public housing facilities.
Juvenile crime, specifically drug sales.
Repeated thefts and related crime by drug addicts.
Repeat domestic assault calls to certain addresses.

FIGURE 5.9   Typical Issues in Need of Intervention

ronment leads to change in the community—not vice versa, an outcome in which the public model has long believed. An "organized" environment takes on the face of cleanliness, cares about the setting, and sends an unmistakable message that the streets belong to the residents, not to the thugs who try to threaten community tranquillity. See Figure 5.10.

Aside from environment, successful community integration programs recognize the need to address each resident in a caring and positive way. Community is nothing more than a collective of individual personalities working toward a common end. Separating individual considerations from collective ones is a surefire recipe for failure. A program that completely avoids the issues of individual character and its growth and maturation is guaranteed to fail. The education of citizenry connotes both vocational and moral training. As Robert Bellah and colleagues so incisively relay,

FIGURE 5.10 Developing Relationships in the Community—Preventative Interaction

> It is part of our classical heritage to see education at the center of our common life. This is an understanding going back to Plato and to Aristotle, which conclude both his *Ethics* and his *Politics* with discussions of education as a central concern of the Polis—a term that is usually translated at "city-state" but that includes the idea of society or community as well.[20]

Hence, CBIP finds ways to allow individuals to grow and flourish and, by implication, the community as well. Here activities with children, parents, and significant relatives become a core principle of the community delivery, and here the residents improve as the community does. Each depends on the other. The idea of moral education in the formation of citizens and states is an ancient ideal, but one that is distressingly lost on modern policy makers. The primary end and aim of community, and of ancient cultures, was the formation of solid citizens.[21] Bellah, Madsen, Sullivan, Swidler, and Tipsta stress this approach in their salient work *The Good Society*.

> For Aristotle, "education" had a considerably broader meaning than we usually give the term. It was indeed the primary function of the *polis* to provide those laws, written and unwritten, that would educate citizens into a life of virtue, for only such citizens would make a good *polis* possible. So it was not schools that Aristotle was thinking of in the first instance when he discussed education, but the laws and the mores of the whole community. These are what educate people, both as children and as adults. And so for Plato and Aristotle the great educators were, above all, the great lawgivers.[22]

Critical Intervention Services, by way of example, has a comprehensive program dedicated to issues of community and personal character known as Community and Character Based Protection Initiatives (CCBPI). CIS describes the systematic process of gaining control of a community and returning it back to its residents, using CCBPI, Figure 5.11.

CCBPI stresses the role of virtue in the reclamation of persons and the communities lived in. Security officers must exhibit the highest level of character, which includes integrity, honesty, and loyalty. Much of the community reorientation is based on an identical emphasis that relates to how character building saves communities. Ethical demands are substantial, as the security policy at Figure 5.12 makes clear. To be successful, the CCBIP program must run through three phases:

1. Reclamation of the environment;
2. Networking with children; and
3. Anchoring with parents, relatives, and others.

In the commentary that follows, the unique and essential qualities of community integration are discovered in three steps. First, the community will be reconquered and positively controlled only when worthy citizens reclaim its environment. Change comes about only because the citizenry, bolstered by the officers, exhibit the moral courage to thwart the offenders. Change comes from the communal whole—involving "community, family and the individual."[23]

Second, the youth of the environment must be made part of the enterprise. In the young, one sees both the present and the future of any community. When the young are on board, the community protection officer has his or her greatest ally. Effective community programs depend on the insights and loyalties of the youth in the community.

Finally, the parents and significant relatives, by and through the children, serve as the last anchor in the bulwark of the strong community. In these three phases, the integration of programs, coupled with the integration and assimilation of people—the residents, both young and old, eventually become stakeholders. Too often in high-crime neighborhoods, the public police appear as occupiers on the soil of a foreign land. This approach cannot engender the types of loyalties necessary for success in community building, whereas CBIP will do so.

A. Reclamation of the Community Environment

Reclamation targets the specific types of criminal activity and quality-of-life issues that allow the felony cycle to perpetuate. It is based on the premise that before any prevention effort can be successful, a coordinated and planned

Critical Intervention Services (CIS) specializes in proactive protective services for communities in need. Since 1992, CIS has earned a worldwide reputation for our effectiveness in dramatically reducing crime and nuisance problems in residential communities.

Local, national, and internatonal televison networks and news publications have produced stories on CIS because our Community & Character Based Protection Initiative (CCBPI) is not only effective, but unique.

CCBPI is based on the phiolosophy that by building relationships with residents, we can establish trust, confidence, and organization in the community. As history has proven, criminals rely on disorganization and fear in order to victimize the community. By restoring order and unity, we deny criminals of the conditions they need to operate successfully.

Please realize that the full result of CCBPI does not appear overnight. We realize that it takes time to earn your trust and full support. We also know that the rewards are well worth the wait. Every officer is committed to doing whatever it takes to make this process enjoyable for both themselves and the community they serve.

Getting to Know You

It is very important that CIS officers get to know each resident living on the property. This enables us to determine who belongs on the property and, more imporantly, who does not. If you are new to the neighborhood, you may have noticed how quickly our officer introduced himself after your

move in. It is our policy to get to know every new resident as soon as possible after they have settled into the neighborhood.

We encourage you to ask our officers any questions you might have about security and safety in the community. Feel free to share your concerns or observations with us. As a member of the community, your input and assistance is invaluable to us.

The relationships we build with you and all of the residents of the community enable us to quickly identify and de-escalate problem situations, such as domestic disputes and disorderly parties, before they turn into serious problems. In many CIS-protected communities, the bond of trust is so strong that residents actively serve as our "eyes and ears"...reporting any suspicious activities they witness.

CIS Officers and the Kids

CIS officers probably interact with children more than any other member of the community. You may see us playing ball with kids, giving them stickers or treats, and just spending time talking and getting to know them.

We believe that children are the future of our community. As part of our long term strategy, our officers work hard to establish trust and rapport among the children. Once trust is established, our officers have a lasting impact and help kids to make positive choices about their lives.

Our Committment to the Community

When a CIS officer agrees to uphold the principles of CCBPI, he or she is making a commitment to help the community in any way that they can. However, despite their tremendous effort and best intentions, CIS officers cannot ensure safety and security without your support. Long term success in crime prevention and public safety requires a partnership with the community. Only by working together can we build a community that everyone can be proud to call home.

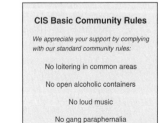

CIS Basic Community Rules

We appreciate your support by complying with our standard community rules:

No loitering in common areas

No open alcoholic containers

No loud music

No gang paraphernalia

FIGURE 5.11 Community and Character Based Protection Initiative

Useful Resources

Hillsborough County

Bay Area Legal Services	232-1343
Children's Services	264-3821
Domestic Violence Program	272-6423
Health Department	272-6200
Metropolitian Ministries	229-1578
Sheriff's Office, Non-Emergency	247-8000
Social Services	272-5040
Victim's Assistance	272-6472

Pinellas County

Legal Aid Service	443-0657
Children's Services	469-5700
Domestic Violence Program	464-3267
Health Department	469-5800
Sheriff's Office, Non-Emergency	582-6200
Social Services	464-8400
St. Vincent de Paul	441-3790
Victim's Assistance	464-6090

SafeTampaBay.Com
www.safetampabay.com

For advice on issues including crime prevention, personal safety, family disaster planning, and response to terrorist incidents, visit our special public safety education web site for the Tampa Bay community: http://www.safetampabay.com.

In addition to general crime and terrorism,other issues addressed on SafeTampaBay.Com include:

- Domestic Violence
- Stalking Prevention/Intervention
- Gang Prevention and Response
- Victim's Support
- More!

Remember...
If you have a true emergency,
call 911 immediately!

To report suspicious non-emergency activity, call the CIS dispatch line during the hours that CIS services your community.

CIS Dispatch Lines
Hillsborough...(813) 221-1911
Pinellas...(727) 444-4465

Critical Intervention Services, Inc.
1261 South Missouri Ave., Clearwater, FL 33756
Tel. (727) 461-9417 • Fax (727) 449-1269
www.cisworldservices.org
www.safetampabay.com

FL Lic. B9200107

CCBPI

Our Commitment
to Your Community

Critical Intervention Services, Inc.

FIGURE 5.11   *(Cont.)*

intervention must take place. This phase directs its efforts specifically at disrupting highly visible criminal activity by using symmetry targeted oriented patrolling combined with other specialized techniques. Symmetry Targeted Oriented Patrolling focuses on the precise environment precipitating crime. The objective for this type of patrolling is to bring symmetry (organization) back to the environment by targeting nuisance, quality-of-life issues, visible criminal activity, vice, and inappropriate conduct. Officers assigned to Symmetry Targeted Oriented Patrolling are referred to as STOP team officers. These officers receive specialized training in the dynamics of violence, community relations, the criminal activity matrix, psychological operations, implementation of shock techniques, and a host of other issues to enhance effectiveness.

The deployment of STOP team officers during reclamation usually starts with a strong focus on specific areas of criminal activity that require immediate intervention. See the photo in Figure 5.13. This method is necessary to gain effective control over nuisance problems and subsequent community participation. Therefore, the main focus in high-crime intervention areas must be directed at criminal activity by order of priority, as determined by threat analysis and assessment.

Criminal activity that involves organized gangs, for example, would take precedence over unorganized drug sales that occur in the open. Next, open drug sales would take precedence over prostitution, and so on. Once these types of highly visible activities are removed, the focus and attention of officers can shift to the real underlying elements that enable a community to decline and deteriorate into a

---

- Restricted -	Critical Intervention Services	- Restricted -
Title: Policy on Officer Conduct		**Uniformed Division Order Series:** 320.00
Intent: To establish guidelines on protocol and conduct.		
Effective Date: January 12, 1997		**Page:** 1 of 3

Critical Intervention Services Code of Ethics	**Uniformed Division Order #320.000A**

"As a Protection Officer, my fundamental duty is to serve mankind; to safeguard lives and property; to protect the weak against oppression or intimidation; the peaceful against violence and disorder; and to respect the constitutional rights of all citizens to liberty, equality, and justice."

"I will keep my private life unsullied as an example to all; maintain courageous calm in the face of danger, scorn or ridicule; develop self restraint; and be constantly mindful of the welfare of others. Honest in thought and deed in both my personal and official life, I will be exemplary in obeying the laws of the land and the regulations of this agency. Whatever I see or hear of a confidential nature, or anything that is confided to me in my official capacity, will be kept ever secret unless revelation is necessary in the performance of my duty."

"I will never act officiously or permit personal feelings, prejudices, animosities, or friendship to influence my decisions. I will protect persons and property appropriately without fear or favor, malice, or ill will, never employing unnecessary force or violence, and never accepting gratuities."

"I recognize the badge of my office as a symbol of public faith, and I accept it as a public trust to be held, so long as I am true to the ethics of Critical Intervention Services. I will strive to achieve these objectives and ideals, dedicating myself to my chosen profession."

Standards of Conduct	**Uniformed Division Order #320.001**

The orderly and efficient operation of CIS requires that all employees maintain discipline and proper personal standards of conduct at all times. CIS has the right to determine the appropriate measure of discipline for its employees, up to and including dismissal. The following is a list of examples of conduct for which the agency may take disciplinary action, including termination, against an employee. This list is representative and is not exclusive.

1. Use of illegal drugs or controlled substances, or possession of same, on or off duty.
2. Sale, trade, or delivery of illegal drugs or controlled substances by an employee to another person is cause for termination and a referral to the law enforcement authorities.
3. Interfering with, obstructing, or otherwise hindering the production or work performance of another employee.
4. Originating or spreading false or disparaging statements concerning employees of CIS or its clients.
5. Leaving a job site without permission, loitering, or sleeping during duty hours.
6. Careless or inefficient performances of duties, including failure to maintain standards of professionalism.
7. Refusal to accept or follow lawful orders or lawful directions from any supervisor of this agency or from any law enforcement agency, or any other form of insubordination.
8. Repeated tardiness or absence, or failure to report to work without a satisfactory reason.
9. Misrepresentation or omission of facts in obtaining employment.
10. False statements to anyone in a position of authority.
11. Falsifying one's own time sheet or that of another employee.
12. Defacing, damaging, or destroying the property of this agency, a client's, or that of another employee.
13. Fighting or causing bodily injury to another person, or engaging in any form of disorderly conduct, on or off duty.
14. Reporting to work or working under the influence of intoxicants or unauthorized drugs or narcotics, or bringing or using such unauthorized drugs or narcotics on agency or client property.
15. Theft, pilferage, or unauthorized removal of property of the agency, client, or that of another employee.

FIGURE 5.12 Professional Expectations for the Community Protection Officer

16.   Bringing, possessing, or using unauthorized weapons, ammunition, or firearms on agency property, client property, in agency owned vehicles, or in privately owned vehicles.
17.   Any violation of agency policies, procedures, and regulations.
18.   Breach of CIS equal employment policy regarding nondiscrimination, including but not limited to derogatory name calling, labels, or actions directed toward any employee, applicant, or any other that one may come in contact with, because of race, color, religion, sex, or national origin.
19.   Consumption of alcoholic beverages (beer, wine, whiskey, etc.) on agency property, client property, in agency or privately owned vehicles while performing duties for this agency, whether paid or not, unless specifically authorized for special events or occasions.
20.   Sexual harassment, including but not limited to: unwelcome sexual advances, request for sexual favors, slurs, jokes, and other verbal or physical conduct of a sexual nature. This conduct cannot and will not be tolerated, and is subject to disciplinary action up to and including termination.
21.   Smoking inside an agency vehicle or in any non-smoking facility of a client or of this agency.
22.   Conduct that is punishable as a felony under state or federal law.
23.   Any conduct that could jeopardize the license or coverage of this agency.
24.   Obscenity of any kind.

CIS utilizes a progressive disciplinary system. The sequence of disciplinary actions is from a verbal counseling, to a written disciplinary notice, to a suspension, to termination. However, CIS reserves the right to immediately terminate any employee without affording the progressive disciplinary system where, in the agency's sole discretion, the conduct of the employee warrants immediate termination. Due to the nature of the security work with this agency, all employees are expected to conduct themselves professionally both on and off duty.

| **Conduct While in Uniform** | **Uniformed Division Order #320.002** |

An officer's conduct while in uniform reflects not only upon themselves, but also upon their immediate supervisor, the chain of command, the division chief, CIS, and the client. Conduct must display pride, professionalism, confidence, and a respectful attitude to those with whom the officer interacts. This pertains to uniform as well as plain-clothes details. .An officer's attitude directly reflects the image of CIS. Officers should display a positive attitude towards clients, civilians, and to fellow officers. Information relayed to clients is to be on a professional level only. Personal relations or feelings should not become part of a professional working relationship. If an employee is wearing his agency issued identification visibly, he will then be considered to be "on-duty" for the purpose of these guidelines, even though said employee may not have been authorized to be on duty and, as such, would not be compensated for this time.

| **Personal Telephone Calls** | **Uniformed Division Order #320.003** |

Initiating personal telephone calls while on duty is prohibited. Returning calls (such as when you are paged by someone else) will be kept to a minimum, short, and to the point. This policy includes personal as well as official telephone calls. When possible, calls will be made from a secure location that is out of view of the public. An officer "lingering" on a public or cellular telephone is not the image that CIS wants to project.

| **Officer/Resident Relationship** | **Uniformed Division Order #320.004** |

All officers of CIS are assigned to their client sites for the purpose of providing safety and security to the client, client employees, and the client property to which they are assigned. CIS has a policy in place on Community and Character Based Protection. This means that the officer should use every available resource to develop good will with residents of the property, including getting to know residents on a first name basis and taking the time to get to know who belongs on the property and who does not. This provides the officer a good understanding of the area. All interactions will be on a professional level, utilizing the utmost courtesy. Any time that the officer has to inquire as to an individual's residency on the property or their reason for being in a particular area, it will be on a professional level. If an individual is found to be a non-resident and cannot adequately explain their presence, the officer will call for a law enforcement officer to issue an immediate trespass. If law enforcement cannot respond, Florida State Statute 776.031 allows security officers to have the option of physically removing the individual from the property. If it appears the situation cannot be handled in a peaceful manner, the officer will contact OPS or the DCO, and the dispatcher will notify the appropriate law enforcement agency to issue the individual a trespass warning.

FIGURE 5.12   *(Cont.)*

FIGURE 5.13   Stop Team Deployment—Proactive Intervention

high-crime area. Some of the nuisance problems addressed by utilizing Symmetry Targeted Oriented Patrolling are activities such as open alcohol consumption, loud music, loitering, abandoned cars, juvenile mischief, and trespassing.

Barriers, whether actual or symbolic, alter the environment as well. Individuals who prey on residents within the intervention area should be confronted with trespass warnings and the subsequent enforcement of those warnings when a violation occurs. See the trespass warning in Figure 5.14. Trespass warnings assist officers in identifying and tracking the criminal element operating within the intervention area as well as the surrounding neighborhood. Of more importance, they enable the arrest of criminals for trespass upon return to the intervention area. Furthermore, reclamation strategy establishes close relationships with law enforcement agencies by shared information and cooperative undertakings. Setting up joint task forces and other mutual operations helps the community to reclaim the environment and facilitates the arrest of countless perpetrators.

Reclamation should be approached flexibly, in order to adapt to the situation as the criminal element changes its modus operandi. The area should be analyzed by crime mapping or through GIS, geographic information systems. See Figure 5.15 for an example.[24] In this phase, officers intensely focus on the street level criminals who work within the targeted intervention area. Knowing that visible crime and the fear it generates has a devastating impact on the community, STOP team officers are given complete freedom to perform their duties and are encouraged to use ingenuity in the removal of community fear.

FIGURE 5.14   Trespass Warnings

During the reclamation phase, especially in a high-crime environment, it is important that officers deploy early so that the community is aware of their presence well before sundown. The reasoning follows that it is not the officers' priority to make arrests and initiate confrontation by surprising the criminal element "in the net." Instead, the message sent out is that with security deployed, criminal acts are unlikely to transpire and will not be tolerated. Confrontation will be minimal but aggressively employed.

Reclamation invites citizen participation and insists on positive and continuous interaction with all facets of community life. Being attentive to the cares, concerns, and questions of residents is paramount in the reclamation process.[25] During this contact, officers ascertain the status of the individual encountered, whether resident, guest, relative, or intruder. If the person is not the guest of a resident and cannot prove a legitimate reason for being in the intervention area, the subject is issued a trespass warning and removed from the location. As an additional tool for tracking people who do not belong in the intervention area, a *field interview report,* similar to that in Figure 5.16, is generated. The report tracks and profiles the troublesome categories of individuals who negatively impact the community. As the intruders are removed, the community begins the slow but sure process of shedding its fear. The visible removal of the "unknown" encourages community members to become involved.

Some security firms contract with the community in an effort to memorialize the parties' intentions in the reclamation effort. The contract lays out specific bound-

Parcel map with buildings.

FIGURE 5.15 Targeted Block in Community Reclamation

aries of acceptable and unacceptable conduct. Critical Intervention Services delivers to residents the *Proactive Resident Contact Policy.* See Figure 5.17.

Planning, intelligence generated by community profiles, and threat assessments are essential initial steps to reclamation. This process includes a study of different environmental factors, such as social, economic, and environmental characteristics and the nature of criminal activity in the area. Furthermore, certain security firms have developed a number of resources specifically directed to high-threat environments. One example of this is the CIS *criminal intelligence system* (CIMATRIX). Criminals in general are not limited in their operations to one

CRITICAL INTERVENTION SERVICES

C.I.S. EVENT #		
POLICE REPORT #		
C.I.S. REPORT #		

F.I.R.
FIELD INTERVIEW REPORT

PAGE   OF

LOCATION OF INCIDENT SCENE:			REPORT DATE:		TIME:
NAME:			RACE:	SEX:	AGE:	DOB:

LOCATION OF INCIDENT SCENE:	REPORT DATE:	TIME:
NAME:	RACE: / SEX: / AGE: / DOB:	
RESIDENCE:	RES. PHONE:	
BUSINESS / SCHOOL	BUS. PHONE:	
ALIAS / AKA MAIDEN NAME / NICKNAME: BUSINESS / SCHOOL	OCCUPATION:	
SOCIAL SECURITY NUMBER:	DL NUMBER:	STATE:
CITY, COUNTY, STATE OF BIRTH:	NATIONALITY:	
HEIGHT: / WEIGHT: / HAIR COLOR: / EYE COLOR: / GLASSES: / TYPE:		
BUILD:	DISGUISE:	
COMPLEXION: / HAND USED: / HAIR LENGTH: / HAIR STYLE: / TEETH:		
CLOTHING:	FACIAL HAIR:	
SCARS / TATOOS (exact location & description)	ASSOCIATION / IN COMPANY OF:	
WEAPON TYPE	DIRECTION AND MODE OF TRAVEL:	

VEHICLE INFORMATION

YEAR:	MAKE:	MODEL:	STYLE:	COLOR TOP/BOTTOM:
VIN:			LICENSE:	STATE:
OTHER:				

COMMENTS

_____
_____
_____
_____
_____
_____
_____

SEND COPY TO:	☐ PROPERTY MANAGEMENT
	☐ SHERIFF'S OFFICE (Circle One) Street patrol Street Crimes Gang Suppression
	☐ C.I.S. OFFICE
	☐ ALL ASSIGNED OFFICERS
	☐ DO NOT DUPLICATE, KEEP CONFIDENTIAL

I CERTIFY THAT THE INFORMATION CONTAINED IN THIS REPORT IS ACCURATE TO THE BEST OF MY KNOWLEDGE:

OFFICER SIGNATURE _____

SUPERVISOR SIGNATURE _____

FIGURE 5.16   Field Report

Resident Contact Policy

As part of our continuing effort to expand on our Community Based Protection Initiative, Critical Intervention Services has established a new policy for all employees to adhere to as part of their prime directive of responsibilities within the areas they patrol. This new policy revolves around creating a proactive positive encounter with residents prior to CIS officers having to enforce community rules and statutory laws.

The concept is a simple one. As of September 01, 2000, CIS officers are required to contact new residents within their properties or patrol sectors once a new resident has moved in and has established residency. Officers are to make every attempt to "welcome" residents to the community and advise them of what CIS' responsibility is as well as some of the basic rules that CIS enforces. Part of the resident contact will involve the CIS officer providing a pamphlet to the resident with the written documentation that gives an overview of CIS as well as some of the information already identified.

This approach is based on the premise that creating a positive interaction first will ultimately enable the officer to get to know residents better as well as gain a foundation of building trust and a positive relationship with that resident. In the event that the resident does violate rules or has problems in the future, it is hoped that the policy will assist CIS officers to deal with that resident in a more proactive non-confrontational basis.

The guideline for officers to utilize is as follows:

- Upon contact with residents, inform them that the purpose of your visit is to give them information on CIS and the community.
- Proceed to welcome them to the community and advise them the CIS officers are here to assist them in any way possible.
- Reassure the residents that they are not in any trouble as many residents may be apprehensive of uniforms upon preliminary contact.
- Advise the residents that the reason for this contact is an effort to get to know new residents in an effort to make them aware of our presence as well as assist them in getting them involved in any type of community awareness program that the CIS officer may be involved with within a particular environment.
- Advise the residents that they can contact CIS officers in a non-emergency to discuss problems, resolve issues, or address concerns by contacting our Communication Center.
- The officer should show the residents on the back of the pamphlet the numbers to contact for Hillsborough and for Pinellas, if it applies.
- Officers should advise residents to feel free to call anytime they may be of help to them.

During the interaction, it is extremely important that officers be professional in their demeanor and polite in the conversations. This encounter will set the first stage for the relationship that CIS personnel will develop with that resident on a long-term basis. Therefore, it is critical that attention to detail be present. Ultimately, it is your responsibility as a professional to conduct

FIGURE 5.17 Proactive Resident Contact Policy

yourself in this manner. Officers should not present themselves or sound like a door-to-door salesman or politician trying to get a vote as those types of approaches do not usually work. A professional demeanor that clearly explains our intent and willingness to aid in any way we can is what we need CIS officers to do. Ultimately, the message is that CIS officers care about the community they are assigned to and the residents who reside within it.

Documentation of Contact

Prior to making any new contact with new residents, CIS officers should contact the Duty Communications Officer and advise that they are about to make contact and at what location or address the resident is at. The Duty Communications Officer should log the time, date, and the resident's name and address at the time they are notified by the community officer. Upon completing the contact, officers should re-contact D.C.O. and advise them that the contact has been completed and give them a summary of the contact whether it was positive or negative with whatever concerns the residents may have brought up and D.C.O. should document the information.

Officers should also document the interaction with the resident on the Area Intelligence Form that is turned into property management for their information purposes. Any concerns whether on behalf of the resident or on behalf of the officer about the resident, should be documented on an Intelligence Form for future use in the event a problem arises with that resident.

FIGURE 5.17 *(Cont.)*

particular community. Usually, street criminals conduct their activities in multiple neighborhoods around a particular area.

Once the criminal players are fully understood, the reclamation project can commence. But reclamation goes even further by carefully considering types of crimes that the community is burdened with and the criminals who reside there. No chance of success exists without full integration into the life of the community. William Walsh and Edwin Donovan's insightful analysis is right on point:

CIS Proactive Resident Contact Policy

Throughout the handout period when CIS is new to the community (reclamation phase), officers stop everyone and make personal introductions. During the exchange, officers hand out a brochure that provides the resident with information about CIS, their commitment to the community, and relevant contact numbers for CIS and for public government services. The contact policy outlines the rules and expectations of conduct for community purposes. New neighbors to the community receive similar information by personal visitation. Not only does this approach serve as a friendly welcome to the community, but also it allows the relationship to begin in a positive light. In this environment, reclamation can take place, since the officers operate from a mutual relationship of commitment, trust, and support. The secondary gain is that new community members know from the outset that crime will not be tolerated.

The CIS Intelligence Database

In order to develop a better picture of criminal activity, CIS developed an integrated system for reporting and recording criminal movements between locations. Today, this system has evolved into a criminal intelligence database cataloging thousands of habitual criminals and suspicious individuals operating in or around CIS communities. Intelligence forms and reports are cataloged. See Figure 5.18.

The criminal intelligence database records the subject's name and contact information, appearance (including photograph if available), automobile and license plate numbers, previous arrest record, trespass warnings, known associates, gang affiliations, and spot reports summarizing suspicious activity. The utility of the information is undeniable. Officers stopping an individual can easily access the database by contact with the operations center. See Figure 5.19.

Special "watch bulletins" can be issued to officers at multiple locations when a subject has been observed committing a crime or is wanted by the local police. In fact, law enforcement agencies have benefited on numerous occasions from the database. As an example, two suspects involved in a shootout with a sheriff's deputy in January 2000 were identified and apprehended partially because of information in the CIS intelligence database. In this case, a sheriff's deputy tried to stop three individuals in a stolen car located in a CIS-protected intervention area. The suspects fired on the officer, turning the routine stop into a firefight. The deputy fatally shot one suspect, and the other two escaped on foot. The suspect was quickly identified as a man cataloged in the CIS database. His query pulled up a listing of five known associates reported by CIS officers over the previous two years. This information was then forwarded to the sheriff's office, in part leading to the arrest of the two escaped suspects.

Incident reports laying out full-blown criminal activity, as well as any type of community contact, be it handing out stickers, talking to a resident, or playing ball with children, are cataloged in the database. See Figure 5.20 for a typical format of an incident report.

CIS created a redundant system that interlinked radio communications, intelligence data basing, statewide paging, and a global positioning satellite system. Having an established "free air" communications network also facilitates the dispatching of suspicious or incident calls to the officer from the operations center. This arrangement allows the officers to exchange information about problematic properties and individuals in a multitude of ways. It also enables the officer to foresee problems and benefit from the assistance and input of other officers when trying to deal with specific problems in the field. See Figure 5.21.

In the event that radios would shut down because of equipment failure, CIS established a backup system for communicating with officers in the field and for dispatching necessary information. This system utilizes digital pagers that are on different cellular towers from those of the main radio system. The pagers are alphanumeric, capable of sending out typed messages from the operations center. Supervisor pagers have a two-way (send and receive) capability in order to respond to incoming information and to give instructions to personnel.

The CIS Intelligence Database (cont.)

INTELLIGENCE FORM

THE FOLLOWING INFORMATION IS TO BE PASSED ON TO FELLOW OFFICERS CONCERNING
INTELLIGENCE GATHERED ON SITES, RESIDENTS AND FOR OFFICER SAFETY.

THIS INTELLIGENCE IS ALSO TO BE PASSED ON TO THE CLIENT.

DATE: 06-23-96   STATION#: 4

OFFICER(S) Bill Smith

GENERAL INTELLIGENCE:
Activity levels are low throughout Area 4, however traffic is
up in next complex. Two vehicles did come in to this area and
then left property after writter began to approach. (see below)

PROBLEM SPOTS OR UNITS: ☐ N/A
South area wall, found beer bottles and empty food wrappers
this could be from party on next property or resident/children
will monitor area.

SUSPECTED DRUG ACTIVITY: ☒ N/A

GANG ACTIVITY OR GRAFFITI: ☐ N/A
Maintaince reported Graffiti in laundry room (A), picture
taken by patrol unit and maintance to paint over tonight.

SUSPICIOUS OR PROBLEM VEHICLES: ☐ N/A

MAKE: Nissan 90s MODEL: Altima(GRN)   TAG# 4V1-02H   APT#na
MAKE: Chevy 80s MODEL: M.Carlo (BLU) TAG# Temp-Tag   APT#na
MAKE:_____ MODEL:_____ TAG# _____ APT#_____
MAKE:_____ MODEL:_____ TAG# _____ APT#_____

USE SUPPLEMENT FORM IF MORE SPACE IS NEEDED

SIGNATURE, *Sgt. B Smith*

FIGURE 5.18 Critical Intervention Services

The CIS Intelligence Database (cont.)

FIGURE 5.19   Gathering Intelligence in the Operations Center

To supplement this secondary system, CIS utilizes a system of laptop computers equipped with cellular digital packet data (GPRS) modems mounted on its patrol vehicles, as shown in Figure 5.22. This system allows the operation center to again use a separate communications link to send typed messages through the Internet to its patrol cars out in the community. In addition, a global positioning satellite system (GPS) is connected with a GPRS modem to the operations computers. This arrangement increases the communication between the operations center and the field units by constantly sending signals to the main operations computer center with the exact location and speed of the CIS vehicles deployed in the community. By utilizing GPS technology, CIS commanders can also review patrol techniques used by its officers by evaluating the information received and recorded by the operations computer systems. A supervisor can review officers' patrol techniques by looking at a computer screen that displays a map, the patrol car, and its routes. By merging the GPS technology and the GPRS modem together with Internet capabilities, a supervisor can also monitor other patrol cars that are on duty and under his or her supervision. See Figure 5.23.

The CIS Intelligence Database (cont.)

CRITICAL INTERVENTION SERVICES

C.I.S. REPORT		C.I.S. EVENT #
10422	**CONFIDENTIAL INCIDENT REPORT**	

DATE:	OFFICER:		POLICE REPORT #
AREA	SHIFT:	PAGE OF TIME:	AGENCY

WRITER: PRIMARY OFFICER ☐   SECONDARY OFFICER ☐   SHIFT SUPERVISOR ☐   WATCH COMMANDER ☐   CIVILIAN STATEMENT ☐

SUPPLEMENT: USE OF FORCE FORM ☐   SEE SUPPLEMENT ☐   SEE SUPERVISOR REPORT ☐   SEE POLICE REPORT ☐

ROUTING: CHAIN OF COMMAND ☐   INTERNAL AFFAIRS ☐   INTELLIGENCE DIVISION ☐   CRIME PREVENTION UNIT ☐

REPORT TYPE: CRIMINAL ☐   CIVIL ☐   FIRE ☐   WARRANT ☐   SAFETY ☐   ACCIDENT ☐

BOLO ☐   JUVENILE ☐   INFORMATION ☐   MEMO/INTERNAL ☐   MEMO/CLIENT ☐

INCIDENT REPORT NARRATIVE

USE SUPPLEMENT FORM IF MORE SPACE IS NEEDED

I CERTIFY THAT THE INFORMATION CONTAINED IN THIS REPORT IS ACCURATE TO THE BEST OF MY KNOWLEDGE:

OFFICER SIGNATURE_____

SUPERVISOR SIGNATURE_____

FIGURE 5.20

The CIS Intelligence Database (cont.)

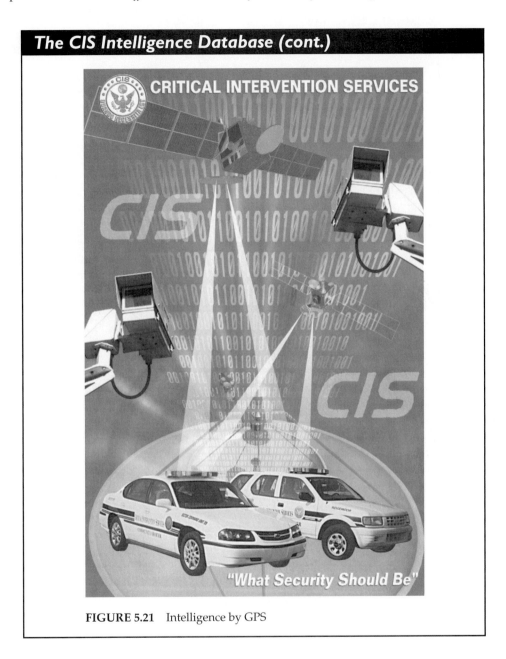

FIGURE 5.21 Intelligence by GPS

The private security officers provide the residents with a level of personal service that is difficult, if not impossible, for public police officers to achieve. This style of policing has helped to integrate the security department and the community. The security officers are not outsiders; they are considered an important part of the community who both serve and protect it.[26]

The CIS Intelligence Database (cont.)

FIGURE 5.22 Intelligence Gathering by Laptop

These interrelationships are manifest in the matrix shown in Figure 5.27.

The criminal relationship matrix displays overlapping rings representing the three different components of the relationship (community, criminal, public safety). The area where these rings overlap represents the specific relationship between the elements and their effect on each other. STOP teams succeed by adapting tactics to interrupt the criminal relationship by targeting these points of intersection or interaction.

As demonstrated in the example, by utilizing a systematic approach, STOP officers are able to insert barriers throughout the matrix and successfully disrupt the relationships between the community, the buyer, and the dealer. This approach to tailoring STOP activities to specific criminal problems is universal, applying to gangs, prostitution, and related criminality. Activities must be dealt with as a priority, before working on the community's quality-of-life issues.

In addition to the actual perpetration of crimes, reclamation also concentrates on the problems created by residents that contribute to the felony cycle. When a

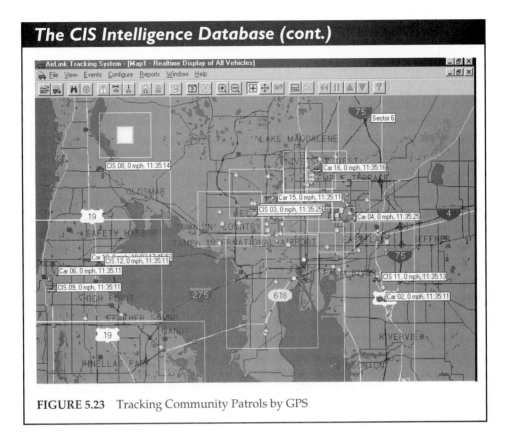

The CIS Intelligence Database (cont.)

FIGURE 5.23 Tracking Community Patrols by GPS

problematic individual resides within the targeted intervention area, officers aggressively employ legal remedies such as evictions or arrest. To accomplish this goal, a novel approach by which private security officers could be classified as a fiduciary or other legal agency relationship for the management companies or other entity that hired them in the first instance. Public police lack this option entirely. Residents in housing complexes can evict by a party designated by the owner/landlord. As standard business practice, some security firms include clauses within service contracts that designate its officers as management representatives and that in turn give officers the ability to issue eviction notices. Some agencies actually have officers who are cross-trained as paralegals to help expedite the process. The role of agent and fiduciary is uniquely suited to private sector justice. With this tool, the environment can be reclaimed in ways unimagined by public policing. Once tenants know the power of this delegation, the cooperation level rises. See a standard violation notice in Figure 5.30.

In the end, reclamation works when residents, the environment, and the criminal absorb change. Once change appears, the private sector specialists can move in even closer to the constituency served.

The CIS Intelligence Database (cont.)

Merging the GPS system, GPRS modem technology and Internet capabilities together also allow for other types of communications to take place. For example, CIS has established a system for filing reports using the Internet. An access-controlled website allows officers to file their intelligence reports or incident reports as needed. Once officers file their reports through the Internet, the dissemination of that report is automatic. Upon clicking the submission button, a copy of the report is sent to both the operation center and the client or representative of the location that the officer is assigned to. A copy of that report is then automatically entered into a master database that contains all of CIS's report files. Through the use of the patrol computers, GPS, and GPRS modems, the patrol officer in the vehicle is able to access the Internet, file his or her report, and transmit the report directly from the car. The report is then either e-mailed or faxed out to the appropriate parties without the officer's ever having to leave the vehicle or patrol area. This arrangement also gives the officers access to the database by utilizing a firewall-protected Intranet. Thus, when a CIS officer wants to track down information on a specific area or a specific person, he or she is able to access any reports in the database and get instant information. These types of communication systems combined together give the officer very strong resources when dealing with situations. Figure 5.24 includes sample datasets for examination.

The GPRS technology also allows CIS officers to monitor cameras that are mounted on client properties through their laptops in the vehicle and through the operations center, by utilizing digital video recorders that transmit streaming video over the Internet. This technique enables officers to assess the environment prior to entering it and gives the officers immediate information as to where the activity is occurring, subsequently allowing the officers to direct their activities to those areas needing immediate attention. By utilizing the techniques discussed, CIS has been able to drop violent and drug-related crime by increasing prevention efforts, citizen contact, and a protective presence in the community.

Critical Intervention Services One Year Snapshot
From 01/01/2003 Thru 12/31/2003 All Pertinent Incidents

"Quando Necessita Est"

Type Of Incident	Total Incidents	Type Of Incident	Total Incidents
Alarm	732	Other	1,956
Area Intelligence	32,809	Prevention Activity	68,840
Local Law Enforcement on Property	938	Property Damage	749
Community Contact	56,275	Quality of Life	26,630
Community Dispute	1,044	Subject Check	15,663
Company Specific	4,173	Susp Vehicle/Person	3,983
Death	13	Terrorist Information	2
Dispatch Call	8,056	Theft	794
Drug Activity	856	Vehicle Crash	175
Medical Emergency	403	Violation Notice	457
Environmental	399	Violent Acts	588
Foot Pursuit	106	Warrant	113
Gang Activity	27		
Illegal Entry	296	Total Events	255,990
Informational	7,066		
Juvenile Delinquency	1,451	Total Trespass's Issued	1,078
Meet With Management	1,255	Total Arrests	630
Nuissance Complaint	15,428	Assist Local Law Enforcement	571

These figures were generated by approximately 80 field officers over a population base of near 80,000 people
The total number of incidents reflects an acurate total of individual incidents we responded to
Incident type totals may vary because some incidents fell into more than one category

FIGURE 5.24   Annual Data Compilation

CBIP Application in the Drug Environment: A Case Study

Open drug sales make plain the criminal's superior position in the community. Aggressive enforcement has occurred from every quarter over the last three decades. See Figure 5.25.

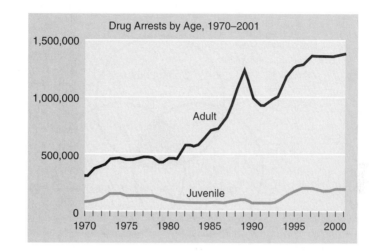

FIGURE 5.25   Data Analysis: Drugs
Source: BJS, Drug Arrests by age, 1970–2000, at http://www.ojp.usdoj
.gov/bjs/glance/drug.htm, 9/3/02.

How to rid the community of this horrid infection can be discerned in the magic of the matrix. Four elements in the drug trade relationship comprise the matrix: *the community, the buyer, the narcotics dealer, and the public safety professionals.* An effective intervention strategy focuses on all four elements of this matrix, shown at Figures 5.26 through 5.29.

In order for open narcotics sale to take place, the community must remain in a state of fear. The degree of the community's fear is directly correlated to a lack of community resolve. In large part, the criminal through the real or perceived possibility of retaliation generates this fear. When fear grips the community, people become isolated. Community members will avoid confrontation and interaction with the drug dealer whenever possible, but may, when confronted, give refuge to a fleeing criminal or refuse to report the criminal to the police—simply out of fear. Often the community becomes both the victims and the protectors of the criminal at the same time. In this sense, the community becomes an unwitting participant in the drug trade.

CBIP Application in the Drug Environment: A Case Study (cont.)

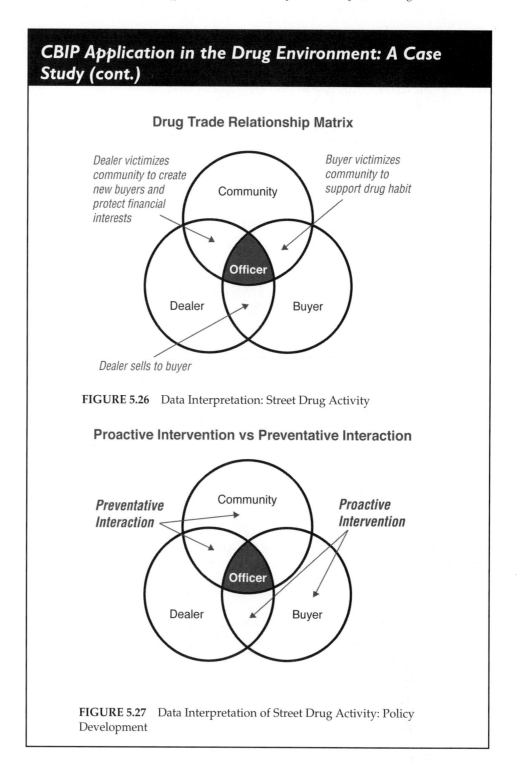

Drug Trade Relationship Matrix

Dealer victimizes community to create new buyers and protect financial interests

Buyer victimizes community to support drug habit

Community

Officer

Dealer

Buyer

Dealer sells to buyer

FIGURE 5.26 Data Interpretation: Street Drug Activity

Proactive Intervention vs Preventative Interaction

Preventative Interaction

Proactive Intervention

Community

Officer

Dealer

Buyer

FIGURE 5.27 Data Interpretation of Street Drug Activity: Policy Development

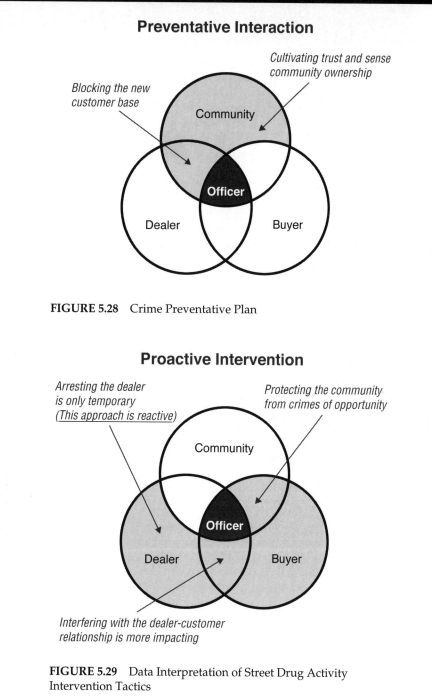

Preventative Interaction

Cultivating trust and sense community ownership

Blocking the new customer base

Community

Officer

Dealer

Buyer

FIGURE 5.28   Crime Preventative Plan

Proactive Intervention

Arresting the dealer is only temporary (*This approach is reactive*)

Protecting the community from crimes of opportunity

Community

Officer

Dealer

Buyer

Interfering with the dealer-customer relationship is more impacting

FIGURE 5.29   Data Interpretation of Street Drug Activity Intervention Tactics

CBIP Application in the Drug Environment: A Case Study (cont.)

STOP team officers address the issue of community fear during the reclamation phase through *proactive intervention* and *preventative interaction* with community members. Proactive intervention involves many techniques that revolve around officers' creating interference, interdiction, harassment, and enforcement. Preventative interaction involves communication, trust building, commitment, and caring for community members.

The dealer is at the other end of the spectrum of the community. Unlike the resident, the dealer will be more than willing to get involved and fight for an obvious self-interest. Unlike the community, the dealer will actually confront, provoke, and even attack when profits are at risk. Curiously, the community becomes both protector and facilitator. The dealer also perceives the community as a customer base and will struggle to maintain accessibility to patrons. See Table 5.2.

In reclamation, STOP team officers intentionally focus on finding the accessibility points and erect barriers to those points (as illustrated in Table 5.2) by placing themselves in the center of the relationship matrix. To break this relationship, the STOP team places relentless pressure on the drug dealer by using a wide range of tactics. Although some of these tactics remain invisible to the public, many are very high-profile and will defrock the preferred and elevated status of the once invincible dealer. Control is reasserted by reclaiming once-conquered territory. Drug dealers do not control the community if the geography has been retaken.

As a result, the community's fear begins to subside, and the drug dealers loose their hold on the population. In essence, a wedge is driven between the community and the dealer by putting the pressure on the dealers (proactive intervention) while restoring courage and ownership to the community through communication (preventative interaction).

The relationship between dealer and buyer must also be analyzed and targeted with the same focus on interruption. A key element in this relationship is accessibility. STOP team officers must focus on disrupting accessibility by creating barriers that interfere with

TABLE 5.2   *The Drug Trade Relationship Matrix*

Agent	Reactive Approach	Proactive Intervention	Preventative Interaction
Buyer		Interferes with relationship with dealer	Indentify and refer for treatment
Community		Protects community from crimes of opportunity	Trust/sense of ownership is cultivated
Dealer	Arrests dealer	Interferes with relationship with customer	Blocks new customer base

CBIP Application in the Drug Environment: A Case Study (cont.)

the sale and purchase of narcotics. The weakest link in this relationship that can accomplish this goal is the buyer. The buyer generally does not instill fear in the community or fight to retain a source of financial profit. It is true that buyers often victimize communities in order to finance drug habits through crimes such as burglary, theft, and robbery. However, it is not the intent of the buyer to instill fear or to control the community; rather, the buyer's intent is to gain the resources needed to purchase narcotics. Generally, the buyer wants to stay as inconspicuous as possible. The buyer, for most purposes, is neutral to the environment in terms of fear and control. The primary goal of the buyer is the purchase of narcotics and, subsequently, the use of narcotics at a convenient and discreet location.

Buyers, then, can be the reclamation lynchpins. When the dealer does not intimidate easily or does not want to stop selling because the customer base is too good, STOP team officers shift focus from the dealer to the customer. The objective is not necessarily to conduct arrests. Rather, the buyer is pressured out of the relationship by intimidation. Officers, for example, may remain on a street corner for eight hours in plain sight equipped with a video recorder, recording drug dealers and their buyers. At the sight of the officers with video recorders, buyers quickly leave the area for fear of identification. Again, the tactic is based on the theory that the buyer is the weakest link in the relationship and therefore that focus must shift to the buyer to ensure success when other techniques are not completely successful. Considering the simple rules of economics, by focusing on the buyer and removing the demand, the dealer will have no other option but to relocate his or her drug sales. This same principle applies to any other businesses that are not capable of attracting customers. They must move, change the way they do business, or ultimately go out of business. Environments can and do change!

Another element of the relationship that exists with drug activity is the dealer's efforts to expand his or her new customer base. A main focus of drug dealers is converting community members into customers, that is, transitioning people from the community ring into the buyer ring. CIS officers attempt to implement barriers by utilizing proactive intervention techniques and preventative interaction with community members, specifically the children. When dealers want to create new customers, children of the area are the preferred targets. Nothing gets a community enraged more quickly than dealers' preying on children. Community support should be enlisted from family groups, churches and temples, nonprofits, and crime prevention groups. Breaking the cycle of sale and use ultimately depends on the strength and character of a community. If the power continuum is upset, then all things are possible.

B. Networking

Phase two, *networking*, continues targeting the undesirable elements in a community by enlisting the support of community constituencies, especially its youth. To network means to enlist, to befriend, and to make stakeholders out of those most

VIOLATION NOTICE

Event # ________________

Property Name ____

Tenant, Occupants, and/or Guests ________________________________

Apartment Address / Unit # ________________________________

City ________________________, Florida, Zip ________________

Property Owner / Property Management Company ________________________

☐ Seven (7) day notice of non-compliance with opportunity to cure. You are in violation of your lease and/or the rules of this property. If you continue to violate the lease and/or rules in any similar manner, at any time during the next 12 months it will result in the immediate termination of your lease and subsequent eviction.

Violation;

- ○ Loitering in stairwells/parking lots
- ○ Alcohol (open container)
- ○ Failure to maintain control of guests
- ○ Loud Music
- ○ Repeated loud noises
- ○ Excessive traffic to the apartment
- ○ Other ____

☐ Immediate Notice to Cease and Desist. The following violations are subject to immediate Termination of lease and subsequent Eviction.

Violation;

- ○ Any criminal activity or behavior that endangers public safety and/or property damage
- ○ Any drug activity
- ○ Vandalism
- ○ Failure to comply with protection officer in correcting a safety hazard
- ○ Other ____

Delivered to ____________________ Apt # __________ on ____/____/____

Posted at Apt# ____________________ on ____/____/____

Signature of Officer ____________________ Signature of Tenant ____________________

☐ Tenant / Occupant / Guest refused to sign

Reorder From NEBS CUSTOM printing service 1-800-888-6327 NEBS, Inc. Peterborough, NH 03458 www.nebs.com Ref. No: G 542700228

FIGURE 5.30 Violation Notice

affected by criminal behavior. Good people look for allies in any war on crime. Practitioners can enlist the community in ways unimaginable to public police. When working with youth, the effects of preventative interaction could not be more marked. The process starts with the children, since they are also the strongest link to the community. Children represent the "path of least resistance" and are not laden with misconceptions about uniforms, race, or trust, and they have yet to garner negative feelings about the police sector. Simply put, children are the most accessible point in the environment and, therefore, the starting point for developing relationships with the community.[27]

As part of this preventative interaction strategy, officers don a playful personality, using stickers, treats, curiosity, "show and tell" sessions with equipment, and engaging in sports activities. Uniformed officers willingly participate in all sorts of activities that are naturally enjoyable to children from the distributor of junior officer stickers and removable tattoos with the police agency designs, giving advice, helping with homework, or just generally "shooting the breeze." See Figure 5.31.

These same officers make continuous efforts to be visibly present in the child's housing complex where matters of safety and security are most acute. Visible presence, and lots of it, constitutes the essence of networking. Being in one's own turf, not in some artificial environment like a police club or an athletic organization sponsored by law enforcement, is what gives credibility and sincerity to the networking. The officers adjust their persona to that of the community member, not the other way around. Where community members are most comfortable is the seedbed for networking. The approach eventually fosters better relationships with protection officers who live in the same community as the residents, who see the officers every day as part of their neighborhood. Over time, a bond between child and officer is solidified, and trust emerges from this interaction. Positive relationships between the children and "uniformed authority figures," whether private or public, are assured. Here the officer integrates into the community rather than rests apart from it. Any activity that enhances the life of the community will enable it members.

The emphasis on child-officer interaction is accomplished in a wide array of programs. The dangers and responsibilities of weapons and gun safety can be illustrated through the McGruff program. Coloring books that educate children on what to do when they find a firearm and that show the dangers associated with firearms are handed out to neighborhood children. Officers utilize the pledge card that reinforces these safety principles. Christmas toy drives deliver to children who are in serious need gifts for the holidays and demonstrate a real and meaningful commitment to the other residents of the intervention area. Private sector officers prefer beat or bike patrols over the shielding and impersonal squad car. Bikes, in particular, are not only accessible to the public but also speak a child's language.

Another worthy innovation that effectively networks with the young is children identification programs. Critical Intervention Services labels its program "Care Port." Care Port is designed to physically identify children through photographs and fingerprints, and to document information such as full name, address, blood type, allergies, social security number, and so on. The actual card is given to the

FIGURE 5.31   Community Integration—Preventative Interaction

parent for safekeeping and for identification purposes in the event that the child is missing, lost, or kidnapped. As a supplemental safeguard in high-crime areas, utilize video documentation of the child and keep it in its custody for a period of five years, labeled and archived for later retrieval by parents. Other community-sponsored activities that directly impact the young and assure positive participation are drug and crime walks that make plain who owns the neighborhood; school visitations; and programs funded by and through the Federal *Weed and Seed Initiative*.

Officers also are accessible to children in ways similar to those of public police forces—allowing children to look at equipment, to test radios, to wear the hats or caps, and to enroll in cadet-type programs for junior officers. In networking, the officers enlist the young and forge the community-officer bond by a caring and concerned approach. The bond is based on mutual affection, trust, and loyalty toward the common purpose of a safe community. The benefits of strong alliances with children are extraordinary. By nature, children are honest and open, and they are not averse to sharing information and intelligence that ferret out the criminal element. Surprisingly, children know who the "bad people" are, what types of drug or juvenile nuisance activity are occurring in the intervention area, and where assistance is immediately needed. In many circumstances, children pinpoint exactly who the unknown or suspected criminal might be. Networking with children opens these doors—not to make them into informants or corrupted snitchs but into willing participants in the betterment of the community. Children often reveal information about situations occurring within in their own home, such as physical or sexual abuse, drug use, and accessibility of firearms.

C. Anchoring

Networking leads to the final phase in community integration and formation—*anchoring*. To anchor is to take root in the community with its significant players, especially parents, brothers, sisters, friends, and relatives. At phase three, community officers are directed to network with the residents (specifically the parents) through the children. As officers befriend children, parents begin to pay attention and interact with officers. Many who were once shy or uncooperative then start looking at officers through the eyes of a child who possesses a positive interaction history. Children who laud the qualities and characteristics of an officer persuade parents on the decency and good intentions of that individual. Children see not only the officer but also the program of community integration and character formation. Anchoring solidifies and eases the officer's way into the family as well as the community. As bonds develop between officers and families, one can see drastic changes emerge in the community's attitude towards "law enforcement" personnel. As the relationships mature, so do the trust and reliance level. Communication comes forth freely and without reservation. Criminal activity, once silently tolerated, will then be reported more readily.

Family anchoring widens the net of available parties to assist in the community protection movement. As the officer enlists more and more individuals who are community stakeholders, extended and even remote family members, the ring of opportunity for the criminal element constricts. As more individuals come on board, the sense of security and protection in the intervention area increases, and the realm of opportunity for crime diminishes. Hence, there is a correlation between the level of "anchored" participants and the tranquillity of a given area. The level of intervention, therefore, depends on the level of control exerted by either the good or the bad elements in the community. Anchoring will not occur overnight, and it demands a full-scale commitment to positive communal change. See Figure 5.32.

Networking in Action

One night, security officers were dispatched to investigate complaints about a party in an apartment. There were over a hundred people at the party, who were in the apartment, the outside stairwells, and the parking lot. Upon arrival, the first officer identified the resident of the apartment and asked for better control at the party. The resident went inside and attempted to gain control of the crowd, and in the process, confronted a man who was armed with a handgun. As the resident asked the individual to stop the disturbing behavior, the individual pointed the firearm at the resident and threatened to kill her if she did not "get out of his face." When a group of onlookers started screaming that the individual had a firearm, the officers responded to the cries for help inside the apartment. The officers, struggling to gain access to the situation, were cautious about immediate confrontation with the gun-holder, especially since the potential for harm was so great. As a fallback position, the officers opted to control the perimeter and immediate area within the apartment, and they allowed the gunman to work his way toward the back door, where he subsequently threw out the handgun.

As the officers were trying to gain control of the scene, the subject slipped out of the apartment and ran into a wooded area. Upon arrival, the sheriff's office took over the scene and took custody of the firearm, which had been located by security officers. As the sheriff's office conducted its investigation, it immediately found resistance and very few signs of cooperation. Community members balked at providing public authorities with information that could lead to the arrest of the individual who threatened the life of the resident. Amazingly, the community indirectly protected the violator from the public police sector. The sheriff's office, unable to get any information, impounded the firearm and left the scene without filing a report of aggravated assault.

Later that evening, a security officer approached a woman and a child who had been at the party. Instead of confrontation, the security officer displayed the traits of networking—understanding, caring, and a desire to be helpful, since that community member was part of the enterprise rather than separate from it. As the conversation developed, the officer realized that the lady and child knew more than had been divulged. As the mother of the child said to the officer, "I don't know where he lives," the child (a nine-year-old boy who knew the officer) gently tugged the officer's pant leg and said, "I know where he lives." The officer, stopping his conversation with the mother, looked down at the child and said, "Does he live where you live?" The child responded, "Yes, I know where." As the officer looked back up to the mother, the mother admitted that she also knew where he was, that he lived three doors down from her apartment (about four blocks away from where the incident occurred). The officer asked the mother if she was willing to identify him, and she agreed as long as the perpetrator did not see her. Immediately, because the security firm had jurisdiction at the apartment community, security officers established a perimeter around the subject's apartment. Upon a second confirmation by mother and child, security officers knocked on the door to find out if the subject was home. The subject's girlfriend answered the door, and the subject made his way to the doorway, partly undressed, as though he had been sleeping. He stated that he had never been to any party. On verification that the suspect was in the residence, security officers summoned the sheriff's office to respond and take over the scene. Subsequently, the sheriff's office took the individual into custody and charged him with aggravated assault with a firearm. During the suspect's criminal background check, the sheriff's office discovered that this particular suspect had a long history of violent criminal behavior and because of that history, could be prosecuted as a "habitual offender."

Because of the level of trust that existed between the child and the officer, the suspect, with his long history of violent criminal behavior, was identified, taken off the street, and subsequently received thirty years in the state penitentiary. Networking with the young reaps enormous fruit in the war on crime. Public officers lack that connection. Private officers can hone and refine the network as it plays an integral role in the shaping and formation of safe communities.

IV. PROGRAM EVALUATION: THE STATE OF THE COMMUNITY

Unfortunately, there is no single tool that can quantify success for all types of community-based programs because approaches are not fully unified and are generally reflective of community characteristics. Public police have intensely studied the structure of the community from varied perspectives, including socioeconomic, demographic, physical, and environmental-density, and neighborhood-makeup. Private sector officers have continually refined these valid inquiries. No two communities are identical, though the pressures and demands associated with crime and criminality impact all walks and ways of life in the American experience. In this sense, the judgment that something either works or does not is probably more

FIGURE 5.32   "Anchored" and Welcomed in the Community

qualitative than quantitative, more art than science, and often the result of trial, refinement, and adaptation. Despite these measuring shortcomings, the security firm must end its journey into the world of community with an honest appraisal of what was accomplished. It must be accountable—and rightfully so. The security industry can argue righteously when it fails in subsequent confirmation. As Rick Sarre puts it, security accountability is derived from many forces, including "market" ones:

> There has long been a suggestion that market forces act as a mechanism of accountability. That is, the poor performer will not survive in any business where client confidence is important. If the operators do not perform satisfactorily and cannot continue to satisfy clients, then they will not remain in business. Bad firms will be culled, so the argument goes, leaving the survival of only the best and the fittest.[28]

Most traditional approaches, such as the evaluation of crime reports, work only partially in the assessment of community-based programs. Public police rightly depend on uniform crime report (UCR) data as computerized by the FBI, as well as a bevy of databases authored at the local, state, and agency level. Crime data sources image the community. Comparison of crime data should be longitudinal rather than short-lived when evaluating the impact of policy on neighborhoods. In the short run, crime rates will likely rise because of increased reporting and a more aggressive and participatory citizenry. Over longer durations, the data can be quite illuminating and predict a community in a state of stabilization and reclamation. Crime data in the nuisance area may be very dependable if the community-based approach is functional. Rapid rates of escalation typify an active community base. But over time the numbers should drop.

Another avenue of input is security officer observations. The officers assigned to a targeted area are able to evaluate rates of criminality. Suggestions for techniques and remedies to improve programs should be solicited.

Another measure of program evaluation requires the use of covert video comparison of neighborhood trouble spots. At the program's inception, the area is videotaped for posterity. As the community-based program unfolds, the surveillance continues during a specific timeline. Finally, at completion of the program's initial phase, the setting is taped and contrasted to its original state, providing a comparison with environmental conditions before and after.

In the end, however, the efficacy of the community-based program can be truly measured only in the hearts and minds of those residents it directly touched. Surveys and polls that measure citizen impressions are compelling evidence of success or failure in the battle over community ownership. Levels of security, stabilization of distressed areas, rates of victimization, and cooperative spirit with neighborhoods and both public law enforcement and the private sector, are just a few of the many measures worth calculating. Interviews with residents, workers, patrons, and visitors can deliver an instructive glimpse into how the community has been altered. Citizens alone can communicate the intimacy of change.

The results of such surveys must be appraised with candor and honesty, leading the way to affirmation of what works and to condemnation of any failed enterprise. Hiding failures continues the pattern of deception and ineptitude that communities too often have unfortunately experienced. Praising what succeeds, and loudly so, just might tickle the ears of those in search of a community integration system that changes lives and uplifts the human condition. Ultimately, the market will adjust for a failed strategy. If the implementation was inadequate, the agency will be replaced.

V. CONCLUSION

The CBIP, the community integration system, the chief subject matter of this chapter, not only drastically reduces criminal activities but also helps foresee problems before they occur. It helps officers control situations that are fluid and developing, such as arguments, out-of-hand parties, and domestic fights. The more officers know the people involved, the more control they have of a given situation. They are able to talk to the people involved and to de-escalate situations that otherwise may become violent or life-threatening. Above all, CBIP helps establish trust, and this trust between the officer and the community is the foundation for that community to protect its own from the criminal elements. Community integration is not an idle ambition but is an affirmative obligation to weave itself and the employer worked for into the fabric of an entire community. Community integration works only when and if the justice professionals see themselves as part of the picture rather than as separate from it. Community integration avoids the historical alienation so prevalent in public police/community relations. New programs, but also new tactics of training, education, and preparation for the security professional represent the vision of CBIP. Specific suggestions in the preparation of community-based officers are provided throughout the chapter.

Community integration occurs in three separate phases. First is the reclamation phase, in which security is most visible and focused on halting the progression of criminal activities. Here the environment is assessed, targeted, and plotted for specific intervention. Phase two, networking, begins the task of enlisting community elements that will aid and assist in the formation of a positive community. First and foremost in the networking plan is the enlistment of children into the enterprise. The networking process will extend to parents, siblings, friends, clergy, and civic leaders. Phase three, anchoring, seeks the bonding with families and specific target areas for maximum effect and deterrence, solidifying and anchoring all the relevant constituencies in the preservation of community. Finally, anchoring generates contacts and intelligence, thereby thwarting criminal activity within the very community in need of protection.

By any reasonable definition, the approach addresses the fundamental premise that a successful program requires the support of the citizenry and community involvement. CBIP creates a multitude of eyes and ears to survey the environment. By networking with the citizenry, officers establish a relationship in which citizens willingly assist in the maintenance of order rather than act under threat of coercion. Community integration programs, conducted by private sector protection specialists, appear the best and brightest hope for stable communities in the twenty-first century.

Notes

1. G.E. commits one million volunteer hours annually to assist high-risk juveniles.
2. Anthony Micucci, *A Typology of Private Policing Operational Styles*, 26 J. of Criminal Justice, at 41, 47 (Jan./Feb. 1998).
3. Nancy E. Gist, *Comprehensive Communities Program: A Unique Way to Reduce Crime and Enhance Public Safety—BJA Fact Sheet* 000276 at 1 (U.D. DOJ Dec 2000).
4. Amitai Etzioni, *The Spirit of Community* 139 (New York Touchstone, 1993).
5. *Youth Violence: A Report of the Surgeon General* at http://www.surgeongeneral.gov/library/youthviolence/chapter5/sec3.html, 9/9/02.
6. Gist at 1.
7. Joanne Ziembo-Vogl and Devere Woods, Jr., *Defining Community Policing: Practice Versus Paradigm*, 19 Police Studies at 33, 38 (1996).
8. J. P. Shaloo, *Private Police* 22 (American Academy of Philadelphia Police and Social Sciences, 1933).
9. Robert Trojanowicz et al., *Community Policing: A Contemporary Perspective*, 2nd ed., 200 Cincinnati (Anderson, 1998).
10. Mahesh K. Nalla et al., *Security Practitioner's Perceptions of Undergraduate Curriculum* 7, J. Criminal Justice ed., at 79, 89 (Spring 1996). *See also* Charles P. Nemeth, *Directory of Criminal Justice Education*, 3rd ed. (1998). This edition was self-published.
11. Nalla, et al. at 7.
12. Bertus R. Ferreira, *The Importance of Law Enforcement Education*, LAW & ORDER, at 26 (May 1997).
13. Skogan, in his book *Disorder and Decline*, makes the case as to why it is so important for officers to approach their duties with this mindset: "Besides the legal concerns, there is another reason for retreating from aggressive order maintenance—the abrasive impact this kind of policing can have on the residents of poor, inner-city neighborhoods. Even if they are conducted in strictly legal fashion, aggressive tactics such as saturating areas with police, stopping cars frequently, conducting extensive field interrogations and searches, and bursting into apartments suspected of harboring gambling or drugs, can undermine police-community relations in black and Hispanic neighborhoods. The police will inevitably err on the side of employing their distinctive advantage on the streets—their capacity to use coercive, and even fatal, force. While Community Policing emphasizes the need to negotiate solutions to problems, police have the power to impose (perhaps short-term) nonnegotiable settlements, and will do so." Wesley Skogan, *Disorder and Decline* 166. Univ. of California Press, Berkely, CA 1992
14. Robert C. Davis and Arthur J. Lurigio, *Civil Abatement as a Tool for Controlling Drug Dealing in Rental Properties*, 11 Security J, at 45–46 (1998).
15. *See* Davis and Lurigio, at 45, 48.
16. Etzioni at 190–191.
17. Gist at 2.
18. Community Oriented Policing Services, *Introductory Guide to Crime Analysis and Mapping* 52 (U.S.DOJ).

19. Robert Bonnie Bucqueroux, Community Policing: A Contemporary Perspective (Cincinnati: Anderson Publishing 1990). Trojanowicz at 282.
20. Robert N. Bellah et al., *The Good Society 145* New York (Vintage, 1991).
21. Aristotle, *Nichomachean Ethics.* Martin Ostwald, trans. New York: Bobbs-Merrill Co. Inc, 1962.
22. Bellah et al., at 145.
23. *Preventing Delinquency: A Path to the Future* 5, Florida Department of Juvenile Justice, (Tallahassee, FL 1997).
24. Community Oriented Policing Services at 22, 30.
25. CPO's must be forever aware of the interplay of race and law enforcement. Part of private sector justice's success is its lack of baggage. *See* Tracey L. Meares et. al., *Urgent Times:* Policing and Rights on Inner City Communities (Boston, Beacon Press, 1999).
26. William F. Walsh and Edwin J. Donovan, *Private Security and Community Policing: Evaluation and Comment,* 17 *J. of Criminal Justice* at 187, 195 (1989).
27. For an interesting survey on how the young perceive crime in the community, *see Kids and Violence: A National Survey & Report* (Tampa, FL: Family First 1998).
28. Rick Sarre, *Accountability and the Private Sector: Putting Accountability of the Private Security under the Spotlight,* 10 *Security Journal* at 97, 101 (1998).

6

Private Sector Community-Based Communication Tactics

The Medium is the Message because it is the medium that shapes and controls the search and form of human associations and action.

Marshall McLuhan

What a man really says when he says that someone else can be persuaded by force, is that he himself is incapable of more rational means of communication.

Norman Cousins

Learning Objectives

1. To delve into communication policy and discern its impact on the community/public safety relationship.
2. To appreciate how individual officer conduct makes or breaks the community effort.
3. To learn how specific steps, such as Notice and Codes of Conduct, play in the establishment of communication in a community.
4. To analyze and assess common pitfalls in the communication domain, particularly between the citizenry and law enforcement.
5. To develop departmental policies that foster positive communication between public safety and the community.
6. To become familiar with the diverse programs of partnership between public and private law enforcement as applied to specific community settings.
7. To avoid repetitive mistakes in the conversation that flows in and out of communities.

8. To be exposed to media challenges that often surround the community crime dynamic.

9. To be proficient in the interaction between police and public safety organizations and the media that often conducts investigative oversight.

10. To become comfortable with communication strategies that promote the free exchange of ideas and information.

I. COMMUNICATION POLICY AND TACTICS FOR PRIVATE SECTOR OFFICERS

Any realistic community-based protection program must stress the essence and nature of communication. Communication involves more than just words. It involves tone, syntax, volume, body language, and other nonverbal indicators such as symbolism, writing, color, clothing style, and actions (or inaction). Every word that is spoken communicates a message of some kind, which can be interpreted in numerous ways, depending on another's complex equivalence of that action, gesture, or word. Interaction is communication and must become an area of focus in the training and subsequent implementation of the public safety effort.

Officers must learn to interact and communicate with residents, patrons, workers, and visitors. Citizens must become comfortable interacting with officers. On this two-way street, the natural flow of information makes the community integration model plausible. Exactly how the citizens of the community or neighborhood engage in communication directly correlates to the level of the protection effort's success or failure. Undeniably, protection officers need to master people skills and become adroit human relations experts who are comfortable in every interactive situation. This capacity can be aptly described as the "art" of security practice in the community. Relying on professionalism alone will not suffice in the community-based model. Couple the science of protection with the art of human understanding, and the security plan assuredly will succeed.

Private security entities must be driven by more than profit motives and reactive strategies. These firms should not shy away from community integration because of liability fears. The traditional "observe and report" mentality will not produce results in the community integration model, which insists on a more substantive investment of human capital and resource. Crime detection and criminalistics cannot achieve the ends of community reclamation. A move that is beyond observation and apprehension, into the world of interaction and proactivism, where community members become stakeholders with security professionals, is a sure path to success.

Community survival depends on this type of intense investment. "Interaction" and "integration" are not hollow words. The word "interaction," which encompasses real communication, should become the chief thrust in the security plan. Communication stresses the interactive, rather than the professionally detached or observant operative. Communication stresses the "art" of the protection business, which relates to people skills and the development of strong interpersonal and communal relations. Communication builds the relationship. Communication fosters trust. Communication assures a commonality of interests.

Communication efforts are a perennial concern for the security firm seeking a foothold in the community. From the outset of the relationship, from the preimplementation stage to contract completion, communication stands at center stage in the delivery of private community-oriented protection services. From the initial day of deployment, the security firm announces its intentions.

A. Notice and Purpose

From the first day of operations, the security officer and firm should give community notice of motive and purpose. An open letter to community members opens the door to lifelong trust and sustainable relationships. See Figure 6.1 for a suitable

---

Sample
(Initial Contact)

Dear Resident(s),

We have requested Protection Officers to patrol the property, effective *(date)*. These Officers are here for the protection of the physical property of *(complex name)* and are not here to serve as Law Enforcement Officers nor for the protection of the Residents or their property. These are Protection Officers and should not be confused with security or courtesy patrol officers.

These Officers will be stopping individuals on our property to confirm their residency. When you have visitors, please ensure that they are accompanied by yourself or an occupant of your apartment. At no time should visitors be unescorted on our property.

All emergencies should be dealt with by contacting—911—, not the answering service nor the Protection Officers.

Please note: We will be enforcing all community rules, including but not limited to, *(example: Rule #29—Loitering)*.

If you observe suspicious activity that is not an emergency, you may contact the Protection Officers at (813-221-1911).

Thank you for your cooperation.

Sincerely,

Management

FIGURE 6.1   Contact Protocol

example. The letter of introduction serves multiple purposes. First, the letter serves as the vehicle of introduction and a statement of intentions. Second, the letter justifies the steps that will be soon taken—some of which may unnerve or rattle previously jaded and hopelessly distrustful citizens. The letter may relay particulars of soon-to-be-implemented operations. In this sense, the letter eliminates the element of surprise and will reduce tension and foster dialogue between the officers and the served constituency. When developing the communiqué, utilize clear-cut and unambiguous language; as a result, the letter itself will generate a certain level of anticipation.

The letter format not only nurtures trust and builds relationships early on in the deployment but also characterizes officers as concerned citizens and responsible, respectable, and trustworthy professionals. The letter lays out the virtuous and honorable intentions of the author—that the security firm will abide by the highest level of integrity and professionalism. When building relationships, it is imperative that the members of the community see the officer or officers assigned to their environment as responsible, respectable, and trustworthy. Whether it is a work environment, a living environment, or a social environment, officers must portray the highest level of honor, integrity, honesty, and dedication to their responsibilities. It must be clear that there is no room for situational ethics while carrying out these responsibilities. Building relationships with these fundamental characteristics is vital to the building of trust and community fiber.

The letter opens the door to communication, even in the worst environments. The more problematic, crime-ridden, or exposed the environment, the more this type of communication is needed.

B. Officer Demeanor and Attitude

Citizens know very quickly the approach that an officer will adopt in problem resolution by how the officer acts or in what manner the officer conducts his or her affairs. Actions often do speak louder than any verbal communication. Officers must be conscious of public image and take into consideration how community members perceive conduct. If an officer, for example, is not actively patrolling within the assigned environment and is instead sitting in a vehicle or reclining on a bench, the message is that the officer lacks a sense of duty rather than having an integrative and proactive mentality. Inactive, lazy, and inattentive officers communicate loudly the level of concern and ambition in the quest for community stability. Active and responsive officers exude the type of confidence citizens find contagious. Officers who do not understand the community relations project will also carry out functions with less conviction than would a professional person who is confident of purpose and strategy. Protection officers are not "rent-a-cops" stressing inactivity and avoidance. Community protection specialists are a unique and special breed of protection professionals who should exude this noble end in both their personal and their occupational approach. Critical Intervention Services instructs officers of the key relationship between community acceptance and behavior. See Figure 6.2. To earn the trust of the citizen requires not just the uniform itself but also an

To: ALL CIS OFFICERS AND SUPERVISORS
From: JAY PACE, DIRECTOR OF UNIFORM SERVICES
Date: NOVEMBER 5, 1999
Subject: FIRST CONTACT PROTOCOL

Operations has recently received complaints about the attitude of officers during contacts with residents and guests on CIS patrolled properties. Following Community Based Protection Initiative (CBPI) procedures can minimize these complaints. We need to remember that the prime directive of all CIS officers is to implement CBPI.

When officers make contact with individuals that they do not know, they are to introduce themselves as protection officers and attempt to establish positive relationships. If individuals become confrontational during the contact, it is the responsibility of the officer to deescalate the situation. This can only be accomplished if the officer remains professional and objective. If the officer becomes argumentative or rude, the situation will escalate rather than deescalate.

Sarcastic, rude, or vulgar language or mannerisms on the part of CIS officers are contrary to the effective purpose of CBPI and will result in disciplinary action.

Please review your Procedures and Executive Orders concerning CBPI and officer conduct and ensure that you are in compliance.

FIGURE 6.2   First Contact Policy

investment of time and energy that manifests real concern about community health and stability. See Figure 6.3 for a directive on conduct in uniform.

Even the appearance of the officers—neatness, cleanliness, and overall appearance—sends a message to the community at large. Protection specialists must appear as organized as the plan undertaken. In equipment and resource, uniform and demeanor, interaction and conversation, the protection specialist needs to be organized in all that is undertaken. Citizens do, in fact, judge appearance, habits,

Practitioner Highlight

Decision Strategies

Decision Strategies is using Link Analysis Software since 2001. Developed primarily for law enforcement drug investigations, the software has been further developed and refined to provide a "graphic view" of many (sometimes, hundreds or thousands) seemingly unrelated data points such as telephone numbers, times of events, bank and credit card numbers, and so on. The CIA, FBI, and others all now use link-analysis to extrapolate piles of data into coherent pictures that may lead to similarities, matches, or conclusions that would not have otherwise been made. The software was developed by i2 technologies.

TO: ALL CIS OFFICERS
FROM: CIS EXECUTIVE STAFF
DATE: JANUARY 11, 1997
RE: CONDUCT IN UNIFORM

It has come to our attention that the behavior of certain Officers, while representing CIS has been at the least, unprofessional. Reports, complaints, and seeing it, for ourselves forms the basis for our new ZERO TOLERANCE POLICY. This should be self explanatory, but, for those whom this memo most relates, we will expand upon the explanation so there are no mistakes in the meaning of ZERO TOLERANCE. After having witnessed some incidents in which the public was the victim of a CIS Officers verbal abuse and indiscretion, it was necessary to instate a policy against such actions. Any Officer who intentionally uses foul language or berates an individual during a situation or conversation, for any reason, will immediately be relieved of duty to face possible termination. There is no reason an Officer has to swear at a person in order to have them answer a question or comply with a command. You as an Officer have the duty and responsibility to the people in the community you serve to be a professional. Being a professional includes not only taking down bad guys, but, also to treat people as you would want to be treated. It includes treating people with the basics of human decency. We are helping to build up communities, not tear them down by degrading the citizens who reside there.

This will serve as the first and last verbal or written warning you will receive on this subject. I expect you will govern yourselves accordingly. BE A PROFESSIONAL.

Thank You,

David Morris, CPO
Director of Uniform Services

FIGURE 6.3

mannerisms, and actions of security professionals. See Figures 6.4 and 6.5. If the uniform shirt is not properly tucked, if stains appear on the shirt or pants, if the pants are too short or too long, or if the brass is not worn properly, the officer displays a lack of personal and professional pride. See Figure 6.6 for a comprehensive security policy on uniform appearance.

C. Avoidance of Responsibility

Officers who begrudgingly engage in professional activities send out a negative and a less than integrative message. Those unwilling to tackle issues outside the normal chain of responsibilities will alienate those expecting the same. Additionally, officers assigned to community-based duties must avoid, whenever possible,

FIGURE 6.4 Community Interaction and Professional Appearance

making statements to community members such as "This is not my responsibility," "I cannot help you," or "What do you want me to do about it?" This type of avoidance conveys a nonparticipatory attitude that is bound to estrange community members. Officers must make every attempt to try and come up with viable recommendations even for problems historically outside the zone of usual tasks.

A failure to tackle problems indicates an unwillingness to delve into the greater and grander issue of community ownership. In this setting, public police often take umbrage with functions outside the job description or traditional expectation for the law enforcement identity. Such pigeonholing will neither open community doors nor foster trust. Private sector operatives know more keenly that success depends on the happy and contented marketplace and that the measure of any community-based program is not only order, but even more critically, full-fledged cooperation.

D. Arrogance and Interaction

Arrogance is another vital issue that must be discussed when attempting to implement public safety efforts within a community. Unfortunately, everywhere in public safety arrogance raises its head. Arrogance alienates its target. Those entrusted with authority who display excess arrogance do substantial damage in police-community relations.

Arrogance, when directed at the community, is an extension of the *"I don't care"* attitude that unfortunately appears in law enforcement settings. But arrogance is even more than indifference—it is a form of contempt for the constituency served.

FIGURE 6.5 The Professional Image in the Community Policy Iniative

It could even be argued that arrogance is at the root of most, if not all, community relationship problems in public safety. Humility is the antidote to arrogance.[1]

Simply put, arrogance at its foundation is rudeness, and "rudeness is an endemic problem in policing because it is an endemic problem in human nature that is magnified by the nature of the police-citizen relationship. Small, seemingly inconsequential, moments of rude interactions can nurture a conflict environment that will continue to serve as an obstacle in the police-community alliance."[2] See Figure 6.7. Good community relationships, such as those demonstrated before, are not fostered by arrogant attitudes. Professional bearing and personal demeanor go hand in hand with the issue of competence. Communities welcome the just and proficient staff and supervisor. Read the memo to CIS command staff outlining expectations relating to image and personality in Figure 6.8.

Practitioner Tip: Measure Attitudes

Security firms and professionals should not shy away from constructive input from community members and leaders. Find a survey instrument that can be administered to community leaders and a sample of residents. The survey should focus on the qualitative measure of officer attitudes—measuring bearing, demeanor, levels of arrogance, and/or respect.

- Restricted -	Critical Intervention Services	- Restricted -
Title: Uniforms and Grooming		**Uniformed Division Order Series:** 310.00
Intent: To establish guidelines on the proper wearing of uniforms and personal appearance.		
Effective Date: January 12, 1997		**Page:** 1 of 3

Proper Dress	**Uniformed Division Order #310.001**

Officers are expected to keep uniforms, insignia, accessories, all issued equipment, and all authorized personal equipment clean and in good repair at all times.

1. Long sleeved shirts may be worn as outer garments or under an agency issued or approved jacket. Long sleeved shirts will be buttoned at the cuff. A shirt may be professionally altered for proper fit. (This does not apply to the BDU jacket.)
2. Trouser legs are to be uncuffed and hemmed at the point where they touch the shoe tops without causing a break in the crease line, or they may be altered with a slight break in the crease line for proper fit.
3. Issued/approved jackets may be worn during cold weather or other inclement conditions.
4. Only black socks are to be worn, and they must be long enough so that skin will not show below the trouser cuffs when walking or sitting.
5. Footwear must be properly shined and in good condition. Shoes/boots must be black in color with black laces and plain toe. Black sneakers are not acceptable footwear.
6. Uniforms are to be kept clean and neatly pressed at all times. This includes shirts, trousers, blouses, skirts, jackets, and any outer garment that is a part of your uniform.
7. Uniform hat or cap, if worn, will be placed squarely upon the head and will not tilt to the sides or the back, or be worn backwards.
8. The tie will be clean.
9. All badges will be clean and shined and worn over the left breast pocket of the uniform shirt or jacket.
10. Shoulder patches will be worn on the left and right shoulders of the shirt, overcoat, or jacket, sewn into place and centered approximately one (1) inch from the top of the shoulder stitch.
11. The nameplate may be of metal or plastic material and silver in color, with 1/4 inch black printed lettering with the officer's last name. If desirable and appropriate, the officer's first initial may be imprinted. The nameplate shall be centered above the right pocket, and flush to the top of the pocket.
12. Officers may wear only the accessories that they are qualified or authorized to wear. If awards are to be worn, they should be 1/8 inch above the nameplate. If only one award is worn, center it above the nameplate; if more than one award is worn, center to the top of the pocket, 1/8 inch above the nametag, in order precedence.

FIGURE 6.6   Uniform Policy

E. Failure to Listen

To understand the community and its citizens, the professional must be a skilled and sincere listener. Different communities have diverse traits and characteristics. Effective communication depends on the ability not only to gather information, but even more importantly, also to detect and monitor the pulse of the people. This is especially the case within areas that are blighted, high-crime or low-income. Since in these environments it will be extremely hard to establish good communication up front, "listening" therefore takes on heightened importance. It may take time, since levels of community alienation and distrust are so entrenched. It took years for the mistrust to develop, so practitioners must be patient in recapturing the hearts and minds of community members. Adept listening skills go a long way toward that reclamation.

FIGURE 6.7   CPO: Preventative Interaction

In these cases, every effort should be made to review any supplemental documents or information that would compensate for that gap in information. Newspaper articles, television interviews, local religious leaders and groups, civic associations, and school counselors are all avenues of added information regardless of the type of environment. Additionally, there are other resources available for cultivating information about the community. Clifford E. Simonsen's *Private Security in America* elaborates as follows:

> A community may translate its concern about crime through the individual and group efforts of its citizens; through the local industries, businesses, and institutions such as schools, youth services bureaus, and religious organizations; and through the responsible and responsive efforts of its governing bodies.[3]

CIS Directive Memo

To: All Supervisors and Commanders

From: K.C. Poulin, President and CEO

CC: All Executive Staff

Date: January 24, 2000

Re: CIS Supervision

Now that you have been promoted to Command status – what does that mean exactly? I'll tell you what it means from my perspective. It means that you are expected to go out there and not only be the professional that we know you are (which is obvious due to the positions that you are in right now), but also to make everybody under you as professional as you. Your responsibilities are to ensure that every officer under your care meets the standards set forth by this agency, mandated by me, by those of our profession and by state. It is your responsibility to ensure that the personnel under you follow each and every rule and every regulation that is laid out for them, without allowing your friendships to interfere with discipline and the professional performance of duties by all CIS employees. Cutting corners, or not following through with duties and responsibilities as a supervisor is just simply not acceptable. You have this agency's liability, its reputation and its future in your hands determined by your actions or your inactions. This is a tremendous responsibility.

That's what it means on the surface, but it's much more than that. I want you to set the tone for supervisors well into the future. I want you to set the professionalism and the personality, just as the officers did in 1992, 1993, 1994, and 1995 and as they do today in the year 2000. Supervisors set that tone and personality that CIS is known for.

FIGURE 6.8   Security Personnel Professional Expectations

When people think CIS, they think of a certain type of person, especially when they think about a CIS supervisor. When a CIS officer thinks of a CIS supervisor, I want him or her to have an image in his or her mind that says first and foremost, that there is honor in that person, as without honor there is nothing. The first character trait is honor. Officers have to see that there is honor in that CIS supervisor, in everything that s/he does, in decision capabilities, in assessments and in the way the supervisor deals with people. Then and only then can the word integrity breathe and get in and take hold as part of the personality I want you to create. Integrity has got to be the cornerstone of the supervision style that CIS portrays. Integrity is simply the cornerstone of personal character and it will not be negotiated. If you don't know integrity, if you don't know the meaning of integrity, I suggest you look it up because it needs to become synonymous with you.

The next characteristic that must exist in the command style is truth; I want you to set the standard of truth so that it becomes embedded into the future of CIS's command structure. But make no mistake, both integrity and truth must be well refined to support each other, as without integrity, there can be no truth. Truth has got to be the foundation, the end all-be all of the CIS supervision style. Truth in dealing with yourself when you are assessing a situation and deciding how to make a recommendation on discipline, truth on how you deal with the troops and truth on how you deal with me and the agency.

Truth, integrity and honor are the three personality traits I want you to bring out into the command structure. That is what I want you to embed for the future supervisors to follow. Have no doubt about it; you are creating the management style of CIS's future. From those three words HONOR, INTEGRITY and TRUTH we can then get real responsibility and professionalism. Responsibility and professionalism will be demanded of every officer in the field. Demanded – not asked for, not begged for, not pled for – DEMANDED!

If an officer cannot deliver responsibility and professionalism, then that officer needs to leave CIS, and if that officer is not willing to leave on his own, then it is your job to help him or her along.

FIGURE 6.8 *(Cont.)*

The bottom line is that you are responsible to supervise officers who themselves are responsible for protecting people who have entrusted us with their safety. Thousands of people... thousands of people every night go to sleep feeling secure that CIS personnel are watching over them... thousands! Your responsibility is to make sure that the reality of our performance is equal to what these folks believe we are doing. You are responsible for thousands of people who put their lives in the hands of CIS officers every night. If you act with that in mind, your potential—and the agency's—is limitless!

"In a social order where one man is a superior and the other is a subordinate; the superior, if he is a gentleman, will never dwell upon it; and the subordinate, if he is a gentleman, will never forget it."

FIGURE 6.8   *(Cont.)*

Part of knowing a community includes understanding the characteristics associated with that particular community. Ethnically based communities, for example, have different behavioral patterns based on the experiences of that community. It is vital that officers understand the cultural diversity among the people they protect. For example, a white officer working in a Hispanic area should understand Latino-American culture. In a Hispanic community, for example, actions such as refusing to look officers in the eyes while talking to them is not a sign of guilt. Rather, this is a sign of respect. Most inexperienced white officers would not know this fact and may misjudge. Understanding characteristics such as this is extremely important in officer/community interaction and communication. White officers are especially vulnerable to cultural misinterpretations. They perceive threats where there may not be any, and the officers' actions may actually trigger an escalation because of their lack of understanding. Some black youths, for example, sometimes do a lot of walking around, have increased hand and arm gestures, and are very verbal. They will also get very loud and give the appearance of being at a point of throwing blows at each other, but then will abruptly stop, turn, and walk away while stating some obscenities. These situations are not necessarily dangerous, but the officer must learn the meaning of actions to effectively understand what they are observing.

Protection professionals should look for reality-based diversity training that may be needed in an effort to meet the community-based program's need. This step can aid in facilitating clear communication and removing any misperceptions that may cause barriers to effective implementation. People who come from countries with serious oppression by the police, such as a Haitian community, are apt to submit to protection officers out of fear instead of respect.

II. PUBLIC POLICE AND PRIVATE SECURITY COMMUNICATION

Active relationships must be emphasized at all levels within the agencies attempting to implement proactive change. Street-level officers must be encouraged to develop relationships among each other on the front line, whether these officers are private, public, or employed by "competing" agencies. Without that specific process occurring, executives at higher levels will have minimal effect when trying to develop official relationships between private and public agencies. One on one, police and security officers and practitioners must learn to communicate with each other on a daily basis in the areas they protect. By having a solid foundation of interaction at the front line, higher-ranking executives will be much more effective in implementing whatever new approaches they choose. This undertaking is extremely difficult to do, however. Many police departments frequently have problems dealing and cooperating with each other, let alone having to extend that cooperation and communication to private agencies. On the other hand, private agencies also have problems with extending communications to the public police, largely because of the perceptions that exist and the fear of not being respected as professionals.

Police executives must be educated as to what role the security industry plays in crime prevention. The unfortunate reality, to a great extent, is that law enforcement practitioners are not aware of the role and resources that the private security industry has to offer. Contributing to the problems, many private practitioners believe that law enforcement personnel often view private security as less than an equal partner in crime prevention efforts. They believe that law enforcement, in general, fails to realize the true effectiveness and professional capability that security practitioners exercise every day toward the overall crime control effort. Some law enforcement professionals actually seem to regard security personnel as secondary in status to law enforcement. By embarking in a partnership with the private sector, law enforcement executives will find that the possibilities offered by increased cooperation are endless. Once police executives understand the dynamics of the security industry and its influence on crime and society, executives will then be capable of setting the tone for the front-line officers as the example to follow in the cooperative partnership effort.

Although enormous progress has occurred in the last few decades, both sectors still appear estranged at times. Predictably, both sectors display with reason some level of distrust, ignorance, or resistance. The issues that so often come up are about the following:

- Status
- Competition
- Ignorance
- False alarms
- Questions of authority

- Constitutional differences
- Profit motives.

The Joint Council of Law Enforcement and Private Security Associations poses some critical lines of inquiry:

- Should the law enforcement officer see his or her private security counterpart as a peer professional?
- Should the law enforcement and property protection objectives of law enforcement be supported by involved corporate and private security agency leaders?
- Can the net cost for both private and public security be reduced through coordinated actions?
- Can the corporation's profit line be increased through cooperative relationships with law enforcement?
- Can corporate citizenship be enhanced through cooperative actions with law enforcement?
- Is there an element of risk on the part of a corporation in joining hands with a law enforcement agency?
- Is there an element of risk on the part of the law enforcement agency in providing police resources and criminal history record information to the private sector?
- Is there a way for the resources of the two sectors to be joined in providing levels of personal or asset protection that cannot be reached independently?[4]

With varying degrees of distrust, both public safety sectors need to remove all forms of enmity and suspicion before full communication can evolve. The problems have been perennial and generally consist of these issues:

- Lack of mutual respect
- Lack of communication
- Lack of cooperation
- Lack of enforcement knowledge of private security
- Perceived competition
- Lack of standards
- Perceived corruption[5]

Sheriff Neil Perry, of St. Johns County, Florida, and founder of the Law Enforcement and Private Security Council of St. Johns County and chairman of the Commission on Florida Law Enforcement Accreditation, has long advocated the necessity of communication between the public and the private sector. These groups believe that law enforcement personnel sometimes miss a valuable asset of sharing information with our counterparts in private security. Private security opera-

---

Practitioner Tip: Habitual Offenders

Private sector professionals, in conjunction with public officers, can target criminal defendants who have long and successful histories of criminal activity. One way to target repeat offenders is to report criminal conduct in known recidivists so that the tough sanctions of the habitual offender laws, commonly known as "three strikes and your out," can be carried out.

---

tives know their property the best, they know what is happening on their property, and they have information and intelligence that those in law enforcement need. It is important for public police to get to know private officers, to become acquainted as friends and partners in a total commitment to fight against crime.[6]

It is ludicrous for these lines of communication to be anything but open and generous. Both sectors are heavily dependent on one another and will not survive without communication and cooperation. As far back as 1976, the National Advisory Committee laid out the following interactive policies for the private and public police:

Goal 6.1: Interaction Policies. Effective interaction between the private security industry and law enforcement agencies is imperative for successful crime prevention and depends to a large extent on published clear and understandable policies developed by their administrators. Policies should be developed to serve as guides for modification by appropriate agencies.[7]

Goal 6.2: Survey and Liaison with Private Security. Law enforcement agencies should conduct a survey and maintain a current roster of those security industry components operating in the agencies' jurisdictions, and should designate at least one staff officer to service as liaison with them.[8]

Goal 6.3: Policy and Procedures. For law enforcement agencies and the private security industry to most effectively work within the same jurisdiction, policies and procedures should be developed covering:
   a. the delineation of working roles of law enforcement officers and private security personnel;
   b. the continuous prompt and reasonable interchange of information; and
   c. cooperative actions between law enforcement agencies and the private security industry.[9]

Goal 6.4: Multilevel Law Enforcement Training in Private Security. There should be a multilevel training program for public law enforcement officials, including but not limited to:
   1. Role and mission of the private security industry;

2. Legal status and types of services provided by private service companies;

3. Interchange of information, crime reporting, and cooperative actions with the industry; and

4. Orientation in technical and operational procedures.[10]

Goal 6.5: Mistaken Identity of Private Security Personnel. Title, terms, verbal representations, and visual items that cause the public to mistake private security personnel for law enforcement officers should be eliminated; security employers should ensure that their personnel and equipment are easily distinguishable from public law enforcement personnel and equipment.[11]

Goal 6.6: State Regulation of Private Security, Uniforms, Equipment, and Job Titles. Each state should develop regulations covering use and wear of private security uniforms, equipment, company names, and personnel titles that do not conflict with those in use by law enforcement agencies within the state.[12]

Goal 6.7: Law Enforcement Personnel Secondary Employment. Law enforcement administrators should insure that secondary employment of public law enforcement personnel in the private security industry does not create a conflict of interest and that public resources are not used for private purposes.[13]

Goal 6.8: Law Enforcement Officer Employment as a Security Manager. No law enforcement officer should be a principal or a manager of a private security operation where such an association creates a conflict of interest.[14]

Goal 6.9: Private Investigatory Work. Law enforcement officers should be strictly forbidden from performing any investigatory work.[15]

The public safety industry today encompasses approximately 2.9 million Americans functioning as security or law enforcement officers, security managers, law enforcement administrators, and other positions. The combined resources of these public safety entities, if effectively coordinated, can more effectively undermine the criminal culture wherever it may be. According to the *Hallcrest Report II,* the security industry is composed of over 15,000 agencies dedicated to providing protective and prevention services to clients across this country.[16]

Both entities are complementary rather than opposed to one another. Although the private sector has more constitutional and administrative leeway than its public counterparts, the public system has access to extraordinary resources in the political and economic realm. Public models are more exclusively driven to service, without regard for profit or other bottom-line efficiency, whereas the private sector can lead the way by implementing innovative and creative approaches that larger bureaucracies are incapable of. Free from civil service requirements, the private sector can adapt and change in communities more rapidly than the public system. Yet even with these differences, the strength and effectiveness of working together far outstrip separate endeavors. Working in harmony will produce enviable results in the community's war on crime. See Figure 6.9.

FIGURE 6.9 Public/Private Communication in Law Enforcement

Even among themselves, both private and public agencies often bicker over jurisdiction or other intrusion. Private security agencies can compete with each other, underbidding on accounts that leads to inevitable cost cutting that is injurious to professionalism. The security industry generally talks the talk of professionalism without delivering the requisite levels of compensation for competent employees, unless quality controls are strictly specified by the client.

Public law enforcement places the administration against the union, the city police against the county sheriff, the highway patrol, and other locality. In turn, the contentiousness extends to the federal domain. Much to the dismay of those urging cooperation and regionalism, the divided and provincial mentality in the public sector is too often witnessed. Although these agencies frequently come together under the guise of special task forces, the normal operating procedure reflects an unhealthy parochialism that cannot lead to any serious and meaningful communication. Tension and turf protection appear more normative. This situation is quite obvious in the Bush administration's current struggle to implement the Homeland Security Office. See that office's web page at www.dhs.gov. Here, as the country sets out to correct the horrid threat from overseas, as well as within, government agencies, unions, and specials interests argue about who is charged with what. Will the Coast Guard replace the DEA, or will Customs forego the INS territory? Such endless, unhealthy provincialism is a condition that must be eliminated if there is to be any chance of success in the war on terrorism. In the community sector, co-

A Model of Cooperation: FLETC

The Federal Law Enforcement Training Center (FLETC) headquartered in Glenco, Georgia, and training headquarters for the Secret Service, DEA, and other agencies at the federal level, is making a valiant effort to cooperate with all sectors of the justice system—including the private portion.

> The National Center for State and Local Law Enforcement Training provides training to local and state law enforcement agencies. These programs have been developed and delivered with the contributions and support of federal, state, local and private agencies. Our office staff is totally committed to providing quality, up-to-date, low or no cost training opportunities to state and local law enforcement officers. As an added benefit, our training programs are not only offered at our Glynco (Brunswick), Georgia, and Artesia, New Mexico, facilities, but also are exported to select sites throughout the country and through telecasts. We are in the process of developing programs to be offered over the Internet. (FLETC website at http://www.fletc.gov/osl/osl_home.htm)

Programs are available to all public and private law enforcement agencies, and they are directed specifically at teaching police and security executives how to build relationships and partnerships. FLETC jointly benefits the private and public sector when it offers programs such as these:

Advanced Airborne Counterdrug Operations Training
Airborne Counterdrug Operations Training Programs
Community Policing Training Programs
Domestic Violence Training Programs
Drug Enforcement Training Programs
Drug Law Enforcement School for Patrol Officers
Drug Task Force Supervisor School
Hate and Bias Crimes Training Programs
First Responder Training Program (FRTP)
Gang Resistance Education and Training (GREAT)

operation must reign supreme. Therefore, any reasonable chance of community success will depend on the cooperation and mutual respect of the dual sectors of the public safety system.[17] Communication cannot occur when barriers remain fixed. It is extremely important that both public and private agencies begin to explore new ways of working together and find common ground. Success stories of mutual cooperation abound.

The Federal Law Enforcement Training Center (FLETC) is a remarkable joint endeavor that illustrates how cooperation works (see box above).

Active and positive law enforcement relationships assure that proactive policies and community integration are not empty ideals. Street-level officers must be encouraged to develop relationships among each other on the front line, whether these officers are private, public, or employed by competing agencies. Executives will have to be just as generous in building relationships between private and public agencies. One to one, police and security officers have to communicate on a wide array of issues, from role and function to areas of responsibility. Discuss ideas and policies and share visions and approaches while seeking input and insight. Do not hesitate to work jointly on a particular project or undertaking. There is strength in numbers. On both ends of the aisle, there is much to learn. Police executives must be educated regarding the role that security plays in crime prevention. Most public law enforcement commanders fail to appreciate for the level of involvement. Many private practitioners operate from similar levels of ignorance about what the public mandate is—failing to understand that constitutional and economic considerations cannot be identical. Too many private security operatives engage in a sort of endless self-pity about a perceived second-class status when compared with the public operative.

When these goals are explored, public law enforcement's tendency to preach from a high moral plain is not as convincing. Richard Kobetz and H. Cooper, in their article "Two Armies: One Flag,"[18] state the following:

> It is no exaggeration to aver that without the aid of those presently engaged in the various tasks of private security, the resources of public law enforcement would have to be expanded far beyond the limits that the taxpayer could afford and would pay. Even those who do not contribute directly to the cost of providing private security services benefit to some notable extent from their existence. Private security is not a public luxury. It represents a substantial contribution to the general security of the community. In their impact on the community public and private law enforcement are one and indivisible.[19]

Private security has long been an underclass when compared with public law enforcement. Differences in the orientation, training, requirements, and social status accorded these positions have a great deal to do with the class or status differentiation. Although much time and energy have been expended in the professionalization of public law enforcement, negative stereotypes still exist concerning private security personnel. The Private Security Advisory Council states that these attitudes

> . . . are based on incorrect assumptions that private security personnel perform the same job duties as patrol officers and investigators in law enforcement, and that a broad generalization can be made about the nature and personnel of all components of proprietary and contractual security—guards, private patrol services, private investigators, armored car guards and armed couriers and alarm response runner and installers. Certainly, the security industry and private practitioners must concede that there is a distinction between the level of training and qualifications for certification. The security industry has been its own worst enemy in this area by failing to promote high-level, sophisticated standards for education requirements.[20]

In response to the call for increased state and local regulation of the private security force, Richard Lukins, in his article "Security Training for the Guard Force," castigates the industry for its lack of action:

This trend has not caught the affected components of the private security industry—the guard services and proprietary security managers—completely by surprise but it does not appear that they were totally prepared either. And certainly no one can say that out industry has established an imposing record of self-regulation.[21]

Lukins further relates that the present impression of a security guard as not more than "half a cop" will be deleterious to future professionalism in the security industry.[22] Professionalism requires more than rhetoric, and to achieve it, the security industry will have to overcome many impediments. Those impediments—a lack of educational discipline or cogent body of knowledge, of an accepted code of ethics, of a prestige or status consensus on occupational roles, or of a mark of social and governmental legitimacy—can all be overcome.[23] To get beyond the characterization that a private security practitioner is nothing more than a play police officer, the industry will have to aggressively implement standards of professionalism.

All these difficulties lead to deteriorating communications. It is distressing that the perception of second-class status is shared and adopted by certain public law enforcement types whose lack of understanding undermines regular conversation between these two forces. Instead of an equal partner, the protection officer is labeled the interluder or interloper. Increased communication will lead not only to understanding but also to endless favorable possibilities. Once police executives understand the dynamics of the security industry and its influence on crime and society, cooperation will emerge and division will dissipate. The strategies to increase cooperation are summarized as follows:

- Recognize certain prescribed standards of performance, education, and high level of professional competence of individuals entering the field or presently employed in the industry.
- Encourage the use of sound practices, principles of security, and loss prevention.
- Promote mutual respect, cooperation, and communication between both sectors as well as increasing the knowledge of each other's functions.
- Speak in a unified voice on issues that promote the industry at large.
- Stress and promote programs designed for increasing professional development at all levels of employment.
- Work to establish liaisons wherever possible that will serve to benefit the entire industry.
- Pursue a program of true professionalism in thought, word, and deed.[24]

Other joint partnerships, in which free-flowing and uninhibited information is shared between the public and private sector, have been regularly witnessed in municipality settings. Although there are limitations on criminal history dissemination, nevertheless, tactical strategies, policy making, and internal data analysis can be readily shared. In North Tampa, near the University of South Florida, CIS and local authorities undertook a clean-up project worth noting as a partnership ex-

Critical Intervention Services and Hillsborough County Sheriff's Department

Over the years, by conducting these types of joint operations, CIS and local law enforcement have been able to target and remove high-level narcotics dealers, illegal gun dealers, and habitual felony offenders. Before any of these events can take place, however, a relationship must be developed, and that effort takes time. CIS joined with the Hillsborough Sheriff's Department for the following operation. This particular operation had taken place in an apartment community that was known for its infestation of drugs and violent crime. This community, which had been under siege for years, had recently been purchased by a new owner. The new owner was committed to clean up this community by hiring CIS and cooperating with the local sheriff's office. A coordinated effort was developed between the property management, CIS personnel, and the Hillsborough County Sheriff's Office under the highly effective proactive leadership of Sheriff Cal Henderson. Just as any operation that CIS conducts, this one began with a community profile and threat assessment prior to any deployment of manpower.

During the threat assessment, CIS profilers were able to identify one particular apartment (through a number of sources) as potentially hazardous to any law enforcement activity within that intervention area. During the threat assessment, it was discovered that the occupants of this particular apartment possessed a number of semiautomatic handguns and possibly some fully automatic weapons with bulletproof vests and other type of equipment. It was evident that this type of firepower and protective gear could be used not only for committing crimes but also in causing potential harm to officers once they deployed in the intervention area. Once this information was attained and CIS profilers were able to verify its accuracy, CIS immediately began cooperating with the joint task force operating out of the Hillsborough County Sheriff's office. The task force was composed of deputies from the Organized Crime Bureau, agents from the Bureau of Alcohol Tobacco and Firearms, the United States Marshals, and others.

Within twenty-four hours of discovering this information and relaying it to the task force, task force members established probable cause from the information CIS had given them and served search warrants on the apartment. One suspect was arrested immediately, and a second individual was later arrested when he returned after a trip from out of town. The task force recovered fifteen semiautomatic weapons along with shotguns and one fully automatic Sten submachine gun. Additionally, the team recovered bulletproof vests, ski masks, and other types of equipment that could have been used for committing bank robberies and other violent crimes.

Once the initial community profiling and threat assessment was complete and the task force had completed their assignment of neutralizing the hazardous situation on this particular community, CIS and the Hillsborough County Sheriff's Selective Enforcement Unit (Street Crimes Unit) coordinated a joint deployment of personnel in an effort to maximize the impact on the community. CIS deployed six protection officers trained in STOP team operations and was supported by another six to ten sheriff's deputies for the duration of the reclamation phase.

Critical Intervention Services and Hillsborough County Sheriff's Department (cont.)

CIS, using its rights under contract to represent management, locked down the entire intervention area perimeter to ensure that no one could walk or drive into the community without being stopped and checked. As CIS officers conducted interviews to ascertain the legal status of individuals coming onto the property, the sheriff's deputies stood by on the interior perimeter ready to respond if a potential situation developed. Specifically, what deputies were looking for was any information that would lead to probable cause and, in turn, allow them to step in for the enforcement portion of the operation. Within the first three nights, by employing this type of combined proactive and reactive effort, Hillsborough County deputies were able to conduct twenty-three arrests, seized three vehicles, and confiscated three handguns. A large amount of crack cocaine was also recovered. One individual had over thirty individually bagged pieces of crack cocaine in his pockets when arrested, while another couple was carrying a thirty-nine gram "crack cookie" that had not even been portioned out for distribution. It was still in its original form after being recently manufactured.

The area was so busy with individuals being arrested for outstanding warrants, possession of drugs, possession of weapons, or simply trespasses after warning, that the Sheriff's office had to station transport wagons at the apartment community. The operation produced so many arrested individuals that at one point, lines of prisoners were formed while waiting for the transport wagon to return after each trip to county correctional facilities. Furthermore, the deployment and arrests generated dozens of eviction notices directed at problem residents.

---

ample.[25] This project produced remarkable results with 43 arrests and 12 evictions within the first three days of the reclamation phase. Hundreds of trespass warnings within the first five days of operation were also issued. To be even more effective, the security firm turned to the public sector for more power and strength against the target audience.

In partnerships, one soon witnesses the value of cooperation and communication. Crimes are solved more quickly, crime is deterred more readily, and safety and security for communities become a sure reality. Once mutual respect is established, communication and intelligence flow between the private and the public agencies, and in turn will proactively impact the community or targeted areas.

Another way to increase understanding is through the delivery of joint training or modular programs that are available to both the private and the public sector. As part of the continuing education requirements, public police departments allow their academy graduates to have interagency training in specialized security topics—subject matter beyond the delivery system of the traditional police department. Private protection specialists present information about the private sec-

Practitioner Tip: Intelligence Sharing

There are many other examples that can be presented as effective steps in the right direction of coordinated activities. Many law enforcement agencies have monthly intelligence meetings with their private security counterparts in an effort to exchange information, debate ideas, and explore the possibilities and the requirements for increasing the effectiveness of public safety overall for the community.

Some agencies are exploring a coordinated officer deployment strategy combined with joint dispatching of officers. Partnerships can allow law enforcement the ability to readjust their manpower according to the security personnel who are deployed within specific zones. In turn, they cooperate in developing dispatching solutions for nuisance problems within properties that security personnel are assigned to. This method allows the law enforcement entities to respond only when truly needed. An example is the Miami SCAN Program (Security Communications Assistance Network), which was initiated by the Miami Police Department in an effort to utilize private security officers equipped with radios to communicate suspicious and criminal activity to the proper law enforcement entities to protect the tourists visiting the city. In comparison, from the year 1995 to 1996, Miami saw a decrease by 33 percent of crimes committed against tourists. Other examples include contingency planning for natural disasters such as hurricanes, earthquakes, and floods. Additionally, this type of dialogue encourages the exchange of intelligence between police and security personnel in order to track and identify criminal trends and activities. Some departments go as far as to integrate security personnel and agencies within their police department's communication infrastructure. In this situation, security personnel are assigned police radios, and they communicate with police dispatchers directly to maximize effectiveness and coordinate response. Another compelling example of mutual cooperation would be the 1996 Olympic Games in Atlanta, where federal, state, local, military, and approximately 16,000 private security personnel worked cooperatively to ensure a safe environment. Thousands of individuals and entities, from diverse jurisdictions communicated effectively. Outside of one pipe bomb, which was found by a private security officer, the events were relatively incident free. None of these undertakings would have occurred without mutual cooperation and communication. (See: Steve Macko, Security at The Summer Olympic Games is Ready, EmergencyNet NEWS Service, Tuesday, July 9, 1996, Vol. 2–191, http://www.emergency.com/olymsec.htm)

tor, its resources, and the way that these resources can be accessed on the front lines on a daily basis by these recent police graduates.

Some agencies are exploring a coordinated officer deployment and dispatch of officers into certain community sectors. This type of partnership allows law enforcement the ability to adjust manpower requirements according to the amount and level of security personnel participation.[26] Joint endeavors between the private and the public sector facilitate and enable strong communication lines in the community integration model.

III. PRIVATE SECTOR COMMUNICATION AND THE MEDIA

Unfortunately, no matter how well an agency screens and trains its personnel, eventually an officer's behavior or improper handling of a situation (on duty or off duty) will subject the agency to negative media attention. Efforts discussed thus far on the communication front mean little when a negative public relation's problem rears its head. Just how the security firm handles this problem will say a good deal about its capacity to communicate with the most visible form of communication media. Public relations must be rooted in an honest and a professional foundation—at all costs, credibility must be maintained and viewed as an irreplaceable commodity. A security firm without credibility will have little, if any, chance at success in a community integration effort based on trust. Hence, when dealing with the media, communication must be in good faith.

Responses to media queries fundamentally fall into these three options.

1. **Proactive.** The proactive approach consists of actively providing information to the media and working with other agencies, if necessary, to bring the situation to a quick conclusion and ensure that the proper conclusion is reached.

2. **Reactive.** The reactive option is for the agency to wait silently and react only to information or accusations that are brought up about the particular incident—trying to maintain control if at all possible. The reactive approach basically boils down to action/reaction, in an attempt to minimize disclosure and deal only with specific issues as they become identified.

3. **Inactive.** The inactive option relies on the famous retort "no comment." The inactive approach tries to restrict all information and to ride out the crisis, and expects nondisclosure to make the problem disappear.

Of the three options, only the proactive approach will maintain and ensure community trust. Honesty and integrity should run through the entire security firm and its employees. It is disingenuous to expect street officers to exhibit candor in community interaction while management engages in parsing and damage control. This hypocrisy will not exist for long. The reactive strategy is essentially a knee-jerk approach and often creates more problems by casting the organization as defensive or hostile. The agency's reputation will be hard to rehabilitate. Likewise, the inactive approach is extremely damaging. It gives the impression that there is something to hide or that the agency is guilty, and thus arouses the community's concern. This outcome can create a level of damage that is extremely hard to recover from.

By utilizing the proactive approach, the agency retains its inherent credibility while dealing with the media or any other source of hostile scrutiny. First and foremost, the proactive approach is cooperative. The agency must be open and willing to expose the facts, no matter how unseemly or distasteful. While employing a cooperative approach, the agency delivers clear information and prevents misconceptions. See Figure 6.10.

For Immediate Release

For More Information Contact:
K.C. Poulin, President and CEO
(727) 461-9417 office

Critical Intervention Services
Retained to Protect Residents' Property
Amberwood Apartments

North Tampa, May 02, 2002, 6:00pm—In light of today's evictions of hundreds of tenants at Amberwood Apartments, due to severe code violations, Critical Intervention Services (CIS) has agreed to provide security to insure the safety of residents' property as they make this sudden transition.

According to K.C. Poulin, President and CEO of CIS, "The residents of Amberwood were forced to leave their apartments, due to no fault of their own, but for their own protection. Many have nowhere to go and are overwhelmed with being suddenly homeless. We have agreed to service this property to insure that personal property is not victimized. It is our hope that we can provide these people with a little peace of mind as they make plans for their future."

Amberwood residents will be able to access their former apartments, to collect their property, during daylight hours until Sunday afternoon.

CIS has been protecting apartment communities and businesses in North Tampa, and throughout the Bay Area, for over 10 years. The agency is well known and trusted throughout the community.

FIGURE 6.10   Proactive Communication with Community

The next step should be to assign one spokesperson to deal with media inquires and a separate representative to deal with legal inquires or interaction with other agencies. These spokespersons should be well briefed on the situation and should have an outline of the points that will be utilized during any interview with the media. It is recommended, in an effort to portray the image of cooperation and at the same time establish clear information with controlled positive statements, that a press release should be compiled and utilized to answer as many questions as possible. This step will help focus the media on specific areas of inquiry beneficial to the spokesperson when that individual is attempting to deal with media representatives. If an employee or officer is the target of the media attention, then the positive letters, commendations, or employee reviews of that officer should be made available for the media along with the press release. In doing so, it will show that the employee had a positive work history, positive reviews, or positive feedback from the people he or she worked with. This information aids in insulating the agency's reputation.

Practitioner Tip: Media Relationships

Successful protection firms develop and maintain strong and credible relationships with a community's media centers, from television to newspapers. Just as the reputation in the community is to be treasured and protected, the protection entity must come to depend and rely on the power of local media. When the firm's reputation is suspect, the media will be uncooperative and rightfully suspicious. When the firm's reputation is credible, the media sources will be of enormous help in community matters.

The last component of the proactive approach is the "be nice" rule. It is highly recommended that the spokesperson be soft-spoken and agreeable, in terms of the positive statements that are given and should in no way become argumentative. Remember that the spokesperson is the "face" of the agency. If the spokesperson seems defensive or aggressive, the agency also will be perceived as defensive or aggressive.

If the agency is accountable, contrite admission should be forthcoming. Even if the agency is innocent, conveying an appropriate sentiment of either apology or concern is always a positive move toward closing the crisis. The community will accept an apology and be willing to move on with minimal damage if the apology is given sincerely. Remember that the actual incident may last only one day, or at the very most a few days, and will be replaced with fresh news from other developing situations. However, if the situation is handled improperly, public relations damage can last for many years.

Once the media attention or "pressure" has come off and the agency is recovering successfully, the agency should quickly follow up with closing letters. Sending these letters directly from the head of the agency to various community entities not only will reinforce the agency's image as a professional organization but also will demonstrate the willingness to communicate. These letters should be directed at any community entities that the agency deals with, its clients, other agencies (private or public), and its own employees. The letter should outline the circumstances very briefly and communicate what was learned from the experience, reaffirming the agency's commitment to the community and the resolve to continue in the future.

Additionally, a letter should be sent to each media organization that covered the story and should reinforce the tone of cooperation, using clear and positive statements. However, this letter is not about the incident. In fact, the letter shouldn't discuss the details of the incident at all but should demonstrate the willingness of the agency to continue working with the community. The media should be thanked for its fairness and its professionalism in dealing with the story. This communication between the agency and the news media will solidify the agency as a proactive community leader and will strengthen relationships in the event that another crisis occurs.

IV. CONCLUSION

The value and merit of communication practice cannot be overemphasized. Whether the policy relates to community intervention and program implementation or to media and interchange between brothers and sisters in the public sector, communication must be ongoing and comprehensive. Strategies for notice and communiqués, as well as methods for press release and problem resolution, are included. Any reasonable chance of success in the community will largely depend on the power to communicate not only what the purpose of the community-based program is but also how it will impact the daily lives of residents.

This chapter lays out particular methodologies for communication in the community and argues that the private security industry is already strategically and ideologically placed in the realm of community communication when compared with the public realm. Communication is key to success in community operations, and the reader has been exposed to techniques that apply from the day of program commencement to wrapping up a community-based project. Special emphasis has been placed on how individual officers must conduct themselves in community settings, how demeanor and attitude are so critical to operational success, and how certain pitfalls, such as a failure to listen or a professional lethargy, can negatively impact public safety success. The chapter provides numerous examples of individual performance criteria and then turns its attention to how the security industry and its personnel must interact with its public counterparts. Clear success stories of mutual respect and cooperation are highlighted in the text. Public and private safety officers can and do work well together. Finally, the chapter delivers instructions on how private safety officers should interact with the media of diverse sorts. Honesty, candidness, and integrity are crucial for the communicator. Trust, in any of these cases, is built on the power of communication.

Notes

1. Ronald D. Hunter, *Officer Opinions on Police Misconduct, 15 J. of Contemp. Crim. Just.,* 155 (May 1999).
2. David L. Carter, in *Police Management & Issues Perspective* 67 (L. Hoover, ed. Police Executive Research Washington DC Fur 1992).
3. Clifford E. Simonsen, *Private Security in America: An Introduction* 1998 Prentice-Hall Upper Saddle River 1998.
4. Edward H. Connors, William C. Cunningham, and Peter E. Ohlhausen, Operation Co-operation *A Literature Review of Cooperation and Partnerships Between Law Enforcement and Private Security Organizations* 12–13 (U.S. Dept. of Justice, Washington, D.C. 1999).
5. National Advisory Committee on Criminal Justice Standards and Goals, *Private Security, Report of the Task Force on Private Security* 267 (1976).
6. *See* Task Force.
7. Task Force at 207.
8. Task Force at 211.
9. Task Force at 214.
10. Task Force at 210.

11. Task Force at 222.
12. Task Force at 226.
13. Task Force at 231.
14. Task Force at 236.
15. Task Force at 238.
16. *See* William Cunningham et al., *The Hallcrest Report II—Private Security Trends 1970–2000* Table 6–11 at 195 (Boston: Butterworth-Heinemann, 1990).
17. Rick Sarre, *Accountability and the Private Sector: Putting Accountability of the Private Security under the Spotlight,* 10 *Security Journal* at 97 (1998).
18. Richard Kobetz & H. Cooper, *Two Armies: One Flag.* 45 *Police Chief,* 28 1978
19. Kobetz at 28 and Cooper.
20. "Law Enforcement and Private Security: Sources and Areas of Conflict and Strategies for Conflict Resolution" Prepared by the Private Security Advisory Council to the Law Enforcement Assistance Administration, U.S. Dept. of Justice Washington, D.C. 1978. *Private Security Advisory Council.*
21. Richard Lukins, *Security Training for the Guard Force* 20 *Security Mangement,* 32 (1976).
22. Lukins at 32.
23. Lukins at 34.
24. Daniel E. McElroy, *A Professional Alliance* 16 Security World 34 (1979).
25. Lonora Lake, *Tampa Tribune. See also* Joseph N. Boyce, *Landlords Turn to "Commando" Patrols, The Wall Street Journal,* 9/18/96.
26. An example is the *Miami SCAN Program* (Security Communications Assistance Network), initiated by the Miami Police Department, in an effort to utilize private security officers equipped with radios to communicate suspicious and criminal activity to the proper law enforcement entities. Statistical data on SCAN shown that from 1995 to 1996, Miami saw a decrease by 33 percent of crimes committed against tourists. Other examples include contingency planning for natural disasters such as hurricanes, earthquakes, and floods. Additionally, this type of dialogue encourages the exchange of intelligence between police and security personnel in order to track and identify criminal trends and activities. Some departments go as far as to integrate security personnel and agencies within their police department's communication infrastructure. In this situation, security personnel are assigned police radios and communicate with police dispatchers directly to maximize effectiveness and coordinate response.

7

Private Sector Community-Based Psychological Tactics

If you leave the volume turned up all the way, all the time . . . you will eventually go deaf.
Sarge's Epitome of Common Sense

Learning Objectives

1. To gain an appreciation for the interplay between psychological tactics and police practices.
2. To learn that PsyOps and its regimen largely depend on the targeted community, its makeup, its state, and its current crime problems.
3. To realize that PsyOps will not be a successful policing strategy if it is lacking in general community support and participation.
4. To become familiar with the usual tactics employed in psychological operations in community-based settings.
5. To understand the nature of appearance, visual imagery, and conspicuous presence in the psychological war on crime and its prevention.
6. To learn about surveillance tactics in the deterrence of crime.
7. To become adept at establishing community-based policies where criminal offenders are exclusively targeted for expulsion.
8. To become proficient in the enlistment of community leaders, media, commercial and business owners, and neighborhood groups in the application of psychological pressure on malefactors in the community.

I. INTRODUCTION

For those who live outside high-crime communities, it seems implausible that residents become acclimated to the ravages of crime. The human condition allows for acclimation to just about any setting—even those plagued by crime and disorder. Another way of describing the phenomena is desensitization. Eventually communities become deaf to the rattles of criminals. Even good citizens have minimal options in the high-crime centers. Police agencies are capable of a similar unawareness, as if in a war zone where the normal appears abnormal, and the abnormal now seems normal. Or people simply withdraw and isolate from others.

In a sense, some communities need awakening from a slumber of indifference and fear. Only then will crime be combated and the streets returned to the rightful owners. Practitioners can deliver the tactics that shake up the community and drive out the intruders. The private sector can engage in psychological warfare that will attack those who undermine the health of a community, put a crimp in criminal opportunities, and reeducate criminals on prospects for future activity. Private sector justice can "jolt" a neighborhood like no other entity by using "shock teams."

> The shock team consists of security officers and support staff, working in conjunction with local law enforcement. The shock team officers act to identify and arrest the criminal element in a massive clean-up campaign. During this time, loitering, drunkenness, loud music, and similar problems are not tolerated.[1]

II. SHOCK TACTICS IN COMMUNITY-BASED METHODOLOGIES

To "shock" the community means what it says: driving out a general lethargy that allows criminal conduct to occur without consequence. The security specialist can adopt practices that pinpoint specific activity in a designated area. What that subject matter will be directly results from previous studies and analysis in the Threat and Risk Assessment and Community Profiling efforts. As part of the community profile, the community is evaluated for conduct; desensitized, troubled areas; juvenile and gangs activity; vice; and other variables. Once these conditions are assessed, the determination regarding what level of "shock" will reasonably be required to capture the attention of the protected community is calculated. The shock strategies will vary depending on the gravity of the activity. Shock activities are broken down into two categories:

1. High Impact Shock Strategies
2. Low Intensity Shock Strategies

The terms seem self-evident, but appropriate shock requirements can vary drastically between environments. For example, an office complex where personnel are accustomed to coming and going at will, without being challenged or monitored, portrays a lax security environment. A practitioner can create a scenario that delivers a sudden shock (low or high) that gains the attention of the target audience. If employees report to work and are confronted with a complete lockdown of the facility, high impact shock takes place. Even access control points at critical junctures of the facility, compartmentalized by different levels of security, will cause a reaction bordering on shock. The sudden implementation of new security procedures prompts unease and anxiety, thereby altering the culture that the employee expects. The less confrontational the tactic, the less the shock value delivered. See Figure 7.1.

The level of shock may require adjustment as conditions modify and the players change in the environment. Whereas the office complex would require a certain level of protection or security another facility might not permit a lockdown. More subtle approaches can be very effective in producing a shock image. Landscaping, lighting, parking arrangements, and signs are just a few. Unfortunately, there is no mathematical equation to abide by in the overall assessment of a combined technique. For this evaluation, the practitioner will have to calculate on the basis of experience and ultimately his or her own professional judgment.

It is very common to mix a combination of high- and low-impact techniques and strategies to meet the exact need of the environment that the practitioner is attempting to bring under control. A high-shock approach can utilize highly visible

FIGURE 7.1 Security in Numbers

Critical Intervention Services: The Shock Continuum

CIS uses a scale for quantifying the level of shock (low or high) required in each different situation. A scale of 1 through 5 was constructed as a continuum. The numerical value (1–5) is assigned to each and every technique that is considered for implementation. The value chosen is meant to identify the intensity level for the technique only. The impact of implementing access control measures, for example, could range from a light controls to a total lockdown. This must be measured in terms of values or levels—1 through 5. A level 1 may entail putting someone at the front door and greeting people. A level 2 would encompass the posted officer plus access control technology that verified identifications. Higher numbers signify complete control and surveillance of all employee movements within the facility.

Uniforms illustrate the continuum. A level 1 is the plain-clothes officer who greets but appears more serious. A level 2 would be an unarmed officer in a light colored uniform. A level 3 would employ an officer in a blazer and slacks, with a patch on the jacket. The blazer looks authoritative and official, but leaves the onlooker with a question about whether the officer is armed or not. A level 4 would be the armed officer in a traditional police style uniform, saddled with utility belt, handcuffs, and other accessories. A level 5 would utilize an armed officer in a high-profile military style uniform called "Battle Dress," shown in Figure 7.2. The military image is bound to stir up some anxiety in wrongdoers, and even in law-abiding citizens. Combine military clothing with canines or other equip-

FIGURE 7.2 Uniforms Relay Intent and Purpose

> ## *Critical Intervention Services: The Shock Continuum (cont.)*
>
> ment, and the shock starts to set in. Deploying officers dressed in suits, with earpieces connected to their radios, and the observer automatically assumes that the officers are armed and highly trained.
>
> CIS shock tactics frequently blend multiple techniques to achieve a higher level of impact. Uniforms blended with canine, cars with police hardware, lighting combined with patrol units, as examples, can complement the effort. Practitioners may mix a combination of high and low impact techniques and strategies to meet exact needs.

techniques combined with other tactics of a lower intensity level to meet the shock value required. This process is done by intentionally coordinating multiple techniques in order to maximize the impact on the overall program within a specific time frame. The possibilities are limited only by the imagination of the practitioners implementing the effort. Weigh and assess the community, and also consult the data derived from the community profile and threat assessment before proceeding.[2]

Security firms, hold a bevy of remedies that usually rest idle. Shock the criminals by the following:

- Actions for ejectment
- Actions for trespass
- Actions for eviction
- Actions for nuisance

Landowners, lessors, and commercial property owners have untapped powers that shock the intruder. "Today, in virtually every jurisdiction, landlords have some duty to protect their tenants from the criminal activities of strangers . . . In addition to these purely private tort duties, increasingly landlords are being held to quasi-public standards for tenants' criminal activities, such as those based on state nuisance abatement laws and state and federal forfeiture laws."[3] To do nothing can trigger liability for negligence or other tort remedy.[4]

A. First-Contact Protocols

Shock does not imply a lack of courtesy and professionalism. Sound practices rightfully insist on a professional decorum. Public policing historically recognizes the interplay of citizen interaction and officer demeanor. Private officers operate under an identical mandate. Protection officers need to remember the basic rules of courtesy and etiquette when dealing with the public that will be subject to these operations. Undoubtedly, shock techniques may upset some people, although most people welcome the intervention if it is truly needed. Officers will have to expend time explaining the purpose and rationale behind these tactics and reassure the law-abiding component of the target audience of the ends that these tactics seek. The explanation phase allows substantial interaction to occur in the community setting, and officers should take advantage of this channel of communication.

Certain parameters to first contact are basic and must be standard operational procedures on all deployments. The officer should always use the terms of Sir or Ma'am when addressing every constituency, and should explain, without reservation, their position as community officers, protection officers, or prevention officers. The officer's tone should be professional, positive, and helpful. Look for ways to intervene and assist as the conversation unravels. First-contact protocols should avoid certain forms of communication such as the following:

- Never engage in condescension.
- Never criticize; offer alternatives.
- Never utilize abusive or profane Language.
- Never be indifferent or uncaring.
- Never engage in racial profiling or stereotyping.

Officers who adopt negative strategies will loose the respect and trust of the target audience, and once lost, it is almost not retrievable. Trust is an extraordinary commodity. See Figure 7.3.

III. HIGH-SHOCK STRATEGIES IN HIGH-CRIME COMMUNITIES

Approaching high-crime communities with shock tactics pressures the criminal element and creates an environment where the criminal becomes apprehensive. The criminal, much to his or her annoyance, gets frustrated by the unwanted attention

FIGURE 7.3   Trust Building with the Young—Preventative Interaction

coming his or her way and expends far too much time avoiding the tactic. This delay cuts into the criminal's normal operating procedure, since he or she is incapable of committing crime and simultaneously avoiding the shock. When the wrongdoer is unnerved, community members sense a chance to remove the malefactor's power base and will, in turn, be more apt to cooperate with lawful authority. The shock heaped on the criminal affects the citizen at the same time. But the shock is both a welcome reality for the lawful and an albatross for the illegal in a high-crime community. With solid networking and understanding of purpose, the relationship between the officer and the community resident begins to flourish. As community involvement grows, the shock techniques that have delivered a structural foundation for a meaningful police-community relationship should be lessened and then stopped. Remember that shock techniques are a short tactic to generate interest and a foundation for environmental change.

IV. LOW-INTENSITY SHOCK STRATEGIES

For situations requiring a lighter and less aggressive touch, low-level shock techniques can be implemented in the protection plan. Low-level shock techniques can be as simple as changing the appearance of security personnel, upgrading the uniforms or style of the patrol vehicles, or even deploying marked vehicles where not usually located. Another example is the introduction of closed-circuit television systems. Additionally, implementing security awareness seminars for community members, employees and, other specific groups impacts the mentality in quiet but very effective ways. See Figure 7.5.

Television stations, with monitors and manned stations, are well-known approaches on the low-shock spectrum, and they do not usually exemplify high-crime environments. Therefore, often personnel who are more sedentary than are the younger and more agile officers will staff the monitor, CCTV system. By switching the retired police officer with a more imposing, younger officer, the low-shock impact will be immediate. Access control becomes more than an afterthought that heavily relies on machines and technology to identify the prospective criminal; now there is a charged and serious environment where nothing escapes the assigned personnel at the computer control center. Energetic officers will continue to shock the community when the task of monitoring is done proactively—by greeting and visually inspecting all contacts. For more significant results in low shock, supplement the CCTV system with personnel patrolling the facility. Instead of a sedentary reaction, the CCTV team is enhanced by an active cadre of security specialists who visually control and interact within the environment. Machines such as CCTV equipment serve many useful purposes, but cannot deliver the level of warning that a team of protection officers interacting with the community can. A group of alert professionals demonstrates to visitors, employees, residents, and the potential criminal their seriousness of purpose. Compare the impact of CCTV products with the imposing professional team highlighted in Figure 7.6. A wide array of California agencies, from policing to education institutions, find merit in the surveillance

High Shock: Lockdown and Layered Interaction

In apartment communities experiencing high levels of crime, Critical Intervention Services established a technique by which the perimeter of the property is "locked down." Security personnel confronted residents, patrons, guests, or visitors to that community various times as they traversed the grounds. This technique, which is called *layered interaction,* creates a rigid cross-checking approach that generates shock and immediately gains control of an environment. See Figure 7.4. Aside from the main gate, visitors were also stopped at random checkpoints and asked questions about purpose and identity. This type of confrontation is considered Level 2. As the visitor moved through the maze, the intensity of officer clothing and accoutrements increased, as did the physical setting where the questioning occurred. Hence, the levels of shock increased too. Although on the surface this technique may appear as nothing more than systematic harassment, the shock tactic serves a critical strategic function. First, the tactic announces a change in normal procedures. Second, criminals soon discover that there will be no safe haven. Third, the criminal who hopes to perpetually avoid detection will not survive in the maze of checkpoints. Fourth, the environment has now become hostile for criminals and troublemakers, and they may find better ground elsewhere. Sixth, no criminal will read this message as one of laxity but rather as one of rigor and commitment. Clothe the armed officers with military battle dress (Level 5 for uniforms), and the shock becomes even more onerous. Then add night vision equipment, camcorders, and canines, and the shock only intensifies.

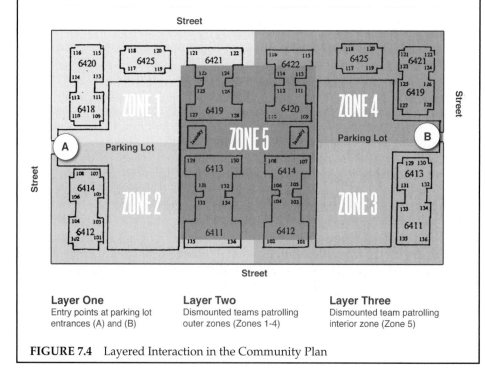

Layer One
Entry points at parking lot entrances (A) and (B)

Layer Two
Dismounted teams patrolling outer zones (Zones 1-4)

Layer Three
Dismounted team patrolling interior zone (Zone 5)

FIGURE 7.4   Layered Interaction in the Community Plan

FIGURE 7.5   Shock and Canine Teams

method. Although there is a natural resistance to technological intrusion, neighborhoods can reap enormous benefits from their use. See Box 7.3 for the rationale for installation.

CCTV personnel are involved with other intelligence and preventive activity and the onlookers are aware of this changed environment. Couple these activities with an escort policy, and the cultural shift continues with both the workers and the undesirable element being slowly but surely affected by these shock tactics. Uniform changes, from the standard security uniform to a corporate-blazer-style uniform with a security ID tag hanging from the pocket, continue the alteration in environment that the target audience cannot help but see.

FIGURE 7.6   Professional Presence as a Shock Tactic

Residential and City CCTV Partnerships

Residential neighborhood initiatives to improve public safety using CCTV video surveillance have been undertaken in the cities of Tacoma, Washington, and Hollywood, California.

The Residential Neighborhood Security Act empowers local organizations and neighborhood associations to participate in planning and funding projects. A framework for volunteer participation would be useful. The plans might specify how CCTV video surveillance would be coordinated with community policing, neighborhood watch programs, and volunteer staffing of surveillance monitors.

Local residential security districts could be created upon meeting standards specified by the office of Criminal Justice Planning (OCJP) or the U.S. Department of Justice. The community security districts could be given authority to install and operate CCTV video surveillance within the district's defined geographical boundary, consistent with state guidelines. Some related activities might include the following:

1. Identify juveniles who violate local curfews or are loitering in the neighborhood. Work with the police to ensure that their activities are consistent with any parole and probation orders.
2. Improve truancy enforcement.
3. Look for and identify people who display firearms in the community. This activity might include pilot projects using new concealed weapons identification surveillance technology.
4. Identify speeding vehicles in order to enhance the effectiveness of traffic laws.

From: Marcus Nieto, *Public Video Surveillance: Is It An Effective Crime Prevention Tool?* (June 1997, CRB-97-005) at http://www.library.ca.gov/CRB/97/05/.

Once the visual changes are implemented, the plan of shock attack continues its evolution. Other programs that might be added to the mix can be continuing education and professional assistance programs. Awareness programs that focus on specific problems in the community are also change agents. Examples of these initiatives are the following:

1. *Bomb and terror countermeasures.* This is a program for the corporate setting where by industry is exposed to prevention measures relating to terrorism and bomb activity. Content is directed to mail room personnel, telephone operators, and heads of departments on how to deal with bomb threats, suspect packages, and outlined contingency plans for an unexpected device detonation. The complexities of this type of protective activity call for esoteric training, such as offered by the Safety and Intelligence Institute.
2. *Workplace violence prevention program.* This is a program that identifies disgruntled employees and the potential liability problems that arise

from a lack of control and supervision. The program further covers the identification and management of situations involving emotionally disturbed employees.

3. *Stalker prevention and identification program.* This is a program that stresses the means and techniques to avoid victimization by stalkers. The program works well in corporate and community settings, and it sends a clear message that the conduct of stalking and harassment will not be tolerated. Victims are trained in how to identify various signs in communication, from physical harassment to inordinate following, and mail sent and phone calls received and the content therein. Content of communications that displayed anger, emotional attachment, excessive adoration, or pornographic materials is highlighted.

These education programs can apply to many other environments and workplaces. The aim is to create more substance in the public safety effort within a short period of time in order to produce a low-intensity shock effect in the target environment.

V. PSYCHOLOGICAL OPERATIONS (PSYOPS) AS SHOCK TACTICS

The infusion of shock into the community environment is often indiscernible. Altering the mentality of residents, business owners, and other community constituencies can be done through both direct and very indirect means. The problems in high-crime communities need to be attacked on many fronts, and for experienced private sector professionals, the best approach is one that is often undetected or difficult to identify. In this way, the security specialist engages in a sort of psychological warfare against the target—and that battle plan works in the background, quietly and without fanfare. Change comes about without the participants' even realizing the full extent of the psychological operation. While high- and low-shock tactics shout their intentions, most of these recommendations can be described only as more subtle.

Practitioner Tip: The Lithium Fence

If a community needs to secure a particular area by perimeter fencing, there is no assurance that the fence can physically control access. A creative approach is to coat the fence with lithium grease, which makes the fence extremely difficult to scale and permanently stains clothing. Lithium grease, which is not visible to the naked eye, is colorless and so is not an eyesore to the physical environment.

PsyOps incorporate creative strategies to disrupt the psychological confidence of perpetrators. PsyOps undercut the "no fear" factor so ingrained in the criminal community. Implemented properly, PsyOps create a state of uncertainty in the perpetrator and impede the ability to identify security vulnerabilities. The degree to which PsyOps impact the criminal elements will depend on their pathology. Those suffering from social or emotional pathology—from the drug addicts to the mentally unstable—are clearly less influenced but in many cases still have impact. Planning, premeditating felons can be keenly targeted by Psyops. PsyOps ultimately force the criminal to move activities to a more predictable environment that is less hostile to individuals with criminal intentions. The program seeks to undermine confidence and replace it with levels of anxiety and consternation that make crime less attractive in the region. Since most criminals select targets on the basis of a perception of the environment, and more specifically, the relative weaknesses that enable the activity, the only defense is the alteration of the environment. Vulnerability and opportunity must be changed to strength and impossibility. Implemented properly, PsyOps generate a climate of perpetrator uncertainty and impede the usual ability to identify security vulnerabilities. Determining an appropriate plan for psychological operations requires an evaluation of the environment and the types of perpetrators that the environment is likely to attract. As stated earlier, the community profile and threat assessment will establish the need and feasibility for using particular tactics in relation to shock techniques to meet environmental needs. PsyOps offer many approaches.

A. Visual Imagery

An environment with warnings is one that puts felons and delinquents on notice of the community's intentions. The criminal trespassers should be bombarded with what would they would perceive as negative imagery. Aside from the no-trespass edict, signs can warn of consequences for conduct, announce the use of technology to track activity, and indicate health risks or hazards resulting from milling around a particular area. Signs convey the message of intolerance and defense when it comes to criminal behavior. Signs stating that an area is under surveillance, making reference to audio and video surveillance, are effective warnings. Visual intimidation, such as "wanted" posters, is one of the most primitive, yet inexpensive tools for protection. See Figure 7.7.

B. Letters, Surveys, and Communiqués

Letters and communiqués should be distributed to the community from the outset of any program of new security procedures and deployments. These forms of correspondence, which lay out intentions in clear-cut and unambiguous terms, provide notice to the troublemakers that the community will undergo alterations that will directly impact the criminal culture, as well as improve the quality of life. The letters take many approaches, including the following:

WANTED

CRITICAL INTERVENTION SERVICES

$ 5,000.00 REWARD

HELP US CATCH A RAPIST AT LARGE

Poster Released by Critical Intervention Services: January 3, 2002

CAUTION Considered Extremely Dangerous

The above composite likenesses were based on descriptions provided by the victims. These likenesses may represent one or more than one individual.

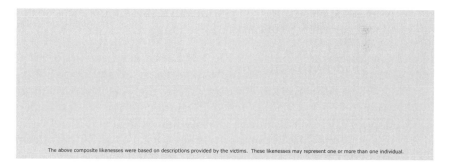

DESCRIPTION

Date of Birth:	unknown	**Hair:**	Black
Place of Birth:	unknown	**Eyes:**	Brown
Height:	5'7" to 5'10"	**Complexion:**	dark
Weight:	180 to 200 pounds	**Sex:**	Male
Build:	Medium	**SSN:**	Unknown
Occupation:	unknown	**Race:**	Hispanic
Scars/Marks:	unknown	**Nationality:**	American
Aliases:	unknown		

"quando necessita est."

CAUTION: If you see someone fitting this description DO NOT attempt to apprehend them. CONTACT LAW ENFORCMENT OFFICIALS

HCSO Sheriffs Office at (813) 247-8655 or Crime Stoppers 1(800) 873-8477 or call your local CIS office, at 813-910-4247

FIGURE 7.7 Reward Poster

- Letters of introduction
- Plan of action
- Descriptions of focused activities
- Descriptions of identified parties
- Announcements of tactical programs
- Announcements of awareness programs
- Announcements of equipment installation
- Results of crime stop initiatives

See the questionnaire issued in an initial deployment in a residential community in Figure 7.8. Flooding the community with strategically crafted literature assuredly moves the psychology of the criminal element in a different direction. Be sure that the literature is balanced with proactive statements that highlight a concentration on improving the quality of the environment, so that it is a more balanced statement of purpose.

C. Visual Intimidation

As the security firm deploys, how it presents itself has psychological implications. The approaches vary widely and can range from the soft to the battle-hardened look. That criminals can be visually intimidated and thereby psychologically adjusted is undeniable. Canine units, shown in Figure 7.9, may deliver the needed effect. See Figure 7.10. Dispensing with the traditional security appearance has effects that are readily measurable.

Despite obvious merits, two issues need consideration before employing visual intimidation. First, minimize the intimidation of residents or employees. Explain and converse with the good citizenry what the purpose for the visual changes are. Adhere to *first contact protocols,* and expend time explaining the program to those who are not its target. If the protocols are done correctly, community members will realize that the public safety effort and its officers work on their behalf. Soon thereafter, community members will become willing partners in the enterprise, if the vacuum of information needed is properly filled. See Figure 7.12. Community cooperation will read this message as beneficial rather than confrontational.

Second, *do not project a false image of capability.* Make the warning with punch behind the words. Intimidate with the ability to respond. False and vacuous threats will eventually backfire. Intimidation without the means and muscle will be perceived as a show and a sham. Under such conditions, the program not only will be ineffective but also will generate safety challenges for the unprepared security personnel.

1. Comprehensive Surveillance.   Surveillance clearly impacts the psychology of any community.[5] Aggressive, comprehensive, and sweeping surveillance tactics surely affect the criminal element and, by any measure, the criminals can

Resident
Your views about crime in the community are very important to us. Please assist us completing the following questionnaire.

Answer each question by filling in the blank or circling the appropriate response. When complete, return the questionnaire to any of the CIS protection officers on duty.

Unit and Apartment Number: _____ Name: _____

NOTE: We only ask for your name and apartment number to identify who has completed the questionnaires for future follow-up in 90 days. Your answers are strictly confidential. Property management WILL NOT see your questionnaire or know who has responded.

Crime & Security

1. How would you describe the level of crime in your apartment community?
    A. Very High
    B. High
    C. Medium
    D. Low
    E. Very Low

2. Do you feel threatened or scared by the presence of drug dealers, gangs, or violent criminals in your apartment community?
    A. Yes
    B. No

3. Have you been the victim of previous crimes in your apartment community?
    A. Yes
    B. No

If YES, did you report these crimes to the police?
    A. Yes
    B. No

4. Do you feel that you can trust the police to protect you and your family?
    A. Yes
    B. No

5. In order of importance, list your greatest concerns regarding crime in your apartment community. (For example: 1. drug dealing, 2. gangs, 3. car theft, 4. burglary)
    1. _____
    2. _____
    3. _____
    4. _____

FIGURE 7.8 Community Survey

Community Organization

6. In general, do you know your neighbors and feel that you can trust them?
   A. Most of my neighbors
   B. Some of my neighbors
   C. Very few of my neighbors
   D. None of my neighbors
7. If you see children behaving inappropriately, do you feel comfortable talking to their parents about the problem?
   A. Yes
   B. No
8. Do you feel that the property managers care about the apartment community?
   A. Yes
   B. No
9. Do you plan on remaining in the apartment community or do you plan on moving in the near future?
   A. Remaining. I plan on renewing my lease when my lease expires.
   B. Remaining until my lease expires.
   C. Leaving as soon as an opportunity permits.

FIGURE 7.8   *(Cont.)*

FIGURE 7.9   Visual Influence in Secure Community Settings

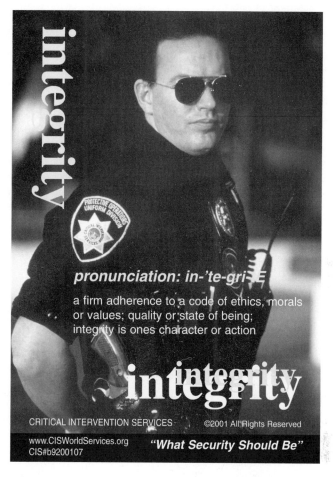

FIGURE 7.10   Professional Literature that Describes Security Personnel

be significantly intimidated. Although a free society needs to perpetually balance the citizen's privacy rights with the desire to rid the community of criminal perpetrators, an equilibrium is not always easy to discover. On the one hand, the imagery of Big Brother may offend our sensibilities because of its seeming intrusiveness. On the other hand, high-crime communities have long since lost any sense of personal sanctity and individualism as rampant crime and social problems rot away their infrastructure. Hard times call for hard measures, and the infusion of serious and pervasive surveillance, both technology-based and human, into a community will psychologically influence its makeup. In high-crime communities, comprehensive surveillance is a tactic of last resort, and its purposes are multifaceted:

Critical Intervention Services: HAZOPS Unit

The CIS Hazardous Operations Unit (HAZOPS) is responsible for implementing Phase One and Two activities in the more challenging and blighted environments. The armed HAZOPS officers are uniformed in black military battle dress uniforms (BDU), ballistic vests, and military boots projecting the appearance that "security means business." See Figure 7.11, from the *Wall Street Journal*'s September 18, 1996, issue.

    This heightened visual effect creates a psychological uncertainty in the criminal who now is desperately trying to assess the effectiveness of these no-nonsense-appearing security personnel. This type of upgraded security appearance communicates to the criminal that the security officers are well disciplined and prepared to handle confrontation. In addition, HAZOPS utilizes specially equipped vehicles, additional specialty equipment, as well as canines and other visually intimidating assets.

FIGURE 7.11   Shock and Siege Officer

FIGURE 7.12 Community Cooperation in the War on Crime

To protect undercover officers or to corroborate their testimony.

To obtain evidence of a crime.

To obtain evidence of a civil wrong.

To locate persons.

To check on the reliability of informants, witnesses, and other parties.

To locate hidden property or contraband.

To obtain probable cause for search warrant processes.

To prevent the commission of an act or to apprehend a suspect in the commission of an act.

To obtain information for later use in interrogation.

To develop leads and information received from other sources.

To know at all times the whereabouts of an individual within a given area.

To obtain admissible legal evidence for use in court.

Surveillance tactics undermine the confidence of criminals who once roamed the countryside without fear and were secure in the belief that their actions remained concealed. Aggressive surveillance strips away the criminal's sense of anonymity.[6]

The surveillance is compelling. If the criminal realizes that security is everywhere, at all times, watching and tracking his or her activities, the criminal's psychology can only shift. And the surveillance can be community- or individually-based. Much depends on legality and community consent, but some form of a visual watch program can be designed. Selectively placed night vision equipment and surveillance cameras, in addition to various modes of observation by officers, that discreetly observe individuals can change environments. What is imperative is the shift in psychology—the criminals now know that other people know. Drug dealers, for example, when under surveillance will suffer from some form of apprehension. If the officer, with camera in hand, makes himself or herself visible to the dealer over a period of time and then confronts the dealer with the equipment in hand, the dealer's confidence loses some its luster.

Visual intimidation by surveillance blends technology and the watchful eye of security professionals. A planned and comprehensive program of surveillance can undermine the psychological confidence of the felon. A program that is difficult to detect adds to the felon's confusion. Surveillance is the invisible eye in the sky that watches at all times, is everywhere, and knows everything. Critical preparatory questions regarding surveillance strategy are included in Figure 7.13.

On a final note, it seems absurd that the skill and acumen of the human player be left out of this equation. Surveillance, in the end, is done by people, or it simply becomes an automated documentation system for review after an occurrence. In this context, surveillance resides within the province of private protection specialists. Although its use is widely praised as a deterrence mechanism, the results will vary according to the skill and training of the officer, type and sophistication of the equipment and method, and the target of observation. One officer alone cannot scan the horizon with a single set of eyes, hoping to detect criminal perpetrators. Neither can too many officers be assigned to too small a zone of surveillance, because such practices diminish returns. Nor should surveillance be strictly mechanical. Technology goes only so far, and the ongoing, persistent, and aggressive presence of individuals is required, who not only watch and observe, detect and

---

1. Is there any alternative to surveillance?
2. Do you know what information is needed from the surveillance?
3. Have you decided what type of surveillance is needed?
4. Do you know enough about the area of surveillance to determine equipment and manpower needs?
5. Do you have the required equipment and manpower?
6. Are proper forms available to record necessary information during the surveillance?
7. Are all signals preestablished?

FIGURE 7.13 Issues in Surveillance Strategy

confirm, but who also are probably the most effective means of psychologically changing the environment. Surveillance depends on the skilled professionals who scan the entire community, with or without machines, and collect information to be used in the public safety effort. Scant debate exists on the tactics effectiveness.[7]

But security professionals cannot succeed in the massive undertaking in isolation. Surveillance and the corresponding psychological shifts that it generates rely heavily on the friendly assistance of community members. A community that feels part of the "watching" is a community that is proactive. This surveillance does not intend to be an intrusive and unwelcome eye on activities but rather a fraternal vigilance of community residents watching out for each other. A recent and very distressing spate of murders in Rochester, New York, has left policy makers and police departments in a state of disbelief. Despite all efforts of the police to integrate into the community, as well as the institution and funding of net stations and programs of every sort, police critics still hammer away at the estrangement that community members either perceive or actually experience. The mayor of Rochester, the Honorable James Johnson, pleaded with the community to become involved, especially urging that the young men of the community report, assist, and watch over this declining community. Mayor Johnson begged for volunteers to be Big Brothers to be caregivers and reporters. The response to this call for assistance was lukewarm, but at least the policy makers appreciate the impossibility of using just the public police and the diverse tactics that they employ, as the sole solution. Community members share the vision of the private protection specialist and must be incorporated into the community-based program. Without community members, actively involved in "community monitoring" surveillance will not be as effective.

2. Conspicuous Presence.   Another form of visual intimidation is through a "conspicuous presence." This tactic demoralizes the criminal by eliminating the privacy and space for criminal commission. Security officers conspicuously post themselves close to the suspected subject and persistently remain close, to the

Practitioner Highlight

Vance International

Vance International has used GPA tracking to its benefit. Its Mexico City office has 24/7 tracking and emergency service center. The service is provided in two distinct ways. First, it is the obvious personnel protection service, which provides a hardened vehicle and security driver and a GPS tracking system that allows for panic communications, constant location determination, and the ability of the monitoring center to control vehicle functions such as locking doors, killing the engine, and listening to the interior of the vehicle. Used in an antikidnapping mode, the service provides for protection, and if that fails, for recovery.

irritation of the subject. This technique not only thwarts criminal opportunity but also eventually causes the criminal to relocate. For example, in the case of a drug deal, officers will use this technique to cut off customers from making purchases and to force the dealer to do business elsewhere.

First, security officers stop and identify all individuals who come to a particular location by conducting *field interview reports,* or in the case of vehicle traffic, by copying down license plate numbers and vehicle information, as well as suspect information when possible. Next, the officer should be equipped with a camcorder to record anyone approaching a dealer. Consumers are averse to this form of intrusion and will soon become strangers to the area under surveillance. See Figure 7.14. This constant intrusion tilts the psychology of both the community and the felon. In the latter instance, the offender will be so unnerved that he or she will have few opportunities to remain in the community. In the former instance, the community will regain its confidence and will feel reenergized to continue driving out the undesirable visitors. One victory builds on another. PsyOps and the tactics of visual intimidation can save communities.

D. Strategic Deception

Strategic deception intentionally provides perpetrators with inaccurate information about security, the community, peers, and criminal ends. False information disrupts the usual bases for assessing vulnerabilities and identifying potential

FIGURE 7.14   Security Operations That Target Known Criminals: Proactive Intervention

victims. When fed deception, criminals tend to lose faith in their once-vaunted abilities to victimize others. In short, the psychological confidence that once supported the criminal mindset is neutralized. Confidence is replaced with fear, anxiety, and distrust. Security specialists can employ a host of psychological tactics to undercut confidence. Deception can be in the form of rumors. A few examples of the deceptive strategy are starting a quiet rumor of impending arrests, of identification of suspects, and of cooperation with local law enforcement in effecting arrest.

Be aware, however, that deception should be used carefully. Study all possible consequences prior to the planned deception. Deception efforts should never be used against the community members who are law-abiding and cooperative in order to achieve a particular end. Trust is too precious a commodity to risk. Deception efforts should be directed only at the criminal element.

E. Media Coverage as Psychological Warfare

Local media outlets can aid in the community integration effort. Media coverage of security operations indicates many things. First and foremost, the story commands attention. In the media culture, what makes the news allegedly is newsworthy. Successful efforts in community control are wonderful stories to relate. Who would not be pleased that drug dealers, prostitutes, gang bangers, and other thugs who rule the streets have met their match? Stories of community victory are the stuff of optimism. Although the media glorifies violence in too many circumstances, it will also be delighted to report success in the war on crime at the street level. The story is so rare that it catches the media's attention. Thus, the aggressive use of media sources, whether print or visual media, further drives the offender into a defensive posture, alters the psychology of his or her operations.

Newspapers, radio, and television glorify the security agency victories over the wrongdoers. As victories multiply, the security firm takes on an air of invincibility, while the criminal retreats in shame. This shift in psychological advantage is fueled by the media coverage. It not only sends a message to the criminal but also enforces the fundamental understanding in the community that a positive change is taking place.

Practitioner Tip: Rumor and Electrical Boxes

Many times electrical boxes become a hangout area for juveniles. The rumor tactic can be used to create concern of health hazards regarding the long-term exposure by close proximity to electrical boxes. For example, a Florida security firm hoping to clean up the area around a power company transformer indicated that close proximity might cause impotence or sterility. A dramatic drop-off in criminal activity occurred after the rumor was circulated.

> ## Critical Intervention Services: Media Coverage and Psychology
>
> Overall, CIS has been shown in the media over the past ten years about 300 times. A quarter of those times has been within the television news media. This news exposure is extremely important to CIS and its community relation's effort, since the community accepts the message as being credible and newsworthy. The development of an informative media kit is paramount. Newspapers, radio, television, and any other opportunities that CIS has been presented with in terms of creating exposure for the agency have been aggressively pursued. As a result, CIS was able not only to create a corporate image toward the public but also more specifically to conduct psychological intimidation toward the criminal elements that perpetrate within CIS-protected environments. Furthermore, CIS personnel have acquired a corporate and an operational personality shaped in the community by the media.

F. Night Vision Tactics

Night vision equipment, which aimed at felons, psychologically intimidates. Similar to surveillance equipment but more mysterious, the equipment shows the lawful authority the collection and delivery of illegal materials. See Night Vision Equipment Company's webpage for an excellent assortment of products at www.nightoptics.com.

Criminals who see the equipment will expect negative consequences from its use. The combination of night vision equipment and video cameras documents criminal activity for use later during criminal prosecution. But the more important impact of the night vision equipment and cameras rests in the lack of awareness of what the officer will do with the results. Psychological imbalance occurs when criminals cannot discern when and where the activities are scoped, and for what purposes the information is collected and cataloged. Routine nightly interaction with the criminal culture, when officers will openly display the equipment to felons and delinquents, further unsettles the psychology.

G. Pay Telephones

Although public police usually call for the removal of pay telephones, the private sector finds pay telephones very useful. With the increased use of cell phones, private sector operatives will have to contend with the new technology. Even so, pay phones are instruments of the criminal actor. One technique used to solve the pay phone problem is to put stickers on pay phones that state, "**WARNING: This phone is being monitored for line integrity.**" The warning is meaningless but sounds official. Under normal circumstances, telephone companies may monitor the line to make sure that the line is working correctly, or an officer may be directed to physi-

---

Practitioner Tip: Graffiti Deterrence

The use of rewards, often funded by business and community entities, gives impetus to community involvement and shifts the psychological edge to the community residents. No longer will people turn the other way. No longer will graffiti artists assume that residents will exhibit a nonchalant attitude about the practice. Economic incentives change the psychology.

$1000.00
REWARD

CIS implemented a $1000.00 reward for any information leading to the identification, apprehension and conviction of any individual(s) involved in committing specific criminal acts on CIS protected properties. The reward is for any information regarding:

Property Damage
(fences, clubhouse, pools and buildings)

Vehicle Theft
Vehicle Burglary
Drug Sales
Home Burglary
Robbery

Please advise your residents, patrons, guests and visitors of this reward through newsletters, memos, and by personal contact.

Information can be relayed to CIS by contacting a CIS officer in person or by calling CIS at 727-461-9417 or 813-910-4247

FIGURE 7.15   Another Reward Format

cally inspect the phone on a daily basis. However, to the paranoid criminal mind, it is perceived as a clear warning that someone is listening to his or her conversation.

The suggestion here is not trivial. The availability and use of pay phones directly correlate with crime rates, levels of fear, and other quality-of-life issues. Sorensen quantitatively analyzes the impact of fewer phones on rates of criminality.[8] Pay phones can in the worst case scenario be completely removed from the community or restricted to outgoing calls, especially in high-crime communities. Keep in mind that many of the residents within these communities have no access to telephones within their homes, and the removal and unchecked restriction of access would create an undue burden on the community members in need of phone service.

H. Rewards

The use of rewards further fuels a negative psychology in criminal perpetrators, since community members now have an economic incentive to turn against them. Using rewards makes sense in all sorts of criminality situations from vehicle theft, robbery, drug dealing, and even violent felony crimes such as rape and aggravated battery. Serial criminals are ripe for the reward program. Rapists who revisit a designated area and repeatedly victimize women will be apprehended more quickly with an intact reward structure. Rewards generate community interest and participation, and they shift the psychology from confidence to nervousness. Even activities relating to criminal mischief activity, such as writing graffiti and vandalism, can benefit from the reward structure. Security firms entrusted with property protection invest in the reward system, since it is cost-effective and assures a satisfied corporate clientele whose property interests are well maintained. See Figure 7.15.

VI. CONCLUSION

When utilized properly, shock tactics and psychological operations are extremely effective against persistent nuisance problems within a community. Security specialists entrusted with the management of psychological operations must be thoroughly trained and briefed on the complexities of these practices. Programs must be tailored to meet the needs of particular circumstances evident in community life. One time approaches are generally unwise. High- and low-crime environments call for varied approaches. Ultimately, shock and PsyOps alter and metamorphose communities—and for the most part, they create an environment that is conducive to a healthy community life but that is ruinous for the miscreant.

PsyOps is as varied as the targeted community. In certain environments, just visibility is satisfactory, from signs to police presence, from uniforms to types of equipment employed. The key to success in PsyOps is knowing which tactics cause people to move in a positive direction and which create the type of unease that the criminal element abhors. PsyOps reflects the stage at which a community has evolved or devolved. Surveillance, for example, will vary according to the place, state of the community, and intrusion by the criminal force. Whatever the tactics chosen, they must be carefully selected to achieve the purposes for which they were chosen. PsyOps can backfire when too overt or too intrusive and unwelcome in a community. In the end, each of these suggestions rests on the fundamental premise that environments belong to those willing to accept and make changes.

Notes

1. Cary Carson, *The Use of Private Security in Public Housing: A Case Study*, 17 J. of Security Admin. 53, 57 (Oct. 1994).
2. B. A. Glesner, *Landlords as Cops*, 42 *Case W. Res.* 679, 682 (1992).
3. Glesner, at 790.
4. *See* Lisa Weil, *Current Topics, Drug-Related Evictions in Public Housing: Congress' Addiction to a Quick Fix*, 9 *Yale L. & Pol'y Rev.* 161 (1991); David B. Bryson and Roberta L. Youmans, *Crime, Drugs and Subsidized Housing*, 24 *Clearinghouse Rev.* 435 (1990).
5. *The Ins and Outs of Video Surveillance*, 20 *Corporate Security* 1 (June 1994).
6. For an interesting assessment of surveillance in the community, see *Title I of the Electronic Communications Privacy Act of 1986* (18 U.S.D. § 2510); *Katz v. United States*, 389 U.S. 347 (1967). In a recent unpublished opinion, *U.S. v. Sherman*, 990 F. 2d 1265 (9th Cir. 1993), the Court of Appeals for the Ninth Circuit held that individuals videotaped in public view have no reasonable expectations of privacy and could not challenge the government's use of videotape at trial as violating the Fourth Amendment.
7. *See* Charles P. Nemeth, *Private Security and the Investigative Process*, 2nd ed. (Boston Butterworth-Heinemann 2000).
8. Severin L. Sorensen, *Empowering Capable Guardians in High Crime and Low Income Settings*, 11 *Security Journal* 29, 32 (1998).

8

Private Sector Community-Based Physical Factors

Learning Objectives

1. To discover the interplay and interdependency between environment, community condition, and rates of crime and deviance.
2. To see how business and commercial interests are negatively impacted by crime-ridden environments.
3. To learn how to conduct risk assessments at designated locations.
4. To learn how the environment and its design can lead to safer communities.
5. To become familiar with Crime Prevention Through Environmental Design.
6. To identify those conditions in the community environment that lead to or maintain community criminality.
7. To review the special problems associated with schools and the workplace environment.
8. To understand that community members and leaders are crucial players in the reconstruction of an environment and that community members must see the neighborhood as part and parcel of their unique interests.
9. To identify environment designs at the community level that are conducive to lower crime rates and to eliminate conditions that foster crime and social problems.

I. PHYSICAL SECURITY AND ENVIRONMENT

For decades, public safety has been tagged exclusively in the war against crime. Money and resources have been expended without caution even as the crime problems increase. Legislation and regulations are passed that proclaim solutions to

FIGURE 8.1   These tragedies are portrayed by children in their artwork. This photo was drawn by a 9-year old boy from an apartment complex in Tampa, FL, depicting an individual armed with two semi-automatic handguns and a knife, firing at another with a young boy caught in the cross fire.

particular problems, and countless programs relating to rehabilitation and punishment for criminal offenses are instituted. Yet the crime scourge goes on and on. See Figure 8.1.

Sometimes policy makers and law enforcement leaders forget about the more obvious solutions. The security industry has been and will continue to be a hotbed for creative ideas in the war on crime. The security industry can provide innovation and expertise undreamed of by the public sector. Within the industry many solutions can be advocated that are resisted in the public sector. One compelling example is the application of *physical security*. In this case, physical means the interplay between the physical environment and the rate or opportunity for crime. Crime is evaluated in light of a larger "ecosystem.[1]" in global or in smaller areas of domain such as political divisions, municipalities, wards and precincts, blocks and neighborhoods, living areas and residential facilities. Physical design of any environment emanates from varied sources—government in the construction of roads, parks and agency offices has the power to effectively design the environment. Police and public safety offices can be constructed with user-friendly architecture. Street lighting and signs can be more intelligently placed. Businesses that anticipate environment can possibly engineer their environment to thwart criminal activity. Nonprofits, neighborhood groups, and religious institutions can also give sound advice on how the community should be constructed. In sum, the costs of physical improvements are really nothing other than a transference of existing fund or a better application of sound planning.

Physical security either enhances or restricts the opportunity for crime in a community. Historically, "physical security is defined as a system of barriers, entry and search controls, intrusion detection, alarm assessment, and testing and maintenance. Collectively this system, along with practices and procedures specific to each site, is intended to deter, delay, detect, assess and appropriately respond to an unauthorized activity."[2] But the definition is far grander than mere access and control. Physical security can also be about larger environments and collective living space. Residents keenly realize the places worth visiting and those to avoid. Citizens are well aware of danger zones in the environment. Common crime risks in a physical environment include the following:

1. Inadequate lighting;
2. Inadequate physical security;
3. Places of concealment for attackers such as vacant structures, dense shrubbery, trash accumulations, isolated parking areas, bus stations, public rest rooms, alleys, and so on; and
4. Situations that create potential access difficulties for police.[3]

Oscar Newman refers to the integration of environment and crime prevention as a question of "defensible space." He relates the following:

> Defensible space is a model for residential environments which inhibits crime by creating the physical expression of a social fabric that defends itself. All the different elements which combine to make a defensible space have a common goal—an environment in which latent territoriality and sense of community in the inhabitants can be translated into responsibility for ensuring a safe, productive, and well-maintained living space.[4]

A strong, formidable physical plan sets up barriers to crime and undermines the criminal element. But exactly how that physical security should take shape is the subject of much discussion.

Communities, businesses, and neighborhoods will not prevent crime by adopting the "armed" camp or lockdown image of an entity in fear or trouble as a main long-term strategy. Indeed, physical security need blend with the life of a community, giving the appearance of safety and simultaneous security, and of most importance, an air of confidence in the quality of life that residents and owners have. Painting the picture of lockdown and defensive survival will not elevate neighborhoods. The Heritage Foundation perceptively describes this awful cycle:

> Another cost of crime is that employers are reluctant to expand or relocate in high-crime neighborhoods even if given economic development incentives. When an of-

fice, store, or factory is said to be in a dangerous neighborhood, employers have difficulties finding and retaining a work force . . . Local residents, fearing crime, are unwilling to patronize neighborhood businesses during evening hours. Business
owners may be willing to bear the risk of crime in order to attract evening
customers, but if residents are too frightened to shop, many of the businesses will
not survive . . . When fear of crime drives out or cuts back the hours of neighborhood enterprises, employment opportunities shrink. This is especially harmful to
teenagers seeking their first jobs. If they are to enjoy productive lives as adults,
avoiding the welfare dependency trap, they must develop marketable skills before
they enter adulthood.[5]

More specific applications of physical security are just as educational. Sexual
offenses, by way of example, are often the direct result of poor environmental design and the enhancement of criminal covert activity. The rate of forcible rape since
1960, although having a slight decrease, as shown in Figure 8.2, gloomily indicates
the pressing need to design safer physical environments. Therefore, physical security is the compatible combination of residence and business and the protection
needed for safety and security without sacrificing the aesthetic quality-of-life issues.

A program of physical security should not appear to be the product of fear and
intimidation but rather of community and business confidence that the neighborhood is not only worth defending but also inhabiting. Here again, the "art" of the
security profession instructs better than science and an overreliance on technology
and equipment. Even so, design for physical security calls for a mix of the two
philosophies.

The physical security plan will often employ a series of barriers that limit or
thoroughly make implausible any criminal conduct. Community-based approaches
should assertively erect or use barriers to increase the quality of life, such as these:

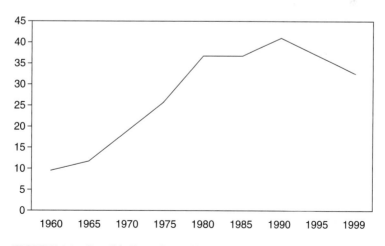

FIGURE 8.2   Forcible Rape Rate, 1960–1999.

Source: Bureau of Justice Statistics' State Level Crime Trends Database

Practitioner Tip: Blending with the Environment

The best and most effective physical security is the least intrusive and noticeable. Physical security should blend into the environment. The imagery of physical security sets the tone and creates the ethos of the community. When possible, the security practice should be consistent with the natural contour and character or the setting applied. For example, one of the common trends in schools today to counteract school violence is to utilize metal detectors, hand searches, closed circuit television camera monitoring systems, clear or see-through book bags, and keycard access to monitor and screen students. Unfortunately, these methods create a prisonlike environment when students are faced with metal detectors, hand searches, locker inspections, and other instruments that portray fear.

1. Fences and other barriers
2. Lights
3. Locks
4. Alarms
5. Doors, turnstiles, gates, and so on
6. Safes, vaults, and other special construction[6]

A combination of natural and man-made designs will be the best tactic. It is important to think carefully before a community zones or allows certain activities to occur in designated areas. Physical security not only prevents injury to the community but also anticipates the possibility of it. The use of lighting and visual openness, for example, inhibits any felon.

The physical environment must warn those who wish to engage in criminal conduct.[7] The environment must send a message to possible malefactors that they have something to fear, something to be concerned about. Street-level drug dealing, for example, is often conducted in the open even when law enforcement is patrolling the area. Using crime-mapping strategies, integrate physical security tactics that target neighborhood locations. See Figure 8.3.[8] The same is true with any street-level criminal who commits robberies, assaults, home invasions, and more serious crimes in broad daylight. The reality is evident. Without an effective physical infrastructure, in addition to the social, political, and moral framework under which communities thrive, crime runs rampant. A community, like a building, needs access control. "Physical barriers are used to control, impede, or deny access, and effectively direct the flow of personnel and vehicles through designated portals."[9]

Flexibility, ingenuity, understanding, and careful consideration of the physical environment are necessary components in the communal protection design. Each environment and the people and purpose within are diverse and multifaceted. Any reasoned plan of crime prevention will be tailored to the specific needs of the environment and its residents. Public transportation facilities are an ongoing challenge for the industry.

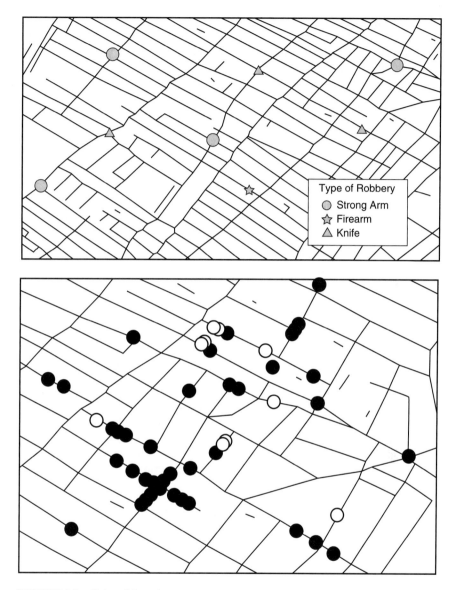

FIGURE 8.3 Crime Mapping

Key among these issues are quality-of-life concerns including disorderly passengers, vandalism and graffiti; fare evasion; trespassing; auto theft and vehicle burglaries at park-and-ride areas; and interfering with rail operations, including obstructions placed on tracks, train stoning and tampering with critical signal devices. Also encountered are employee theft and fraud, counterfeit fare media and, to a lesser degree, passenger assaults, robberies, purse snatchings and other crimes.[10]

Office buildings, gated communities, subsidized housing, government facilities, retail establishments, inner-city blocks, and suburbia have distinct environmental demands. In environment, the only plan worth preserving is that "which can be employed by inhabitants for the enhancement of their lives, while providing security for their families, neighbors, and friends."[11] It is environment that shapes minds and hearts.

A. Crime and Environmental Design

Environmental design of buildings, facilities, parks, and entertainment complexes are seminal matters for the public safety specialists. The University of Wisconsin at Madison's School of Architecture appreciates the correlation between design and the inhibition of crime:

> Traditionally, security has been a concern in banking and some government and low-income housing facilities. Now, clients with high-tech structures, education facilities, corporate headquarters, office complexes, and residential structures need security, but it might be up to the architect to suggest this . . . In planning security, architects must accept constraints related to traffic and access of outsiders and insiders to certain building areas. Planning for security begins in the conceptual stage just as it does for many other building requirements.[12]

In the present age of terrorism, those who design communities and the buildings that compose them must be mindful of how design inhibits and advances the criminal plotter. Richard Healy's *Design for Security* foretells the interplay between environment and the opportunity for crime.

Philosophies, such as *crime prevention through environmental design (CPTED),* should be integrated into all planning for public safety. Security specialists need to adopt proactive approaches, which create "defensible space." Transit systems across the United States have paid serious attention to CPTED, and the results have been dramatic.

> Better lighting, emergency phone systems, more and better directional signs, and the closing off of dead-end passageways in which riders could become lost or trapped by assailants are built-in features today of new systems and receive high priority when old systems undertake station renovations. The importance of landscaping for safety is well known.[13]

CPTED creatively mixes criminology with architecture and seeks ways to negate or inhibit the criminal activity.

> A comprehensive CPTED analysis attempts to identify central problems and craft changes in the physical and social environment that will reinforce positive behavior. Posed rules and theme-oriented artwork to reinforce pro-social curriculum, greater use of windows to enhance visibility and reduce isolation, student art displays to build a sense of pride, altered seating arrangements to encourage supportive group interactions, or changes in scheduling the use of space to avoid conflict, are all potential CPTED measures that could be implemented.[14]

It is environment and the physical protection system that forge mindsets and conceptions. In other words, people are intensely influenced by the environment experienced.

For example, picture the different states of mind between shoppers in a mall and the person experiencing the rigors of the new and improved airport security. These corresponding environments shape mindsets and attitudes. The physical barriers and controls impact the psyche and internal workings of those who come in contact. The same effect is certainly true for citizens living and laboring in high-crime regions, whose outlook radically varies from the affluent community member. Physical security reflects the needs and characteristics of the community.[15]

In a sort of perverse elitism, planners and community designers at the public and private level have assumed less concern about safety and security in low-income areas. The entire infrastructure of 1960 through 1980 public housing designs, with its penchant for high-rises and cement-block compaction, was arrogantly built on this disregard for quality-of-life questions. Oscar Newman cuts cogently to this issue:

> Defensive space, it may be charged, is middle-class thinking. The poor have their own culture. They don't want the peaceful, secure, dull life of middle class. They don't want property. They don't want the value middle-class society wishes to foist upon them. Violence, it is contended, is part of their culture. So, apparently, is communality. They don't want walls, whether real ones, or the ones you place in their minds by the design of space.
>
> The romantic view of the poor is without foundation. Interviews with hundreds of low-income housing residents reveal that most hold the goals and aspirations of the middle class. The desire for security is not limited to the middle class.[16]

Design critically illustrates the interplay between design and safety.

That insight has been incorporated into the literature on design against crime, and is also covered under at least three other keywords: environmental criminology, defensible space, and crime prevention through environmental design or CPTED. An underlying concern of design is to enhance individual responsibility to look after places.[17]

B. The Mall as an Environment

Just as schools, hospitals, and other community sectors possess environmental qualities, so does the retail establishment. With the dawn of mega-malls and super-stores, the demands on the private sector have been rapidly rising. Malls have been labeled self-sustaining cities with a full-fledged environment.[18]

The program initiated at the University Square Mall in Florida represents a significant alteration of an environment. In this mall that was once roamed by gangs, the aggressive intervention in what conduct was acceptable within the environment mirrored a differing culture. In the previous setting, the gang types found a home worth visiting. In the adjusted environment, the attraction was lost. Here, the proactive approach paves the way for success in any environment. In short,

Case Study: University Square Mall: Tampa, Florida

When a retail environment loses its reputation for safety and security, it is on a sure road to economic decline. University Square Mall of Tampa, Florida, was under siege by gangs and turf battles. The mall, approximately 20 years old, contained a sixteen-screen theater with a food court, housed 162 stores in over 1,300,000 square feet of lease space spread out over three-quarters of a mile long, and was utilized by 14,000,000 customers a year. With the arrivals of gangs, the mall lost both its profit base and its reputation with the community as a safe haven. The general manger of the mall, Tom Loch, authored a bold approach in dealing with the growing problem of juveniles out of control.

The first issue that Mr. Loch addressed was the institution of a code of conduct for the mall. At all doors, the mall posted its new rules and regulations. Security personnel were ordered to enforce the new policies to ensure compliance. The rules, which struck at the heart of the gang culture, sought to undermine the status symbols and other signs of authority in gang activity. For example, dressing left or right, which is common within gang groups, was prohibited within the mall facility. This meant that wearing watches, hats, belt buckles, and shoe laces *all* to the right or *all* to the left was not allowed for any patron of the mall. Juveniles had to make sure that pant legs were down and not rolled up, because many juveniles like to keep one pant leg up to identify them as part of a particular gang. All bandanas or "colors" that gang members are known to wear were prohibited from being worn in the mall. The mall rules went even as far as not allowing jockey shorts to be hanging out, which is a common style among many juveniles today. Other rules were enforced on a broader scale. No personal radios and no weapons were allowed, and security personnel tolerated no abusive or foul language of any kind.

To ensure that the new policies were communicated with the target audience, the mall's rules and regulations and a code of conduct were printed on business cards and given out to juveniles encountering security personnel. The good kids whom the security personnel interacted with were rewarded with movie passes. Little children were given stickers and security badges, just to name a few of the proactive methods used by the security department.

gang behavior and imagery were vanquished from the environment. As a result, the customer base lost the negative participation of those who undermine safety and security, and gained the law-abiding citizen whose business is always welcome. By this change in the environment and the conduct of the juvenile patrons, a large facility that was exposed to serious criminal activities and problems reclaimed its rightful sense of ownership.

II. PHYSICAL SECURITY AND RISK

Any plan of physical security depends on a learned view of the environment. To set the foundation for making sound judgments about security planning, plan designers often begin by conducting a risk assessment. In this context, risk assessment is a systematic analysis of an organization's characteristics to determine the probability and potential severity of asset loss or damage. Three primary factors are evaluated to derive the risk estimate: assets, threats, and vulnerabilities.

Although there are many models for conducting risk assessments, most assessment methodologies follow a five-step process. See Figure 8.4.[19] During the first phase of the assessment, *the asset evaluation*, the security planner focuses on identifying and valuing the organization's assets. In many cases, this process also includes the identification of undesirable events that can negatively impact the organization's assets. When the asset evaluation is complete, all of the organization's assets (tangible and intangible assets) and possible events that could negatively impact the assets have been identified, and all negative events and assets have been evaluated to determine their potential impact on the organization.

During the second phase of the assessment, *the threat assessment*, possible sources of threat (adversaries) are identified and evaluated to determine the likelihood that they would target the organization. Likelihood of attack is usually determined by evaluating known characteristics about the adversary to determine whether the potential adversary possesses the intent and capability to execute an attack against the organization. This phase of the risk assessment also often includes the identification of specific assets that probable adversaries would most likely target (by considering their previous targets) and the development of design basis threats (DBTs). Design basis threats (DBTs) are characterizations of an adversary's capabilities and methods of operation that are used for the purpose of evaluating vulnerability to different types of attacks.

Once assets and threats have been identified and evaluated, the focus of the assessment shifts to vulnerabilities. This phase of the risk assessment is aimed at determining the likelihood of adversary success if an attack was launched against the organization's assets. This vulnerability assessment usually includes an analysis of existing security measures to estimate the level of vulnerability to each asset or undesired event and to identify conditions that would permit occurrence of risk events.

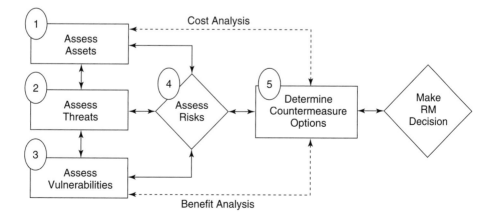

FIGURE 8.4   Risk Assessment Continuum

The methods used for evaluating security countermeasures vary considerably. For the purpose of evaluating physical security, many assessors use vulnerability survey checklists that walk the assessor step-by-step through the process of identifying and evaluating physical security measures. Although security surveys are very useful in identifying specific concerns or possible vulnerability issues, compliance surveys do not measure the integrated performance of the physical security system. To address this need, many assessors supplement security surveys with the use of performance-based evaluation methods. For example, an assessor may use Sandia National Laboratories' Estimate of Adversary Sequence Interruption (EASI) model to evaluate the integrated effectiveness of barriers, detection and alarm systems, and response elements in "interrupting" attacks along a possible intrusion path. In addition to EASI, there are other evaluation models designed to derive similar estimates of system effectiveness that account for a range of additional issues, such as guard force engagement capabilities. In addition to Intrusion Path Analysis, many organizations use additional measures such as penetration tests to directly evaluate the effectiveness of physical security measures. Penetration testing is particularly useful in evaluating security systems that are heavily reliant on human performance (such as airport passenger screening). See Figure 8.5.[20] Also see Tables 8.1 and 8.2 and Figure 8.6.

Performance-based evaluation of physical security requires a true understanding of the limitations and capabilities of physical protection system elements, such as barriers and intrusion detection sensors. For example, barrier effectiveness is measured in terms of the time required for an adversary to breach the barrier using various tools. This is referred to as barrier delay time. Performance-based evaluation models, such as EASI, use the barrier delay times in conjunction with delay sensor locations, probability of detection, response force time, alarm assessment time, and other factors to provide a true estimate of the effectiveness of a physical protection system.

After all three risk factors have been explored, the assessor would evaluate each asset and undesirable event in context with the identified threats and vulner-

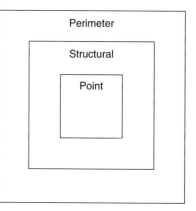

FIGURE 8.5 Zones of Penetration and Lines of Defense

TABLE 8.1 *Barrier Delay Times*

Barrier Type	Method of Breach	Breaching Aids	Low Delay (sec.)	Mean Delay (sec.)	High Delay (sec._	Std. Dev.*
Door, Industrial Pedestrian, 16-gauge, rim set, butt hinges	Pry Lock Frame	Pry Bar	6	12	18	
Door, Industrial Pedestrian, 16-gauge, rim set, butt hinges	Axe Through Metal	Fire Ax	22	56	90	X
Door, Industrial Pedestrian, 16-gauge, rim set, butt hinges	Place, Blow, & Through	Linear Shaped Charge	30	60	90	X
Fence, 4', No T.G.	Climb Over	None	1	2	3	X
Fence, 8', No T.G.	Climb Over	Gloves	3	6	9	X
Fence, 8' Security	Cut Hole	Boltcutters	8	16	24	X
Fence, 8' Security, Unsecured Bottom	Pry Up & Climb Under	10-ft Pipe	3	6	9	X
Fence, 8' Security, Concrete Sill or Buried 2-ft Mesh	Dig, Cut, & Climb Under	Pick, Shovel	> 75 min.	> 75 min.	> 75 min.	X
Fence, 8' Security, Barbed T.G.	Climb Over	Gloves	4	8	12	X
Lock, Padlock, Warded	Pick	Lock Picks	4	27	50	X
Lock, Pin Tumbler	Pick	Lock Picks	6	150	300	X
Wall, Wood Frame, 2 × 4 Studs, Gypsum	Hammer & Through	Sledge	4	6	8	X
Wall, Wood Frame, 2 × 4 Studs, Gypsum	Hammer, Cut, & Through	Brace & Bit, Sabre Saw	42	84	126	.27
Wall, 4" Cinder Block, No Fill, No Rebar	Hammer & Through	Sledge	12	24	36	.08

(continued)

TABLE 8.1 *Barrier Delay Times (Continued)*

Barrier Type	Method of Breach	Breaching Aids	Low Delay (sec.)	Mean Delay (sec.)	High Delay (sec.)	Std. Dev.*
Wall, 4" Cinder Block, No. 4 Rebar on 8" Cntrs, Mortar Fill	Hammer, Cut, & Through	Sledge, Boltcutters	30	60	90	.2
Wall, 8" Cinder Block, No Fill, No Rebar	Hammer & Through	Sledge	18	36	48	X
Wall, 4" Reinforced Concrete, 3000 psi, No.5 at 6" Ctrs	Hammer, Cut, & Through	Sledge, Hand Saw, Bolt-cutters	150	290	420	X
Wall, 8" Reinforced Concrete, 3000 psi, No.5 on 6" Ctrs	Hammer, Cut, & Through	Hand, Thermal, Power Tools	420	840	> 22 min.	X
Wall, 4" Fibrous Concrete, 6500 psi, No.5 on 6" Ctrs	Place, Blow, & Through	Explosive Platter Charge	30	60	90	.2

Source: *Barrier Technology Handbook* (Sandia National Laboratories, 1978).

*EASI works most effectively if a standard of deviation value is provided for each adversary task and response time. According to Sandia Natl Labs, if the standard deviation is unknown, a value of 30% of the mean time is usually an accurate representation of the standard deviation for most adversary and response tasks

TABLE 8.2 *Task Times for Common Sabotage Methods*

Attack Type	Method of Attack	Tools	Delay Time (sec.)	Est. Std. Dev.
Arson	Pour accelerant, ignite accelerant	1 liter of accelerant in bottle, windproof lighter	10	3
Arson	Ignite Molotov cocktail and throw	1 liter Molotov cocktail, windproof lighter	6	1.8
Explosive	Detonate primed suicide bomb in close proximity of target	5–10 lbs. TNT, primed, w/ command activation system	1	.3
Explosive	Attach magnetic charge to target surface, prime charge, and set time delay	1–5 lbs. TNT w/ magnets, time delay system	15	4.5
Explosive	Attach charge to target surface using adhesive strip, prime, charge and set time delay	1–5 lbs. TNT, adhesive strips, time delay system	18	6
Physical	Don protective mask and open exit valve	Gloves, protective respiratory mask	15	4.5
Physical	Force open screwed sheet metal side panel and hammer internal components	Claw hammer	17	5.1

Source: Simple testing conducted by Critical Intervention Services.

abilities to determine the level of risk. This objective risk evaluation (step four) then forms the basis for all risk reduction decisions.

Once risks have been identified as acceptable or not, the assessment moves into the fifth phase, the *countermeasures identification*. During this phase, the assessor identifies possible countermeasures that could reduce the level of risk, estimates the potential risk reduction forced by the proposed countermeasure, and conducts a cost-benefit analysis to determine which countermeasures offer the greatest reduction in vulnerability (or severity) for the amount of money allocated to risk reduction.

The principles of risk management and planning based on objective risk assessment are universal and apply to virtually any type of organization (including public and private communities). Some of the tools used in evaluating risk in community environments is similar to the methods and approaches used in assessing risk in closed, facility environments. Other tools are unique. For example, as part of the threat assessment, a community risk assessor may use crime mapping techniques to generate an accurate estimate of the types of crimes affecting specific

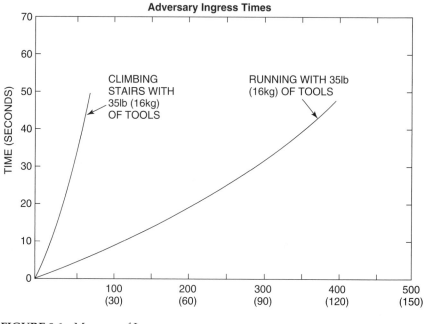

FIGURE 8.6   Measure of Ingress

Source: MIL-HDBK-1013/01.

areas (Figure 8.7).[21] In small-facility environments, this type of analysis would not be necessary.

Regardless of the specific tools or methodologies used for conducting the assessment, practitioners will always benefit by using an objective, risk-based planning approach in developing community-based programs.

A. Image and the Risk Plan

Once the actual risks are identified, the plan of physical protection and security should be sensitive to community needs. Put another way, not only must the security professionals weigh the means to eliminating or minimizing crime and nuisance in the community, but also they must accomplish these purposes with style and positive grace that enhances community life. Accomplishing this is an art. The last thing a community under siege needs is to look like a community under siege. In this sense, risk plans communicate a certain image. Hardened, lockdown imagery, manifest in bars and bolts at every corner, sends a negative message—one of fear and hopelessness.

On the other hand, physical security devices that look or appear to be something other than what they truly are—such as glass over iron rods, hidden versus visible cameras—portray an entirely different image. The message emanates from

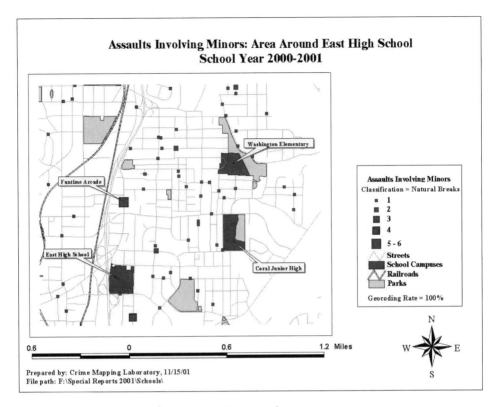

FIGURE 8.7 Crime Mapping: Targeted Zone or Sector

the image of protection. Thus, physical security measures contribute to the self-image of a community, and not only do they send to the criminal agents a negative series of images but they also, just as capably, transmit positive feedback to the good citizenry. In turn, physical security shapes the ethos of a given community. Practitioners must tailor approaches that uplift the community and communicate messages of hope rather than of fear. The imagery of physical security is one that can be labeled only an impression, and impressions are easily received but much harder to dispose of. In areas where bars on windows, cameras, and other types of control measures have to be implemented, practitioners should attempt to use a variety of methods to reduce the image of fear and control. Bars, for example, can be replaced with a laminate protection and other plastics made by the 3M Corporation. See their security product catalog web page at www.3m.com/security/en/sec_products.jhtml.

For the slight deterrence value that bars have on windows to perpetrators, other methods can accomplish more with less bleakness. Images of bars are a constant reminder to the community that they are not safe and that victimization is round the bend. Small window stickers announcing electronic monitors are better deterrents than bars. Bars are physical objects that can be overcome; to outmaneuver electronic surveillance requires more expertise and effort than the average criminal is capable of and willing to circumvent. Cameras can be hidden behind domes or recessed in the wall with two-way mirrors or other types of aesthetically pleasing camouflage.[22] The criminal will know that they are present, but the community will not continually be reminded of their presence. Physical security specialists must craft a "first impression" that is long-lasting and positive.

Projecting messages through imagery must be thoroughly assessed and balanced, since its purpose is twofold: to protect and uplift the community and to warn and drive out the criminal element. For instance, some security practitioners advocate the image of a fortress that communicates impenetrability and that therefore deters the criminal from taking action. On the surface, the physical security plan appears attractive, but what impact will the strategy have? What ordinary person desires a fortress for a home? Does not a fortress convey the image of siege and attack where the citizenry is under constant attack and confrontation? Although a fortress appears strong, its very existence defines a certain sense of insecurity and fear that ultimately messages dark and foreboding events or that constantly communicates the potential for present threat. Physical security should surely protect but not undermine individual freedom and self-image. Fortresses essentially imprison the community and project a certain inability to control the criminals and change the pattern of community victimization. The fortress message locks everything up, including the community, and indirectly fosters a siege mentality. It gives a message that practitioners are prepared just to focus on the easier solution of locking everything up, including the members of the community, making them hostages in a hostile environment.

There is a fine line between using tools of the trade such as locks, lighting, alarm systems, fences, and cameras and creating a secure, positive environment. Security is not about equipment, but is about people. Physical security that forgets people is security not worth promoting. Unless the environment is one where a high level of security must be present (e.g., nuclear plants, federal buildings, etc.), an open, free, and "balanced" environment is the most desirable image. Entrenchment and paranoia should be avoided. For example, one of the common trends in schools has been a continuous laboratory for environmental experimentation. Violence and misbehavior can be put in check by all sorts of alterations in physical security. Metal detectors, scanners, closed circuit television camera monitoring systems, clear or see-through book bags, and keycard access are just a few examples. Unfortunately, the indirect result of these security "improvements" is the creation of an environment that is anything but comfortable. Like an armed camp, the schools alter the mindsets and the environments without intending to do so. As if a self-fulfilling prophecy, students adopt the ways of the environment. Instead of being scholarly, many tend to become survivalist or penal in manner. The 1999 school shooting by an 11-year-old, Andrew Golden, and his companion, 13-year-old Mitchell Johnson, illustrates how difficult it is to prepare for such levels of irrationality.[23]

B. Technology and the Physical Environment

How technology impacts the environment is becoming the focus of intense academic study.[24] Technology alters life in every quarter from family to communities. Technology makes possible, for example, the elimination of public safety positions in favor of squad cars and monitoring devices. Computer scans of faces have replaced police artistry, and databases of known or suspected felons are kept in cyberspace. Companies like Visionics have crafted software programs such as FaceIt® to replace the police artist's depiction or witness description. "FaceIt® is an award-winning facial recognition software engine that allows computers to rapidly and accurately detect and recognize faces and enables a wide array of real-world applications in both commercial and government market segments." Viisage Technology delivers similar products and services. See their web page at www.viisage .com.

In the United Kingdom, for example, current public safety wisdom has been the installation of thousands of cameras that are mounted over the countryside in order to monitor criminal activity. Implementing technology as preferential to using officers alters the community and its corresponding environments in significant ways. Technology, moreover, may lead to certain advances in public safety processes but will not replace the effectiveness of officers in human relations' settings. Few would argue that the environment would continue to see erosion of community as machines replace the human being. The unseen unsettles both the criminal and the good citizen. Privacy rights and other expectations of personal sanctity have to be undermined to some extent. Clearly, the conversation of camera and citizen is a factual impossibility. Hence, the vaunted English bobby, with the rightfully earned reputation for community skills, has been under challenge for the last few decades. See Figures 8.8 and 8.9. Bobbies, like all other law enforcement officers, should be part and parcel of the community, not detached or separate from it. Machines have no sense of ownership in the community—but officers should and must have this sense. The replacement of officers with over utilization of technology such as cameras tells the community that the government is not willing to make a full commitment to developing a community-based approach.

Furthermore, this technology can also instill a false sense of security within the members of the public because they assume that someone is actually monitoring these cameras. Yet these thousands of cameras will never be able to predict a single bank robbery or make judgments or professional insights that foretell and deter crime in its many facts. Most technology can do no more than merely report information—impersonally and without analysis.

C. Schools as Experiments in Physical Security

Schools are a prime example of overkill in the science of physical security. Strategies that ferret out the troublemaker before the trouble and that remove the troublemaker from the environment should be the basic rationales for physical security. See Figure 8.10.

FIGURE 8.8   English Bobbies and Community Interaction

1. Safe School Initiatives.   With school shootings reaching alarming proportions, the role of physical security has increased in significance. The National Institute of Justice has extensively examined the problem in its study *The Appropriate and Effective Use of Security Technologies in U.S. Schools.* Topical considerations are the following:

Practitioner Highlight

Palladium Media Group (PMG)

PMG developed a very sophisticated training program on bomb countermeasures that would rival any such training program within the public or private sector. In 1999, PMG produced training media that comprehensively addressed the risk of terrorist and criminal bomb attacks. Most of the books and videotapes produced on bomb security by traditional security publishers and government agencies were outdated or addressed only a small aspect of the threat. To fill this need, PMG developed a multimedia training CD-ROM called "Bomb Countermeasures for Security Professionals." The CD-ROM was designed using an interactive multimedia format to present a detailed examination of explosive-related threats and countermeasures, including a considerable amount of information never before assembled in publication.

FIGURE 8.9 Police in London

Analysis of vulnerability points	Installation and capital investment
Site modifications	Staffing and training
Video surveillance	Scanners and walk-through devices
Entry controls	Duress alarms
Weapons detection	Parking
CPTED	Drug and alcohol sensors
Graffiti sealers	Radios
Fencing	Detection sensors

Although much of the analysis for school integrity is now largely physical, the planners must not lose sight of the reality. "Safety and security technology can only be one tool in a comprehensive program that each school must develop to create a safe learning environment that is perceived to be safe by all students and staff."[25] And this is true in many other types of environments.

Physical security measures are correctly directed to the identification and elimination of guns and other weapons in the school environment. But for some, no

FIGURE 8.10   Environment, Design and School Facilities:
Pearl High School, Pearl, Mississippi

matter how much technology intercedes, the unpredictability of it all will make it
impossible to thwart these bizarre cases. Francis Hamit offers another perspective
on these gun events in the schools. "As shocking and sad as these events are, we
must remember they are exceptional rather than ordinary."[26] It is sad that our halls
of innocence are now consumed by fear and trepidation. The ingenuity of the private sector can go a long way toward finding suitable solutions.

   2. Uniforms.   How students conduct and clothe themselves is another critical environmental factor in the search for controlling human behavior, which is
the ultimate goal of implementing physical security that works. The matter of
uniforms in the schools has been hotly debated throughout the United States but
is one alternative to technology that has proved promising. Although the wearing
of uniforms has long been a part of private, religiously affiliated or academy settings, proponents see immediate benefits with students caring less about material
things and being unlikely to engage in the wars that have erupted over clothing
in school environments.[27]
   Critics charge that uniforms negate individuality and do not allow for differences. But it is this stripping away of individuality that alters the environment and
the corresponding perceptions that students have. A larger, more collective perspective that devalues what one has over another, replaces individualism. The trifles and pettiness of students about questions of clothing and dress can be excessive.

Admittedly, juvenile motivation stems from image-oriented issues. Peer pressure is a glaring reality for too many of our young. As petty as the issue appears, uniforms can make a difference in the cultural and physical environment. School uniforms undercut the status symbol within schools. Also, uniforms neutralize personality and make difficult much of the outlandish behavior in schools. Restrictions go beyond clothing in the case of pagers, cell phones, gaudy jewelry, or profane materials. Uniforms can counteract by providing an organized environment free from status-seeking—an issue critical to any control of gang behavior. Uniforms shift the center of attention from individual to the collective enterprise known as school, where a wide array of individuals gather in the pursuit of knowledge. Removing superficiality in the school environment forces kids to search for positive ways to stand out.

III. CONCLUSION

Physical security comprises far more than a discussion of locks and anti-theft technology. Even communities have a physical space in need of defense and protection. This chapter lays out community as a subject matter of physical security and urges the security specialist to appreciate and interlock the community environment with its general integrity and safety. Safe communities, put another way, have a safe and defensible environment. Whether it is the more specific locations of school or workplace, which are components of the environmental whole, a plan of risk assessment on the entire community is natural to securing it. Whole communities either contain the defenses to withstand high levels of criminality or have long since lost the ability to withstand the onslaught. Physical security provides the planner, the community leader, and the private security specialist with the tools to ensure the safe environment.

Communities are protected by their environmental design. Indeed, engineers and architects know only too well of the dependency. With the group Community Protection Through Environmental Design, (CPTED) the planner assures the safest possible environment. Through specialized risk assessment, the security professional weighs and assesses not only the quality and content of particular locations but also whole neighborhoods. From mall to elementary school, the community officer is mindful of the environment that he or she labors in. This approach is especially critical within high-crime high schools where individual status is the most important thing in school life.

Notes _____

1. Marcus Felson, *Crime Prevention, Apartments, and the Larger Ecosystem*, 22 *Security Journal* 61 (1998).
2. IOPA Website, *Physical Security Systems*, at http://www.oa.doc.gov/sase/physical-sec.html, visited 8/29/02.
3. "Inhibiting Crime Through Design" Univ. of Wisconsin, Madison. Dept. of Engineering Professional Development at http://aec.engr.wisc.edu/resources/rsrc06.html

4. Oscar Newman, *Defensible Space* 3 (New York, Macmillan, 1972).

5. Carl F. Horowitz, *An Empowerment Strategy for Eliminating Neighborhood Crime*, Background 84. The Heritage Foundation. 3/25/91 at http://www.heritage.org/Research/Urban Issues/BG814.cfm

6. Richard J. Healy, Design for Security at 6. New York: Wiley 1968.

7. The displacement of the criminal offender alters the physical in and of itself.

8. COPS, *Introductory Guide to Crime Analysis and Mapping* 56,59 U.S. Dept. of Justice, Washington, D.C. (2001).

9. *Physical Security Systems Inspectors Guide* 5–1 (U.S. Department of Energy, Washington, D. C., 2000).

10. John P. Sullivan, *A Planning Blueprint for Security in Commuter Railways, Crime & Justice Internat'l* 19 (Feb. 1997).

11. Newman at 3.

12. Univ. of Wisconsin School of Architecture web page.

13. Dorothy Moses Schulz, *Private Security Comes on Board, Security Management* 225 (Apr. 1997).

14. Tod Schneider, *Safe School through Environmental Design, ERIC Digest* Number 144.

15. The National Institute of Justice's recent Research in Brief that studies Baltimore neighborhoods produced surprising result. In part, the study argued that "[p]hysical conditions had deteriorated significantly on the street blocks assessed in 1981 and 1994. Graffiti and abandoned houses occurred more frequently. Despite the worsening physical conditions, residents did not report that local physical or social problems in the neighborhood were significantly worse." Ralph B. Taylor, *Crime, Grime, Fear and Decline: A Longitudinal Look—Research in Brief—*NCJ 177603, 7 (1999).

16. Newman at 19.

17. Felson at 1. *See also* Barry Poyner, *Designs Against Crime: Beyond Defensible Space* (London: Butterworth, 1983); Patricia L. Brantingham and Paul J. Brantingham; *Police Use of Environmental Criminology in Strategic Crime Prevention*, (Police Practice, 1991) 211–240; Oscar Newman, *Creating Defensible Space*, Washington, D. C., U.S. Dept. of Housing and Urban Development, 1996; and Timothy D. Crowe and Diane L. Zahm, *Crime Prevention through Environmental Design*, Land Dev., Fall 1994.

18. Gang Lee, Richard C. Hollinger, and Dean A. Dabney, *The Relationship Between Crime and Private Security and U.S. Shopping Centers*, 23 *American J. of Crim. Justice* 2 (1999); L. Sherman, P. R. Gartin, and M. E. Buerger, *Hot Spots of Predatory Crime: Routine Activities and the Criminology of Place*, 27 *Criminology* (1989).

19. Carl Roper, *Risk Management for Security Professionals* Figure 1.1 (Boston, Butterworth Heinemann, 1999).

20. Robert J. Meadows, *Fundamentals of Protection and Safety for the Private Protection Officer* Figure 6.1 (Upper Saddle River, NJ, Prentice Hall).

21. COPS at 72.

22. For supporting case studies, *see* James J. Vardalis and Suman Kakar, *Crime and the High School Environment*, 23 *J. of Security Admin.*, 37–48 (2002); Michael D. Kelleher, *New Arenas for Violence: Homicide in the American Workplace* (Westport, CT: Praeger Press, 1996), which examines the work environment and physical security measures that contribute to the "best" environment; Grant R. Grissom and William L. Dubnov, *Without Locks and Bars: Reforming our Reform Schools* (New York: Praeger, 1989); Allan Wallace, Daniel Ford, and Westinghouse Electric Corp., *Crime Prevention through Environmental Design: The Commercial Demonstration in Portland, Oregon* (Washington, DC: U.S. National Institute of Justice, 1980); and, Robert A. Gardner, *Crime Prevention Through Environmental Design*, 25 *Security Mgmt.* 36–42 (1981).

23. *See* "Boys Charged in School Shooting" *U.S.A. Today Online*, 3/31/98, last visited 1/7/99.
24. See Lawrence J. Fennelly, *Effective Physical Security:* (Boston: Butterworth-Heinemann 1997); Deborah Marie Galvin, *Management Information and Executive Information System Technology Applications in the Field of Security*, 2 *Security Journal* 25 (1991); Joel Konicek and Karen Little, *Security, ID Systems and locks: The Book on electronic access control* (Boston: Butterworth-Heinemann, 1997).
25. National Institute of Justice, *The Appropriate and Effective Use of Security Technologies in U.S. Schools*—NCJ 178265, iii (1999).
26. Francis Hamit, *School Security: Dealing with Kids & Guns, Security Technology & Design* 73 (July 1998).
27. James Sterngold, "Taking a New Look at Uniforms and Their Impact on School," 149 *New York Times*, 6/28/00, B-11; Ihsan K. Taylor, "Majority of Dade School Back Uniforms for Students" 16 *Education Week* 3 (4/30/97).

9

The Future of Public Safety: Preparing for the Challenges

Change is the law of life, and those who look only to the past or present are certain to miss the future.

John F. Kennedy

Learning Objectives

1. To discover the extraordinary preeminence of private sector justice in the delivery of community-based public safety.
2. To recognize that private sector justice will be a critical player in the health and maintenance of communities.
3. To discern and discover the bevy of legislative initiatives that advances the private security industry in the community model.
4. To appreciate the increasing recognition by public law enforcement that they can no longer assure communities without novel and aligned policy making with private sector justice.
5. To be assured that the future of private sector public safety is not only bright but also enviably dynamic.

I. ADVANTAGES OF THE PRIVATE SECTOR IN COMMUNITY-BASED EFFORTS

With the increasing role of security in society and the trend toward privatization of public safety functions, it is plain that the two systems of public and private must operate under one flag. Privatization is driven by an important principle—cost efficiency and cost effectiveness. Whereas public monoliths and civil service constructs limit creativity and innovation, private security has the means and the will to step in where its public counterparts cannot. The public system can no longer efficiently deliver community-based police services while remaining shackled by the reactive 911 system.

According to the Independent Institute of California, private services reduce costs by up to 30 percent.[1] Privatizing support services, for example, will enable departments to allocate police resources that directly concentrate on violent crime or other criminal activity that calls for esoteric training.

Public law enforcement is struggling in its most fundamental mandate of law and order to become overly concerned with community-based programs. To do so adequately would drain a large portion of the available resources. The public sector may advocate the community-based model but lacks the infrastructure and philosophical approach to effectively deliver. To be truly effective, the private sector must, to a greater extent, implement community-based programs while authoring public safety partnerships.

Today, the private security industry represents the largest public safety resource in the United States. The security industry that employed 200,000 officers during World War II now employs 2 million officers. Its expansion shows no sign of waning. The marketplace is driven by what The Security Group, of Cahners Business Information, labels "growth drivers." They are the following:

- Contributing to growth generally: systems integration, security video, access control and information/computer security.
- New technologies driving market growth: CCTV, wireless technologies, and the Internet/Web. Biometrics, smart cards voice transmissions and asset-tracking systems are also expected to impact the security service market over the next decade.
- The growing concern about such security risks as work violence, industrial espionage, and employee theft.
- Other developments: new concepts such as home automation, intelligent buildings, and service bundling.[2]

Current expenditures for the private sector are over $100 billion per year and growing progressively.[3] Private business continues its massive transference to contract, proprietary and independent contractors in private sector justice. In addition, government entities using taxpayer receipts achieve significant cost savings by outsourcing to the private sector. As long as public governments strain to do more with fewer resources, delegation to the security industry will be assured. These growth trends trump the public sector twofold. The security industry is the workhorse of the justice system, filling the void, picking up where the public sector fails, and most importantly, innovating while the public model contorts to survive. With more resources and institutional flexibility, a better sense of cost/benefit analysis, and a willingness to be creative in the justice marketplace, the future belongs to the private sector. Private security specialists for nuclear plants, privatized correctional facilities, private communities, and courthouses and judicial centers are being secured. The private sector is the premier choice to get the job done when it comes to the prevention of crime; this trend is proven every time that private entities contract the private sector to provide public safety services. See Figure 9.1.

As privatization of safety responsibilities grows, the future will witness an age of specialists and the technically proficient public officer whose reactive capabilities in emergency situations will be further refined. A cadre of officers forensically trained in sophisticated investigations will be a substantial occupational role in the public sector. Although community policing will still be touted as a solution to crime and violence in the high-crime community, public policing will be stretched in time and resource and will be incapable of delivering on its promise. The public sector will soon learn that its incapacity can be ameliorated by its colleagues in the private sector and will delegate a large portion of community-based policing responsibilities and other nonemergency related efforts, as the demands tighten around the public safety infrastructure. Partnerships and joint ventures

FIGURE 9.1 Professional and Prepared.

will significantly increase. In the final analysis, communities will go to those who operate from a compatible vision. It will be the primacy and superiority of art over science. Communities will yearn for a greater good than the technically proficient. Communities will pine for those practitioners who put art ahead of the scientific model.

II. A CASE OF ART OVER SCIENCE IN THE DELIVERY OF PROTECTIVE SERVICES

A recurring theme throughout this text has been the distinction between the "art" and the "science" of protection services. Private protection services rest firmly in both art and science. Yet science alone will never be sufficient. By art, the industry carries out its diverse and demanding tasks with interpersonal communication skills, interactive sophistication, and professional sensitivity. Whereas the science of enforcement grabs and intensely keeps our attention, from forensic inquiry to the employment of technology to target malefactors, it will be the "art" of human interaction and community involvement that marks the security industry. Although science should not be devalued, it cannot be the primary underpinning of police operation, because science delivers a managerial method, in which it systemizes policies and procedures and fosters intelligent planning and resource usage. Science implies the wise and prudent distribution of personnel and budgetary allotments. Science also will study and compute the effectiveness of protection plans and will calculate data and results to the design. At times, the "plan" becomes the single most important factor in the delivery of public safety services, and its maintenance often directly thwarts the creative mind, the innovative thinker, and the fringe analyst who can offer a broader or even more specialized perspective. The "plan" or the "system" itself should not become the be-all and end-all of protection practices—especially in communities distressed by frequent ravages. Private sector operatives consider things with the type of flexibility that needs both science and the art of interaction.

Community services cannot be adequately delivered without these dual approaches. It is the art of protection that allows the professional observer to see holistically and to grasp the social, political, and economic picture of a community, and to gain awareness about the lifeblood of the particular community. Science can go only so far: it may and should be used as a support to the art of public safety strategies: help detect and apprehend, but it cannot engage the community. Science can impress but not befriend and enlist support. Something substantially more humane is needed. Communities need to have the sense that their protection officers care intensely, share the victories and failures, and become stakeholders in how the communities evolve. Art means conversation and friendship between those entrusted with security and those who require the service. Art connotes honesty, character, and integrity in the functional aspects of public safety. Also, art implies a meaningful understanding of the constituencies served, with the promise to listen and react on the basis of communal interest, not strict adherence to a plan that has become inconsistent with community needs. Art expressly requires that the protection firm be engaged for the long haul in the life of the community instead of the 911 contact who pops in and out of the lives of residents. In addition, art prods the safety professional to think about alternatives to both criminal defendants and the communal problems identified and to be open to approaches that may or may not be centered in the legal system. Whereas the science of enforcement zealously employs arrest, apprehension, and prosecution, the art of protection may proffer another approach outside the system, whether it is community watch groups, religious tribunals, neighborhood courts, or the enlistment of the youth to detect and prevent crime from occurring. Art implies creativity and a willingness to adapt to particular circumstances instead of mindlessly adhering to SOP's and plans that must succeed. Clearly, the future belongs to the scientifically proficient, but only when guided by the art of protection. Assess the distinction in the chart in Table 9.1.

TABLE 9.1

Art of Protection	Science of Protection
Community viewed in relational way.	Community viewed as area of responsibility.
Community assessed for diverse perspectives, social/economic, and political.	Community assessed from narrow perspective of order maintenance.
Community members deemed essential to order maintenance.	Community members are potential suspects.
Community members can and should be befriended.	Community members should be distanced for objectivity purposes.
Resources and technology are secondary to human relations.	Resources and technology are primary instruments in the war on crime.
Human interaction is the chief means to crime prevention and community control.	Human interaction is important but only after control has been established.
Community members jointly cooperate in the war on crime.	Community Members are sources in the war on crime.
Crime prevention and proactive management is the primary philosophy.	Reaction, apprehension, and control is the primary philosophy.
Alternative approaches favored over plan and SOPs.	Plans and SOPs are favored approaches.
Partnering with community members deemed essential.	Listening to community members deemed sufficient.
Community success measured qualitatively (reduced crime and tension, freedom of movement, business, etc).	Community success measured in system's evaluation, data tabulations and crime reporting mechanisms.

III. THE RISE OF PUBLIC/PRIVATE PARTNERSHIPS IN THE JUSTICE MODEL

Few would contest that the merger of services in the public/private sector is now well under way.[4] In the United States, Canada, England, and Continental Europe, the idea is far from revolutionary. The Canadian government's Law Commission clearly presents the state of affairs:

> We suggest that what is emerging in Canada are networks of policing composed often of a mix of public police and private security providers. To what extent does the current law reflect the reality of policing in Canada? Given the evolving nature of private and public policing, does the public/private distinction which exists in our laws make sense any longer?[5]

George Rigakos, in his recent text *The New Parapolice*, types these private/public approaches as "strategic partnerships."[6] He portrays an entrenched relationship between private sector operations and community policing. "The police are becoming not only institutional partners with private security firms—often under the umbrella of community-based policing—but also advocates for those firms."[7] See Figure 9.2.

As profound as these insights are, this phase is just the beginning of a remarkable story. Policing has been transformed and "is in the process of changing from a system in which public forces provided almost all of our policing services, to one in which policing services are provided by a range of public and private agencies."[8] Privatization has become a familiar term. All that remains to be done is what Ron Hauri calls "the synergy of cooperation."[9] Since the 1970s, there has been a strong recognition of the need for cooperation (see Figure 9.3).[10] The Private Security Advisory Council originally funded by the federally funded Law Enforcement Assistance Administration (LEAA),[11] strongly suggested the need for joint ventures and posed various recommendations on how to achieve that goal. See Figure 9.4. Hauri remarks that "The leading professional societies on both sides of the dividing line not only advocate cooperation but also are working actively to foster it."[12]

Practitioner Highlight

Miami SCAN Program

In a move to strengthen communication between private building security forces and police, a new radio system is in place linking the two crime-fighting forces. The SCAN system enables condo and commercial building security guards who in emergencies use radios to switch to a nonprivate channel that is picked up by the police. With this new link, guards with criminal emergencies on their hands bypass the need to find a phone and go through a 911 operator. The overall goal of the system is to cut down response time for police when getting to the site of a crime in progress.

Dallas/North Texas Regional Law Enforcement and Private Security Program (LEAPS)

Developed around 1983, LEAPS operated for several years but fell somewhat dormant due to turnover. The program was revitalized in 1993.

LEAPS has a steering committee and formal bylaws, but no budget or legal or corporate status (a possible hindrance to fundraising and partnership institutionalization). The steering committee contains the deputy chief of the Dallas Police Department (DPD) and one to three private security members from each of nine business sectors. One officer from each DPD patrol division also is assigned to support the program, and more than 50 private sector organizations participate. Major projects include:

- *Security officer training.* Police train security officers on topics of interest to both, such as protecting crime scenes. The training, at police substations, gives security officers increased status and assures police that security officers have received training. The sessions also build relationships.
- *Police officer training.* A video about LEAPS is shown at police roll call and recruit training to encourage street-level cooperation.
- *Special-interest relationship building.* Corporate security executives wanted a better relationship with the police department's Criminal Investigation Division, so LEAPS arranged a meeting between the two groups.
- *Fax Net 1 information service.* Fax Net 1 disseminates crime information between public and private agencies.
- *Publicity.* LEAPS activities are chronicled in police and private sector newsletters. Also, LEAPS members speak to professional and trade groups, and the organization built an exhibit booth for display at trade shows.

The program has enabled police to enlist the support of the private sector, whose private security officers outnumber police officers in the Dallas area by five to one.

FIGURE 9.2 LEAPS: A Cooperative Public/Private Partnership

Typical Activities of Collaborative Programs

Networking

- Breakfast and lunch meetings (to discuss common problems and help each side understand the pressures, motivations, and constraints on the other).
- Lectures by private security professionals at police recruit training.
- Speeches by one field at conferences of the other field.
- Sponsorship of law enforcement appreciation functions and scholarships by security organizations.
- Directories of local law enforcement and private security contacts.
- Honors and awards (from private security to law enforcement and vice versa).

Information Sharing

- Information (provided by law enforcement to the private sector) on criminal convictions (if authorized by law), local crime trends, modus operandi, and incidents, shared via e-mail trees, Web pages, mailed newsletters, fax alerts, or telephone calls.
- Information (provided by the private sector to law enforcement) on business crime and employees.

Crime Prevention

- Joint participation in security and safety for business improvement districts (BIDs).
- Consultation on crime prevention through environmental design and community policing.
- Special joint efforts on local concerns, such as check fraud, video piracy, graffiti, or false alarms.
- Joint public-private support of neighborhood watch programs.
- Joint participation in National Night Out.

Resource Sharing

- Lending of expertise (technical, language, etc.).
- Lending of "buy" money or goods.
- Lending of computer equipment needed for specific investigations.
- Donation of computer equipment, cellular telephones, etc.
- Donation of security devices to protect public spaces.
- Creation of a booklet that makes it easier for law enforcement to borrow equipment and resources from private security, listing specific contact information for using auditoriums, classrooms, conference rooms, firing ranges, four-wheel drive vehicles, helicopter landing areas, indoor swimming pools, lecturers on security, open areas for personnel deployment, printing services, and vans or trucks.

Typical Activities of Collaborative Programs (cont.)

Training

- Hosting speakers on topics of joint interest (terrorism, school violence, crime trends, etc.).
- Exchange of training and expertise (corporations offer management training to police; private security trains law enforcement in security measures; law enforcement teaches security officers how to be good witnesses or gather evidence in accordance with prosecutorial standards).
- Police training of corporate employees on such topics as sexual assault, burglary prevention, family Internet safety, drug and alcohol abuse, traffic safety, and vacation safety.

Legislation

- Drafting and supporting laws and ordinances on such topics as security officer standards and licensing, alarms, and computer crime.
- Tracking of legislation of importance to law enforcement and security operations.

Operations

- Investigations (of complex financial frauds or computer crimes).
- Critical incident planning (for natural disasters, school shootings, and workplace violence).
- Joint sting operations (cargo theft).

Research and Guidelines

- Review of, distribution of, and action on research papers and protocols regarding false alarms, workplace drug crimes, workplace violence, product tampering, mobile security devices, non-sworn alarm responders, closed-circuit television, security personnel standards, etc.

---

*Networking and the personal touch
*Collaboration on specific projects
*Increased crime prevention and public safety
*Cross-fertilization
*Information sharing
*Leveraging of resources

FIGURE 9.3   Benefits of Cooperation

Developing public law enforcement and private security protocols or guidelines for cooperation
Cataloging and publishing success stories
Making criminal history information available to the private sector
Exchanging expertise, training, and technology between the private/public sectors
Enhancing working relationships between both sectors in crime prevention
Setting selection and training standards for private security
Suppressing drugs in the workplace
Improving understanding of private security role by law enforcement
Privatizing selected law enforcement functions
Conducting joint public/private operations (e.g., VIP protection, hazardous materials transport, overseas threat information)
Providing cooperation and honesty in background checks
Improving public/private sector operational communications
Reviewing polygraph legislation
Developing guidelines for police moonlighting in private security
Reducing false alarms

FIGURE 9.4   Areas for Cooperation

Of most significance has been the vital support of the International Association of Chiefs of Police, especially by and through the established Private Sector Liaison Committee (PSLC). The committee has been particularly active in police stress, drugs in the workplace, product tampering, and telecommunications fraud. See Figure 9.5.[13] ASIS has been just as influential in advancing cooperation by and through its Law Enforcement Liaison Council (LELC), which has advanced some striking initiatives in the area of educational materials, accreditation programs, and partnering. See Figure 9.6.

Private security firms can do a great deal to advance mutual cooperation and respect. If respect and cooperation are promoted, they will eventually rub off. The balance of respect and integration is delicate. See a sample company policy in Figure 9.7. The trend is plainly unstoppable. Partnering can only increase as public budgets shrink and role expectations expand. Shearing and Stenning term this part-

Private Sector Liaison Committee
This committee is composed of representative members from all facets of the private security sector and the law enforcement community. The role of the committee is to strive to improve the relationship between the private sector and public sector by the discussion and dissemination of meaningful data on a continuing basis.

Source: International Association of Chiefs of Police webpage at http://www.theiacp.org/div_sec_com/committees/pslc.htm.

FIGURE 9.5   International Association of Chiefs of Police—Committees, Divisions, and Sections

Vision Statement:
The American Society for Industrial Security will be the foremost organization advancing the Security profession worldwide.

Mission Statement:
To achieve its vision, the American Society for Industrial Security will establish, develop, and promote excellence in the security profession.

Goals:
Further, the American Society for Industrial Security will achieve its Vision and Mission by assuring:
1. High quality educational programs
2. Responsiveness to members needs
3. Standards for Professional and Ethical Conduct
4. A forum to debate and the Exchange of Ideas
5. Promotion of the Organization & Profession
6. Strategic Alliances with Related Organizations
7. Enhancement of Volunteer Leaders
8. A commitment to Continued Growth

Source: ASIS Online at http://www.asisonline.org/councils/noframe/law/plan.doc.

FIGURE 9.6   ASIS Law Enforcement Liaison Council—Business Plan

nering a form of interaction. The work of the two groups together will increase along these lines:

1. Joint public/private investigations;
2. Public agents hiring or delegating authority to private police;
3. Private interests hiring public police;
4. New organizational forms in which the distinction between public and private is blurred; and
5. Circulation of personnel between the public and the private sector.

Although these five forms are described using examples of undercover investigations, they represent more generic forms of interdependence.[14] Public police cannot carry out an unreasonable mandate.

Although these steps bode well for the future of both systems, perceptions of individual officers, according to some, are still fixed in the two-tiered mentality. Nalla and Hummer's recent study of perceptions graphically lays out the chasm of status that exists in the opinions and attitudes of so many officers. As the study indicates, public police still maintain a "superior" perspective, whereas private officers resent that attitude.[15] Results from a study by Nalla and Hummer can be read only as a continuance of the peripheral divide—a condition that must be eliminated for real cooperation to exist.[16] But along with growth come further responsibilities and questions that the security industry must take seriously, such as these issues:

Interaction with Public Law Enforcement	Uniformed Division Order #420.004

It is of utmost importance that CIS officers operating in the field be able to engage in good, courteous, and mutually beneficial professional relationships with law enforcement officers of various agencies. There are a number of things that can be done to facilitate interaction with law enforcement. From the very first contact a CIS officer has with a new police officer or sheriff's deputy they should make it clear that CIS is willing to do all that it can to cooperate and assist them. When a CIS officer is involved in a situation that law enforcement is dispatched to, upon their arrival they need to be provided with all details as quickly and as reliably as possible. At this point, the CIS officer should step back and allow the law the enforcement officer to carry out their duties, but let them know that you can offer assistance if and when needed.

This approach does a number of things. It shows law enforcement that CIS is not going to interfere with their duties or override what they're saying and become a hindrance. It also establishes CIS as separate from the actual incident that is occurring, and shows law enforcement personnel that CIS officers are professional and do not have the "wanna-be" syndrome. Officers should make sure that when law enforcement personnel are dispatched to their location it is for valid reasons and not merely petty problems. This will show them that when a CIS officer calls, there is a legitimate crime that will most likely lead to an arrest. This establishes the CIS officer that much more as a professional because they are not calling for non-criminal related problems.

Within the realm of professional respect and courtesy it is important that law enforcement personnel understand the scope of CIS's powers under state statutes. Occasionally, CIS officers will encounter law enforcement officers that question these powers. Therefore, CIS officers must be knowledgeable in the areas of state statutes that not only govern them but apply to them on a regular basis, such as trespass, burglary, battery, aggravated battery, assault, aggravated assault, etc. The more CIS officers understand these statutes, the more they understands their rights according to state statute to exercise those rights.

> **Example** Some law enforcement officers refuse to issue trespass warnings because they think that security personnel need criminal reasons to be able to trespass individuals. However, according to state statutes, security officers have the power and the right to trespass individuals whenever they, or the management company they are representing, deem it necessary.

Officer interaction with law enforcement should always be professional. Law enforcement is on site to either interact with CIS in a situation, or they are just stopping by to see how the CIS officer is. Officers should always be careful with verbal communications and not over-talk law enforcement to the point that they will not be interested in future interactions.

When law enforcement requests assistance, officers must provide it. It is a misdemeanor under state statutes to refuse assistance to any law enforcement officer. Cooperation will help to build a bond. Law enforcement will respond to calls without back-up knowing that CIS officers are on site to assist.

Maintaining good, accurate Intelligence Reports is an important aspect of an officer's responsibilities. The more intelligence collected on particular individuals within a given area, the more law enforcement will come to rely on CIS to provide information about the whereabouts of an individual, or his actions, when they come looking for him. Time and time again, CIS

FIGURE 9.7 Interaction Protocol and Guidelines

- To what extent does the fragmentation of the industry restrict its organizational development?
- What measures can be taken to assist the private security industry in developing an effective industry association?

personnel prove themselves to be of assistance to law enforcement because they are the only ones who can provide the high quality information needed.

All CIS employees will extend their full cooperation to all public law enforcement personnel on a professional level at all times. This will include the local police, deputy sheriffs, state and federal officers, and fire department officials. Officers should always identify themselves to any law enforcement personnel, so that they may get to know one another since they will be working in the same area. Officers must never compromise themselves, the agency, organization, or client-company that they are charged to protect. If in doubt about what interaction to take, they should seek guidance, verification, and/or assistance from their immediate supervisor or from the senior ranking officer/field supervisor who is on duty. Remember, the bottom line is professionalism.

1. Never interfere with police officers performing their official duties.
2. When police scanners are monitored, be especially cautious when responding to crimes in progress on CIS sites, as this may inadvertently interfere with police response.
3. If possible, do not respond too quickly to the scene of recent crimes, as this may inadvertently interfere with police apprehension tactics.
     Example: Officer may cross the path of a suspect, thereby possibly, or unknowingly, ruining the ability of a Police K-9 to track the suspect.
4. If ordered by a police officer to provide assistance, officers must always comply. Failure to do so is a misdemeanor under state statutes.
5. At the scene of a crime, a CIS officer must not ask to view or interfere with the scene, as the police must maintain and protect the crime scene, in order to not contaminate any evidence.
6. Officers should identify themselves to any police officers (as long as they are not investigating or responding to a call), so as to build relationships with law enforcement working in CIS areas.

Anytime that there is an issue with reference to the manner in which CIS personnel are treated by law enforcement, or when law enforcement refuses to assist with such things as issuing a trespass, etc., the box "Code 6 Issue" is to be marked and accompanied by a brief narrative. This is also to be done when law enforcement is contacted and a dispatcher is rude or hangs up on CIS Operators.

FIGURE 9.7   *(Cont.)*

• To what extent would the collection of systematic data about the private security industry assist the industry in developing a professional orientation?[17]

IV. THE RISE OF REGULATIONS, STANDARDS, AND ACCREDITATION

An organized framework with standards and regulations across the states has yet to materialize for an industry with so much influence. Extraordinary variety in the types and classifications in the industry exists, but the future will likely see some standardization. The Bureau of Justice Assistance already has detected this trend. "In addition, increasing professionalism in private security has slowly been improving law enforcement's attitude toward security practitioners, and 'each successful contact aids in establishing further ties and acts as a building block for increased communication and joint programs.'[18, 19] As far back as 1980, law en-

Washington Law Enforcement Executive Forum (WLEEF)

WLEEF was founded in 1980 by law enforcement executives and private security representatives, originally to lobby for a law that would give some businesses access to criminal records. Legally, WLEEF is part of the Washington Association of Sheriffs and Police Chiefs (WASPC), which is recognized for lobbying purposes, can get federal grants, has an office building, and provides WLEEF with staff support. The WASPC connection provides operational consistency over the long term and cases transitions from one chair to the next.

WLEEF itself has a minimal structure, relying mainly on tradition and a circle of highly motivated members. The presidency of WLEEF alternates between a public sector and a private sector member.

The organization's 30 members include top law enforcement executives from around the state and corporate representatives who, when not the actual corporate presidents, at least have access to the top corporate executives.

WLEEF has been especially productive. It holds bimonthly meetings, produces draft legislation, helped set up a toll-free number for reporting drunk drivers, coordinates corporate donation of computer equipment to law enforcement agencies, and produces informative brochures on such topics as medical fraud, insurance fraud, check fraud, real estate fraud, workplace violence, identification document fraud, bankruptcy, product tampering, substance abuse, money laundering, securities fraud, telecommunications fraud, counterfeiting, white-collar crime, computer crime, and children and the Internet. Funding of those brochures has sometimes come from the affected industries.

California High Technology Crime Advisory Committee

This public-private collaboration, first funded by the state in 1998, helped establish and continues to assist regional high-tech crime task forces. The committee's public sector members represent the California sheriffs' association, police chiefs' association, attorney general's office, highway patrol, high-tech crime investigators' association, office of criminal justice planning, and district attorneys' association. The private sector members represent associations of computer hardware manufacturers, software publishers, cellular carriers, Internet-related companies, cable television providers, film producers, and telephone carriers. About half the private sector members have security backgrounds.

The program works on two levels. First, the committee developed a statewide strategy for combating high-tech crime. Second, it awards large grants to regional law enforcement task forces (of which there are currently three), which have conducted hundreds of investigations and recovered millions of dollars in lost property.

The committee now is working to develop a statewide high-tech crime database. In the future, it may add to the number of regional task forces.

For years the world has recognized a need for competent professionals who can effectively manage complex security issues that threaten people and the assets of corporations, governments, and public and private institutions. As the emphasis on protecting people, property, and information increases, it has strengthened the demand for professional managers. To meet these needs, the ASIS International administers the Certified Protection Professional program. Nearly 10,000 professionals have earned the designation of CPP. This group of professionals has demonstrated its competency in the areas of security solutions and best-business practices through an intensive qualification and testing program. As a result, these men and women have been awarded the coveted designation of CPP, and are recognized as proven leaders in their profession.

Source: http://www.asisonline.org/certification/cpp/index.xml

FIGURE 9.8   ASIS International Website Certified Protection Professional

forcement executives in both the public and private sector recognized the need for professional cooperation. WLEEF represents a solid example.

The industry itself should zealously rectify any deficiencies in the matter of regulation. Its credibility depends upon enactment.[20] Consequently, as the security industry's role escalates, regulations are needed to ensure the quality of performance and to announce adequate standards of professional conduct. See Figure 9.8. Academic analysis still paints a picture of both public and private officers failing to achieve high levels of education. "Only 1% of local law enforcement agencies require a 4-year degree, and 75% have no formal policy linking education with promotion. It is argued that a four-year degree standard has not been adopted because police organizations and police work have not changed in ways that require it."[21] On a positive note, Barton Protective Services has recently expanded its master security officer training program in Texas and California, and then it will go nationally. The training consists of in excess of 48 hours of classroom instruction on numerous topics.

Collective bargaining units such as AFL-CIO's Service Employees International Union (SEIU) have been extraordinarily critical of the private sector's empty promise to professionalize. The very fact that the SEIU is now targeting security professionals for union membership signifies the "hotbed" issue of poor credentials and living standards. See Figure 9.9. The SEIU and others in the security work-

Who We Are
We are the largest union of security officers in the AFL-CIO, made up of over 20,000 officers who work for private security companies and 30,000 officers who work in the public sector. The major security companies and building owners we work for operate all across America. Through SEIU, we've been able to win better wages and benefits and more respect on the job.
Source: http://www.seiu.org/building/security/who_we_are2/.

FIGURE 9.9   SEIU—Security

force of the future have much territory to cross before the words leap beyond puffery. The "new environment" of 9/11 alone has changed the equations.[22]

Legislatively, there is momentum, particularly since the terrorist attacks of 2001. At the federal level, *The Law Enforcement and Industrial Security Cooperation Act of 1996* (HR2996) was introduced, though not passed. HR 2996 encouraged cooperation between the private and the public sector. If passed, this bill would have been a solid step for the security industry to take toward an active roll in opening lines of communication with law enforcement and, in turn, in sharing ideas, training, and working in conjunction with each other, all indirectly influencing standards. The content of the proposed bill is instructive and certainly foretells an active future for the security industry. The rationale for bill adoption is fourfold:

1. Seventy percent of all money invested in crime prevention and law enforcement each year in the United States is spent by the private sector.
2. There are nearly three employees in private sector security for every one in public law enforcement.
3. More than half of the responses to crime come from private security.
4. A bipartisan study commission specially constituted for the purposes of examining appropriate cooperative roles between public sector law enforcement and private sector security will be able to offer comprehensive proposals for statutory and procedural initiatives.[23]

The most significant piece of legislation passed at the federal level involving aviation security is the *Aviation and Transportation Security Act of 2001.* Although the Act "federalizes" certain security employees and hands over operational control to the Department of Transportation, the act aggressively mandates sweeping security measures at all transportation modes. The provisions are clear:

> Federal transportation law to establish in the Department of Transportation (DOT) the Transportation Security Administration, to be headed by an Under Secretary of Transportation for Security responsible for security in all modes of transportation, including: (1) civil aviation security, and related research and development activities; (2) security responsibilities over other modes of transportation that are exercised by DOT; (3) day-to-day Federal security screening operations for passenger air transportation and intrastate air transportation; (4) policies, strategies, and plans for dealing with threats to transportation; (5) domestic transportation during a national emergency (subject to the Secretary of Transportation's control and direction), including aviation, rail, and other surface transportation, and maritime transportation, and port security; and (6) management of security information, including notifying airport or airline security officers of the identity of individuals known to pose a risk of air piracy or terrorism or a threat to airline or passenger safety.[24]

As recently as April 2002, the Senate assessed bills that upgrade security officer standards and licensure requirements and access to criminal records. *The Private Security Officer Employment Standards Act of 2002's*[25] preliminarily finding include the following:

1. Employment of private security officers in the United States is growing rapidly;
2. Private security officers function as an adjunct to, but not a replacement for, public law enforcement by helping to reduce and prevent crime;
3. such private security officers protect individuals, property, and proprietary information, and provide protection to such diverse operations as banks, hospitals, research and development centers, manufacturing facilities, defense and aerospace contractors, high technology businesses, nuclear power plants, chemical companies, oil and gas refineries, airports, communication facilities and operations, office complexes, schools, residential properties, apartment complexes, gated communities, and others;
4. sworn law enforcement officers provide significant services to the citizens of the United States in its public areas, and are supplemented by private security officers;
5. the threat of additional terrorist attacks requires cooperation between public and private sectors and demands professional security officers for the protection of people, facilities, and institutions;
6. the trend in the Nation toward growth in such security services has accelerated rapidly;
7. such growth makes available more public sector law enforcement officers to combat serious and violent crimes;
8. the American public deserves the employment of qualified, well-trained private security personnel as an adjunct to sworn law enforcement officers;
9. private security officers and applicants for private security officer positions should be thoroughly screened and trained; and
10. standards are essential for the selection, training, and supervision of qualified security personnel providing security services.[26]

Given the diversity of services delivered by the private sector, records access is critical.

The Homeland Security Act, while federalizing some aspects of the transportation industry, reaffirmed its dedication to the security industry. Some of the more pertinent parts are the following:

1. prevent terrorist attacks within the United States;
2. reduce the vulnerability of the United States to terrorism;
3. minimize the damage, and assist in the recovery, from terrorist attacks that occur within the United States;
4. carry out all functions of entities transferred to DHS;
5. ensure that the functions of the agencies and subdivisions within DHS that are not related directly to securing the homeland are not diminished or neglected except by a specific Act of Congress;
6. ensure that the overall economic security of the United States is not diminished by efforts, activities, and programs aimed at securing the homeland; and
7. monitor connections between illegal drug trafficking and terrorism, coordinate efforts to sever such connections, and otherwise contribute to efforts to interdict illegal drug trafficking.[27]

It is obvious that private sector industry will have a crucial role to play in this far-reaching mandate. California has adopted far-reaching legislation as to the conduct and powers of security officers. Its Bureau of Security and Investigative Services oversees the entire industry. (See box on p. 307.)

Unified standards can also come about through the accreditation process. The private security firm solicits some designated professional body or entity empowered to make quality assessments for accreditation. In higher education, regional accreditors like Southern or Middle States review universities and colleges; nursing and physician-based programs by the American Medical Association; and lawyers by the American Bar Association. Essentially, accreditation represents a seal of approval that the entity is meeting a minimum standard of professional competence. The security industry would benefit from this type of peer analysis. An independent organization such as The American Society for Industrial Security or The International Foundation for Protection Officers would be appropriate candidates for accreditation oversight. Although talk of professionalism is rampant, the industry will have to invest in its people and infrastructure. Standards of all sorts must rise.

V. THE PRIVATE SECTOR SOLUTION

In the final analysis, the central thesis of this text is the need for the paradigm shift–from public to private in the matter of community-based policing. Private sector firms can formidably deliver rejuvenated communities. Current policing models have historically shown an uncanny incompetence in the maintenance order in troubled communities and offer even less optimism in the rehabilitation of these forgotten and troubled areas. The current police model fails, since it merely reacts to reports and calls—the sort of mindless reactionism that pays scant attention to the root causes of the disorder in that community. As if they were in survivalist mode, the public police declare success when reaction time beats the clock.

Given the paucity of resources, civil service and union rules, and a general bureaucratic mentality, innovation and creativity are hard to come by in the public sector. Only the private sector is capable of redeeming the community. Increasingly, criminologists are quantitatively demonstrating the reduction of crime by the transference from public to private.[28] Only private protection specialists can expend time and energy on nonreactive functions that are nearly impossible for the emergency approach of the public command. Of course, law enforcement must continue to carry out its mission of responding to emergencies and its enforcement responsibilities.

With a rising and an unceasing plague of crime, the United States—the industrial giant and leader in the world—still lacks a unified, coordinated approach that utilizes all of our resources to seriously impact the crime epidemic. The methodology of public policing cannot save the culture from the onslaught of wrongdoers in American communities.

It is, as Jason Lloyd-Leonard tags it, a devolution of sorts in which public protection devolves only to be replaced by private sector systems. Private sector

- Countermeasures Selection
- Financial Management
- Management Systems
- Personnel Management
- Planning, Organization, Leading, and Communications Management
- Vulnerability Assessment
- Risk Assessment
- Countermeasures
- Policies
- Internal Relations
- External Relations
- Identification and Disposition of Abusers
- Prevention Programs
- Types of Solutions
- Loss Prevention
- Liaison
- Substance Abuse

Investigations

- Investigative Resources
- Methods of Investigation
- Results and Reports of Investigation
- Types of Investigation

Legal Aspects (United States, Canada, and United Kingdom)

- Administrative and Regulatory Agency Requirements
- Civil Liability Torts
- Civil Rights and Fair Employment
- Contract Considerations
- Crimes, Criminal Procedures, and the Criminal Justice System
- Due Process and Constitutional Immunities

Personnel Security

- Employment Selection and Retention Standards
- Evaluation of Information
- Screening Techniques
- Security Awareness Programs
- Disciplinary Action

Physical Security

- Employee and Visitor Control
- Alarms
- Barriers
- Facility Planning
- Guard Patrols and Weapons
- Materials Control
- Mechanical, Electrical, and Electronic Devices and Equipment

FIGURE 9.10   ASIS International Website—CPP Exam Structure and Content Security Management

- Perimeter Boundaries, Gates, and Lobbies
- Protective Lighting
- Security Surveys
- Parking, Traffic Control, Communications, and Security Transportation

Protection of Sensitive Information

- Control
- Identification
- Sensitivity

Emergency Management

- Implementation
- Plan Development
- Types of Emergency

http://www.asisonline.org/certification/cpp/steps/examStructure.xml

FIGURE 9.10 *(Cont.)*

protection, working in unison with the public sector, can achieve greater results than witnessed thus far. Rethinking the overall police approach is a radical undertaking that includes a coordinated effort of public officials, private sector practitioners, community leaders, and a host of other for profit and nonprofit entities and individuals. It will take more than, as Braiden call it, "hitchhiking" on waves of popularity.[29]

Furthermore, community members who are experiencing conflict and misery are part of the equation too. Citizen input and insight breed a sense of ownership that is sorely missing in the present police/citizen relationship. What is needed is a clear commitment—a focus on what creates real relationships and trust rather than on what makes policing appear to be effective through enforcement.

Whereas public policing thinks that technology is the smart route and the answer to cumbersome problems and that forensic science will replace common sense and footwork, the private sector will engineer a better road into the heart of the community. Human interaction, detection, defusion and de-escalation, communication, networking, observational psychology, community anchoring, relationship building, economic empowerment, confrontation and shock tactics—all of these factors typify an industry with the creative edge necessary to win in the battle over community victimization. Bruce Benson even argues that privatization will increase the probability of arrest and successful prosecution. Not only are private sector practitioners efficient, but they also operate from noble motives.[30] In doing so, the private industry can create environments that encourage and promote the human spirit and instill a sense of citizenship, pride, and a virtuous disposition that can only benefit the collective. In truth, this is a story about more than apprehension and arrest; it is about the capacity to balance the ends of enforcement and prevention and of knowing when peace is assured for the good. See Figure 9.10.

VI. CONCLUSION

This chapter summarizes the communitarian approach that can be delivered by private sector justice. From the available evidence, it appears that this is a trend that will not be halted. Legislatively, the industry continues to see its role expanded in the delivery of justice services across the nation. Numerous examples of this legislative confidence are found within the chapter. Additionally, the merger—and a willing one at that—of public safety and private justice is equally unstoppable. More and more public justice agencies are reaching out to the private sector in the complicated world of crime prevention. In communities, the thrust of these alliances has become undeniable. In the final analysis, private sector justice seems to be the more capable player in the matter of community protection and oversight—not that public law enforcement will ever be out of the mix. In fact, its place could not be more entrenched or more crucial to community maintenance. But the area in which private sector public safety shines rests in the world of reclamation and community maintenance. Instead of the "lost" neighborhood caricature, private security offers up an optimistic plan for the salvation of communities, since its philosophical underpinnings rest side-by-side with what the inhabitants of any community really want—pride, safety, and a sense of home.

Notes

1. Vail Symposium *1997 Briefing Book.* Vail, Co: The Vail Symposium 1997
2. *See* The Security Group, *Reed Business Information* a division of Reed-Elsevier New York, NY. (2000).
3. *See* William Cunningham et al., *The Hallcrest Report II—Private Security Trends 1970–2000* (Boston: Butterworth-Heinemann, 1990).
4. *Experts Salute Public & Private Sectors on Crime Reduction Collaboration,* 32 *Security Letter* (7/8/02); Chris A. Bradford and Clifford A. Simonsen, *The Need for Cooperative Efforts Between Private Security and Public Law Enforcement in the Prevention, Investigation, and Prosecution of Fraud-Related Criminal Activity,* 10 Security Journal, 161 (1998).
5. Law Commission of Canada, *In Search of Security: The Roles of Public Police and Private Agencies* 11 (ottawa, Ontario, Canada 2002).
   http://www.lcc.gc.ca/en/themes/05/2002-04_15.htm
6. George S. Rigakos, *The New Parapolice* 42 (Univ. of Toronto Press Toronto 2002).
7. Rigakos at 40.
8. Law Commission at 12.
9. S. Ronald Hauri, *Public-Private Security Liaison: The Synergy of Cooperation, Crime & Justice International* 16 (Oct. 1997).
10. Operation Cooperation, *Guidelines for Partnerships between Law Enforcement & Private Security Organizations* 2–3 (Washington, D.C., U.S. Dept. of Justice 2000).
11. James Kakalik and Sorrel Wildhorn, *Private Police in the United States,* Volume I (R-869) and Volume II (R-870) (Washington, D.C.: U.S. GPO, 1971).
12. Hauri at 16.
13. Operation Cooperation at 8.

14. C. Shearing and P. Stenning, *The Interweaving of Public and Private Police Undercover Work* in *Private Policing* (Sage, Newbury Park, CA 1987).
15. See Mahesh K. Nalla and Don Hummer, *Relations between Police Officers and Security Professionals: A Study of Perceptions, Security Journal* (1999).
16. Nalla and Hummer, Table 2, at 36.
17. Law Commission at 34.
18. Jack R. Greene, Thomas M. Seamon, and Paul R. Levy, "Merging Public and Private Security for Collective Benefit: Philadelphia's Center City District," vol. 14 American Journal of Police. 5 (1995).
19. Edward F. Connors, William C. Cunningham and Peter E. Ohlhausen, *A Literature Review of Cooperation and Partnerships Between Law Enforcement and Private Security Organizations,* 22 (Washington, D.C. U.S. Dept. of Justice, Jan. 1999).
20. *Security Business,* Vol. 32, 7/8/002. This is a newsletter and all that was on it.
21. Agnes L. Baro, *Law Enforcement and Higher Education: Is There an Impasse? 10 J. Crim. Just. Ed. 57* (1999).
22. SEIU's Executive Summary for the security workforce of the future calls for (1) the identification of private security needs in this new environment; (2) the creation of a professional security workforce, including better training, compensation, standards, and career opportunities; (3) the development of partnerships with all stakeholders to set standards and work toward goal implementation; (4) the establishment of labor-management training programs as part of a certification process for all private security employees; and (5) efforts to improve the standards, regulations, and integration of security personnel's responsibilities with the responsibilities of other players as well as improved enforcement of standards and regulations.
23. H.R. 2996, 2/29/96, 104th Congress, 2nd session.
24. S. 1447, 11/19/01, 107th Congress, 1st session, P.L. 107–71.
25. S.2238 6/24/02.
26. S.2238 at Sec. 2.
27. H.R. 5005 11/25/2002, 107th Congress, 2nd session P.L. 107–296.
28. For example *see* Lloyd Klein, Joan Luxenburg, and Marianna King, *Perceived Neighborhood Crime and the Impact of Private Security, 35 Crime and Delinquency* 370 (1989).
29. *Police Management: Issues and Perspectives* 107 (Washington DC, Police Executive Research Forum Larry Hoover, ed., 1992).
30. Bruce Benson, *To Serve and Protect* New York: New York Univ. Press 318 (1998).

Appendix

Environmental Threat Assessment & Residential Property Security Survey

1. CONTACT INFORMATION

Name of Property:_____

Property Manager:_____ Asst. Property Mgr:_____

Property Mgr Tel:_____ Alt. Tel:_____

Management Company:_____ Company Dist. Mgr:_____

Company Dist Mgr Tel:_____ Fax:_____

Property Address:_____

Mailing Address (if different):_____

Police Jurisdiction:_____ District/Zone:_____

Police Crime Prevention Officer:_____ Tel:_____

Local Area Supplemetary POC:_____ Tel:_____

Local Area Supplemetary POC:_____ Tel:_____

2. PROPERTY DESCRIPTION

2.1 Layout & Construction

Obtain and attach a copy of the property layout diagram. Be sure that the diagram indicates apartment buildings, offices, clubhouses, pools, laundry facilities, parking areas, entrances, and apartment numbers.

2.1.1 How many apartment units are located on-site?_____

2.1.2 How many units are located in each building?_____

2.1.3 How many floors are located in each building?_____

2.1.4 How many buildings are located on-site?_____

2.1.5 Where do residents and visitors park?_____

_____

2.1.6 When was the complex built?_____

2.2 Resident Population

2.2.1 What is the ethnic composition of the resident community?_____

2.2.2 What are the age demographics of the resident community?_____

2.2.3 What are the economic demographics of the resident community?_____

2.2.4 What is the level of tenant turn-over in the neighborhood?_____

_____

2.2.5 What is the level of unemployment in the resident community?_____

2.2.6 Approximately how many children are present in the community?_____

2.2.7 Is the property declared as Section 8?_____

2.3 Surrounding Environment

2.3.1 In general, describe the surrounding community (e.g., residential, other apartment communities, mixed residential/commercial, office buildings, etc.):

   North:_____

   South:_____

   East:_____

   West:_____

2.3.2 What are the demographics of the surrounding community?

   Ethnicity:_____

   Age:_____

   Economic status:_____

   Employment:_____

2.3.3 What types of indicators of community disorganization or social disorder are present?

Check cashing businesses?_____

Liquor stores?_____

Trash/abandoned bldgs/general decay?_____

_____

Barred windows/heavy roll-away doors?_____

Abandoned or stripped cars?_____

Pawn Shops:_____

Porn Shops:_____

2.3.3.1 Are there banks present in the area? ☐ Yes ☐ No

2.3.3.2 Do pizza drivers deliver to the area? ☐ Yes ☐ No

2.3.3.3 Do taxi drivers take pick ups in the area at night? ☐ Yes ☐ No

3. CRIMINAL ACTIVITY

Conduct in cooperation with local police crime prevention officer. Request a list of reported crimes for the property and adjacent areas for a period of at least last six months prior to the survey. If the property is located in the Tampa Bay area, refer to the TBO crimetracker if necessary.

3.1 General

3.1.1 Does the property management have an accurate record of previous incidents including police reports and in-house documentation?

3.2 Violent Offenses

3.2.1 What types of arrests have been conducted over the past year related to assault or battery?

_____

_____

3.2.1.1 Were the perpetrators residents or non-residents?_____

_____

3.2.1.2 Were the acts committed by gang members or directed at gang members?_____

_____

3.2.2 Have there been any incidents of assault reported by residents that have not been reported to police?_____

_____

3.2.3 What types of arrests have been conducted over the past year related to domestic violence?

_____

_____

3.2.4 Have there been any incidents of domestic violence reported by residents that have not been reported to police?

_____

_____

3.2.5 Have there been any complaints by residents of violent arguments in apartments that have not been reported to police?

_____

3.2.6 Have there been any incidents of murder, attempted murder, or assault with a deadly weapon (aggravated battery)?

_____

_____

3.2.7 What types of arrests have been conducted over the past year related to sexual battery (rape) or sexual harassment?

_____

_____

3.2.8 Have there been any complaints by residents of violent sexual encounters or harassment of women in the environment?

_____

_____

_____

3.3 Non-Violent Offenses

3.3.1 What types of arrests have been conducted over the past year related to drug sales or possession?

_____

_____

3.3.2 Are there any known or suspected drug dealers living on-site?_____

_____

_____

_____

3.3.3 Are there any known or suspected non-resident drug dealers doing business on-site?

_____

_____

_____

3.3.4 Have residents complained about open use of drugs or alcohol?_____

_____

_____

_____

3.3.5 Have there been any reports or observations of suspicious activity associated with specific apartments? Suspicious activity including:

- High volume of traffic in and out of the apartment
- Youths hanging out in front (often with cell phones or radios)
- Darkened or blocked windows
- Signs of reinforced doors and windows
- Unusual smells
- Changed locks (without management approval)
- Persistently "burned-out" light bulbs
  (Residents replacing or breaking new bulbs after burned-out bulbs are replaced)

_____

_____

_____

_____

_____

3.3.6 What types of arrests have been conducted over the past year related to prostitution?

_____

_____

3.3.7 Have there been any complaints by residents or evidence of high volumes of male traffic in apartments occupied by single females?

_____

_____

3.3.8 What types of incidents of burglary have occurred on-site within the past 12 months?

_____

_____

_____

_____

_____

3.3.8.1 Were most burglaries accompanied by theft?

If YES, what types of articles were stolen?_____

_____

3.3.8.2 Were burglarized apartments also vandalized?

Describe:_____

3.3.8.3 Was there evidence of alcohol consumption, drug use, or other activities during the burglaries?

_____

3.3.9 What types of incidents of vandalism have occurred on-site within the past 12 months?

_____

_____

_____

_____

_____

_____

_____

_____

3.3.10 What types of incidents of auto theft have occurred on-site within the past 12 months?

_____

_____

_____

_____

3.3.11 Has there been a history of stolen cars being "dropped" on the property?_____

_____

_____

3.4 Rules Violations

3.4.1 What types of complaints have been issued by residents or observations made by managers regarding loitering in stairwells, common areas, and other locations?

_____

_____

3.4.2 What types of complaints have been issued by residents or observations made by managers regarding open alcohol consumption?

_____

_____

3.4.3 What types of complaints have been issued by residents or observations made by managers regarding unregistered or unserviceable cars?

_____

_____

3.4.4 What types of complaints have been issued by residents or observations made by managers regarding unruly public behavior?

_____

_____

3.4.5 What types of complaints have been issued by residents or observations made by managers regarding loud music and uncontrolled parties?

_____

_____

3.4.6 What types of complaints have been issued by residents or observations made by managers regarding illegal residents and unreported guests?

_____

_____

3.5 Gang Presence & Activity

3.5.1 Are there any known gangs operating on-site or in the local area?_____

_____

    3.5.1.1 If YES, are the gangs legitimate sets of national alliances?_____

    3.5.1.2 What appears to be the primary motive for gang affiliation locally (peer acceptance, money, "something to do", etc.)?

    _____

3.5.2 Do police gang officers have any information about gang members, affiliates, or "girlfriends" living on the property?

_____

_____

_____

3.5.3 Have juveniles been observed on-site displaying any of the following signs of gang affiliation?

    Gang Indicators:

- Clothes of similar colors
- Similar tattoos (often with unusual symbols)
- Slanting clothes completely to one side
- Unusual gestures when meeting or conversing

_____

_____

If YES:

3.5.3.1 Are the juveniles residents, non-residents, or a combination?

_____

3.5.3.2 Do the juveniles spend a majority of their time on-site?

_____

3.5.3.3 Is the activity new?

_____

3.5.4 Has there been any graffiti on-site or in the local area that possibly indicates gang activity?

Common motifs in gang graffiti include:

- stars
- pyramids
- pitchforks
- crowns
- numbers

_____

_____

3.6 High Activity Areas

3.6.1 Where (what locations on-site) have previous crimes and nuisance activities been reported?_____

_____

_____

3.6.2 Where (what locations on-site) do people tend to loiter or gather?_____

_____

_____

3.7 Surrounding Environment

3.7.1 Are there any locations in the surrounding environment where people loiter for extended periods of time (gas stations, street corners, parks, basketball courts, etc.)?

_____

_____

3.7.2 Are there any locations in the surrounding area identified by police as "high-crime" or "drug sales" locations?

_____

_____

4. COMMUNITY ATTITUDES & INTEGRATION

4.1 Crime Perceptions

4.1.1 Do residents regard the property as a high crime location?_____

4.1.2 Do parents allow children to play outdoors after dark?_____

_____

4.1.3 Do families use the outdoor recreational facilities (pool, playground, etc.)?_____

_____

4.2 Community Unity & Trust

4.2.1 Do residents appear to know and interact well with each other?_____

_____

_____

4.2.2 Do residents report misbehaving children directly to their parents?_____

_____

4.2.3 Do residents verbally discipline other parent's children?_____

_____

4.2.4 What is the turn-over rate for residents?_____

4.2.5 Does the community hold organized crime prevention meetings?_____

_____

     4.2.5.1 How many citizens show up for the meetings?_____

     4.2.5.2 How often do they meet?_____

4.3 Community Care & The Environment

4.3.1 Do residents report broken windows, doors, lights, and similar maintenance requests?_____

4.3.2 Who is the first to discover or report a maintenance problem (Property Maintenance personnel or residents)?

_____

4.3.3 Do residents volunteer to help with painting and grounds keeping?_____

4.3.4 Do residents plant flowers or decorate the outside of their residences?_____

_____

4.3.5 Do children attend school regularly or are children frequently seen on property during school hours?

_____

4.3.6 Are young children unattended while playing outdoors?_____

4.4 Perceptions About Law Enforcement & Property Management

4.4.1 Do residents look apprehensive or suspicious in the presence of uniformed security or law enforcement personnel?

_____

4.4.2 Do residents talk openly and volunteer information to police while police are on-site?_____

_____

4.4.3 Do residents stand outside to see what is going on or do residents "hide" indoors when law enforcement officers are on-property?

_____

4.4.4 Do residents report the majority of crimes committed on-property to police or do they seem resistant about reporting directly to police (rather, preferring to complain to management or amongst themselves)?

_____

_____

4.4.5 Do most residents report maintenance problems promptly to property management?_____

_____

4.4.6 Do residents report community rule violations and suspicious behavior to property managers or their representatives?

_____

_____

4.5 Resident Interviews

If possible, interview several residents. Ask:

- How would you describe your community in terms of crime frequency (low crime, high crime, average, etc.)?
- Do you feel safe walking alone (or allowing your children to play outside) at night in your community?
- What is your greatest concern regarding crime in your community?
- How fast do the police respond to emergency calls here? Do they seem to respond slow or fast?
    - If SLOW, why do you think so?
- Do police interact well with people here?
- Do you feel that the police treat you the same way as other people?

5. PHYSICAL SITE SURVEY

Daytime Survey

The following sections (5.1 to 5.5) are to be evaluated by conducting a daytime survey of the property and adjacent areas. Emphasis during the daytime survey is to evaluate potential physical security and crime prevention issues associated with design and maintenance of the property, identify potential indicators of criminal activity and community disorganization, and identify any open criminal activity occurring during daytime hours (such as street-corner drug dealing).

5.1 Grounds & Outdoor Community Areas

5.1.1 Is there trash, cigarette butts, or other items littering the ground?_____

5.1.2 If litter is observed, does the manager stop and pick it up of his own initiative?_____

_____

5.1.3 Are there any indications of drug or outdoor alcohol abuse? *Look carefully in the bushes and around garbage cans for any of the following:*

- "Roaches" (Burnt hand-rolled cigarette ends)
- Cigar tobacco (from inside the cigar, hollowed out to create a blunt)
- Empty rolling paper boxes or wrappers
- Very small zip-lock plastic baggies
- Discarded syringes

- Burnt coke cans with punctured holes
- Burnt spoons
- Burnt brillo pads
- Beer bottles & cans
- Wine & liquor bottles

_____

_____

_____

5.1.4 How well are the grounds kept and maintained (paint, grass, shrubbery, etc.)?_____

_____

_____

_____

5.2 Apartment Buildings

5.2.1 How well are the apartment buildings kept and maintained (paint, grass, shrubbery, etc)?

_____

_____

5.2.2 Are there any indications of possible drug and alcohol abuse (as suggested by indicators described in 5.1.3)? *Particularly look around the stairwells, bushes, and trash dumpsters.*

_____

_____

_____

5.2.3 Are there any signs of forced entry or tampering on doors, door jambs, windows and window frames, and patio doors?

_____

_____

5.2.4 Are there any broken windows, doors, light bulbs, or other items?_____

_____

  5.2.4.1 If YES, when were these items reported to property management or maintenance?_____

  _____

5.2.5 Are there any signs of "suspicious activity" around any of the apartments? Note any indicators such as:

- Blocked or covered windows
- Reinforced doors and windows
- Unusual smells
- People hanging around building—making a discreet call or quickly going inside when you appear during the inspection
- Broken or burned out light bulbs

_____

_____

_____

_____

5.2.6 Are there any shrubs or vegetation near apartment windows that obscure view from the surrounding area?

_____

5.2.7 Are all apartment doors secured with deadbolts, door chains, and latch locks?_____

_____

5.3 *Pools & Clubhouses*

5.3.1 Is the pool fenced?_____

5.3.2 Do families with younger children use the pool during the day?_____

5.3.3 Are there any indications of possible drug and alcohol abuse in the pool or clubhouse area after hours (as suggested by indicators described in 5.1.3)? *Particularly look around bushes and trash receptacles.*

_____

_____

_____

5.3.4 Does the pool look maintained?_____

   Is the water clear and free of floating contaminants?_____

5.3.5 Have there been any reports or complaints about non-resident juveniles or "pool crashers" using the pool or clubhouse facilities?

_____

_____

5.3.6 Is there an access control policy or procedure for establishing the identity or credibility of pool patrons (such as issued pool passes, gate keys, etc,)?

_____

_____

5.4 Parking Lots

5.4.1 Where are the parking areas located?_____

5.4.2 Is the parking area monitored by CCTV or observed by frequent foot patrols?_____

5.4.3 Are there indications of abandoned cars present? Some indicators include:

- Car without license plate or temp tag (unregistered car)
- Vehicle with expired registration
- Missing tires (vehicle on blocks)
- Vehicle with broken windows
- Vehicle with dead battery
- Vehicle has not moved for one week or more

_____

_____

_____

5.4.4 Do residents lock their vehicles when they are parked?_____

5.4.5 Do residents with valuable cars use anti-theft devices, such as clubs, alarms, etc?_____

5.5 Surrounding Neighborhood

5.5.1 Is there a fence separating the property from the surrounding community?_____

   5.5.1.1 If YES, is the fence made of mesh fabric and designed and maintained properly?_____

   _____

5.5.2 Are there any locations in close proximity where people are likely to loiter (gas stations, bus stops, parts, etc.)?

_____

_____

5.5.3 Is there a lot of pedestrian "through" traffic in the area?_____

_____

    5.5.3.1 If so, where does it originate and where does it go?_____

    _____

    _____

Nighttime Survey

The following sections (5.6 to 5.7) are to be evaluated at night. This evaluation should be conducted more discreetly and is often well conducted as a discreet surveillance of the property over several nights.

5.6 Lighting

5.6.1 Is lighting in parking areas and outdoor walk ways adequate to permit safe travel and discourage opportunistic attacks?

_____

5.6.2 Is lighting around apartment buildings adequate to permit safe travel and discourage opportunistic attacks?

_____

5.6.3 Are there any locations around or within apartment buildings where lighting is inadequate (areas that serve as possible ambush locations or where darkness obscures possible drug activity)?

_____

_____

_____

_____

_____

5.6.4 Are there any burned-out or broken lights?_____ If YES, list:

_____

_____

5.7 After Hours Activity

5.7.1 Are there any potential signs of drug sales activity?

For example:

- Units with high entry and exit traffic
- Cars driving up, quickly conversing with someone in the parking lot, then driving away
- Individuals hanging out—One or more people talking on cell phones or pay phones, then quickly going somewhere and returning
- Individuals hanging out—One or more people talking on cell phones or pay phones, followed several minutes later by outsiders that visit briefly, then depart

_____

_____

_____

_____

5.7.2 Are there any potential signs of prostitution activity?

For example:

- Units occupied by females with high entry and exit traffic of unaccompanied men
- Cars driving up, quickly conversing with a female, then driving away with female—She later returns, only to repeat the pattern
- "Streetwalkers" hanging out

_____

_____

5.7.3 Where do outdoor groups tend to gather after dark?_____

_____

_____

_____

_____

5.7.4 What types of nuisance problems are observed after dark (loud music, etc.)?_____

_____

_____

5.7.5 Are children observed after dark?_____

5.7.6 Do police patrol the community visibly at night?_____

5.7.7 Do local pedestrians and drivers pass through the community at night to get to other locations?_____

_____

_____

5.7.7.1 If YES, can any of the property entrances be closed at night to minimize through traffic?

_____

6. POLICIES & MANAGEMENT PRACTICES

6.1 Applicant Screening

6.1.1 How are applicants screened?_____

_____

_____

_____

6.1.1.1 As a minimum, does applicant screening include:

- State criminal records check
- Felony wants & warrants
- Credit history
- Previous residence check

6.1.2 Are tenants clearly advised in both writing and verbally about the following policies:

- Illegal activity
- Illegal tenants
- Nuisance activity
- Community rules & violations
- Care of property

_____

_____

6.1.3 Are mandatory follow-up (or "welcome neighbor") visits conducted by property management or security to evaluate the condition of the apartment and presence of illegal guests within 3–14 days after the tenant has moved in?

_____

_____

_____

6.2 *Community Orientation*

6.2.1 Do property managers appear to genuinely care about the property and the residents?_____

_____

6.2.2 Do property managers live on-site?

_____

6.2.3 Do property managers have friends that live on-site or do they converse informally and regularly with residents?

_____

_____

6.2.4 Does property management host and coordinate unifying community events (such as barbeques, clean up days, kids events, and other activities)?

_____

_____

_____

6.2.5 Is the property manager recognized by people around the property? Does the property manager appear to know the residents?

_____

_____

_____

6.2.6 Does the property manager actively encourage interaction between residents (making introductions, etc.)?

_____

_____

6.3 *Resident Problem Resolution & Eviction*

6.3.1 Does the management team have a system for documenting offenses and rule violations?_____

_____

6.3.2 Are all "community rules" well documented in policy statements and signed as part of the contract or as addendums by all residents?

_____

6.3.3 Does management follow up and investigate "Guest stay" claims and other similar items?_____

_____

6.3.4 Are violation notices issued quickly to residents?_____

_____

6.3.5 What are the procedures for issuing eviction notices?_____

_____

_____

_____

6.4 Trespassing & Outsider Interdiction

6.4.1 Do property managers and security officers stop and identify suspicious individuals on property?

_____

6.4.2 Do property managers and security officers issue trespass warnings to individuals that do not belong on property or to non-residents involved in on-site altercations?

_____

_____

If YES:

   6.4.2.1 Are trespass warnings documented by police?_____

   6.4.2.2 How are trespass warnings documented and maintained?_____

   _____

   _____

   6.4.2.3 Are Polaroid or digital photos taken of trespassed individuals?_____

   6.4.2.4 If YES, is there a Polaroid book or some other location where images are kept for reference?

   _____

6.4.3 Are individuals that return after previous trespass warnings reported to police for arrest?_____

_____

7. LOCAL RESOURCES

7.1 Are there any banks located within close walking distance that can service the needs of the community?

_____

_____

7.2 Are there any affordable and reputable childcare facilities within close walking distance of the property?

_____

_____

7.3 Are there any after-school activity organizations (boy scout troops, girl scouts, YMCA, 4H, PAL, etc.) within close walking distance of the property?

_____

_____

7.4 Are there any conventional medical clinics (that accept medicare) or hospitals within walking distance of the property?

_____

_____

7.5 Are there any free medical clinics or charitable organization offices (food banks, etc.) within close walking distance of the facility?

_____

_____

7.6 Are there any LARGE grocery stores (Publix, Alberson's, etc) within close walking distance of the property?

_____

_____

7.7 Is there close access to public transportation from the property (within two or three blocks of a bus stop or train station)?

_____

_____

7.8 Where are the nearest schools?

- Elementary?_____
- Middle School/Jr. High?_____
- High School?_____

SUPPLEMENT A. POSSIBLE INTERVENTION TARGETS

Use this sheet to identify any specific residents or habitual local offenders that have been identified as problematic influences in the operational environment. These individuals should be specifically targeted for trespass warning and/or evidence collection to support eviction and possible prosecution.

Name:_____   Resident ☐   Non-Resident ☐

Address:_____

Reason for Targeting:_____

Name:_____   Resident ☐   Non-Resident ☐

Address:_____

Reason for Targeting:_____

Name:_____   Resident ☐   Non-Resident ☐

Address:_____

Reason for Targeting:_____

Name:_____   Resident ☐   Non-Resident ☐

Address:_____

Reason for Targeting:_____

Name:_____   Resident ☐   Non-Resident ☐

Address:_____

Reason for Targeting:_____

Name:_____   Resident ☐   Non-Resident ☐

Address:_____

Reason for Targeting:_____

Name:_____   Resident ☐   Non-Resident ☐

Address:_____

Reason for Targeting:_____

Name:_____   Resident ☐   Non-Resident ☐

Address:_____

Reason for Targeting:_____

Name:_____   Resident ☐   Non-Resident ☐

Address:_____

Reason for Targeting:_____

Name:_____   Resident ☐   Non-Resident ☐

Address:_____

Reason for Targeting:_____

Name:_____   Resident ☐   Non-Resident ☐

Address:_____

Reason for Targeting:_____

Name:_____   Resident ☐   Non-Resident ☐

Address:_____

Reason for Targeting:_____

Name:_____   Resident ☐   Non-Resident ☐

Address:_____

Reason for Targeting:_____

Name:_____   Resident ☐   Non-Resident ☐

Address:_____

Reason for Targeting:_____

Name:_____   Resident ☐   Non-Resident ☐

Address:_____

Reason for Targeting:_____

Name:_____   Resident ☐   Non-Resident ☐

Address:_____

Reason for Targeting:_____

Name:_____   Resident ☐   Non-Resident ☐

Address:_____

Reason for Targeting:_____

Name:_____   Resident ☐   Non-Resident ☐
Address:_____
Reason for Targeting:_____

Name:_____   Resident ☐   Non-Resident ☐
Address:_____
Reason for Targeting:_____

Name:_____   Resident ☐   Non-Resident ☐
Address:_____
Reason for Targeting:_____

Name:_____   Resident ☐   Non-Resident ☐
Address:_____
Reason for Targeting:_____

Name:_____   Resident ☐   Non-Resident ☐
Address:_____
Reason for Targeting:_____

Name:_____   Resident ☐   Non-Resident ☐
Address:_____
Reason for Targeting:_____

Index